Cyber Safety: An Introduction

Cyber Safety: An Introduction

Edited by
Rutger Leukfeldt & Wouter Stol

eleven
international publishing

Published, sold and distributed by Eleven International Publishing
P.O. Box 85576
2508 CG The Hague
The Netherlands
Tel.: +31 70 33 070 33
Fax: +31 70 33 070 30
E-mail: sales@budh.nl
www.elevenpub.com

Sold and distributed in USA and Canada
International Specialized Book Services
920 NE 58th Avenue, Suite 300
Portland, OR 97213-3786, USA
Tel.: 1-800-944-6190 (toll-free)
Fax: +1 503 280-8832
E-mail: orders@isbs.com
www.isbs.com

Eleven International Publishing is an imprint of Boom uitgevers Den Haag.

© 2012 E.R. Leukfeldt & W.Ph. Stol (eds.) | Eleven International Publishing

Printed in The Netherlands

ISBN 978-94-90947-75-0
NUR 741

www.elevenpub.com

Preface

This book is an initiative of the Cyber Safety Research Group of NHL University of Applied Sciences and Police Academy of the Netherlands. It could not have been produced without the effort of 28 authors from 18 different organisations in the Netherlands, Belgium, the United Kingdom and Malaysia. We would like to thank all the participating authors for their contributions.

The concept of cyber safety refers to safety in cyber space. Cyber safety is thus wider than the commonly used concept 'cyber crime'. Indeed the latter term relates purely to crime (the committing of an offence). Scholars frequently draw the conclusion that little scientific research has been devoted to cyber safety. Such knowledge as exists is fragmented, and it is difficult for students and professionals to get an overall view.

This book is an introduction to the field of cyber safety. Its aim is to present an overview of current knowledge in that area. It is targeted at university students reading for a bachelor or masters degree (for example, in Safety and Security, or Police Sciences) and at professionals who encounter the negative effects of digitization in their working environment (for example, police officers and the courts, who will increasingly have to deal with digital elements in traditional cases, as well as youth workers wishing to know more about the world in which young people actually live).

The book is divided into four parts. The first covers the introductory concepts, looking at cyber safety from different perspectives. After dealing with the concept of cyber space and safety as such, it reflects on related technical, sociological, criminological and juridical factors. It ends by addressing two important themes in the area of cyber safety: privacy and the impact of technology, and the (potential) rise of the Orwellian society.
In Part 2, the various types of cyber crime are described individually, addressing issues such as definition, nature, scale and offender characteristics. The cyber crimes reviewed include hacking, e-fraud, child pornography, unauthorised file sharing, cyber warfare and criminal techniques like botnets, social engineering, phishing and DDoS-attacks.

Part 3 deals specifically with youth and cyber safety. Specific themes are: online sexual solicitations, sexually explicit internet material, cyber bullying and the perils and pleasures of playing video games.

Part 4 is about the organisations that play a part in safeguarding internet security. It addresses the role of the police, commercial organisations such as Internet Service Providers, and information security.

Developments in the field of cyber safety move fast. This book is published in 2012, but due to the lengthy process of determining the appropriate subjects for a book in this new field, and then selecting the right authors and editing their contributions, most texts were written in the course of 2011. Their shelf life is limited in the sense that technological possibilities and trends in cyber safety are continuously changing. At the same time, research is producing new insights into the nature and scale of the issues at hand – or so we hope. Nevertheless, we believe that the fundamental principles of technology and safety under discussion here will remain relevant at least until the second edition of this book.

Success in this field depends crucially on cooperation, not only between the organisations seeking to make the internet a safer place, but also equally between scholars and other knowledge workers. Information on a number of collaborating groups and institutes in The Netherlands can be found at www. cybersafety.nl, the online hub of the Cybersafety Research and Education Network (CyREN). Anyone wishing to contribute to the next edition of this book can get in touch with us through the CyREN website.

Rutger Leukfeldt
Wouter Stol

Table of contents

Part 3   Youth and Cyber Safety

Part 4   Internet & Regulation

Abbreviations

ACPO	Association of Chief Police Officers
ADSL	Asymmetric Digital Subscriber Line
AIVD	General Intelligence and Security Service (in Dutch: Algemene Inlichtingen- en Veiligheidsdienst)
AMPM	Adolescents' Media Practice Model
AMS-IX	Amsterdam Internet Exchange
ARPA	Advanced Research Projects Agency
APWG	Anti-Phishing Working Group
BDE	Bureaus of digital expertise
BOGO team	Team for Assistance and Investigation in Automated Environments (in Dutch: Team voor Bijstand en Opsporingen in Geautomatiseerde Omgevingen)
CAPTCHA	Completely Automated Public Turing tests to tell Computers and Humans Apart
CCU	Censorship Compliance Unit
CCU	Computer Crime Unit
CEOP	Child Exploitation and Online Protection
CIA	Confidentiality, Integrity & Availability
CID	Criminal Investigations Department
CIRCAMP	Cospol Internet Related Child Abusive Material Project
CNIL	Commission nationale de l'informatique et des libertés
COTS	Commercial 'Off The Shelf' Games
CP	Cyberpunks (hacker)
CPNI	Centre for Protection of the National Infrastructure
DDoS	Distributed Denial of Service
DNS	Domain Name System
DPA	Data Protection Authorities
DSM-IV	Diagnostic and Statistical Manual of Mental Disorders
EC3	European Cyber crime Centre
ECO	Association of the German Internet Industry (in German: Verband der deutschen Internetwirtschaft)
ENISA	European Network and Information Security Agency
EU_ICS	European Survey of Crime and Safety
EULA	End User License Agreement
FAQ	Frequently Asked Questions

FCCU	Federal Computer Crime Unit
FTP	File Transfer Protocol
G8	Group of Eight
HADOPI	Haute Autorité pour la Diffusion des Oeuvres et la Protection des Droits sur Internet
HTML	Hypertext Markup Language
HTTP	Hyper Text Transfer Protocol
HTTPS	HyperText Transfer Protocol Secure
IC3	Internet Crime Complaint Center
ICANN	Internet Corporation for Assigned Names and Numbers
ICMEC	International Centre for Missing & Exploited Children
ICT	Information & Communication Technology
ICVS	International Crime Victims Survey
IGCI	Interpol Global Complex for Innovation
IM	Instant Messaging
INACH	International Network Against Cyberhate
INCRP	Interpol National Central Reference Points
INHOPE	Internet Hotline Providers in Europe
IP	Internet Protocol
IPR	Intellectual Property Rights
ISP	Internet Service Provider
ISPA UK	Internet Services Providers' Association
IRC	Internet Relay Chat
IRDSD	Innovation, Research and Digital Security Directorate
ISACs	Information Sharing and Analysis Centers
IT	Internal (hacker)
ITC	Information Technology Crime
IW	Information warrior (hacker)
KLPD	Dutch National Police Services Agency (in Dutch: Korps Landelijke Politiediensten)
LAN	Local Area Network
MAC	Media Access Code
Malware	Malicious software
MMORPG	Massive multiplayer online role- playing games
NCIS	National Criminal Intelligence Service
NCRP	National Central Reference Point System
NCSC	National Cyber Security Centre
NCSS	National Cyber Security Strategy
NCVS-ITS	National Crime Victimisation Survey
NFIB	National Fraud Intelligence Bureau

NFRC	National Fraud Reporting Centre
NHTCU	National Hi-Tech Crime Unit
NICC	National Infrastructure against Cybercrime
NIST	US National Institute of Standards and Technology
NRF	New Regulatory Framework
NV	Novice (hacker)
OECD	Organisation for Economic Cooperation and Development
OG	Old guard hacker (hacker)
OPTA	Independent Post and Telecommunication Authority (in Dutch: Onafhankelijke Post en Telecommunicatie Autoriteit)
P2P	Peer-to-peer
PA	Political activist (hacker)
PAC	Program Against Cybercrime
PC	Professional criminal (hacker)
PCeU	Police Central e-crime Unit
PET	Privacy Enhancing Technologies
PIA	Privacy impact assessments
PII	Personal Identifiable Information
PIN	Personal Identification Number
PT	Petty thieves (hacker)
PPP	Public-Private Partnership
RCCU	Regional Computer Crime Units
RIFD	Radio Frequency Identification
RMT	Real Money Transfer
SEIM	Sexually explicit internet material
SMTP	Simple Mail Transfer Protocol
SOCA	Serious Organised Crime Agency
TAC	Transaction Authorisation Code
TCP	Transmission Control Protocol
THTC	Team High Tech Crime
TLD	Top Level Domain
UDP	User Datagram Protocol
VoIP	Voice over IP
VPN	Virtual Private Network
VW	Virus writers (hacker)
W3C	World Wide Web Consortium
WoW	World of Warcraft
WWW	World Wide Web

Part 1: Introductory Reflections

1 Cyberspace and safety[1]

Wouter Stol

1.1 Prologue: a brief sociological analysis of the origin of cyberspace

For about century now, we, the human race, thought that we had just about finished mapping our world. After we had reached the North Pole, and shortly afterwards the South Pole, in the first decades of the twentieth century, it seemed as though there was not much undiscovered space left, at most a few remote places in the vast jungles of the southern hemisphere and one or two deep troughs in the ocean. No Major Missions remained, no final frontiers of an unknown world that appealed to everyone's imagination. The Norwegian Roald Amundsen claimed the last great trophy when he reached the South Pole. Explorers, seeking new worlds with unknown horizons, had to rely on the space between the planets and the stars for new discoveries. To discover new worlds we had to travel further and search harder. This was the privilege of an extremely limited elite: a handful of astronauts and a few mainly western scientists with exorbitantly expensive equipment. Humanity as a whole was trapped as it were, both physically and mentally, within the boundaries of the world around it. But then, from a position of distress, through a yearning to expand and from a sense of creativity, *homo technologicus* created a new world within existing space: cyberspace. Once again there was air and space, space to see possibilities, space to take new paths, space for hope and optimism, space for inspiration and discovery, space for creativity and freedom (box 1.1). Space not only for a few scientists, but for many.

Box 1.1   Tonee Ndungu's and Barack Obama's cyberspace

'As opposed to the older hippo generation, that still complains about colonialism and imperialism, the cheetahs are taking charge. They are connected to the web, are joining online networks and are urging others to join in. (...) The internet has given them the key to drag Africa out of the gutter. Or, as Tonee Ndungu from Kenya puts it: "We lived on a glimmer of hope. Finally, finally we can reach it and grasp it." Ndungu, too, is a real cheetah.' (*de Volkskrant*, 25 March 2010).

---

1   This chapter is based on Stol (2010).

Tonee Ndungu is not the only one who shows us the relationship between the internet and this new living space. The current president of the United States, Barack Obama, made intensive use of the internet to win his presidency. And after he became president he announced that he wanted to put an end to the programme for manned space travel.

This brief sociological analysis can be placed in the tradition of optimistic social scientists, among whom the American Lewis Mumford deserves to be mentioned as an important exponent of this movement. The optimism that he brings to the fore in his unparalleled study *Technics and civilization* – from 1934 – encompasses two points.

Mumford demonstrates convincingly that it is not so much technology that determines the path of history, but the mental development of man, in other words: culture. It is not the chance technological inventions of ingenious or disturbed engineers that decide the path of history, but the mental state in which society finds itself that determines which technology society produces. In the social analysis just sketched, it is no coincidence that the internet arose at a time when, for decades, people no longer had the prospect of pioneering new territories. The fact that the majority of people never roam the earth anyway does not detract from this. The issue here is the lack of prospects, the shortage of space to explore. Contrary to what we are told, worldwide cyberspace is not merely the result of a few boffins stringing together a bunch of computers. That explanation is too simple. Cyberspace is the result of the fact that humanity, because of a lack of room to explore in its everyday world, found itself in a state of mental imprisonment. Cyberspace is the answer to the shortage of opportunities to pioneer and explore. Or to put it differently, it is not so much that people like to use new technologies simply because engineers have developed them, but that engineers have developed modern technologies because people (and they themselves) so much like to use them.

Secondly, Mumford vehemently, and in my opinion successfully, defends the claim that people are not only capable of launching new technologies, but also of steering them, and even changing their direction. We are not doomed to be destroyed by the technological force we unleash – provided we do not want to.

Mumford died in 1990 aged 94 and missed seeing the breakthrough of the internet. Yet his approach to technology is appropriate even when it comes to the internet. After all, there is no point in making an effort to improve things unless you are convinced that man's intellectual force and his capacity to influence things is more powerful than 'technology' or some other invisible hand that determines the course of history for us. We, you and I, do live in the world of the internet. It is therefore our responsibility to allow cyberspace to be an environment that inspires people and gives them the opportunity for progress and new, promising discoveries.

This is not an easy task; it is demanding of those who take it on. Roald Amundsen and his fellow explorers had to battle cold, exhaustion, malnutrition, polar bears, injury, sledge accidents and many other hazards. This is not hard for us to imagine. Yet within their teams these pioneers struggled with boredom and bad relationships, to the point of treachery, theft and murder. When people live together, they must not only defend themselves against the elements, but also – and I think especially – against each other. Safety is a basic requirement for any human endeavour, be it the conquering of the North or South Pole or developing the *terra incognita* of cyberspace.

People are always the instigators behind the dangers of cyberspace. Safety in cyberspace is not so much a technological problem or aspect of 'physical safety' – as some experts call it. Instead it is first and foremost a question for the social sciences such as sociology, psychology, criminology and law. The technological sciences play a supplementary role.

The concept that is central to safety in cyberspace is behaviour, and the main issue ultimately is how to influence people's behaviour in such a way that it does not cause unsafety. Or better still: so that people can effectively protect themselves and others from dangers. This practical 'how question' ('How can people's behaviour be influenced in such a way that it enhances safety?') is not simple to answer. The first thing is to identify the safety issues, what their background is and how they develop. Only then is it possible to consider properly how to tackle the problems, and decide what can be done to make cyberspace safer. But there's the rub: we still know very little about safety problems in cyberspace. And we therefore know very little about how to effectively tackle them.

1.2   Cyberspace

Internet belongs to the category of technology that has been of immense importance in social development. Other technologies in the same category include the art of writing (3,200 BC), printing presses (1,000 AD), the telegraph (1833), telephone (1876), television (1927), computer (1943) and mobile phone (1973). The invention of writing is without doubt the greatest innovation of all time. To be able to invent writing, people had to dare to believe that their thoughts could go their own way, separate from their bodies, that spirit and body were not an indivisible unit. That seems to be the biggest mental adjustment in the history of humanity. The internet is an almost direct extension of this.

The internet belongs to the above category of innovations, but it is different to the rest. The internet is not merely a method of communication; people also build social structures on the internet. Social structure is the sum of all more or less fixed patterns of human interrelationships. Alongside communication between people, this includes the rules, the infrastructure and all the other aids that people use to maintain their relationships. People cannot act as if structures do not exist, or even ignore them; they have to take them into account. Social structures arise through the comings and goings of people, and once structures have been formed, they in turn give direction to what people do. Giddens (1984) called this characteristic the duality of structure.

Even if no one were on the internet, there would still be domains, websites, profile sites, search engines, chat rooms and all their interconnections. Whoever enters the internet has to take its structure into account. The social structure within the internet is what we call cyberspace.

The social structure on the internet channels people's behaviour. In this sense, cyberspace has compulsory aspects. Yet the structures are not only compulsory, they also offer opportunities. Thanks to these structures people with similar interests who would never have found each other in the past now meet through search engines, websites, social media and virtual communities.

Because the internet has a social structure it resembles a real society. An important difference is its virtual character: the absence of a physical environment. This means that distance and time differences on the internet play a minor role. In terms of safety, it is more important that people are physically absent. To summarise, the two most important characteristics of the internet are:
- It has a social structure that we call 'cyberspace' and that compels people's behaviour in certain respects but at the same time offers new opportunities.
- The social structures of the internet do not have a physical environment: distance and time play a minor role and people are physically absent.

1.3   Cyber safety and cyber crime

The theme of this book is cyber safety, or in other words: safety within the social structure of the internet. Safety is the effective protection against personal suffering: protection against the infringement of physical or mental integrity. Safety is a broader concept than crime, a concept that only refers to acting against the law. Cyber safety therefore encompasses more than cyber crime. It is most obvious in the context of youth and cyber safety, where internet addiction, cyber bullying and communication with unwanted sexual connotations come to mind (see part three of this book). Unsafety begins as soon as someone is harmed or as soon as they perceive that they are being harmed.

A somewhat flexible approach should be taken to the physical or mental integrity of individuals. If we were we to adhere strictly to the integrity of individuals, then phenomena that do not form a direct threat to individuals, but rather to social integrity, might be overlooked. Examples are the so-called victimless offences (e.g., illegal trade) and the rise of criminal structures or links between the underworld and lawful society (e.g., money laundering through business activities in cyberspace).

Although cyber safety encompasses more than cyber crime, the latter plays an important role in the cyber safety field (see part two of this book). Several definitions of cyber crime are in circulation (e.g. Grabosky 2004; McCusker 2006; Yar 2005; Leukfeldt et al. 2010). There is no common definition or consistent conceptual framework for this area of crime. An arsenal of terminology is used, whether or not combined with the prefix cyber, computer, e-, internet, digital or information (Van der Hulst & Neve 2008). Several definitions distinguish between different sub-categories of cyber crime (see for an overview Van de Hulst & Neve 2008). These definitions use many different concepts, but some key points can be distilled: there are crimes where ICT (Information & Communication Technology) is both the goal and the means (e.g. hacking or spreading viruses); and there are crimes where ICT is *essential* for the execution of the offence, but where ICT is not the target (e.g. e-fraud or the spread of child pornography).

Consequently, cyber crime can be used as the umbrella concept for all forms of crime in which ICT plays a crucial role. Subsequently, there are two distinct subcategories. The first subcategory is 'cyber crime in the narrow sense'. This subcategory includes all forms of crime in which ICT is used both as a means and a target, such as hacking and the spread of viruses. The second subcategory is 'cyber crime in the broad sense', a category including all crimes where ICT is essential for the execution, but where ICT is not a target. One could also speak of old crimes in a new form or, as some prefer to say, 'old wine in a new bottle'.

An important question related to the concept of 'cyber crime in the broad sense' is: when is ICT essential for the execution of an offence and when is ICT only used as a tool? In the latter, the offence is not a form of cyber crime (i.e. a burglar who uses Google maps to create an escape route). Some people argue that it would be better to abandon the term 'cyber crime in the broad sense'. Just as the police have reserved the label 'car crime' for crimes targeted at cars (car theft, ringing, handling stolen cars), the term cyber crime – as Van der Hulst and Neve (2008) claimed – will in future be reserved for crimes targeted at ICT. The phrase 'cyber crime in the broad sense' will then be redundant. The use of ICT in 'ordinary' crimes will be no more than the way in which the crime is committed or its *modus operandi*.

Dropping the term 'cyber crime in the broad sense' will not bring an end to the discussion about what cyber crime is and what it is not. Empirical research, for example, showed that many hacking cases are the work of young people abusing each other's email or Facebook account (Leukfeldt et al. 2010; Kerstens & Stol, forthcoming; Domenie et al., forthcoming). According to law, using someone else's account without permission is hacking. The above-mentioned cases however are about a social phenomenon that consists of the brutal behaviour of young people towards each other, not about (technological) acts against ICT. Should we still speak of cyber crime and cybercriminals when trying to characterize this behaviour among youth? I would not be surprised if someday we come to the conclusion that hacking is not always necessarily an act of cyber crime.

Perhaps in the end the term cyber crime will be abandoned altogether since, basically, we do not need the term to study crime and the way technology is used to commit it. Nor do the police need the term to fight crime in the internet era. The concept 'cyber crime' clarifies nothing. We should not name crimes after the means used to commit them, because then each new technology would require the design of a whole new taxonomy of crime. What it boils down to in more academic terms is that we should not try to understand the social relevance of information technology starting from the technique but rather from the social processes the technique relates to (De Sola Pool 1983, 1994; Danziger 1985, Brissy 1990). In legal terminology: attributing the meaning of crime should be done on the basis of the legal interests that are endangered (Kaspersen 1990) – and not on the basis of which technology is used (see box 1.2). In more common words: fraud is still fraud, even when computers are used.

Box 1.2   from a focus on technology to a focus on crime

The former English National High-Tech Crime Unit was taken over by the Serious Organised Crime Agency (SOCA) in April 2006. After all, the 'hi-tech techniques are used across the whole range of organised criminality, not just by specialised "hi-tech criminals". That is why our e-Crime Unit is integrated into SOCA, providing the specialist knowledge and techniques needed to fight today's organised criminal enterprises.' (www.soca.gov.uk, 2006). So, in the UK attention has shifted – moved back is perhaps a better phrase – from the instrument used (ICT) to the crime itself (in this case: organised crime). This can also be expected to happen in other countries because the focus on technology blocks the sight of social reality.

1.4   The relationship between the internet and safety

25

The internet relates to safety in two ways:
–   It offers people new opportunities to behave contrary to the norm (and this gives rise to new problems).
–   It presents new opportunities for regulating behaviour (new opportunities, therefore, to do something about abnormal behaviour).

New opportunities for behaving contrary to the norm
To start with, the internet significantly increases opportunities for people. In her research into communication technology in 1983, before the internet era, Ithiel De Sola Pool (1983: 226) concluded: 'Computers, telephones, radio and satellites are technologies of freedom, as much as was the printing press.' Through all of these technologies, people started to become part of a more extensive network and their opportunities to act increased accordingly. With their personal computers, laptops and mobile phones, they participate in the international network through the Internet, for their hobbies or for work. They order goods through webshops, they download the latest hits and they visit sex sites. Through these communication channels, it has become possible for people, more so than in the past, to form and maintain relationships with others, without their environment being aware of them.

On the internet people are able to take part in social traffic more anonymously than in the offline world. The average internet user is not able to establish the true identity and address of their fellow users. Generally speaking, they cannot see each other and therefore cannot recognise each other or tackle each other about things afterwards. They also do not risk being accosted for things because they are not physically present. This means that behaviour on the internet that contravenes the norms carries fewer risks than the same behaviour would do in the offline world. Because people all over the world who behave in the same aberrant fashion can find each other easily, deviant social networks form where previously that was impossible. According to Frissen and Van Lieshout (2003: 21), cyberspace enables citizens 'to search for, extend and even transgress' the boundaries of what is permissible. They speak of 'unconstrained behaviour'.

The above is in line with the familiar thinking of both scientists and those in the field, in brief: the internet facilitates crime. This claim is easy to defend and fairly popular, but there is more to it.

One objection to this claim is that since the rise of the internet, i.e., the mid-1990s, there has not been a noticeable increase in crime that can be attributed to the internet. The counterargument is that crime facilitated by the internet may not be reflected in police statistics. This subject will be dealt with later.

More important than this quantitative discussion is the question of how this assumed facilitating of crime works. After all, only once you know how things work, once you know why things are the way they are, is it possible to work towards putting measures in place to address them.

The rationale behind the claim that the internet facilitates crime is generally as follows. Because people can act more anonymously on the internet than they can in the physical world, and because less monitoring takes place on the internet, people are more likely to behave differently to the norm than they would offline. The question of whether people are really more anonymous online than offline, and whether they are less subject to monitoring online than offline is not the main issue here. Here the Thomas theory applies, and that is: 'If men define situations as real, they are real in their consequences' (Merton 1968). In other words: if people are of the opinion that they are anonymous, and that they are not being monitored, then they consequently behave as though that is the case.

New opportunities to regulate behaviour

In cyberspace, too, there are norms, and people hold each other to account according to these norms. This is particularly so on the social networking sites that people are often part of. Here cyberspace is similar to the offline world. Anyone searching for norms in cyberspace will soon find them. To start with: when you're on the internet, you probably feel as though you have to behave yourself. You wouldn't start behaving like an animal the minute you enter cyberspace. What's to stop you? It is all the norms that you have internalised from your upbringing and schooling that you take with you to cyberspace. In part these norms are fixed in a general 'nettiquette', for instance, or in smaller communities on a list of frequently asked questions (FAQ). On Hyves (a Dutch social networking site) it is considered 'not okay' to bully, stalk, discriminate, spam, create a false profile or to post pornography. Norms apply everywhere, including in cyberspace (see also box 1.3).

Box 1.3   norms in internet communities

> Svensson and Van Wijk (2004) concluded in their research into codes of conduct among student communities on the internet: 'The copying of copyright protected works is judged positively, sharing pornography as neither positive nor negative and spreading child pornography is emphatically condemned. (...) whoever downloads should also share files; hacking and spam is out of the question, as is the spreading of computer viruses.' (2004: 79). De Pauw and colleagues (2008) report that it is not acceptable to cheat in the world of online gamers. Various studies point out that in hacking circles there are strict codes of conduct, such as safeguarding one another's anonymity and not committing acts of vandalism (Jordan & Taylor 1998; Stol et al. 1999; Turgeman-Goldschmidt 2005).

In cyberspace, too, people who deviate from the norm can expect sanctions. In the student communities mentioned by Svennson and Van Wijk, internet users call offenders to account for their behaviour; if this is not effective then a moderator – a discussion leader within the internet community – takes measures, for example, by issuing a warning, removing a contribution or excluding the offender, either temporarily or permanently. In extreme cases, the service provider may disconnect the offender (Zouridis & Frissen 2004).

In their research into internet gaming communities, De Pauw and her colleagues detected sanction mechanisms: 'Online communities developed a monitoring and regulation system through a moderator to tackle inappropriate behaviour. The most efficient punishment is "shaming" whereby cheaters are stigmatised. This is more effective than a ban or a warning because it undermines the players' reputations' (2008: 20-21). On Hyves, users can make 'not ok' reports. In the information it states: 'Items are automatically removed temporarily after a number of "not oks". We then assess the situation to see if they should be put back or permanently removed.'

Partly on the basis of the studies mentioned, four types of reactions to behaviour in cyberspace that contravene social norms can be differentiated:

The first is 'non-action': no measures are taken against the offender. Their behaviour is tolerated or ignored, or those who are bothered by it retreat to some other part of the internet.
The second is informal social control: other internet users undertake actions against the offender. This may entail someone speaking to the offender, or a large group of internet users closing ranks against the offender, or the offender being nailed to the virtual cross.
The third reaction, which is really a differentiation of informal social control, is mediation. Internet users call in a mediator to resolve the conflict. This could be done through a mediator of a specific internet community or, in extreme cases, the Internet Service Provider (ISP).
The fourth reaction to abnormal behaviour in cyberspace is formal social control. Internet users call upon the intervention of a formal body to take monitoring and corrective action. Incidentally, formal authorities also act on their own initiative.

While non-action may be a reaction to deviant behaviour in cyberspace it does not regulate the offender's behaviour, since they are able to carry on unhindered. In order to mediate and apply informal social control, other internet users must be able to find offenders and approach them. This works well provided the offender regularly visits more or less open, visible and stable internet communities, such as gaming sites, internet communities or profile sites such as Facebook or LinkedIn. It is then possible to approach and hold the offender accountable. Technical measures are also possible in cyberspace, such as removing texts, barring someone's access to a community or organising an email bombardment (DDoS attack). Mediating and informal social control can be effective against crime, but formal social control is frequently called for. The most important organisations for meting out formal social control are of course the police and the justice department. This is not only the case for tracing cyber crimes, but also for the prevention of crime, the timely apprehension of criminals, and building an information base and monitoring – in short a complete arsenal of police methods.

Although they normally only take action when other corrective mechanisms fail, and cannot do much without the active input of others in society, the police play an essential role. It is therefore of vital importance for safety in cyberspace that the police are able to take action effectively – obviously within the limits of the law and common decency.

What options are available to the police? In theory, many. When people use modern technology they invariably leave a digital trail in their wake. For instance, Internet Service Providers have records of who is online and when; computers and mobile phones record which sites have been visited; mobile phones automatically connect to transmission stations; those who pay electronically not only reveal their location but also their spending patterns; those who take part in social networks on the internet show the outside world where their interests lie and in which circles they move, and so on. The movements and particulars of people are better registered than ever before. While it is true that a handful of whizz kids know how to stay off the radar, this does not change the principle. The comings and goings of citizens are registered more than before and this allows for stricter control. This applies not only retrospectively in the sense of tracing movements, but also in advance in the sense of 'knowing who you're dealing with'.

Although investigation is only part of the picture, I would like to make a remark about it at this point. I once heard a police detective say the following about police investigations at the scene of a crime: 'perpetrators always leave tracks, always: hair, skin, specks, an imprint, whatever. The problem is that we often don't find tracks because we are not in a position to discover them – often simply because we don't have enough manpower to search for them intensively enough.'

Perpetrators of cyberspace crime also leave tracks. And there too the police don't always find them; quite frankly: they mostly don't. The police detective's statement just paraphrased applies here too: 'we often don't find tracks because we are not in a position to discover them – often simply because we don't have enough manpower to search for them intensively enough.' More specifically: why are the police not in a position to discover tracks in cyberspace?

The biggest problem that the police are faced with in their operations in cyberspace is a lack of knowledge, and not only in terms of investigations. This is nothing new; the police themselves have repeatedly pointed it out (Stol et al. 1999; Stol 2003; PWC 2001; LPDO 2003; Griffith 2005; Van der Hulst & Neve 2008; Toutenhoofd et al. 2009). It has to be added that the police are taking action to address this shortage of knowledge, but it won't happen overnight.

1.5   A balance?

I argued earlier that cyberspace gives people new opportunities to behave against social norms, and that they make use of these opportunities. Behaviour regulating mechanisms also operate in cyberspace, and the police make an essential contribution to this. But are the two in balance? Or are there insufficient mechanisms to regulate behaviour in cyberspace? Is deviant behaviour getting the upper hand? Are the police consigned to the sidelines and does crime in cyberspace have a free rein? Or is the opposite the case: do the authorities have a stranglehold thanks to new technology?

As it stands the police have a lot of catching up to do, this much is clear (see also chapter 19). But that is no cause for serious concern because the police are not the only barrier against deviant behaviour in cyberspace. Citizens and countless private organisations and enterprises also work towards safety in the digital world, from mediators on small websites to the security divisions of large banks (see also chapter 18). These are the first line of defence against unsafety. Society is resilient, and certainly not totally dependent on the police. Only if citizens and businesses cannot prevail under their own steam does it become a matter for the police. Obviously the police need to be prepared for this. The lack of knowledge mentioned earlier as the biggest problem facing the police needs to be addressed.

Key concepts

Cyber space
Safety
Cyber safety
Cyber crime
Social structure

2   The Internet: Historical and Technical Background

Marko van Eekelen & Harald Vranken

2.1   A brief history of the internet

The internet is a relatively young medium, but it already has a considerable history. The internet was born at the end of the 1960s when the *Advanced Research Projects Agency (ARPA)* of the U.S. Department of Defense initiated the ARPAnet project for connecting computers at some university research centres into a network. These research centres were funded by ARPA for carrying out both military and fundamental research. Although they were spread over the USA, they had to cooperate closely and exchange research results. Another goal of the intended computer network was to share computer resources. At the time, it was already difficult to set up communication paths between computers of the same vendor, let alone to connect computers of different vendors. For exchanging small amounts of data, a point-to-point telephone connection between two locations could be used. Exchanging larger amounts of data required physically transporting punched cards, punched paper tapes or magnetic tapes.

The design principles of the ARPAnet laid the foundations for the internet. It was important that the intended network could survive if some of the connected research centres or network connections were to be destroyed in a disaster such as an earthquake or a nuclear attack. A centralised network architecture would not meet this requirement. For that reason a decentralised network architecture was created, containing redundant pathways between the connected computers. Each computer formed a node in the distributed network, offering services to other nodes or using services from other nodes in the network.

The ARPAnet initially connected four computers in 1969 and subsequently continued to grow. In the 1970s similar networks were created, such as ALOHAnet and Telenet, followed by many more. Many of these networks were interconnected or merged, evolving into today's worldwide *internet* with two billion users in 2010.

In The Netherlands, for example, 91% of households and nearly every business had access to the internet in 2010 (CBS 2010). The internet is used for many different things, like communication via email or chat, searching information on the world wide web, online banking and shopping, playing games, downloading audio and video, and social media. Criminals also make use of the opportunities offered by the internet, and it is expected that internet-related crimes will increase in the coming years (KLPD 2010).

In the remainder of this chapter a brief outline of the technical background to the internet is given, addressing how the internet is operated and organised, its key components, and how it is used. There is a vast body of literature describing these technical topics in depth, of which (Kurose & Ross 2009) and (Tanenbaum & Wetherall 2010) are good examples.

2.2   A brief technical background of the internet

When the internet was formed various technical choices were made. These choices made it work in the way we are used to. Without them the internet would not be the same today. In this section we describe some key choices on how messages are sent and routed over the internet, how the complexity of the communication protocols is managed, how hosts connected to the internet are identified by unique addresses, and how these addresses are managed.

Circuit switching versus packet switching

The ARPAnet took a new direction in network technology. In traditional networks, such as the analogue telephone network, *circuit switching* is used. When making a phone call for instance, first a connection is set up between the caller and the callee, and next this connection is used exclusively for the phone call until the conversation is ended. This results in inefficient usage of the network, since only a small amount of the network capacity is actually used. The solution used by the ARPAnet and the later internet is to divide message data into packets. Each packet is sent separately to the destination, and subsequent packets may take different routes to reach the destination. At the destination, the packets are glued together to assemble the message. Hence, in this approach there is no notion of a single, persistent connection between sender and receiver, and the network connections can be time shared for transporting packets corresponding to multiple messages from different users. This technique is called *packet switching*.

Addressing and routing

In packet switching there is no notion of a fixed connection between source and destination. Each packet therefore contains the address of the receiver.

The network uses this address to route the packet via some path from the sender to the receiver. This routing is done by routers: special nodes in the network that send packets into the right direction from source to destination. Routers try to avoid congestion in the network, and hence two subsequent packets may be sent over different paths to the destination. Since packets may take different routes, the packets may arrive at the destination in a different order than they were sent. Also, packets may get lost or corrupted during transmission, for instance due to interference or overload in the network. In that case, retransmission of a packet is required. The internet has been designed to deal with these issues and end users don't have to worry about them. The internet provides reliable communication between end users even if parts of the underlying network infrastructure are unreliable or unstable.

Protocol layers

In general, a *communication protocol* defines what messages can be sent in what order between two partners. The communication protocol used in the internet is very complex. There can scarcely be any notion of a single protocol, since different applications such as the world wide web, email or file transfer require different protocols. Also, the protocols have to provide reliable communication, dealing for instance with reordering and retransmitting packets. In order to deal with this complexity, the internet protocols have been divided into a stack of layers. Each *layer* provides some basic functionality that can be used by the next layer.

The layered approach resembles in some respects how letters are posted and delivered. A sender puts a letter in a post box, the postal service collects the letters, sorts them in the post office, and the mailman delivers the letter in the mail box of the intended receiver. The protocol of interest to the sender and the receiver is sending a letter. In order to do so, they use the service offered by the post company. The sender and receiver do not have to bother how the post company performs the sorting and routing of the letters. Hence, in this example we have two layers: the layer of the sender and the receiver, and the layer of the post company.

The initial ARPAnet also had two layers, but this proved to be too restricted for coupling the different kinds of computers from different vendors. Also, the networks consisted of various communication media such as radio waves transmitted by satellites, electrical signals through all kinds of cables, and light signals through glass fibre. By dividing the communication functions over layers, and clearly describing the interfaces between the layers, it became possible to connect heterogeneous networks. Also, when introducing a new kind of application, or a new kind of communication medium, only the relevant layers have to be adapted or extended.

In 1983, ARPAnet introduced the so-called TCP/IP protocol stack and the term internet came into use. The communication protocols were split into a stack of five layers (see figure 2.1): application layer, transport layer, network layer, datalink layer, and physical layer. One or more protocols reside in each layer, and the interfaces between the layers are clearly defined. The name *TCP/IP* refers to two of the most important protocols: the *Transmission Control Protocol (TCP)* in the transport layer, and the *Internet Protocol (IP)* in the network layer. The protocols in the *application layer* use the protocols in other, lower layers that manage the actual transportation. The application layer contains protocols like *Simple Mail Transfer Protocol (SMTP)* for email, *File Transfer Protocol (FTP)* for file transfer and *Hyper Text Transfer Protocol (HTTP)* for the world wide web. Each protocol defines what information is exchanged between the sender and receiver for a particular application.

The *transport layer* contains two protocols: *Transmission Control Protocol (TCP)* and *User Datagram Protocol (UDP)*. TCP is used when it must be ensured that each packet is correctly delivered at the destination. Hence, TCP provides reliable communication, which however requires some overhead. For instance, the receiver sends an acknowledgement for each packet back to the sender, to indicate that the packet arrived correctly at the receiver. If a sender does not receive an acknowledgement, it will send the packet again after a certain amount of time. Although TCP is reliable, it is not fast. UDP is a fast alternative for TCP, but is however less reliable. Acknowledgement of received packets and retransmission of packets is not included in UDP. For application where reliability is important, like sending a file, TCP is the preferred protocol. For applications where reliability is less important, like listening to streaming audio in real time where a slight amount of noise is acceptable, UDP is preferred. Also tasks like dealing with network congestion are arranged by TCP and UDP in the transport layer.

The *network layer* contains one protocol: *Internet Protocol (IP)*. IP couples different networks and routes packets through these networks based on IP-addresses.

The *datalink layer* contains a large variety of protocols, related to the physical network. The datalink layer is used to move packets between two hosts connected to the same communication link. A well known protocol is the *Ethernet protocol* used in local area networks.

The *physical layer* is the layer where the bits are sent as signals on the physical medium. The protocols in the physical layer relate to the network transmission technologies, in which raw bits are sent over a physical link.

Figure 2.1   TCP/IP protocol stack

| Application layer (e.g., HTTP) |
| Transport layer (TCP/UDP) |
| Network layer (IP) |
| Datalink layer (e.g., Ethernet) |
| Physical layer |

As an example, we consider the transmission of a simple email (see figure 2.2). The user composes an email using a mail program. The email is contained in an SMTP message in the application layer. Besides the actual text content, the message also contains information such as the email addresses of sender and receiver, the subject, and the time and date of sending. The SMTP message is passed to the transport layer. Since we require reliable communication, TCP is used in the transport layer. The message is divided into packets. A *header* is added to each packet, which contains information like the sequence number of the packet. The packet with header is referred to as a *segment*. Each segment is passed to the network layer. Again a header is added, which contains information like the IP addresses of the sender and receiver. The segment with IP header is referred to as a *datagram*. The datagram is passed to the datalink layer. Again, a header is added, which contains information to send the datagram correctly to the next host in the local network. The datagram with header is referred to as a *frame*. The frame is passed to the physical layer, where it is actually sent over the physical communication medium.

Figure 2.2   Sending an email

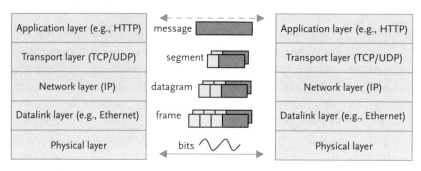

At the receiver, the physical layer receives the bits and assembles them into a frame that is passed to the datalink layer. The information in the header of the frame is processed and removed. The resulting packet is the datagram that is passed to the network layer. This is repeated, until in the transport layer the segment is revealed. The segments corresponding to the email are gathered and used to assemble the email message in the application layer. Finally, the receiver can read the email.

Port numbers, IP addresses and MAC addresses

Each packet in the transport layer is equipped with a header. This header also contains a so-called *port number*. The port number indicates to the application in the application layer to which the packet corresponds. For instance, SMTP corresponds to port number 25. At the receiver, by reading the port number in the transport layer header, the message can be sent to the email application. Many port numbers are standardised. For instance, port number 80 is reserved for the HTTP protocol used in the world wide web.

The header in the network layer contains the *IP address*. This IP address is used by the routers in the internet to route the packet through the network.

The header in the datalink layer contains the *Media Access Code* (*MAC*) address which is a unique address identifying an Ethernet device. The MAC address is used to route a packet in the local area network. Usually, the sending host sends the packet over the local area network to a *gateway host*, which is connected to the internet.

Managing IP addresses

A unique *IP address* is assigned to each device that is coupled to the internet via a network interface that uses the IP protocol. The IP address is used to route packets to the device over the internet. When developing the IP protocol, it was assumed that the number of available IP addresses would be sufficient for a very long time. However, due to the explosive growth of the internet, the number of available IP addresses became insufficient. It is predicted that the internet will continue to grow, for instance due to *'the internet of things'* consisting of all kinds of devices, ranging from refrigerators to mobile phones, that get connected to the internet. An intelligent refrigerator could for instance signal 'short of' milk or other products, and automatically order these products from the supermarket by sending a message over the internet.

Users or companies wishing to access the internet need to get an IP address from their *Internet Service Provider (ISP)*. In turn, ISPs get IP addresses from the *Internet Corporation for Assigned Names and Numbers (ICANN)*, an independent organisation that issues IP addresses worldwide. ICANN assigns blocks of IP addresses to the ISPs. Hence each ISP has a supply of IP addresses that can be assigned to customers. This means that not all IP addresses are actually used, even if all possible IP addresses have been issued by ICANN.
Worldwide there is a large number of ISPs that have coupled their networks. Each ISP is typically connected to multiple other ISPs. Nodes like the *Amsterdam internet exchange (AMS-IX)* connect the networks of multiple ISPs. Parts of the physical network infrastructure are owned by many organisations, some of which operate worldwide. These companies offer their network infrastructure to the ISPs. Hence, ISPs may not own the physical network infrastructure; they only operate it.

37

The internet is formed from the physical and logical networks that are all interconnected and owned by many different organisations. The internet is therefore called a network of networks. Figure 2.3 gives a visual representation of parts of the internet. Nodes represent IP addresses; lines represent connections; the length of a line is indicative of the delay between two nodes.

Figure 2.3   Partial map of the internet (source: www.opte.org)

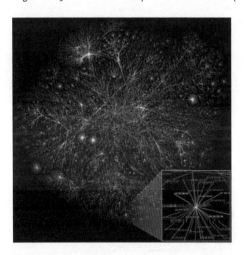

IP addresses initially had a length of 32 bits, and hence there are 2^{32} (nearly 4.3 billion) different IP addresses. This IP numbering structure is named IPv4. In 2011, the last IPv4 addresses were issued by ICANN. The successor of IPv4 is IPv6, using IP addresses with a length of 128 bits. With IPv6 there are 2^{128} ($3.4 \, 10^{38}$) different IP addresses, which exceeds the number of atoms on the surface of the earth. In theory there should therefore be plenty of IPv6 IP addresses.

ICANN not only issues IP addresses, but also domain names. A domain name is a human readable string of characters that is coupled to an IP address. Humans can much better remember meaningful names than arbitrary sequences of numbers. For humans, it is obvious that the domain name www. google.nl corresponds to Google. The extension .nl indicates the *top level domain (TLD)*. Most countries have their own TLD, such as The Netherlands (.nl), Belgium (.be) and the USA (.us). There are also TLDs for other organisational structures. Well known examples are .com for companies, .edu for educational organisations in the USA, .net for network organisations, and .org (initially) for non-profit organisations. ICANN has issued a large number of other TLD's, such as .info and .biz.

Domain names have become important for marketing and profiling on the world wide web. A meaningful domain name, often corresponding to a brand name or the name of an organisation, makes the organisation easily traceable on the web. Some smaller countries earn money by selling domain names. For instance Tuvalu, a small island nation located in the Pacific Ocean, earns millions of dollars by leasing its .tv TLD.

2.3 Technical components building the internet

The internet has various kinds of components that each have their own role. In this section we briefly describe the main components: routers, access networks, local area networks, and hosts.

Routers

The internet has a hierarchical structure consisting of a backbone network, access networks, and local area networks (LANs). Routers are placed at the nodes where different networks are connected. Routers are specialized computers that route packets through the internet to the correct receiver, based on the IP address of the receiver. Routing is done with complex algorithms.

Not only the shortest or fastest path between source and destination is considered during routing, but also the costs involved, based upon agreements between ISPs and network companies.

Access networks

Private users and small companies were initially physically connected to the internet over the analogue telephone network. A special device called a *modulator/demodulator* (*modem*) was needed to transform the analogue signal on the telephone line into a digital signal as input/output by the computer. Usage of the analogue telephone network implied that costs charged were based on the amount of time that the connection was actually used, similar to traditional phone calls. Nowadays, connections to the internet over the telephone network mostly use *Asymmetric Digital Subscriber Line* (*ADSL*), which offers a permanent connection and larger bandwidth against fixed costs. Cable networks, initially exclusively used for broadcasting television signals, are also used to connect to the internet. Cable networks initially consisted largely of copper wires, but are being replaced by glass fibre offering larger bandwidth.

Local area networks

Within organisations, computers are connected in a *local area network* (*LAN*). A LAN can be connected to the internet by means of a modem and a router. The modem takes care of the physical connection and transformation of physical signals. The router manages the traffic between the LAN and the internet. The router often also plays a role for security, for instance also implementing a firewall to filter unwanted traffic.

In recent years wireless connection has become very popular. A wireless network may be part of a LAN, and mobile devices like laptops can be easily connected. There are also many wireless networks that allow public access.

Internet hosts

Hosts are the computer systems that form the endpoints of internet connections. Such hosts can be the computer systems of individual users connected to the internet, but hosts can for instance also be refrigerators connected to the internet, or servers located at companies.

Many applications on the internet are distributed, involving the *client-server model*. A *client* is a host that uses the services offered by servers; a *server* is a host that offers services to clients. Examples of servers are web servers that offer services for the world wide web. Clients can contact web servers and download web pages. Other examples are email servers. Clients can send and receive email by using the services offered by the email servers. The email servers contain mailboxes for incoming and outgoing messages, and ensure that the messages are delivered to the mailbox of the intended receiver.

Servers also play an essential role in the operation of the internet. The *Domain Name System* (*DNS*) is a worldwide distributed database system that stores the relations between IP addresses and domain names, like a telephone catalogue. The DNS is composed of DNS servers that are organised in a hierarchical structure. For instance, when a user wants to surf to www.google.nl, the DNS is first accessed to retrieve the IP address corresponding to this domain name. Based on the IP address, the web server of Google can then be contacted.

2.4   Applications and services

The internet is the network infrastructure, a network of networks, that can be used for all kinds of services and applications. In this section we describe some further aspects of the internet: the world wide web as the most popular internet application, access restrictions to parts of the internet, and services offered on the internet.

World wide web

Since the mid-1990s, the most popular internet application is the *world wide web* (*www*). The organisation W3C (World Wide Web Consortium) has guided the development of www standards. ISPs operate many services on the internet such as hosting services to store and manage web pages, mailboxes and domain names. Using the HTTP protocol the world wide web is accessed via a *browser* (e.g. Internet Explorer, Firefox, Safari or Chrome). Since the internet is most commonly accessed using a browser, many people identify the world wide web with the internet. But the internet is more than that; it is the infrastructure of connected devices. World wide web is one of its applications.

Shielded internet domains

The initial idea of the internet, where clients could access services from servers without constraints, has been refined over the years. Today, many servers and services are accessible only for limited groups of users. The shielding of services and servers is implemented by measures at the network level and the server level. This gave rise to intranets and extranets.

An *intranet* is a private computer network in which the same protocols are used as on the internet. Intranets are typically internal networks within organisations that have connections to the internet, secured by firewalls. The firewalls ensure that the public internet can be accessed from the intranet, but access from the public internet to the intranet is prohibited. The services on an intranet are usually only available inside the intranet. Internal websites are an example of this.

An *extranet* can be considered as an extension of an intranet. The services on the extranet can be accessed from the public internet. Extranets typically offer services like email or web servers to the public internet. Other services on extranets may only be accessible by certain groups of users, such as partners or suppliers of the organisation. Access control techniques, for instance using usernames and passwords, are used to control which external users have access to the extranet.

Employees of organisations who are travelling or who work at home can often still access both the organisation's extranet and intranet. This is achieved by setting up a *Virtual Private Network* (*VPN*) which provides a secured connection between the employee's computer and a firewall at the perimeter of the intranet. When access is granted by the firewall, the employee can access the intranet.

Operational aspects

Besides the separation of internet, intranets and extranets, it also has become common to separate *applications* (e.g. programs that use internet like email clients) and *services* offered by servers. An example of a service is the service offered by Google to search the world wide web. Google's search engine is a large distributed system, involving thousands of servers. Users expect services to be available 24 hours per day, while flexibility is required to service large amounts of users. Hence, services should be reliable and scalable, which can be achieved by offering services from many servers spread over different networks and different locations.

Security is an important aspect. Networks are divided into intranets, extranets and VPN's for security reasons. For instance, the databases of an organisation containing private data such as financial data or information about employees and customers should only be accessible from the intranet. Access can even be more restricted to certain users within the intranet. The organisation's public web servers typically reside in an extranet, since they should be accessible from the public internet. DNS servers should also be accessible from the public internet.

An organisation itself does not have to provide all kinds of services. The ISP, connecting the organisation to the internet, can offer additional services on behalf of the organisation. This typically includes hosting services.

2.5   Web browsers

Web browsers are used for retrieving and presenting information from the world wide web, using the HTTP protocol in the application layer. *HyperText Transfer Protocol Secure* (*HTTPS*) is a security enhanced version of HTTP, providing data encryption and authentication of server and client.

The layout of a web page is described in *Hypertext Markup Language* (*HTML*). The HTML code is passed to the browser's layout engine, which presents the web page on the screen. The web page can contain text and also images, audio and video. Web browsers have a modular structure and can be extended with plug-ins to support for instance Flash applications.

A web page can also contain interactive elements. Interactivity in a web page can be provided by Java applets or JavaScript code. *JavaScript* is a scripting language that is supported by most browsers. JavaScript code is downloaded from the server and executed by the client's web browser. This allows interactive web pages, but it is also notorious since users may download and execute malicious JavaScript code without knowing.

HTTP is a *stateless* protocol. A web server does not remember any information about clients that retrieve web pages from the web server using HTTP. This is inconvenient for applications such as on-line shopping web sites, since the web server should store the products that customers select in their shopping carts. *Cookies* provide web servers with a memory function stored at the client side. When a client retrieves a first web page, the web server sends a cookie to the client. When retrieving subsequent web pages, the client's web browser automatically sends the cookie along with the request message to the web server. The cookie allows the server to identify the client. On the web server, this identity can be used to store all kinds of information about the customer in a database. The cookie mechanism can be used not only for shopping carts, but also for gathering other information about users. Cookies may therefore violate the user's privacy. Web browsers allow users to decide whether to accept cookies or not, but rejecting cookies often makes websites unusable.

2.6   Structure and growth of the internet

Communication over the internet is done by sending packets that are routed through the network based on IP addresses. In general there are many paths possible for routing packets from source to destination. The internet clearly does not have a centralised architecture, which makes it very scalable. Both the physical communication infrastructure and the logical infrastructure, consisting of protocols and services, can be easily extended.

This scalability also holds for the world wide web. Users can publish websites composed of multiple web pages, and the links between web pages form a logical network: the world wide web. The world wide web is even more scalable than the internet itself, since it is easy to add web pages and links.

Searching information on the world wide web is facilitated by means of search engines like Google. However, not all information on the world wide web is accessible. First of all, a search query usually returns thousands of links. The most popular links show up first, and less popular links are last in line. In practice, these less popular links are therefore harder to find, but in theory they can be found. The network of public web pages that are linked together and that can be searched by search engines is called the *surface web*. However, beyond the surface web lies an even larger web, the *deep web*, which is much harder to access. This is not because these web pages are shielded behind firewalls or only accessible in intranets. The deep web refers to information that is accessible through the world wide web, but stored in databases that can be queried producing web pages on demand. Product catalogues are an example of such web pages. The structure and size of the deep web is hard to measure.

Key concepts

Internet
IP address (Internet Protocol address)
Packet switching
Protocol layer
Router
TCP/IP
World wide web

3   Sociological and Criminological Theories in the Information Era

Majid Yar

3.1   Introduction

It is now commonplace to observe that the development of Information and Communication Technologies (ICTs) has transformed the world, impacting upon many and diverse domains including the social, cultural, economic and political. Analysts and commentators have attempted to capture these changes by suggesting variously that we now live in an 'information society', an 'information era', a 'virtual society', a 'post-industrial' society, a 'knowledge society', or a 'network society'. All such accounts place central emphasis upon the transformative power of ICTs to reconfigure and reorganise human action and interaction, thereby creating a new social order that differs markedly from its antecedents. With respect to matters of crime and deviance, criminologists have of late started to direct concerted attention to the ways in which the informational era changes both the nature and patterns of law-breaking behaviour, and how it presents new and unprecedented challenges for crime prevention and crime control. In this chapter I undertake a twofold task: firstly, to overview sociological perspectives on the information society (so as to identify its key defining features and characteristics) and secondly to consider how discourses of criminology and crime control have sought to capture the implications of the new informational order.

3.2   Theorising the information era

Social scientific accounts of the new informational order now abound, and different accounts inevitably offer their own analysis of just what is distinctive about this new informational era, how its emergence can best be explained, and what its impacts and consequences might be. Given the limitations of space, I will confine this section to describing some of the main lines of thought that have shaped our understandings of the information era.

The first and most enduring influential work on the information society was *The Coming of Post-Industrial Society*, written by American sociologist Daniel Bell, and originally published in 1973 (two subsequent editions have appeared, in 1976 and 1999, each including an extensive Foreword containing Bell's reflections on social and economic changes occurring in the intervening years). In this and subsequent commentaries, he uses the term 'post-industrial society' interchangeably with 'the information society', viewing information and knowledge as the primary distinguishing features of an emerging new socio-economic order. Bell's starting point is an evolutionary theory of history rooted in the sociology of Max Weber, and adopting an explicitly anti-Marxist stance. Bell distinguishes the historical development of Western socio-economic systems into three phases: the agrarian, the industrial, and the post-industrial. The pattern of transition and supersedure from one to another is explained through the development of ever more efficient *productive technologies*. Thus, for example, agrarian society was once characterised by subsistence existence – the majority of the population was occupied with producing those goods necessary for the reproduction of their own existence. However, with the 'agricultural revolution' of the 16th century onwards, ever greater technological efficiencies began to release labour from the land, making possible the development of urban industrial production. In other words, productive efficiencies in agriculture made it possible for the whole population's basic needs to be met through the labour of only a proportion of the population, freeing the remainder to engage in other forms of productive activity. During the industrial phase of society, this pattern of increasing productivity through techniques and technological efficiency (steam power, electrification, the 'Taylorist' division of labour, and so on) has been repeated. Bell argued that by the late 1960s, in America and other advanced economies, these productive gains had reached such a point that large parts of the working population were in transition to a new 'post-industrial' economic sector. This sector was characterised above all by the provision of *services* (rather than material goods), and based upon the exploitation and mobilisation of information and knowledge. Basically, the underlying motor of social change, driving society on from agrarianism to industrialism, and now from industrialism to post-industrialism, was the search for instrumental efficiency or 'instrumental rationality' which generates a tendency to produce 'less with more'. Bell saw this movement generating profound changes in the social structure, with a declining industrial working class, and the steady rise of new strata of post-industrial 'knowledge workers' such as professionals (doctors, accountants, architects, lawyers, and so on), educators, managers, administrators, and other providers of inter-personal services. Bell furnishes empirical support for such changes in the form of statistical studies of labour force participation. For example, in the 25-year period between 1974 and 1999, the percentage of the US workforce employed in manufacturing fell from 26% to 15%; by 1996, the proportion of workers employed in professional, technical, managerial, administrative and sales capacities had risen to almost 60% (Bell 1999: xv). For Bell, ICTs play a crucial enabling role in facilitating work and productivity across all these domains, since they furnish the means through which knowledge and information can be codified, ordered, managed and communicated, thereby enabling the provision of informational or knowledge-based goods and services. In Bell's view, the development and deployment of information technologies drives a process of social transformation, giving rise to a new economic order and a corresponding new social class structure. To summarise, according to Bell the term information society refers to a stage of socio-economic development in which the importance previously allocated to the production of material goods and resources is superseded by the centrality of knowledge and information in economic activity.

While Bell's account focuses most directly on economic change and the corresponding restructuring work, Manuel Castells takes the basic tenets of the information society thesis and mobilises it to chart what he sees as a wholesale revolution across all domains of life, including community, identity, politics and culture, as well as labour. In his monumental account of the 'network society' (3 volumes, 1996-1998), he argues that central to these changes are not only the development of ICTs per se, but also their connection into globe spanning networks of interconnectivity. For example, they enable real-time communication and coordination of complex design, manufacturing and marketing activities that underpin the multinationally and transnationally based activities of corporations, thereby binding spatially distant locales into a single global system of economic exchange. Not only do these technologies enable a new information-based economy to emerge, but they also enable the radical reconfiguration of human inter-relations and institutions, which now transcend locality and place, existing instead in a global 'space of flows'. Increasingly, Castells argues, it is ICT-based interaction that permits the formation of network-based social collectivities, communities and social movements, comprising a web-like nexus of manifold individuals brought together via near instantaneous electronic connectivity. State power, based as it is upon sovereign control over a clearly delimited territorial domain, is incrementally eroded by flows of activity and association that blithely transcend all borders. Notions of culture-specific identities and ways of life are also challenged by these global flows, as the circulation of cultural codes and discourses integrate far-flung individuals into new identities and value orientations. The network, based upon digital ICTs, is for Castells nothing less than a new morphology of social life, the organising force behind a dynamic new global order. This process of globalisation may be summarised as the social, economic, political and cultural processes in which local and national spatial limits on interaction are overcome, and come to span the globe.

A further range of thinkers, broadly concerned with the emergence of a 'post-modern' society, place primary emphasis on informationalism as a cultural phenomenon. For the likes of Jean Baudrillard (1983), Jean-Francois Lyotard (1984) and Mark Poster (1990), the contemporary world is one characterised by the ever-intensifying circulation of mediated signs and symbols. For Baudrillard, what we now experience as society comprises a series of simulations, a 'hyperreality' in which culture becomes a self-referential system, divorced from any underlying reference to anything 'real'. Poster, building on Baudrillard's analysis, argues that our immersion in new informational technologies transforms our very selves, liberating us from fixed identities and enabling the creation of new, multiple, ever-changing subjectivities. For Lyotard, the proliferation of cultural codes spells the end of singular, over-arching notions of truth, being displaced by a multiplicity of different cultural realities each with their own 'local' conceptions of knowledge and belief. Crucially, for Lyotard, this multiplication and fragmentation of knowledge is closely linked to the emergence of the ICT revolution from the 1970s onwards. Building on such analyses that connect the cultural shifts of postmodernity with the development of information and communication flows are the likes of Castronova (2007), who discern in the emergence of virtual reality a whole new mode of existence liberated from the exigencies of the 'real'.

Accounts of the kind offered by both Bell and Castells, as well as the 'postmodernists', tend to emphasise wholesale (indeed epochal) social transformation and a break with the past supposedly brought about by the development of informationalism. Other theorists and analysts have however taken a more cautious stance. It is not that they deny the increasing prominence and importance of ICTs, electronic flows of information and culture, or knowledge-based activities. As Webster (2002: 124) puts it: 'the 'information explosion' is a striking feature of contemporary life and any social analyst who ignores it risks not being taken seriously'. However, it is possible to understand these developments not as harbingers of a new society, but as part of longer-term historical developments closely bound-up with pre-existing social forms and processes. Thus for Herbert Schiller the mobilisation of information and communication represents a continuation of the capitalist economic system's dynamic. Behind the development of new technologies and the information flows they generate, we find very familiar patterns of capitalist activity, property ownership and profit seeking. Consequently, the rise of informational activity is driven by

48

market criteria. It is embedded in corporate capitalist activity, and ultimately serves to reproduce long-standing class structures and inequalities (Webster 2002: 128-9). For Schiller and other Marxian analysts of the 'information age', it represents not a new kind of society but the consolidation of a social formation that took shape with the emergence of modern capitalism itself. As we shall see below, disputes about societal transformation versus societal continuity have also come to figure within criminology's more specialised considerations of informationalism and cyber-society.

3.3   Criminological accounts of cyber-society

Sociological debates about the information society have certainly created an intellectual climate in which criminology has moved (albeit slowly and incrementally) to widen its focus so as to consider the significance of informationalism for crime, deviance, and security. Broadly speaking, these efforts have focused primarily on the development of computer-based information and communication networks, particularly those associated with the internet, such as the World Wide Web. Crime is any act that contravenes law and is subject to prosecution and punishment by the state. Deviance is behaviour that may not necessarily be criminal, but which may transgress collective norms about appropriate or acceptable behaviour. While crimes are subject to formal legal sanctions, actions that are deemed deviant may be subject to informal sanctions such as social stigmatisation and denunciation. The term *cyber crime* has come to be used as a convenient shorthand to denote patterns of criminal and rule-breaking activity that take place within or by utilising networks of electronic communication such as the internet – where internet refers to the publicly accessible network of computers that emerged in the 1970s and came to span the globe by the late 1990s (see also chapter 2). Criminologists have variously considered how the advent of the internet has potentially transformed patterns of criminal activity, possibly generated new forms of crime and deviance, and created unprecedented challenges for policing and security (Yar 2006).

From the outset, criminologists have debated whether cyber crime denotes the emergence of a 'new' form of crime and/or criminality. Would such novelty require us to dispense with (or at least modify, supplement or extend) the existing array of theories and explanatory concepts that criminologists have at their disposal? Unsurprisingly, answers to such questions appear in positive, negative and indeterminate registers. Some commentators have suggested

49

that the advent of 'virtual crimes' marks the establishment of a new and distinctive social environment ('cyberspace' as opposed to 'real space') with its own ontological and epistemological structures, interactional forms, roles and rules, limits and possibilities. In this alternate social space, new and distinctive forms of criminal endeavour emerge, necessitating the development of a correspondingly innovative criminological vocabulary (see, for example, Capeller 2001 and Snyder 2001). Sceptics, in contrast, see 'cyber crime' at best as a case of familiar criminal activities pursued with some helpful (at least for the offender) new tools and techniques – in Peter Grabosky's metaphor, largely a case of 'old wine in new bottles' (Grabosky 2001). If this were the case, then cyber crime could still be fruitfully explained, analysed and understood in terms of established criminological classifications and aetiological schema.

In light of the above discussions, it is critically important to gain a clearer purchase on issues of continuity and change with reference to cyber crime. One of the most useful analytical schemas for addressing these matters has been developed by David Wall (2001, 2007). In analysing the emergence of cyber offences, Wall distinguished between 'computer integrity crimes', 'computer assisted crimes' and 'computer content crimes'. These forms of offence each has a different bearing on matters of 'novelty', and depend on exploiting different facets of the information and communication infrastructure. They will be considered below in turn.

Computer integrity crimes are those aimed at the network of electronic communications itself, targeting variously its computer hardware and the software that enables it to function. These crimes include hacking (unauthorised access, intrusion and potentially interference with a computer system); the distribution of 'malware' (malicious software, such as viruses, worms and Trojans) that can affect the operation of the devices targeted; and 'denial of service' attacks that take web-based services offline, often by flooding them with an unmanageable number of communication requests. What is noteworthy about such integrity crimes is that they can be seen as wholly new forms of offence – they are only made possible by the existence and architecture of the computer network itself, and in the absence of that ICT-based order they could not exist.

The second kind of offence identified by Wall, computer assisted offences, represent in contrast a reworking of established forms of offending in the new informational environment. They include various forms of theft and fraud. They may target goods and services, money and finance, or information itself (such as confidential data, personal details, private communications or, as is extremely common, the various forms of legally-protected intellectual properties that are bought-and-sold online). They also include a variety of forms of interpersonal victimisation, such as sexual harassment, virtual abuse and stalking. These are all offences that predate the existence of modern ICTs – history is, after all, replete with instances of thefts, frauds and assaults, and the practices associated with media 'piracy' have certainly attracted attention since the rise of home taping of music in the 1970s. However, while they may not be qualitatively unprecedented, their transposition to the medium of digital communication does transform them in significant ways that must be criminologically recognised. For example, fraudsters are now enabled to make their 'pitches' electronically to millions of potential victims though spam emailing, and can do so simultaneously and at virtually no cost. The increasing use of ICTs for financial transaction (ranging from e-shopping to e-banking) renders users vulnerable to appropriation of sensitive information, including details of credit cards and bank accounts. Through communication channels such as email, instant messaging and social media, individuals are made vulnerable to abuse, bullying, and threats. The ability to reproduce and virtually distribute digitised content creates seemingly ungovernable levels of unauthorised copying and sharing of musical recordings, motion pictures and computer software. Moreover, all of these offences can be committed at-a-distance, and with varying degrees of anonymity, which means that the offender can communicate without having his identity revealed to others. As we shall see later, these characteristics generate major challenges for policing and security in the information society.

The third type of offence identified by Wall centres on the content of computerised communication itself. Of particular note are those communications that breach legally defined limits on speech, where for example certain types of communication and representation are considered harmful to society and its various social constituencies. These include high profile and widely debated practices such as the circulation of obscene and violent images, sexualised images of children, expressions that incite political violence (such as 'terrorism'), and messages that express and incite hatred against ethnic, religious, sexual and other minorities. Again, these forms of communicative content have long existed, but take on a new lease of life in the online environment. Networked communications enable such content to be globally disseminated, enable the bypassing of restrictions imposed on established media channels, enable the exploitation of variation in legislation concerning restricted speech in different countries, and also afford those responsible a degree of anonymity that makes them difficult to identify and act against. This capacity for extended communication is not entirely negative of course, as it can also enable a variety of social actors to bypass state censorship and ensure the circulation of truths and opinions that authorities may otherwise be able to silence.

What then can we deduce in general terms from these developments, insofar as they shape our wider understandings of the cyberworld and its criminological implications? Firstly, we can suggest that the availability of networked communications systems acts as a 'force multiplier', significantly extending the potential scale and scope of illegal activities. Secondly, the actions and interactions enabled by modern information systems have a significant impact on social ontology. Specifically, they play a crucial role in driving a process of space-time compression, wherein spatial and temporal limits on action are transcended by near-instantaneous, globe-spanning interactivity. Criminology's conventional, spatially-bounded notions of crime are brought into question when offending becomes 'disembedded' from any clearly identifiable spatio-temporal location, and can indeed exist in what Mitchell (1995: 8) describes as the essentially 'anti-spatial' environment of the virtual realm (also Yar 2005).

3.4 The information society: implications for cyber security

The aforementioned characteristics of the new informational environment, and the shifting parameters of crime and deviance they entail, carry some important implications for managing security and crime control in contemporary society.

Firstly, the spatial extension of offending carries implications for territorially bounded security and crime control. 'Terrestrial' crime, as a spatially located phenomenon, has generated a corresponding apparatus of security and crime control that is based on geographical sub-division. For example, the organisation of policing is based on the enforcement of national laws within a specified territory, and further differentiated into sub-national regions and locales. However, the cyber sphere transcends such spatial fixities and thus facilitates crime threats that regularly transgress regional, national and continental borders. The existing apparatus of policing is ill equipped to deal with such threats, in which criminal predation emanates from distant places, and flows of illicit activity appear indifferent to political borders. The challenge is further accentuated by the problem of legal pluralism, by which we mean the divergences and differences in criminal law between different sovereign nations (Yar 2006: 143). These differences can be exploited by offenders so as to insulate themselves from effective regulation, as for example where they base their illicit activities in countries with weak or non-existent criminal prohibitions or sanctions in relation to various cyber offences. One clear example of this phenomenon is the way in which far-right extremist groups host globally-available hate material in nations such as the United States, where measures to protect freedom of speech are much more wide ranging than in other territories, and there are corresponding limitations on the criminalisation of offensive communications (Whine 2000). Undoubtedly the rise of such transnational flows of computerised offending have in recent years inspired moves to harmonise national cyber laws, for example through the development of binding international agreements (such as the Council of Europe's *Convention on Cyber crime* – Williams 2009). However, there remain major challenges for national legal systems and law-enforcement authorities in responding to the transnational character of cyber crime.

A second challenge emerges from our increasing societal dependence on ICTs, and the new forms of risk and vulnerability this entails. An inevitable correlate of living in an information society is that systems of electronic communication will play a central role in organising and performing the widest possible array of activities. The contemporary economy and its underlying financial system are crucially dependent on the functioning of ICT networks. However, this dependence now also extends to the operation of other parts of society's key infrastructure, including communications and transport, energy and water supply, healthcare and disease control, defence and security, and so on. This very centrality of ICTs creates a situation of heightened risk, as vulnerabilities in these systems make possible catastrophic failures with wide-ranging consequences. Awareness of this situation has inspired the emergence of a security discourse oriented around the 'critical information infrastructure', and corresponding strategies to try to protect this infrastructure from either accidental or deliberate disruption (Dunn & Wigert 2004). Particular attention has centred upon the ways in which societal dependence on ICTs can be exploited either as part of state-centric 'information warfare' or by 'terrorist' organisations and their sympathisers. Both, it has been argued, have the capacity to generate major social disorder by targeting networked communication systems (Denning 2009).

A third kind of challenge arises from the ways in which the sheer scale of cyber-offending threatens to overwhelm the existing apparatus of security and crime control. Jewkes (2009) notes that the ever-increasing penetration of

53

networked technologies has brought with it a massive increase in the number of cyber crimes. Moreover, for a complex variety of reasons, such offences remain significantly under-reported, with potentially as few as 10% of these crimes actually being brought to the attention of relevant authorities. Even where the offences are reported, law enforcement agencies may well allocate a low priority to their investigation, with the lion's share of time and resources being already committed elsewhere, in particular to those terrestrial crimes that generate the greatest amount of public and political concern (Yar 2009). A lack of technical expertise amongst investigators can further exacerbate the problems. Taken together, these factors have served to create a security deficit, with public authorities offering only a limited and inadequate response to the challenge presented by the rise of cyber crime. This deficit has been met by the emergence of a wide range of non-state actors (located in both the private and voluntary sectors) who have assumed the burden of cyber crime prevention, detection and investigation. Although other parties than the police become engaged in controlling activities, we still speak of 'policing', since this term refers to the wide range of activities that serve to monitor and control social behaviour. Policing may be undertaken by official state-sanctioned bodies (such as the police), by private organisations, by communities or by individuals. Yet this pluralisation and privatisation of cyber security brings its own challenges. Firstly, the multiplicity of actors creates potential for confusion about roles and responsibilities, with problems of overlap, duplication and indeed competition between different actors. Secondly, where cyber security is offered via the market, it risks excluding those without the financial resources to buy in security goods and services; this can lead to a new 'digital divide', a world of users divided into security 'haves' and insecure 'have-nots' (Yar 2008). Thirdly, the co-option of security provision by private actors raises issues related to public accountability – how are the actions of a private 'cyber-police' to be monitored and regulated? How can we ensure that their conduct is itself lawful and equitable, and that their responses are proportionate and justified? Tension points have already arisen in this area, as with internet-monitoring organisations (such as the Internet Watch Foundation) acting effectively as judge and jury, and making unilateral decisions about blocking access to websites that they deem to host illegal content. Similar issues arise in cases where holders of intellectual property rights pressurise Internet Service Providers (ISPs) to block access for those they allege to be guilty of unauthorised file-sharing or 'piracy'. Such activities inevitably lead to concerns that the rights and liberties of users may be curtailed without the observation of proper legal process, and that policing activities may be dictated more by private commercial interests than the public good.

3.5   Conclusion

This chapter has outlined the ways in which the 'information revolution' has been theorised in both sociology and criminology. While accounts vary in their explanations for the emergence of 'informationalism', all share the conviction that ICT networks, and the communications that they facilitate, have come to figure centrally in the organisation of social, political and economic life. Criminologists have sought to think through the implications of this societal transformation, focusing upon the ways in which crime and deviance are reconfigured as a result of our increasing dependence upon ICTs. It is clear that the information society has both brought new forms of criminal activity in its wake, and wrought a transformation of long-standing patterns of offending. Equally, it carries significant implications for the organisation of security, generating societal challenges that we are only just starting to address.

Key concepts

Anonymity
Crime
Cyber crime
Deviance
Globalisation
Information Society
Internet
Legal pluralism
Policing
Transnational crime and policing

55

4 The Development of International Legal Instruments

Arno Kentgens & Evert Stamhuis

4.1 Introduction

The promotion of cyber safety has been recognised by states all around the world as a target for their national policy as well as an issue for joint effort. Either by way of bilateral agreements or by composing multilateral conventions, states are advancing on the road to more safety in cyberspace. A convention is an agreement between a large number of states, reflecting positions that are shared among many. Other states may join later. One of the main avenues towards greater cyber safety is to prevent and combat criminal behaviour in cyberspace. The powers to investigate, prosecute and punish crime are largely confined to national states. For common law enforcement in the field of cyber crime, states have to join forces on a voluntary basis. European states have done so under the umbrella of the Council of Europe. We can see moreover that the common legal instruments of the EU are also relevant. In order to achieve a starter's level of knowledge on the legal instruments and limitations for cyber safety policies, this chapter will deal with two Council of Europe conventions in turn. The substance and purposes of those conventions will be demonstrated. EU regulation will be addressed to a limited extent, that is to say only to illustrate what effect it has had on further pursuing the uncorrupted use of cyber space. Two examples of implementation in national jurisdictions will be given just before the concluding paragraph. A brief explanation of legal instruments can be found in box 4.1.

Box 4.1 Legal instruments, a brief explanation

When states want to join forces in order to reach a certain goal they formulate a common text, usually after negotiations. In that text one can read what the common goal is and which instruments have been agreed upon to achieve progress towards that goal. The text is often signed at a ceremony and is called an agreement or a treaty, often accompanied by an explanatory memorandum or commentary, highlighting certain issues or dealing with questions of interpretation or implementation. When a large number of states is involved the term convention is often used, and implies that the ideas laid down in the text are widely accepted. The variation in instruments is enormous and a combination of instruments is usually included in modern international cooperation agreements. Examples of instruments are: harmonisation of existing national laws and policies, common initiatives, alignment of state actions, establishment of an international organisation or agency, new regulations, instruments for cooperation etcetera. The ceremonial signature of the text marks the start of a process of implementation. The agreement has to pass through a process of ratification and implementation as prescribed by the treaty and the different national laws before the instruments become available for national authorities. For example, in many countries the agreement is subject to parliamentary approval. Amendments to a treaty or convention are effectively new agreements, but are often presented with a close link to the original text as Additional Protocols. Those protocols supplement the treaty or convention, but usually have to undergo the same process of accession and ratification, before entering into force.

4.2   Cyber crime Convention 2001

Development
The awareness that the growing use of computer technology in society was relevant for criminal law grew over the course of the last quarter of the 20th century. The first remarkable result of that development was an initiative of the Organisation for Economic Cooperation and Development, which issued a recommendation in the mid-1980s to incorporate certain computer related acts into criminal law.[2] The common idea was that the use of ICT was increasingly indispensable for economic activity, which legitimized its protection by the criminal law. This initiative was carried forward by the Council of Europe, leading to a recommendation in 1989,[3] dubbed "Computer-related crime" that contained recommendations on the harmonisation of national criminal law and international cooperation instruments; mainly referring to a report of the European Committee on Crime Problems with the same title.[4]

---

2   OECD, Computer-related Crime: Analysis of Legal Policy, ICCP Series No. 10, Paris 1986.
3   Council of Europe R(89)9, dated 13-09-1989.
4   European Committee on Crime Problems, *Computer-related crime*, Strasbourg: Council of Europe 1990.

In the course of the next decade it became apparent that a firmer approach was necessary to achieve the desired level of harmonisation and cooperation: recommendations should be replaced by a multilateral agreement. After having issued a last recommendation on problems relating to criminal procedure,[5] the members of the Council of Europe began the process of creating a more binding instrument. After a programme of negotiations that agreement was signed at Budapest on 23 November 2001.[6] Although it is an agreement concluded in the Council of Europe forum, it received support from the European Union and is open to accession for non-European states. Japan, the USA and Canada have consequently signed the convention. At the moment it represents one of the main outcomes of international cyber safety promotion and reaches far beyond the European arena.

The Convention contains four chapters. Chapter I gives definitions of terminology in the convention, notably "computer system", "computer data", "service provider" and "traffic data". Chapter II lists the measures that States have to take at the national level. For the main part it prescribes legislative action in the field of substantive criminal law in section 1 (i.e. definitions of crimes), procedural law in section 2 (i.e. powers, procedures and safeguards) and jurisdiction in section 3 (i.e. establishing the power to take legal action against crimes). Chapter III contains provisions for international cooperation relating to extradition, mutual assistance and spontaneous information sharing. Chapter IV sets out regulations for the signing and entry into force, and the accession and application etc. of the convention itself.

Substantive law

A main objective treated in the Convention's first chapters is harmonisation.[7] Uniformity of substantive criminal law not only provides for criminal liability for cyber crimes throughout the states that implemented the convention, it also facilitates cross border assistance in law enforcement. Where states have more or less the same definitions in their respective criminal jurisdictions, their cooperation will run more smoothly. Many national laws require the criminal offences for which assistance is requested by another state to be crim-

---

5 Council of Europe R(95)13, dated 11-09-1995.
6 Convention on Cyber Crime, CETS 185; on http://conventions.coe.int/Treaty/en/Treaties/html/185.htm with Explanatory Report and ratifications list.
7 Harmonisation is the development to change national law and/or policy towards similarity to an agreed standard; example: introduction of uniform descriptions of criminal behavior.

inal offences in the own national jurisdictions too. That is the so-called double incrimination requirement. In cases where definitions of criminal behaviour are closely similar on both sides of the border, this requirement for cross border cooperation is easily fulfilled.

The Convention expects the signatories to have established criminal liability for a range of criminal acts. These are defined in Articles 2 to 10: illegal access, illegal interception, data interference, system interference, misuse of devices, computer-related forgery, computer-related fraud, offences relating to child pornography, offences relating to infringements of copyright and related rights.

Some additional substantive provisions are collected in title 5, for example relating to accessory liability, corporate liability and sanctions (see Articles 5 and 6 in box 4.2 and 4.3).

Box 4.2   Article 5 – System interference

Each Party shall adopt such legislative and other measures as may be necessary to establish as criminal offences under its domestic law, when committed intentionally, the serious hindering without right of the functioning of a computer system by inputting, transmitting, damaging, deleting, deteriorating, altering or suppressing computer data

Box 4.3   Article 6 – Misuse of devices

1. Each Party shall adopt such legislative and other measures as may be necessary to establish as criminal offences under its domestic law, when committed intentionally and without right:
   (a) the production, sale, procurement for use, import, distribution or otherwise making available of:
      (i) a device, including a computer program, designed or adapted primarily for the purpose of committing any of the offences established in accordance with the above Articles 2 through 5;
      (ii) a computer password, access code, or similar data by which the whole or any part of a computer system is capable of being accessed, with intent that it be used for the purpose of committing any of the offences established in Articles 2 through 5; and
   (b) the possession of an item referred to in paragraphs a.i or a.ii above, with intent that it be used for the purpose of committing any of the offences established in Articles 2 through 5. A Party may require by law that a number of such items be possessed before criminal liability attaches.

2. This article shall not be interpreted as imposing criminal liability where the production, sale, procurement for use, import, distribution or otherwise making available or possession referred to in paragraph 1 of this article is not for the purpose of committing an offence established in accordance with Articles 2 through 5 of this Convention, such as for the authorised testing or protection of a computer system.

3. Each Party may reserve the right not to apply paragraph 1 of this article, provided that the reservation does not concern the sale, distribution or otherwise making available of the items referred to in paragraph 1 a.ii of this article.

In the text of Article 5 we can see that the Convention provides a fairly detailed description of the behaviour that States are obliged to include in their criminal law codes. The article even prescribes the inclusion of the subjective element of intention, which is repeated in other definitions. The actual meaning of intent is not defined and consequently left to national implementation. With the phrase 'without right' the legitimate interference with computer systems foreseen for example in procedural law or in contract conditions between users and providers, is excluded. In this way the drafters of the text seek to limit criminal liability to really serious and illegal infringements of cyber safety. Under Article 5 the parties only partially categorised the uninvited distribution of mails, usually for advertising, for which we use the term spam. Those interferences with the mailbox, experienced by almost all email users, are extraordinarily irritating but were not accepted separately as an infringement of proper behaviour in cyberspace. Spam would fall under the terms of the Convention only when it resulted in "serious hindering without right". Otherwise it was not considered to involve the required level of severity that had been negotiated.

The EU member states have met the challenge to arrive at a uniform approach to spam, not surprisingly because it touches upon issues of free markets inside the Union area. Spam is simultaneously the use of as well as a threat to free digital highway traffic and for that reason required further attention. It is important to note that the Explanatory Report refers to administrative sanctions as well as criminal sanctions. Obviously both avenues of law enforcement are in the picture regarding safety in cyberspace.

In Article 6 we can see that the Convention not only aims at the repression of criminal acts, but also deploys a preventive approach. It prescribes the criminalisation of activities that chronologically precede the offence, such as the possession of items with which a person can commit the offences listed in the articles of the Convention. Article 6 defines offences in the stage before the actual harm is done and is intended to supplement the liability for criminal attempt. That was a delicate affair in the negotiations, which is demonstrated in Articke 6, paragraph 3, which allows states a degree of freedom to opt out of the obligation to criminalise the preparation stage. Instruments to prevent an overly broad definition of criminal behaviour, that is to say a definition that might include all kinds of legitimate actions, were already incorporated in the text of the article ("without right", "intentionally", "with the intent"), but an extra paragraph was clearly found necessary.

Procedural law

The procedural law section of chapter 2 of the Convention contains a variety of provisions. It sets out specific powers and procedures necessary to investigate computer crime (Articles 16-21) and defines scope and safeguards in Articles 14 and 15, to which the following articles continuously refer. Harmonisation of national procedural systems was not the aim of the Convention, that being too complicated and not necessary for the purpose of combating cyber crime internationally. As Article 15 paragraph 1 says: *Each Party shall ensure that the establishment, implementation and application of the powers and procedures provided for in this Section are subject to conditions and safeguards provided for under its domestic law, ...* The text then continues with a reference to human rights conventions that shall be respected adequately in these conditions and safeguards. In the field of powers and procedures national differentiation is less affected by the Convention, as long as the safeguards are on or above a certain minimum, to which the state parties already committed themselves by joining conventions on human rights.

The powers and procedures listed in Articles 16 to 21 can be summarised as follows:

- Ordering the preservation of computer and traffic data and related powers, Articles 16 and 17;
- Ordering the production of computer data, subscriber information and related powers, Article 18;
- Searching and seizure of stored computer data, Article 19;
- Real-time collection of traffic data, Article 20 (see box 4.4);
- Interception of content data, Article 21.

Box 4.4   Article 20 – Real-time collection of traffic data

1   Each Party shall adopt such legislative and other measures as
    may be necessary to empower its competent authorities to:
    a   collect or record through the application of technical means
        on the territory of that Party, and
    b   compel a service provider, within its existing technical
        capability:
        i   to collect or record through the application of technical
             means on the territory of that Party; or
        ii   to co-operate and assist the competent authorities in
             the collection or recording of, traffic data, in real-time,
             associated with specified communications in its territory
             transmitted by means of a computer system.
2   Where a Party, due to the established principles of its
    domestic legal system, cannot adopt the measures referred
    to in paragraph 1.a, it may instead adopt legislative and
    other measures as may be necessary to ensure the real-time
    collection or recording of traffic data associated with specified
    communications transmitted in its territory, through the
    application of technical means on that territory.
3   Each Party shall adopt such legislative and other measures
    as may be necessary to oblige a service provider to keep
    confidential the fact of the execution of any power provided for
    in this article and any information relating to it.
4   The powers and procedures referred to in this article shall be
    subject to Articles 14 and 15.

As can be seen from box 4.4, the Convention prescribes the empowerment of
national authorities to certain specific actions and refers to the general provisions in Articles 14 and 15. According to Article 20 the national authorities
must be able to obtain (a record of) traffic data in real time, either by its own
collection or through the service provider. If necessary, the provider can be
subjected to compulsory measures, either incidentally or structurally. A general mandate to store traffic data for a certain period of time has been negotiated
but was not included in the Convention.[8] Paragraph 3 provides for the introduction of the power to order confidentiality upon the provider, because this

8   This controversial issue was tackled by the EU in Directive 2006/24/EC, OJ L105/54.

service provider could inform the participants in the data traffic and thereby frustrate the investigation.

Cooperation between states

Chapter 3 of the Cyber crime Convention pays attention to instruments for international cooperation in concrete cases and represents a key issue in the agreement. Without adequate arrangements for cross border law enforcement the entire effort of the Convention would lose much of its effect. What would have been the use of the harmonisation of substantive law, when the results thereof in the national jurisdictions would never be put to use to support law enforcement action of another state? The various forms of cross border cooperation are addressed in the text of Articles 23 to 35. In addition to the ordinary forms of cooperation assistance, activities are regulated that are specific for cyber crime. The point is repeated here that the inclusion of those instruments in the Convention is not in itself enough to empower national authorities to make use of them. Almost all jurisdictions require national legislation as a legitimate basis for any invasion of individual rights, which is also required by provisions such as Article 8 of the European Convention on Human Rights. Article 8 requires a regulation by national law in order to attain a certain level of predictability for individuals. By becoming party to the Cyber crime Convention states have pledged to assist each other to the widest extent for the purpose of combating the breaches of cyber safety that are defined in chapter 1 of the Convention. Article 23 provides for this.

These general principles are elaborated further in the succeeding articles, firstly for extradition, that is: the surrender of a person to another state in order to be prosecuted or subjected to execution of an earlier conviction (Article 24). Articles 25 to 28 then continue to pave the way for an expeditious and smooth cooperation between state authorities in the investigation of cyber offences by way of assisting the collection of information and/or evidence. Article 35 provides for a communication network of contact points available around-the-clock to ensure timely assistance when requested. The factual material in cyberspace can be highly volatile and immediacy can be called for in investigations. In this context the Convention uses the term mutual assistance, admittedly confusing language but it is traditional in international law to indicate this type of assistance by using those specific words.[9]

---

9 Mutual assistance is the activity of state authorities to help their colleagues from other countries in the investigation, prosecution and adjudication of crime and the execution of sentences; example: collection and surrender of information, obtained from a computer search.

We now refer to the text of the Convention and pay some attention only to those forms of assistance that are specific to combating cyber crime, also categorised as mutual assistance. Articles 29 to 34 deal in turn with assistance in the preservation of stored computer data, the disclosure of preserved traffic data, the search and access of stored computer data, the real time collection of traffic data and the interception of content data. Article 32 regulates trans-border action that a state may take without actual assistance or prior authorisation. According to its provisions one state may gain access to data publicly available in another state or benefit from the consent of the competent person in another state to share stored computer data. This may appear to be self evident, but it is still the investigative activity of one state in the territory of another state. It is therefore advisable to provide for an explicit legal basis. Other forms of this self-help activity are available under international law, but almost always subjected to prior or posterior approval. By the way, this article, like the others, reflects a geographical perspective on data location that may need some adjustment in the era of cloud computing. Currently, locating data in a certain hosting territory cannot be based on the appearance and requires extra investigation. Fortunately for the authorities, Article 32 makes that extra work redundant. Whatever can be accessed by way of ordinary clicks is available to investigating officers, without the duty to locate the data in a hosting state. This does not include the power of cross border invasion and search in computer systems or networks, because data retrieved thereby are not publicly available. This type of activity is quite relevant for the investigation of cyber crime, but no agreement was reached to include it in the Convention of 2001. For our introductory tour of the Cyber crime Convention chapter IV is less important. As already mentioned, it contains provisions that are relevant for the situation under international law, but not for the subject matter of this contribution.

We can now conclude that the previous section has demonstrated the actual substance and purpose of the Convention in the international and national combat against certain cyber offences. As we shall see later, this largely explains its national legal status, but to complete the legal picture it remains important to know about its domestic implementation. When adopting the legislation prescribed by the Convention, national states have followed the systematic features already present in their own criminal law. After full implementation Parties to the Convention will have adopted the same instruments but these may differ in form. That is a feature of the law which, despite its success, the Convention cannot remove.

The Convention reflects the state of affairs as concluded in 2001. In this ever changing playing field, new forms of criminal behaviour have emerged that fall outside the terms of the original agreement. The Council of Europe has responded to new developments by initiating negotiations to supplement the terms of the Convention to address more forms of distribution of illegal content. The negotiations leading to the 2001 agreement did not take the content-related offences further than child pornography. In 2003 the text of the first additional protocol was open for signature, dealing with racist and xenophobic material. Following the framework as highlighted above, the protocol prescribes the criminalisation of the distribution to the public of such material through a computer system (Article 3), as well as threats and insults of a racist or xenophobic nature (Articles 4 and 5). Article 6 deal with the criminalisation of denial or minimisation of genocide and crimes against humanity when distributed through a computer system.

4.3   Convention of Lanzarote 2007

The joining of international forces to prevent and combat cyber crime is not only represented in the specific cyber crime initiatives, but can also be found in other international agreements. To familiarise the users of this book with that reality, we briefly pay attention to the contentious area of sexual abuse and exploitation of children. In that area the Council of Europe developed an initiative and concluded an agreement in 2007: the Council of Europe Convention on the Protection of Children against Sexual Exploitation and Sexual Abuse, signed on 25 October 2007 on the Spanish Island Lanzarote (CETS 201). Among the official observations that precede the actual text of the agreement, one is particularly interesting for the present; see box 4.7.

Box 4.7   sexual exploitation and sexual abuse

Observing that the sexual exploitation and sexual abuse of children have grown to worrying proportions at both national and international level, in particular as regards the increased use by both children and perpetrators of information and communication technologies (ICTs), and that preventing and combating such sexual exploitation and sexual abuse of children require international co-operation;

The parties to the agreement are quite clearly aware of the connection between suppression of sexual exploitation and cyber safety. Consequently the text of the convention contains provisions that deal with the promotion of safety for children in cyberspace. In chapter VI on substantive law the parties agree on criminalisation of many sexually abusive or oppressive acts. A clear reference to ICT can be found in the provision relating to child pornography (Article 20) where the obtaining of access to child pornography through ICT is included in the acts that should be criminalised: Article 20, paragraph 1.f. The same article refers implicitly to ICT where the transmission of child pornography is listed in paragraph 1.c, which certainly embraces the digital transmission of such illegal material.

For the promotion of child safety in cyberspace Article 23 is particularly interesting. That provision prescribes the criminalisation of "intentional proposal, through information and communication technologies, of an adult to meet a child who has not reached the age …" set by national law for a child to be engaged in sexual activity by an adult, for the purpose of committing forbidden sexual acts or producing child pornography. This so-called 'grooming' of a child should be a criminal offence when the proposal has been followed by material acts leading to a meeting.

We can thus see that the states that become party to the agreement on child protection not only have to reconsider and reformulate their criminal law relating to sex crimes against children, but also take a look at the cyber crime provisions in their national legislation. The community of states obviously accepts that in modern society the territory of crime is no longer limited to the real world but includes electronic highways and digital spaces around the globe. One particularly controversial part of this awareness was the criminalisation of virtual child pornography, which is the construction of pornographic images by manipulating photographic material or by producing graphic material of a non-existent child. Some states objected to the inclusion of this activity as an offence where others argued that child safety also suffers from the production and circulation of that type of child porn, now that rapid developments in technology allow for the production of extremely lifelike images.[10] A result of the negotiations was the duty to criminalise, in combination with an explicit opportunity to opt out. The Lanzarote Convention carries such combination in Article 20, paragraphs 1 and 3.

---

10   See Explanatory Report to CETS 201, nr. 144.

4.4   Examples of implementation

As an example of the way in which national governments dealt with cyber crime, we discuss the criminalisation of some forms of cyberc rime in the Dutch and German Criminal Code below, with particular emphasis on the role of the above-mentioned international instruments. We will demonstrate that national states follow their own systematic features when implementing treaty obligations. The outcome of the implementation process will consequently differ from country to country. States have their separate histories, and criminal legislation reflects their different choices in the course of that history. The offences are sometimes hard to find and national legislators have often not introduced any new provisions in the criminal code at all after the ratification of relevant international and EU instruments. In many cases they have come to the conclusion that the international duty to criminalise was already covered by an existing offence in its present form, or by a change of interpretation of the existing offence for which the text does not require to be reformulated. So where the international picture may represent a high level of unity and uniformity, the national scene is one of differentiation and diversity. Where the aim of harmonisation is the most relevant for substantive law, we will introduce readers only to the diversity in offences at the national level. Differences in procedural law are less surprising, one might say.

In the Netherlands specific legislation on cyber offences started in the early 1990s by including computer crimes in the criminal code.[11] The Dutch legislator adopted a computer variety of classical offences such as illegal trespassing and illegal damaging and inserted those in the criminal code immediately after the classical offence. A revision introduced in 2006 covered the implementation of the Cyber crime Convention.[12] The Lanzarote Convention did not warrant more legislative action than the inclusion of access through ICT (Art 20; see above) in the child pornography offence, the introduction of the offence of inducing the presence of children at sexual acts and of the offence of grooming in the Criminal Code. Other criminal acts in the Convention were already present in the chapter on sexual crimes, including the ban on virtual child pornography.

---

11   Act of 27 December 1992, Staatsblad (State Gazette) 1993, 33; entry into force 1 March 1993.

12   Act of 1 June 2006, Staatsblad (State Gazette) 2006, 300; entry into force 1 September 2006.

The offences are distributed over the various chapters of the Dutch criminal code. The safety of public networks was already included in title VII of the second book in the Code, which title deals with offences against public safety. Offences relating to the safety of the public ICT network can be found in that title (Arts 161sexies and 161septies Criminal Code). Illegal access to computers was classified as a version of illegal trespassing, thus placing these offences under title V on public order. This includes illegal access (Art. 138ab Criminal Code) and e-bombing/DoS attacks (Art. 138b Criminal Code), illegal data tapping (Art. 139d, paragraph 1 Criminal Code) and the preparatory offences (Art 139d, paragraph 2 Criminal Code).

The contamination of computer systems with viruses, malware etcetera is classified as a specific variety of criminal damage and included in title XXVII on damaging property. The offences under Dutch law are the erasure, disabling or damaging of digital data, either intentionally (Art 350a Criminal Code) or through negligence (Art 350b Criminal Code). It is interesting to note that the deliberate choice of the legislature in the 1990s not to include cyber versions of illegal appropriation and fraud in the Criminal Code has been maintained until today. Fraud by way of interfering with internet banking systems, for example, is therefore to be classified (and prosecuted) either as one of the offences mentioned above or as a form of classical fraud or theft. Case law has shown that the courts are prepared to give a modern interpretation to classical terminology in the Code. For example the withdrawal of money from a bank account by using an illegally obtained password or personal identification code has been successfully prosecuted as theft by using a false key.

The Dutch Criminal Code reflects the same mixed approach in the case of digital forms of sexual abuse. In title XIV on vice crimes we can find the inclusion of pornographic images on data carriers alongside real objects and images, as well as the virtual images in the offence relating to child pornography (Articles 240a and 240b Criminal Code). On the 1th of October 2002 article 240b was adjusted in such a way that this article became applicable to all persons under the age of 18 instead of 16.[13] Grooming is explicitly criminalised in the

---

13 Act of 13 July 2002, Staatsblad (State Gazette) 2002, 388; entry into force 1 October 2002. Based on the 'International Labour Organisation (ILO) Convention No 182 of 17 June 1999 concerning the prohibition and immediate action for the elimination of the worst forms of child labour' (www.ilo.org/public/english/standards/relm/ilc/ilc87/com-chic. htm<http://www.ilo.org/public/english/standards/relm/ilc/ilc87/com-chic.htm>).

same title in Article 248e Criminal Code, as a consequence of accession to the Lanzarote Convention.[14]

In Germany, as in the Netherlands, the provisions relating to cyber crime are scattered throughout the Criminal Code. Their place in the code is determined on the basis of their similarities with traditional (offline) crimes. To give some examples: child pornography (sections 184b to 184d Criminal Code) is included in chapter 13 'Offences against sexual self-determination'; data espionage (by means of unauthorised access; section 202a Criminal Code) is included in chapter 15 'Violation of privacy'; and computer fraud (section 263a Criminal Code) is included in chapter 22 'Fraud and embezzlement'.

Germany's legislators took their first steps in the field of computer crime as early as 1986, when the Second Act to Combat Economic Crime came into force.[15] This act introduced, inter alia, the above-mentioned criminal provisions on data espionage (section 202a Criminal Code) and computer fraud (section 263a Criminal Code). The second relevant legislative action is the Information and Communication Services Act of 1997.[16] As far as the Criminal Code is concerned, this law brought only a few changes. The main change is the clarification of the term 'writings' (in German: 'Schriften'). For this purpose, section 11 subsection 3 Criminal Code was extended to include 'data storage media'. The subsection now reads: 'Audiovisual media, data storage media, illustrations and other depictions shall be equivalent to written material in the provisions which refer to this subsection'.[17] As a consequence, in every section that contains a reference to this subsection, data storage media should be understood as equivalent to writings.

The third act that played an important part in this context is the Act against computer crime.[18] This act is designed to implement – to the extent necessary – the Council of Europe Convention on Cyber crime[19] and the EU Council Frame-

---

14 Act of 26 November 2009, Staatsblad (State Gazette) 2009, 544; entry into force 1 January 2010.

15 Zweites Gesetz zur Bekämpfung der Wirtschaftskriminalität, BGBl. 1986 I Nr. 21, p. 721 (proposed law: BT-Drs. 10/318).

16 *Gesetz zur Regelung der Rahmenbedingungen* für Informations- und Kommunikationsdienste (Informations- und Kommunikationsdienste-Gesetz - IuKDG), BGBl. 1997 I Nr. 52, p. 1870 (proposed law: BT-Drs. 13/7385).

17 Translation : www.gesetze-im-internet.de/englisch_stgb/german_criminal_code.pdf.

18 Einundvierzigstes Strafrechtsänderungsgesetz zur Bekämpfung der Computerkriminalität (41. StrÄndG), BGBl. I 2007 Nr. 38, p. 1786 (proposed law: BT-Drs. 16/3656).

19 Budapest 23 November 2001, *ETS* No. 185.

work Decision [20] on Attacks Against Information Systems[21] into substantive criminal law. For example, on the basis of Article 2 of both the Convention and the Framework Decision, Germany has to criminalise 'hacking'. Until then it was not completely clear whether merely gaining unauthorised access by circumventing a protection (without 'spying' on data) was covered by section 202a subsection 1 Criminal Code (data espionage) (Heckmann 2011). For that reason the criminal provision was modified so that no doubt remained in this respect. Another important modification to the Criminal Code was the criminalisation of acts preparatory to data espionage and phishing in section 202c Criminal Code, in order to implement Article 6 subsection 1 under a. of the Convention on Cyber crime.[22]

On the basis of Article 9 of the Convention on Cyber crime, the provision on child pornography needed to be adjusted with respect to the age of the person involved. In Germany, section 184b Criminal Code on child pornography only covers children under 14 years of age, while the Convention demanded that criminalisation be applicable to all persons under 16 years of age, and preferably even 18 years of age. This age limit was addressed together with the required modifications on the basis of the EU Framework Decision on Combating the Sexual Exploitation of Children and Child Pornography[23] in the 'Act to implement the EU Framework Decision on combating the sexual exploitation of children and child pornography'.[24] For this purpose, section 184c Criminal Code was introduced, which deals with juvenile pornography (pornography with persons between the ages of 14 and 18).

71

---

20 A EU Framework Decision is a regulatory text from the competent EU institutions, that is binding for the member states to implement minimum rules or a minimum situation for a common purpose (under the law before the Lisbon Treaty, used for justice and home affairs).
21 Council Framework Decision 2005/222/JHA, Official Journal of the European Union 2005, L 69/67.
22 BT-Drs. 16/3656, p. 11-12.
23 Council Framework Decision 2004/68/JHA, Official Journal of the European Union 2004, L 13/44.
24 Gesetz zur Umsetzung des Rahmenbeschlusses des Rates der Europäischen Union zur Bekämpfung der sexuellen Ausbeutung von Kindern und der Kinderpornographie, BGBl. 2008 I Nr. 50, p. 2149 (proposed law: BT-Drs. 16/3439).

4.5 Summary and conclusion

In order to support a starters' level of knowledge we have demonstrated two international legal instruments with which states seek to promote cyber safety. Those instruments aim at the harmonisation of criminal law, the empowerment of national authorities to take appropriate action for criminal law enforcement in cyberspace, the formulation of minimum safeguards and the improvement of mutual cross border cooperation by furnishing legal support for various forms of assistance.

So far the most inclusive instrument is the Cyber crime Convention of 2001 and its Additional Protocol, specifically designed to promote the common combating of cyber crimes. Other international agreements may also contain provisions that are relevant for this purpose. To illustrate that point we have discussed the Convention of Lanzarote on the Protection of Children against Sexual Exploitation and Sexual Abuse, concluded in 2007.

Much of the cyber crime territory has been covered, but new forms of crime surface not only as a consequence of new digital technologies and practices, but also as a result of smart exploration of new opportunities by individuals and criminal organisations. Drawing up a supplement to an international convention is a very lengthy process, but in the meantime national courts are able to adapt the current cyber crime definitions to new circumstances. That has to be done by way of interpretation, and there are limits to the scope of criminal law. New legislation may be found necessary in the near future. In the area of powers and procedures, the cross border search in non-public computer systems is greatly missed. In that respect the contemporary international instruments adhere too closely to a geographic approach to data and systems.

International agreements forcefully determine the content of the law on cyber safety. However, the current criminal legislation of national states also mirrors their separate histories and the deliberate choices they have made in responding to the development of computer crime. In order to underline this statement we briefly discussed Dutch and German substantive criminal law. The extent to which this national diversity influences the success of joint actions against cyber crime is a topic for further research. The overall conclusion still stands: that the necessary instruments are to a large extent available. It is for the national authorities to add to that by giving a high priority to combating cyber crime, whether within their borders or internationally. Cyber safety is not a matter that is confined within national boundaries, and that should also not be the case with the issue of combating cyber crime.

Key concepts

Convention
Treaty
(Additional) Protocol
EU Directive
EU Framework Decision
Harmonisation
Mutual assistance

5   Privacy

Jaap-Henk Hoepman & Marc van Lieshout

5.1   Privacy: a fundamental right

What is privacy?

The definition of privacy presented by Zureik et al. (2010) captures most relevant dimensions that are usually encountered: (1) the right to be left alone (no intrusion by third parties if not wanted), (2) limited access to the self (e.g. refuse to open the door of your house if you don't want to), (3) secrecy (e.g. correspondence such as email must remain confidential)), (4) control of personal information (e.g. being able to know what data the supermarket or the tax office have collected about you), (5) personhood (e.g. you may experiment with your identity, if that makes you happy), and (6) intimacy (no one can enter the very private sphere around you if not allowed to do so). These six dimensions are loosely related to a classical distinction made by Westin (1967), differentiating between various spheres of privacy: solitude, intimacy, reserve and anonymity. These two definitions show that privacy is a relatively broad concept that captures various aspects of ordinary life.

When we take the point of view of information and communication technology, the focus is primarily on the informational dimension of privacy. It relates to personal data that floats around and may be used – outside direct control of the subject to which the data relate. In this context one can define privacy as the right to control the release of personal information about oneself, even when that data is collected and stored by a third party.

Although proper security mechanisms are needed to protect personal information and prevent unauthorised access and use of that information, it is important to understand that privacy is not the same as confidentiality (or data security). The right to privacy also stipulates that personal data is only collected when that is necessary, that no more personal data is collected than needed, and that such data should only be used for the purpose for which it was originally collected. Also, people have the right to view and update personal information held by others about themselves

The importance of privacy

Privacy is not only a personal value, but also a common societal value. Offering a personal shelter to all has potential benefits for society as a whole. It is a prerequisite for realising all of one's own potential and the ability to develop one's own opinion, which contributes in turn to the development and innovation of society as a whole (Solove 2010). Privacy has always been related to freedom: being free from intrusion against one's will, and being free in choosing one's own life path, thus being autonomous. The origins of this position stem from liberal thinkers such as John Locke who state that free individuals are for the benefit of a free and open society.

But what about people who say 'I have nothing to hide'? This frequently heard argument (sometimes phrased as 'If you have nothing to hide you have nothing to fear') is wrong for several reasons. First of all, it assumes that privacy is about hiding wrong, illegal, things. But all of us have many innocent, perhaps even irrelevant things that we would not like to reveal to others, such as our salary, our PIN code (Personal Identification Number), our sex life, and much more. Secondly, things that are legal or harmless now, may be illegal in the future. If you reveal them now, they may harm you later. Similarly, things that are normal in one context (a party, a holiday) are frowned upon in another context (at work).

The threat to privacy

The invention of computers has made it possible to store data in digital databases that can be searched very efficiently. Furthermore, the rise of the internet has made it easier to interconnect databases. This allows for more complex searches and mining for more complex patterns. Data collected in one context (e.g. your work) becomes connected to data collected in another context (e.g. your private life).

In fact we live in an 'information society'. In economic terms, information has become a resource (like oil, water, etc.). Information, including personal information, has economic value. In societal terms, information is increasingly used as the fabric we use to build relations with our peers, our friends and family. We use mobiles, email, or social networks (like Facebook) to stay in touch. In fact we increasingly use such social networks to build and expose our own self-image or identity. Much of that information is very private in nature, but is stored centrally by the social networks, and accessible to 'the whole world' (unless you have applied the correct privacy settings[25]). This personal information is the main economical resource of these networks. It is therefore in the interest of such networks to collect as much (personal) information as possible, in order to increase company value.

Another threat to privacy is the increased aversion to risk in our current society. In the 20th century, the western world has experienced tremendous economic growth. People are much better off now than they were a century ago, and as a result they stand to lose much more. In recent decades this has led to the development of a 'risk-averse society' where increasingly stronger levels of control are implemented to prevent 'mishappenings' and to limit risks. Camera surveillance is one example of this trend (Beck 1990; Giddens 1992).

The 9-11 terrorist attacks and the events that followed have further increased the need for so-called homeland security, to protect our society from outside attacks. This has resulted in invasive anti-terrorism laws and increased surveillance. Airport security has intensified because of this, including the development of so-called body scanners. And governments surreptitiously gain access to more and more sources of data, like the US government that monitors international bank transfers of EU citizens through the international banking network SWIFT (COM 2010).

5.2   Protecting privacy

Legal measures

One typical approach to protecting privacy is using legal measures. Most prominent is the Universal Declaration of Human Rights. In Article 12 this states that 'No one shall be subjected to arbitrary interference with his privacy, family, home or correspondence, nor to attacks upon his honour and reputation. Everyone has the right to the protection of the law against such interference or attacks.' This right to protection is repeated in the European Charter of Fundamental Rights (2000) which states that everyone has the right to respect for his or her private and family life, home and communications (Article 7) and everyone has the right to protection of personal data (Article 8). The distinction between these two articles is telling: while Article 7 relates to privacy,

---

25 Note however that sometimes, privacy settings are ignored or adjusted by organisations. Facebook did so in 2010 when adjusting all privacy defaults to 'open to the world'. This was heavily criticised and as a consequence Facebook had to change its privacy policy back again.

Article 8 relates to personal data. In our approach we would consider Article 8 to relate to the informational dimension of privacy. As we will show, in current practices both articles become more closely related.

In national legislation the right to privacy is generally recognised in the Constitution. The Dutch Constitution for example states that all Dutch citizens have a right to privacy (Article 10). Though not referring to an absolute right (even constitutional rights need to be balanced against each other) privacy can thus not easily be 'traded away'.

It is the right to protection of personal data that is of particular relevance for this chapter. This right has led to some important European Directives.[26] The two most relevant are the directive 'on the protection of individuals with regard to the processing of personal data and on the free movement of such data' (Directive 95/46/EC) and the directive 'concerning the protection of personal data and the protection of privacy in the electronic communications sector' (Directive 2002/58/EC). This latter Directive has meanwhile been inserted in a larger Directive (2009/136/EC) that integrates two directives (one on Universal Service as well) and a Regulation on consumer laws. Some aspects of the 2002/58/EC directive have been elaborated in greater detail in the new Directive.

Directive 95/46/EC formulates a number of criteria for the lawful processing of personal data. These criteria refer in turn to a set of privacy principles which had already been formulated by the OECD (Organisation for Economic Cooperation and Development) in 1980 (OECD 2011). Each processing of personal data may entail a possible infringement on the privacy of the people whose data are collected and processed. That is only allowed when it can be justified on the following grounds:
–   it serves a legitimate aim
–   it is lawful
–   collecting and processing the data is necessary (for instance to deliver a service or a product).

When data collection can be justified, the process itself should meet the following criteria:

---

26 Directives oblige Member States to develop national laws which implement the content of the Directive.

- it should serve a clear purpose
- the purpose cannot be achieved in another, less invasive way (subsidiarity)
- the data collection should be proportionate (not excessive, and in line with the purpose)
- safeguards should be in place (security measures, quality of data)
- the rights of the 'data subjects' should be guaranteed (informed consent, the right to access and correct the data)

An important exception to the safeguards presented is the need to infringe upon someone's privacy on grounds of national interest or a relevant public interest (Data protection directive 95/46/EC Article 3). The fight against serious crimes and terrorism may make privacy infringements necessary. A relevant tool in this respect is the possibility of retaining data for a specific period of time. The European Data Retention Directive (2006/24/EC) prescribes that all European countries are obliged to determine a specific period of time in which traffic and location data need to be retained. The Netherlands opted for a period of 12 months, which is double the standard minimum period prescribed by the European Data Retention Directive. Protecting the borders of Europe against illegal immigrants requires the exchange of personal data between border authorities. Emergency services are also at liberty to infringe upon an individual's privacy in the event of an alert that requires direct intervention. In all these cases the main question is the acceptable extent of privacy infringement and the safeguards that ought to be in place to support citizens in exercising their democratic rights. This is not an easy playing field. A relevant phenomenon is *function creep*: over time the functionality of a system may change and grow, encompassing functions which diverge from the original purposes of the system. An illustration of function creep is provided by the public transport card. Today's public transport cards are RFID-based cards. Travel data are stored for the purposes of optimising transport efficiency and reducing fraud. Every now and then intelligence services request travel data in order to track criminals. The increase in such requests has been manifold since the introduction of the RFID-based public transport card. What is not known however is how many additional criminals have been caught by using these data. It is thus difficult to assess whether such privacy infringement is justified. Data were never collected with the aim of using them to track criminals. National interest may play a role here and may – as stated above – legitimate the use of these data. Commercial objectives form another purpose for data collection (to offer non-travel-related services, for instance). The Dutch owner of the public transport card, TransLink, had formulated the provision of commercial services with no direct link to travel functionalities as a purpose for the intended data collection. The Dutch Data Protection Authority considered this to be outside the scope of the original purpose of the data collection and therefore requested TransLink to reconsider and reformulate its strategy concerning the use of collected and aggregated travel data.[27]

Technical measures

Informational privacy deals with the release and control of *personal identifiable information (PII)* – information that can be linked, with reasonable effort, to a natural person. A reasonable effort in this context is for example to use data in several different databases (even if some of those are not under your immediate control) to establish such a link. This is why the European Article 29 Working Party (an organisation formed by the European Data Protection Authorities and initiated in consequence of Article 29 of the European Data Protection Directive 95/46/EC) expressed the opinion (Article 29 WP 2010) that an IP address is personal information: using the database of the Internet Service Provider (ISP), the name and address of the account holder corresponding to that IP address can be identified.

The goal of technical measures to protect privacy is to make it difficult (if not impossible) to link a piece of information to a natural person, and to give a user control over his or her personal data once that data has been given to someone else. We note that surprisingly few tools are available to control data once it has been released. We therefore focus on the so-called Privacy Enhancing Technologies (PET) to hide the link between persons and their personal data. These technologies aim to achieve a certain level of *anonymity, unlinkability* or *unobservability* (Hansen & Pfitzmann 2011).

Anonymity is defined as 'the state of being not identifiable within a set of subjects', which captures the intuitive notion of 'hiding in the crowd'. *Unlinkability* guarantees that two events or data items cannot be linked to each other. Examples of such events are visiting several websites, or sending several emails. Examples of such data items are your subscription to a newspaper, or your current place of work. Finally, *unobservability* guarantees that nobody is able to tell whether a certain event (like sending a message) did or did not take place.

---

27 Although it did not in fact prevent the subsequent introduction of the OV-chipcard in the Netherlands.

A powerful onslaught against these privacy properties is called *traffic analysis*. This can be used to identify the sender and receiver of a message without looking at the content of the message, and therefore works even if such messages are encrypted. It typically involves monitoring several network links under one's control, and trying to correlate the messages one sees on different links. Traffic analysis (and the related concept of network analysis that maps relationships among people based on user profiles on social networks) is a powerful tool to determine the mutual relationships between people in a group, and is often used in criminal investigations (for example requesting the phone and/ or email records of suspected individuals). Data retention ensures that the relevant (historic) communication data is available to achieve this.

Some techniques
We will briefly describe some of the basic privacy enhancing techniques that can be used to combat traffic analysis and implement certain levels of unlinkability.

Pseudonyms can be used to hide the relationship between a real natural person and some personal data. Nicknames or arbitrary numbers can serve this purpose, as long as the relationship between pseudonym and a real person is unknown.

Mix networks are deployed to thwart traffic analysis and to achieve unlinkability. Traffic analysis works under the assumption that incoming and outgoing messages at a server can be related to each other by looking at their content, size and the time and order they came in and went out again. Mix networks make this harder, by re-encrypting incoming messages before sending them out, and padding all messages with extra bits to make them the same size. Mix networks also use a store-and-forward process whereby a server stores incoming messages until a certain number of them have been received before sending them out in random order. A well-known implementation of a mix network is Tor.[28]

Secret sharing is a technique that allows one to split a message (or a key) into several shares such that each share in itself contains no information about the message. To reconstruct the message, all, or a subset, of the shares have to be brought together.

Anonymous credentials are a form of anonymous attribute certificates. Similar to attribute certificates, such credentials express a property of a subject (like 'the bearer of this credential is over 18 years old'), that is signed by an authority

81

---

28 http://www.tor.org.

that can verify the validity of the claim. Traditional attribute certificates are not anonymous, because the same certificate is presented whenever one wants to convince someone about the validity of a claim.

Privacy by design

The technical opportunities to prevent the misuse of personal data can be complemented with other measures. Organisational measures may help prevent unauthorised access to personal data. These may include specific privacy officers who seek to create greater awareness of privacy aspects throughout the organisation. Large companies like Google and Nokia employ officers whose main task is to formulate and safeguard a privacy policy for the company, raising awareness for privacy issues within the company and representing the company in the outside world when privacy is at stake. In the Netherlands, the Dutch Data Protection Agency also had such a role.

Since all information systems need to comply with national and international regulations and laws, a variety of tools have been developed that support a more integrated or holistic approach to the role of privacy in developing and using new systems. This approach is known as *privacy by design*. Privacy by design adopts the perspective that privacy should not be regarded as an issue that needs to be taken into account when a system is ready for use but that privacy should already be adopted as one of the *design parameters* of a system in the early stages of systems design. Privacy by design not only considers technological measures as means to safeguard privacy of individuals, but also includes physical and organisational measures. This requires an analysis of the privacy risks *before* a system is developed. *Privacy impact assessments* (PIA) offer a methodological framework to assess these risks (Van Lieshout et al. 2011).

At the 2010 annual meeting of data protection agencies in Jerusalem a resolution was adopted that was based on the notion of privacy by design. The resolution stipulates that technology, business practice and physical measures go hand in hand. The following seven privacy principles show the way forward:
- Be *proactive* instead of reactive.
- Privacy should be a *default* setting.
- Privacy should be *embedded* in the design.
- Privacy-embedded systems still should offer *full functionality*.
- Privacy-embedded systems should offer *end-to-end security*.
- *Visibility* of measures taken and *transparency* on processes should be guaranteed.
- Keep *users* in the centre of the development process.

Notwithstanding any intuitive appeal these guidelines may have, not many systems are being developed today on the basis of these principles. One positive example, however, is the design of a body scanner for use at airports (Cavoukian 2011). In the case of body scanners, technological, business practice and physical measures are integrated to shield off private data as much as possible without negative consequences for the functionality of the system (detecting objects that could pose a threat in airplanes).

5.3   The future of privacy

Revocable privacy: resolving the tension between security and privacy

Security and privacy are seen as conflicting requirements (Cavoukian 2010). It is widely believed that they are a 'zero-sum' game (Schneier 2008): security cannot be achieved without sacrificing privacy, and vice-versa. This tension between security and privacy is felt in many areas of public policy making. Examples include camera surveillance, systems for road pricing, interconnecting national and international databases for law enforcement purposes, national ID-cards and their integration into national systems for identity management and e-government. Due to the high political importance given to homeland security, this has resulted in approaches to increasing societal safety that disregard the privacy of the citizens. Similarly, in designing privacy enhancing technologies (PET) no attention is being paid to the quite reasonable request to consider societal security issues at the same time.

This is an unfortunate state of affairs. In fact, it is our belief that in a democratic society the terms and conditions for using a public infrastructure are determined by society as a whole, as part of the democratic decision making process, balancing several societal needs. PETs as well as security mechanisms for public infrastructures should be designed in compliance with these terms and conditions. One approach to reconciling security and privacy requirements can be found in the concept of *revocable privacy*.

It is essential to realise that legal or regulatory attempts to remedy the imbalance between security and privacy are inadequate in themselves. Rules and regulations may change over time, allowing for more possibilities to gather information about people. Such 'function creep' occurs frequently, as we indicated earlier: once a system offers certain means of collecting data, sooner or later politicians, government officials or law enforcement will request an

extension of powers. The solution must therefore be sought in limiting possibilities in the architecture and design of the system at the outset, through
technical means. That makes it impossible to change the rules after the fact.
This line of reasoning emanates from the idea that 'architecture is politics'[29]
and 'code as code'[30] (Lessig 1999), and is inspired by the 'Select before you
collect' principle (Jacobs 2005). To change the rules, the system has to be rede-
signed completely. Should such a redesign be performed, old data collected
with the old system remains inaccessible.

In essence the idea of revocable privacy is to design systems in such a way that
no personal information is available, unless a user violates the pre-established
terms of service. A system implements revocable privacy if the architecture of
the system guarantees that personal data is revealed only if a predefined rule
has been violated. Examples of such rules are 'spending digital money twice
is illegal', or 'users should pay for services rendered' or 'you should not access
data unless you have the right to do so'. Technical measures (comparable to
the use of unlinkable pseudonyms, secret sharing or mixing networks as discussed earlier) are used to guarantee this.

EU developments

Ten years after 9/11 we can observe that homeland security has left its traces
in the 'privacy landscape'. A recent communication of the European Commission identifies 18 different information systems and approaches that have been
developed or are under development for the purpose of safeguarding European
countries and citizens against terrorism, organised and serious crimes and
illegal immigration. Examples of such systems are the Schengen Information
System, the Visa Information System, EuroDAC (for collecting fingerprints),
the Customs Information Services, and the Advanced Passenger Information
system. Systems not yet in place but under development are a fully-fledged
Passenger Name Record system and an Entry-Exit system.[31] Co-operation and
legislation is practised in a number of initiatives and directives. A relevant
directive in this respect is the Data Retention directive we mentioned earlier
that regulates the storage of traffic and location data. This directive serves as a
test case since two European countries (Germany and Rumania) have declared
the directive to run counter to their constitution.

---

29 Attributed to Mitch Kapor, see http://blog.kapor.com/index9cd7.html?p=29.
30 'Code (the executable code of a computer program) as code (norms, laws, i.e. the code of
    conduct)'.
31 For a complete overview see COM (2010) 385 final.

The widespread introduction of information systems that serve to protect Europe against terrorism etc. has consequences for the privacy of European and non-European citizens. Function creep can be demonstrated to have occurred in the application of DNA profiles for solving serious crimes. Over time more detailed profiles could be exchanged and the use of these profiles was broadened from serious crime to much more mundane and ordinary crimes (Dahl & Saetnan 2009).

The European Commission and related parties such as the European Data Protection Supervisor and the Article 29 Working Party are discussing the follow-up of the Data Protection directive (95/46/EC) and the elaboration of recent communications and directives that regulate specific parts of the 'privacy landscape'. A new Data Protection directive should further harmonise data protection laws across member states, and should take into account new technological developments (internet of things, for instance) as well as new social developments (the emergence of social media) with their associated risks and problems. It also introduces an explicit 'right to be forgotten'. This development goes hand in hand with a revision of tasks and responsibilities of the national Data Protection Authorities. Within the Netherlands the revision of the Dutch DPA (*Commissie Bescherming Persoonsgegevens*) is moving in the direction of a stronger supervisory role with less attention for awareness raising and information provision.

85

Fundamentally different approaches

Most legal and all technological protection for our privacy focuses on limiting the amount of personal information that is collected in the first place. This is a limited approach, and also one that is not very effective when people are willingly revealing very personal information on social networks (like Facebook), and seem generally quite eager to provide personal information for a small benefit (for example when applying for loyalty cards). Instead people like Hildebrandt and Van den Hoven argue for a harm-based approach (in what Hildebrandt (2008) calls 'Ambient Law') that protects a person against unwarranted application of profiles one is not aware of, by requiring that people are treated equally despite obvious differences. The benefit of this approach is that it allows people to be more open and thus obtain the advantages of sharing information on the internet (as when using social networks like Facebook), while having legal protection against abuse of this information. A drawback is that users have to rely on government and businesses really not to abuse the data, and on enforcement agencies to enforce this.

Another radical different approach is presented by Koops (2010), who promotes data maximisation and dual transparency. Data maximisation should offer all of us access to all available data, thereby creating a 'level playing field' that makes no distinction between parties. Dual transparency means that both the data subjects and the process of data collection and storage are fully transparent.

5.4   Conclusions

This chapter has explored the various aspects of privacy. Privacy is closely related to data protection (of personally identifiable information) but also embraces spatial and corporeal dimensions. It represents a social value that is safeguarded in the Dutch constitution and the European Charter for Fundamental Rights. As appropriate tools for safeguarding privacy we have cited privacy by design and privacy enhancing technologies. These present a starting point that reconciles privacy requirements with requirements posed by homeland security. Though often positioned as a trade-off (more privacy means less security and the other way around) the alternatives presented show that privacy and security can be reconciled. This leads us to the following conclusions: Privacy requires a multidisciplinary perspective: technological, social and legal perspectives should be integrated.

New information technologies have generated many more opportunities for gathering and using data; not only has this had an impact on (informational) privacy, it also requires a broadening of scope to include spatial and corporeal dimensions (since these dimensions are currently not covered by data protection legislation).

Over the past decades new approaches to protecting privacy such as privacy enhancing technologies and privacy by design have emerged, which reconcile seemingly opposing interests (such as privacy viz-a-viz homeland security). One example of how these interests can be reconciled is Revocable Privacy More radical approaches to privacy exist, given todays' developments. These adopt a different perspective on how privacy should or could be safeguarded such as a harm-based approach, data maximisation rather than minimisation, and dual transparency.

Key concepts

Privacy (in the context of information systems)
Personal Identifiable Information (PII)
Privacy by design:
Anonymity
Privacy Enhancing Technologies (PET)
Function creep
Revocable privacy

6 Digitisation and the Orwellian Society[30]

Wouter Stol

6.1 Introduction

Just about every single new regulation to enforce the law in cyberspace attracts words of approval as well as strong criticism. The latter generally comes from the minority but expresses an anxiety that is deeply rooted in our society. This anxiety relates to the creation of a so-called police state. The combination of new technology in the hands of the police apparatus, together with ever increasing powers, bring the vision of an Orwellian society to many minds. Critics often interpret new powers as an infringement of their right to privacy. But what is happening in our society today is not what Orwell predicted in 1984. He was wrong in one important aspect. It is important to recognise this because there are lessons to be learned for policing in cyberspace. Let us stop to refresh our memories, consider the book in question and the discussion that accompanies it.

6.2 Orwell's 1984 ... and more

George Orwell's novel, 1984, was published in 1949. He looked 35 years into the future and did so almost 30 years before IBM launched their first personal computer onto the market (that was in 1981). Orwell wrote about a society in which the authorities monitored citizens via omnipresent 'telescreens' that could not be switched off. These machines were televisions, video cameras and intercoms all in one. The views of the leader are continuously to be heard on the television, a leader who goes by the comforting name of Big Brother. The video camera part of the machine comes equipped with an intercom function and is intended to observe people and correct them should they display deviant behaviour. The authorities make no secret of the fact that they are constantly watching their citizens. On the contrary, everywhere posters on the walls remind them 'Big Brother is watching you' (see box 6.1).

---

32 This chapter is based on Stol (2010).

Box 6.1   Orwell's *1984*

Winston and Julia are the protagonists in the novel. We are first introduced to Winston, who feels that he is different to the rest, that he has the right to his own thoughts and time to himself. This is of course highly suspect. Julia and Winston fall in love, so much so that they dare to flout the supervision of Big Brother. Together they create their own world in a room above a junk store, somewhere in a forgotten and somewhat shady neighbourhood. In the climax of the novel it turns out that the shopkeeper is connected to the Thought Police. 'There was a snap as though a catch had been turned back, and a crash of breaking glass. The picture had fallen to the floor, uncovering the telescreen behind it. "Now they can see us," said Julia. "Now we can see you," said the voice' (Orwell 1949: 230-1). Winston and Julia stand naked against the state apparatus and are arrested. The Thought Police instil in them state discipline in the Ministry of Love until they are physically exhausted and spiritually broken. 'Almost unconsciously he traced with his fingers in the dust on the table: 2+2=5. "They can't get inside you," she had said. But they could get inside you. (...) But it was all right, everything was all right, the struggle was finished. He had won the victory over himself. He loved Big Brother' (Orwell 1949: 303, 311).

This is how the expressions 'Big Brother' or 'Orwellian society' became proverbial for a government that uses information technology to discipline its citizens. The authorities acquire information technology and use it everywhere and constantly to monitor its citizens. These same authorities have far-reaching powers and citizens who don't toe the line are picked up and put under pressure for as long as it takes for them to let go of their idiosyncratic thoughts and adopt the philosophy of the state as the truth. In this society, privacy is suspect, for traitors have thoughts that undermine society and customs. And this is why more information technology in the hands of the authorities is, for many, linked to far-reaching infringements of privacy and other civil rights. Orwell's novel falls within a philosophical tradition involving tension between rational-technological thinking on the one hand and essential human aspects, such as ethics, feelings, intellect, emotions, originality and aesthetics on the other. In short, the tension between machinery and humanity. Various authors refer to the mechanical aspect of this, using terms such as Rationalisation (Weber 1922), The Machine (Mumford 1934), Technology (Ellul 1954), Technological Rationality or 'Techno-logic' (Marcuse 1968), Discipline

(Foucault 1975), Surveillance (Lyon 1994) and Technology (Fukuyama 2002). Some are more radical than others, but they all arrive at a common conclusion: the technological complex is becoming more and more dominant. This immediately raises the question of what room remains for being human.

Some authors point to the possibility that the problem will solve itself because people will gradually become reconciled to the technological complex. They will transform into machine-people that Haraway (1991) calls *Cyborgs* for short, and will no longer struggle with it. 'He loved Big Brother,' is how Orwell summarises this. Mills (1959) speaks of 'cheerful robots'. In Aldous Huxley's dystopia *Brave New World* (1932), people have succumbed en masse to a life controlled by technology. According to Fukuyama, this is the biggest fear that people have of modern technology, 'that we could undergo this change without realising that we have lost something of great value' (2002: 128).

Orwell does not debate the issue in abstract terms like many of the other authors generally do. He was not a scientist or philosopher, but worked for the police, in the army and in education – and he was a writer.[33] Orwell's strength in *1984* was that he got to the core of the discussion, magnified it and sketched the dilemma in concrete images, in images that large groups of people can understand. There are no conflicting concepts in his work, no invisible hand of history and no structures without acting subjects, but real-life characters – Winston and his lover Julia – in a body and mind conflict with real-life police officers that have at their disposal the power and the technology.

The police, the authorities and technology find themselves at the heart of this discussion. The government apparatus comprising a combination of the police, authorities and technology forms the very concrete machinery for which we should be afraid, according to Orwell, that is.

The police in our society are indeed the strong arm or power apparatus of the authorities. In the Western world, the police have the monopoly of violence, but it is not theirs to do with as they please (Newburn 2008). When it comes to law enforcement – in cyberspace as elsewhere – the police are under the command of the public prosecutor. He in turn answers to parliament. The press record the process. So the powers that be are under supervision. Yet are we

33 According to the preface of *1984*, Penguin Books edition, London, 1990.

paying sufficient attention? Or is it the case, as Fukuyama claims, that something precious is being lost?

Critics claim that extensions to police powers in cyberspace bring in their wake the loss of things of value – namely our privacy and our fundamental rights.

The French sociologist Jacques Ellul was decidedly negative about the combination of police and technology. In *The Technological Society*, he writes about the police and technical methods. As long ago as 1954 Ellul put into words the fear for police with technology to much better effect than many webloggers of today (box 6.2).

Box 6.2   Jacques Ellul about The Technological Society

'Another example is the police. The police have perfected to an unheard of degree technical methods both of research and of action. Everyone is delighted with this development because it would seem to guarantee an increasingly efficient protection against criminals. Let us put aside for the moment the problem of police corruption and concentrate on the technical apparatus, which, as I have noted, is becoming extremely precise. Will this apparatus be applied only on criminals? We know that this is not the case – and we are tempted to react by saying that it is the *state* that applies this technical apparatus without discrimination. But there is an error of perspective here. The instrument tends to be applied *everywhere* it *can* be applied. It functions without discrimination – because it exists without discrimination. The techniques of the police, which are developing at an extremely rapid tempo, have as their necessary end the transformation of the entire nation into a concentration camp. This is no perverse decision on the part of some party or government. To be sure of apprehending criminals, it is necessary that *everyone* be supervised. It is necessary to know exactly what every citizen is up to, to know his relations, his amusements, etc. And the state is increasingly in a position to know these things. This does not imply a reign of terror or of arbitrary arrests. The best technique is one that makes itself felt the least and which represents the least burden. But every citizen must be thoroughly known to the police and must live under conditions of discreet surveillance. All this results from the perfection of technical methods.' (1954: 100)

Ellul wrote this in 1954 when the police had no computers to be seen anywhere. The first experiments with computers by the police in the Netherlands, for example, were carried out in 1966, when they computerised the Identification Service (Stol 1996), more than 10 years after Ellul wrote his critical text. Ellul's work is very gloomy; his take on the police and technology is very dark. Just like Foucault, Ellul ascribes substantial powers to the police and, just like Foucault and Orwell for that matter, he concentrates on what the police are capable of doing with technology and how they can use it to observe and regulate the way citizens behave. But that's not the whole story. The reality nowadays reveals a different picture.

Our police have considerably more technology to hand than the police in the Ministry of Love in *1984*. Modern computers, databases, tapping equipment, analysis and investigation tools, tracking devices and so on make child's play of Orwell's telescreens in *1984*, with which the police had to keep their citizens under control. Yet we have to admit that our police are anything but in control. Citizens make use of the extra degree of freedom that technology, and cyberspace in particular, affords them (compare De Sola Pool 1983) and expand their opportunities by doing so, as do criminals. The authorities are active too. More and more activities in cyberspace are being regulated in terms of the law and the police are being given more powers. But despite their technology and their powers, the police cannot keep up with developments, and they do not have their citizens in their grasp (PWC 2001; Stol 2003; LPDO 2003; Van der Hulst & Neve 2008; Toutenhoofd et al. 2009; Stol et al. 2012). Cyberspace leads to an increase in unlawful acts. On balance, the authorities (the police) have lost rather than gained control over citizens' behaviour.

At the beginning of the 1990sin The Netherlands, Stol (1996) researched the effect of new information technology on police officers on the beat. At the time, something revolutionary was afoot: for the first time ever, police officers stored all the information about citizens and addresses on a police computer that they could consult later, as though it was a huge police memory bank. Project leaders and police chiefs expected that this would result in a more vigorous police performance, particularly when called out to fights and disturbances, such as domestic violence, loud music and disputes between neighbours. Those running amok – because their details were all on file now – would be confronted with police intervention and a police record, arrest and confiscation. During the study, when he made participatory observations on the streets, Stol did not see any more rigorous police interference with citizens – no glimpse of an Orwellian society (Stol 1996). Today we can see a police force wrestling with cyberspace and cyber crime (Stol et al. 2012). At the same time, the police do not seem to know how to turn the existing technology that they have at their disposal into more rigorous, or if you like, more vigorous or more effective police supervision; the police do not know how to employ these new tools so that they have a greater influence on the comings and goings of citizens. Why is it that, despite this wealth of modern technology, the police in our society are not developing in line with the expectations of Orwell (1934) and Ellul (1954)?

6.3 Beyond Orwell: the theory of technological enforcement

Orwell was right in one respect: if it is possible for a police state such as the one he sketches to come into being, then it is through a police apparatus with far-reaching powers and advanced information technology. You might say: if the police are so far behind in terms of knowledge, if they know so little about cyber crime, then it is no wonder that they do not know how to convert this new technology into more rigorous police action, and it will never amount to anything. This gap in knowledge plays a part in the current situation, but this is not a definitive and lasting impediment. Deficits can be dealt with. Expertise can be acquired or sub-contracted through collaborative efforts. The crux of Orwell's concept lies in the combination of intention and technology.

The intention of Orwell's government is to have total control of all citizens, everywhere and at all times. The authorities strive to eliminate individuality, to have total subordination to the state, so that people think and act as prescribed by 'the party'. The question of why the government would want this is not important here. The vision of 'the state' as the only social entity, with citizens who are no more than uniform and powerless – and preferably without will – cogs in the wheel, is a vision that has been around for a long time thanks to Sir Thomas More, an Englishman who described possibly the archetype of this kind of society in his novel, *Utopia*, in 1516. The Utopians have everything they want, but they too are under the constant eye of a malevolent government that intervenes rigorously at the slightest departure from the norm (More 1516). Utopia is therefore not a paradise but a nightmare, a vision that is more than four hundred years old. Information technology is the new element that Orwell introduces, centuries after More. That is what Orwell brings to the table. The more or less implicit message in his novel is that authorities are striving for total control and that information technology is the vehicle with which they may finally achieve this. Information technology may thus trigger an evil streak in the authorities. Information technology carries the promise of absolute knowledge about citizens, and with it absolute power – because power is knowledge and it generates more power, and so on. Information technology makes it possible for the authorities to expand into a fully-fledged control machine.

Again, the question whether authorities have essentially evil, machine-like intentions does not really matter. Our main concern here is with the principles of information technology and in particular how this translates to policing in cyberspace. In Orwellian terms, the question is: is more information technology in the hands of the state really the strategy for Big Brother? Regarding our own police and cyberspace, the question is: in order to effectively fight the increase in cyber crime, do the police have to use more information technology, as Orwell suggests?

Now we have arrived at the point where the analysis deviates from Orwell's representation of the matter. The answer is: no, because authorities that seek to influence the way citizens behave should not start to employ information technology *themselves*, but should ensure first and foremost that the people who employ it are the citizens they have in mind. This is where the theory of technological enforcement applies (Stol 2004). This reads as follows: 'technology primarily regulates the behaviour of those who actually use it.'
This theory is based on various observations. The principle is actually old, and was used at the beginning of the 20th century in the American automotive industry. The first assembly line technology used in Henry Ford's factory tied the employees to their workplace and regulated their behaviour extensively. In this way, the management kept their hands, not only figuratively, but literally free (Pieterson 1981).

In Stol's research into police work and information technology (e.g., Stol 1988, 1996; Stol & In 't Velt 1991), the theme concerning behaviour regulation is that the comings and goings of police officers becomes more visible to their superior officers and that they have to align their behaviour to what the machine asks of them (information collection, inputting of data, and work speed) when they use a computer. Police computers regulate the behaviour of police officers themselves to a far greater extent than the behaviour of citizens. This effect is so obvious that police officers invariably complain about the pressure that the machines exert, particularly when recording a statement or documenting work that has been carried out. If we explore further, even more consequences can be seen for the comings and goings of people within the police organisation: computer users have to be trained, systems have to be developed, and new versions have to be implemented. Managers spend time in meetings about computerisation, every now and again politicians have to report on the state of affairs regarding police computerisation, and so on. All of this keeps the police busy. The question remains: what effect does information technology have on the behaviour of citizens in general and criminals in particular? Here is a finding from a different neck of the woods. In 2006 and 2007, the municipality of Leeuwarden, The Netherlands, carried out an experiment in the city centre using cameras to tackle nightlife related violence. The experiment had clearly observable effects on the behaviour of the local authority personnel involved. Police officers changed their surveillance patterns, recorded work related incidents more often and had to go through the camera recordings. Police chiefs had meetings about the project, at the municipality the various people responsible were constantly running around organising the camera surveillance and the city council had to be appraised of their activities. When the project was evaluated, however, it was clear that the people the cameras were focussed on hardly changed their behaviour at all. The goal of 'reducing violent crime' was not achieved at either location. The aim of 'increasing feelings of security' was achieved, albeit only among one of the four target groups – people on a night out. The question remains, however, whether this was a result of camera surveillance or because of the more active police surveillance that accompanied it (Kerstens et al. 2008).

The last example is about the combating of cyber crime. In 2007, the Dutch police started blocking websites containing pornographic images of children. The project was costly in terms of time for the detectives who had to filter the material, time that they would rather have used to track criminals. 'One of the detectives mentioned the disproportionate burden on the available capacity within the corps. "This experiment is somewhat out of control, in part because of the commotion surrounding it. We've taken a path and it seems as though there is no turning back, added to which it is not clear what the results will be"' (Stol et al., 2008: 128). The latter was confirmed by the project evaluation: it showed that there was insufficient reason to assume that this technical measure affected the behaviour of internet users intent on searching the web for child pornography.

Technology primarily regulates the behaviour of those who actually use it, and only indirectly – if at all – the behaviour of others at whom the technology is directed. This is according to the theory of technological enforcement. There is evidence to suggest that in their attempts to enhance safety, a government that is concerned about safety in cyberspace should therefore avoid using the very same technology that they want to use to regulate people's behaviour in cyberspace. The government would be better off encouraging citizens to use technology. Those who use information technology become more visible to their environment, sometimes directly and very literally, sometimes because they leave a digital trail in their wake. They do this when they use the internet, discount cards, access cards, client cards, railway season tickets, credit cards, debit cards and mobile phones. People's movements can be fairly accurately reconstructed on the basis of this usage. The population has signed up for technology on a massive scale and report, several times a day and on a voluntary basis exactly where they are, what they are doing, with whom they've been in touch and which route they've taken. Twitterers take it a step further and give continual explicit accounts of what they're doing. Big Brother in 1984 couldn't have done a better job.

Citizens can also use technology to monitor one another informally. The Dutch police project *Kiezen of Helen* (a play on the saying 'take it or leave it') is an example of this. The aim is that citizens are given access to an internet facility that allows them to check for themselves whether things offered for sale on websites are registered as stolen or not. In an unrelated case, a police officer once told me about a proposed project regarding the theft of consignments from trucks. The idea was that truck drivers could use their mobile phones to keep an eye on their parked vehicles through webcams mounted in parking lots. It is not known whether the project was implemented, but the police officer's way of thinking is refreshing: don't get involved with technology yourself, rather let the people concerned do it. The police too readily apply old reflexes: reaching for new technology to combat crime through surveillance. The police still have to learn not to get involved themselves. They don't have the capacity to solve the problem of criminality on their own, regardless of the technology at their disposal, and that applies equally to cyberspace.

The theory of technological enforcement puts the police onto a different track and warns them, as it were, against embracing technology too hastily and too ambitiously as a new instrument to tackle delinquent behaviour. There will always be exceptions, and on the basis of these, the theory can be fine-tuned. With this theory in mind, what can we say, for example, about the 'twittering officer on the beat' – a phenomenon that recently made the news? 'The Netherlands has about 50 of these officers. They are pioneers who see Twitter as a means of expanding the accessibility of the police' (*De Volkskrant*,

24 August 2010). An initial reaction might be: they are moving with the times, that's a good thing. Moreover, it is good that the police experiment with what new technology can deliver. But it will have become clear that the theory of technological enforcement contains a warning against this initiative. The police are using new technology themselves. However, 'being accessible' is not a police task and should therefore not be a goal in itself. It is a means to an end. The goal is enforcing law and order. The question is how using twitter can contribute to this police task. It clearly impacts on the behaviour of the police officers involved and their comings and goings become more visible. 'So, time to relax. Watching football with Kasabian's "Fire" blaring on the headphones. Wife giving disapproving looks' according to one of the tweets (ibid.) Wasn't the original idea behind police information technology that the police would gain more insight into the comings and goings of citizens? It looks as though the opposite is happening. According to the theory of technological enforcement, it should be citizens who are doing the twittering. Then local police officers will get more insight into their activities – instead of the other way round. Nevertheless, this twitter experiment has to be continued and the police have to check carefully how this new technology contributes to the enforcement of the law.

Obviously a good relationship with the public is a prerequisite for gathering information and for getting support when the police need it, for example for solving cases or controlling public disorder in the neighbourhood. The benefits of this new way of working will reveal themselves over time; that is not a problem. Drawbacks arise when the police use new technology and fail to seriously evaluate how that contributes to their goals, something that happens too often for my liking.

Another novelty in the force is 'internet surveillance'. What does theory have to say about this? For internet surveillance, police officers use technology to carry out surveillance in cyberspace. Whenever we see that officers are the people using technology, we should be cautious according to the theory. After all, it is the behaviour of the officers that is being regulated and made more visible. That is not a goal but an investment. What advantages does it have? Internet surveillance is a tool that should be used sparingly, only if the police are searching for something very specific. The use of the term 'internet surveillance' should be avoided. It sounds too much like unfocussed monitoring. Surveillance may be useful in the neighbourhood, in a shopping centre or in an entertainment area, but as things stand, surveillance in cyberspace cannot be seen as a useful way of employing police capacity – unless they are specifically searching for an individual or information about a particular incident, in which case it should not be called internet surveillance but an investigation.

The theory of technological enforcement points out that as soon as the police use technology, they must constantly ensure that they are not tying themselves down and thus do not have enough time to exercise their influence on the behaviour of citizens. Technology acts like syrup: if you touch it too much, you get stuck and bogged down. Your movement slows down, you get distracted by it, and it takes more and more effort to rid yourself of it. The citizen you're trying to find stays out of reach. This should be a strong warning to the police in cyberspace. Cyberspace is a world that can only be accessed through technology. How can you enforce the law in a world where you get bogged down as soon as you enter it?

As an aside, an obvious thought is: why don't cyber criminals get bogged down? Cyber criminals run the same risk, and they know that. They are very familiar with the theory of technological enforcement, but in their circles it is the theory of technological crime. They have derived two strategies from this. Firstly, they make sure that they remain as invisible as possible, for example through false identities and cryptography (encryption). That is how they avoid becoming visible through their use of technology. Secondly, they themselves use technology as sparingly as possible: they let others do it, generally their victims and potential victims, but also their gullible sidekicks. That is how cyber criminals avoid becoming stuck behind the computer and addicted to it, or worse still, becoming visible. They let their victims download and activate viruses, they let their victims log on to false websites and enter their own information, they let their victims unwittingly transfer money, and so on. Together these two strategies form, as it were, a Teflon layer for cyber criminals.

99

Cyber criminals who do get stuck because they become too involved with technology get noticed and picked up. Botnets are by all accounts a clever criminal strategy. (Botnets are networks of computers that criminals have command of without the owners knowing about it, see chapter 12.) Criminals let others do the work on their computers while they stay in the background as much as possible – to avoid getting bogged down. The police have given priority to tackling botnets in the hope that, by doing so, they will scratch the criminal cyber Teflon layer.

Now, back to the main theme of the argument. Citizens have signed up to technology en masse and voluntarily reveal their whereabouts, what they are doing, with whom they are in contact and which route they have taken, several times a day. They do so willingly. Twitterers take this a step further and continuously give an explicit report on their comings and goings. Orwell could never have predicted that citizens would voluntarily succumb to technology in this way. In his world, it is the authorities that get busy with technology, and gain more control as they apply more technology. As we have just learned, this is a mistaken assumption. The theory of technological enforcement maintains that you should not use technology yourself, you should hand it over to others! Let others work with it. Observe how the banks have mobilised us with technology. Witness how chain stores have seduced people with loyalty cards into handing over their personal information and revealing their purchasing habits. In short: the authorities should make good use of the fact that citizens love using technology.

They can do this in two ways. To start with, the authorities can supply citizens with information technology that they can use to help combat cyber crime. The police project 'Kiezen of Helen', mentioned above, is an example of this. The idea behind this is that citizens are given software which they can use to establish whether second hand goods offered for sale online are stolen or not. This is the right line of thought.

The second way is that the police should analyse the digital tracks that criminals leave, should they have a suspect in their sights. Use the fact that they are linked to technology and as such have become visible. Perhaps it is possible to encourage suspects to use more technology and by doing so expose themselves even more – obviously within the limits of the law.

Key concepts

Orwellian society
Theory of technological enforcement

Part 2
Cyber crimes

7 Hacking

Rutger Leukfeldt & Erik de Jong

7.1 Introduction

The term hacking in combination with technology dates from the 1960s. It was a positive description of someone who is skilled in developing elegant, creative and effective solutions to technical problems (Yar 2006). Hacking was the innovative use of technology. The hacker community that was formed in the sixties and seventies had its own ethics, influenced by social and political movements of that time. This ethic emphasised the right to free information and knowledge. These hackers were mostly concerned with 'research' of other computers out of curiosity. Damaging systems during this research was deemed incompetent and unethical (Stol et al. 1999; Yar 2006).

The term hacker could mean different things to different people (Warren & Leitch 2009). The difference between hacking and cracking is often described in literature, see for example Rogers (2000) and Van Geest (2006). Originally the term hacker was used for people who break security systems with bona fide intentions, for example, to demonstrate security holes. The term cracker stands for similar activities, but made with malicious intent, typically with destruction as a goal. Over time, the distinction between hacking and cracking diminished, not in the last place because in practice the distinction between hackers and crackers is not clear (Van Geest 2006; Stol et al. 1999). Today, only a very small group of people still use that distinction. In general usage, the term cracker has almost completely disappeared and hacker is used for all who break into someone else's computer. We therefore use only the term hacking in this chapter.

In conformity with Europe's Convention on Cyber Crime, we define hacking as the intentional and unlawful intrusion into an automated work. Literature shows that a hacking attempt usually meets three criteria: it is illegal, simple but well thought through, and it shows a high degree of technical skills and expertise (Van Geest 2006; Van der Hulst & Neve 2008). In practice, however, hacking attempts do not always comply with these criteria. Not invariably can one can speak of an act of someone with exceptional technological skills. For example there are tools available on the internet that anyone can use to hack. Furthermore, from a legal perspective, it is a case of hacking if someone logs on to a computer without the permission of its owner, whether or not high tech tools or skills were used. In a secure system, moreover, it is often not possible to immediately gain the highest level in a system (that of administrator) (Ianelli & Hackworth 2005). A hacker will therefore try to gradually acquire more and more rights, using various weaknesses in security.

7.2 Types of hackers

We can distinguish between different types of hackers by looking at how the hack was carried out or by looking at the type of offender. The latter is quite common in literature. Hackers are divided into different types, including old guard hackers, script kiddies, crackers, hacktivists and so on. The way the hack is technically committed, such as using social engineering, keyloggers or password crackers, does not determine to which group a hack is classified, but is part of the *modus operandi* of the offenders within a particular group. In practice, it appears that the various methods and techniques in existence are not strictly bound to groups. Looking purely at the technology, the way in which a hack is executed does not directly indicate a particular type of offender. Additional information about the complexity and timing of an attack and the intended target may be significant clue material in this regard.

In literature, hackers are categorised in different ways. The simplest distinction can be made between bad and good hackers, or black hats and white hats. The intention of a good hacker is only to expose weaknesses in security, and these hackers do not have a financial motive. However, if these hackers enter an electronic work without the consent of the owner, they are still punishable. A slightly more nuanced distinction is made by Gelderblom (2004). He distinguishes three categories: hackers, crackers and script kiddies. This basically means the good, the bad and wannabees. Europol (2003) and Dasselaar (2005) show us even more categories (figure 7.1).

Figure 7.1   Black hats, white hats and other types of hackers (Europol 2003 and Dasselaar 2005)

White hats. People who use technical skills for legitimate purposes. Such hackers usually abide by the law and use technology for constructive purposes.
Black hats. Also called crackers. Use knowledge and skills for illegal purposes.

Grey hats. Hackers who fall between the first and second group. An example is a hacker who breaks (illegally) into a computer for the purpose of security testing.
Hacktivists. Politically or socially engaged and use ICT to achieve their goals.
Script kiddies. Use techniques developed by others. They have little technical knowledge themselves and their ignorance can cause much damage.
Political or religious extremists. Use ICT to commit acts of terrorism.

Rogers (2000, 2001, 2006) uses nine categories in his 'hacker taxonomy'. The taxonomy of Rogers is based on different studies[34] that distinguish different types of hackers (figure 7.2).

Figure 7.2   Hacker taxonomy (Rogers, 2000, 2001, 2006)

Novice or newbies. Lack of technical knowledge, cannot program and use toolkits.
Cyber Punks. Are able to do a little programming but their knowledge of programming and computer systems is limited. Vandals.
Internals. Disgruntled (ex-)employees with a good technical knowledge.
Petty thieves. Hacking for criminal opportunities. The classic criminal. Victims are online stores and naive internet users.
Old guard hackers. Driven by the intellectual challenge.
Virus writers or coders. Writing scripts and automated tools used by others. Acting as mentors to novices.
Professional criminals. Underworld figures with knowledge of the latest technological possibilities. Are not looking for fame or reputation.
Information warriors. Mingle politics and criminal activity. Their job is to protect vital infrastructures or to attack vital infrastructures of others (possible former employees of intelligence organisations from Eastern Bloc)
Political Activists. Are engaged in hacktivism.

---

34 Adamski 1999; Chantler 1996; Hollinger 1988; Landreth 1985; Parker 1998; Post 1996; Post et.al. 1998; Power 1998; Shaw et.al. 1998.

Rogers's taxonomy also has categories that cover the good (old guard hackers), the bad (professional criminals and information warriors) and the followers (novice or newbies). But Rogers also distinguishes some subcategories. There are vandals who destroy things to hack (cyberpunks), there are criminals who only want to make money (petty thieves) and there are hackers who support other criminals (virus writers or coders). In addition, Rogers creates a separate category for disgruntled employees or former employees who seek revenge (internals) and there is a category with hackers that have a clear political objective (political activists). It is possible that these categories have some overlap (Van der Hulst & Neve 2008). The practice is always more complex and diverse than a model suggests.

Another classification is that of McAfee (2006). According to McAfee, cyber criminals range from amateurs with limited programming skills who rely on pre-set scripts to carry out their attacks, to well-trained professional criminals who use the latest tools (figure 7.3). McAfee distinguishes fewer categories than Rogers. Again, a rough distinction is made between good, evil and followers. The 'goods' are the innovators. This group is motivated by the technological challenge; this type represents the old guard hackers of Rogers. The bad are the organised cyber gangsters, whose motive is financial gain. Furthermore, according to McAfee, there are two groups of followers who have little or no technical skills (the fame seekers and amateur copycats). Finally, there is also the disgruntled group of current or former employees (insiders).

Figure 7.3   Categories according to McAfee (2006)

Innovators. Hackers who spend their time searching for security holes in computer systems or exploring new environments to see if they are vulnerable for false codes. They do it for the challenge. The danger of this group factor is low. This is an elite group and, according to McAfee, represents only 2% of the hacking and malware authors.

Amateur fame seekers. Novices in the field of computer crime, with limited computer skills and programming capabilities. Seeking media attention, use ready-made tools and tricks. They have a moderate risk factor: the danger of this group is that they carry out attacks without really understanding what they are doing and what the effects may be.

Copycats. Wannabe hackers and malware authors. A group that copies the formulas of others in order to become famous (thanks to the 'status' of the cyber criminal community). Focus on the repetition of simple attacks and do not develop anything new. The hazard factor is moderate.

Insiders. Disgruntled ex-employees, contractors and consultants. Revenge or petty theft. Abuse poor security measures or their privileges from their position within the company. The hazard factor is high, because technical security measures are less effective.

Organised cyber gangsters. Highly motivated and organised cyber crooks. Limited group, but with considerable power. They break into vulnerable computers for profit. At the heart is a strong core of leaders who try to profit by using all possible ways to exploit others and use humans and computer resources to do so. The hazard factor is high.

Figure 7.4 compares the categories from Europol (2003), Dasselaar (2005), Rogers (2000, 2001, 2006) and McAfee (2006).

Figure 7.4   Different categories of hackers compared

Rogers (2000, 2001, 2006)	McAfee (2006)	Europol (2003), Dasselaar (2005)
Novice or newbies	Copycatters	Script kiddies
Cyberpunks	Amateur fame seekers	Black hat
Internals	Insiders	
Petty thieves		Black hat
Old guard hackers	Innovators	White hat
Virus writers of coders		
Professionals criminals	Organised cyber gangsters	
Information warriors		
Political Activists		Hacktivist / Political or religious extremists

The different classifications do have some main characteristics. Six categories are recurrent: 'novice and newbies', current or former employees, old style hackers, petty thieves, organised criminals and politically motivated hackers.

The first two categories of Rogers, 'novice and newbies' and 'cyber punks' are comparable with 'copycatters', 'amateur fame seekers' and 'script kiddies', and to some extent with 'black hats'. These hackers are characterised by a lack of technical knowledge. They thrive on copying the scripts of others. In this group we find the unskilful hackers who are exploring their possibilities and trying to expand their knowledge. They are not worried or ignorant about the potential damage their actions might cause.

The 'internals' of Rogers are similar to the 'insiders' of McAfee. Both groups are described as (ex-)employees with feelings of revenge.

Rogers's category 'petty thieves' is similar in part to the 'black hats' of Europol and Dasselaar. These are hackers who act like petty criminals (or petty criminals who have mastered digital technology).

The 'old guard hackers' are the same as 'innovators' and 'white hats'. The group is driven by intellectual challenge and curiosity. The hackers in this group are probably those who have most to do with old hacking values such as freedom of information.

The 'professional criminals' that Rogers identifies correspond with the 'organised cyber gangsters'. Both are groups of organised criminals. The 'virus writers or coders' can be hired by organised cyber criminals. Hence, these two groups are interrelated and are both linked to organised crime.

The final group is the politically motivated hacker: 'information warriors' and 'political activists'. Hackers who work for political purposes or fight cyber warfare are no imaginary threat. That became clear with the Russian hackers attack on Estonia in 2007 and Georgia in 2008, and the large number of websites defaced with political pamphlets (see chapter 11).

Although such a classification may well be used in discussions about hacking, it is not always the most useful way to describe everyday reality. For example, in their study based on police files, Leukfeldt et al. (2010) came to the conclusion that most hacking cases were small cases with a low tech character, which could be best labelled as 'hacking out of curiosity', 'hacking for profit' or 'hacking for revenge (e.g. classmates, ex-partners). They therefore distinguished cases by looking at the goals and/or targets of the hack instead of looking at the 'real identity' of the hacker involved – not least because, empirically speaking, it is difficult if not impossible to determine a hacker's 'real identity' and put him/her in the right box of a model.

7.3 Offender characteristics

It is impossible to give a general profile of 'the' hacker (Van der Hulst & Neve 2008; Leukfeldt et al. 2010). According to literature, hacking attempts usually are simple but well thought through and show a high degree of technical skill and expertise on the part of the offender (Van Geest 2006; Van der Hulst & Neve 2008). But because the internet is increasingly becoming a fixture of our everyday life, hacking seems to become more and more democratised

(Leukfeldt et al. 2010). Nowadays, hacking is not *only* for whizz kids, but also for the man in the street.

A thirst for knowledge and personal challenge, but also financial gain, are cited as primary motivation (see figure 7.5). The 'real' hackers originally focussed on the detection of security gaps in systems (old guard hackers). The more difficult the task, the more status they acquired when they succeeded in 'entering'. There was a hacker culture with its own rules and regulations, with a specific status hierarchy, specific language, norms and symbols (Turgeman-Oldschmidt 2005). Within the hacker community, members shared a social identity that is based, according to Jordan and Taylor (1998), on six indicators:
- pleasure in using technology and the innovative use of it;
- a tension between confidentiality (staying out of the hands of law enforcement and private investigators) and publicity (sharing information in order to be recognised);
- anonymity (the real 'offline' identity is concealed);
- fluidity (an informal culture to which people may or may not belong);
- masculine and misogynistic attitudes;
- continuous explicit reflection on the motivation of hacking (addiction, curiosity, excitement, power, recognition, and the 'service function' of the discovery of security holes).

Section 7.2 showed that there are more types of hackers than only the old guard hackers. In their study which specifically focused on identifying offender characteristics Van der Hulst and Neve (2008) show generally three types of offender:

The juvenile criminal. According to a few studies hackers are men between 12 and 28 years old (Turgeman-Goldschmidt 2005; Yar 2005). Yar therefore refers to hacking as a form of juvenile delinquency. Based on 54 unstructured in-depth interviews with hackers, Turgeman-Goldschmidt (2005) concluded that fun, excitement and challenge are often the main motives. Van der Werf finds in her research that hackers can be compared with young vandals who '... in the physical world would demolish bus shelters or mess around on the playground of a school (Van der Werf 2003: 8).
The financially motivated hacker. According to Van der Hulst & Neve (2008), hackers are increasingly financially motivated and hacking is more and more linked to other forms of cyber crime (e.g. fraud).
The ideological hacker. Most hackers are intelligent people with an explicit need to enrich their knowledge (Casey 2002). The preliminary findings in the current Hacker's Profiling Project (Biancuzzi 2006; Chiesa & Ducci 2006, in

Van der Hulst & Neve 2008) describe hackers as intelligent people with an explicit need for knowledge, personal challenge, power and a strong sense of civil liberty.

Leukfeldt et al. (2010) add a fourth category: the common criminal. They conclude that a large portion of cyber crimes are committed by ordinary people and that hacking is democratised. An analysis of 159 Dutch hacking files shows that hacking is mainly a matter for men under 45 years old who commit their crimes alone – as is the case with most other forms of crime. Additionally, their research shows that many hacking cases are committed in the relational sphere (e.g. ex-lovers, jealous husbands or schoolmates). Suspects and victims usually know each other. The primary motivation is revenge, curiosity and financial gain. The researchers conclude furthermore that it is unclear whether suspects, as claimed in the literature, have a high degree of technical skills. It is quite certain that not all suspects are technically literate.

In their literature review, Van der Hulst and Neve (2008) have linked the offender characteristics of hackers as described by Rogers (2000, 2001, 2006), Casey (2002), Furnell (2002), Morris (2004) and Nykodym et al. (2005) to the different types of hackers who are distinguished by Rogers. According to Van der Hulst and Neve (2008), this format is currently 'the most comprehensive categorisation of hackers in which divergent views on hackers are integrated' (2008: 108). Figure 7.5 gives a summary.

Such a classification may suggest that characteristics can be combined fairly exactly with certain types of hackers. However, as Van der Hulst and Neve themselves indicate, that is of course not the case. Precisely distinguishing between the groups by assigning a unique set of characteristics to each is a precarious issue. Rather, we should interpret a schedule with types of offenders and characteristics as a figure that shows accents. That is, in a sense, the approach that Rogers himself (2006) choose. He works on the basis of distinguishing four primary motives:
Revenge: focuses on individuals, organisations, countries and continents;
Financial gain: greed and personal financial gain;
Curiosity: knowledge, excitement, intellectual challenge;
Fame: media attention, bragging, folk hero.

Figure 7.5   Offender characteristics of hackers (Van der Hulst & Neve 2008)

	NV	CP	IT	PT	OG	VW	PC	IW	PA
Social demography									
Age 12-30	X	X				X			
Age 30 +			X				X		
Middle class family		X							
Poor school performance		X							
Well educated			X				X	X	
Disgruntled (ex-)employee		X							
Technical occupation			X					X	
Primary motivation									
Sensation (media attention)	X	X				X			
Status (prove themselves)	X	X				X			
Financial gain		X	X	X		X	X	X	
Revenge	X	X	X	X		X			X
Malice / vandalism	X	X		X		X			
Power		X				X			
(Intellectual) challenge		X		X	X	X		X	
Curiosity					X				
Nationalist								X	
(Political) ideological			X					X	X
Criminal career									
Criminal history				X	X				
Organised crime							X		
Type of cyber crime									
DDoS attacks	X								
Malware / Trojans		X				X			
Spamming		X							
Defacing		X							
(Identity) fraud		X	X	X					
Business information systems			X						
Credit card fraud				X					
Espionage							X	X	X

Legend: NV = Novice, CP = Cyberpunks, IT = Internal, PT = Petty thieves, OG = Old guard hacker, VW = Virus writers, PC = Professional criminal, IW = Information warrior, PA – Political activist

According to Rogers these motives can be linked to the degree of expertise in each category. The novices or newbies (NV) have a low expertise rating and act out of curiosity, revenge, fame or financial gain. The cyber punks (CP) have reasonable expertise and are mainly aiming for fame. Internals (IT) have a fairly high expertise and are aimed at getting revenge and, to a lesser extent, financial gain. The petty thieves (PT) also have a fairly high expertise, but are only aiming for financial gain. Old Guard Hackers (OG) have high expertise and act mainly out of curiosity. Virus writers or coders (VW) also have a high expertise, but in addition to curiosity act mostly out of revenge. Professional criminals (PC) have a high degree of expertise and want financial gain. They are diametrically opposed to the old guard hackers, who also have a high degree of expertise, but are not aiming for financial gain at all. Additionally, information warriors (IW) have a high degree of expertise, but they have immediate financial gain and revenge as primary motives. The political activists (PA) also have high expertise, but fame is their main motive and to a lesser extent financial gain.

Rogers (2006) has put these features in a circumplex (figure 7.6). However because of a lack of empirical data the circumplex is a hypothetical model and ought to be empirically tested (Van der Hulst & Neve 2008). The circumplex is divided into four parts: the primary motives. The degree of technical expertise can be seen from the axis; the farther out, the higher the experience. The circumplex shows how the different categories of hackers (may) relate to each other. It reveals, for example, that old guard hackers (OG) and the professional criminals (PC) are diametrically opposed, while the petty thieves (PT) are closer to the professional criminals (PC). According to Rogers (2006) the circumplex is a basic tool for identifying offender profiles. Based on the shifts in motivation and skills, the criminal careers of hackers can be identified.

Creating such offender profiles is difficult. Little scientific research has been done on the behavioural principles of offender profiling. The preparation of offender profiles based on scant empirical data is a truly hazardous undertaking. The finding of Leukfeldt et al. (2010), that hacking is closely interlinked with many other crimes, also raises the question of when we should speak of a hacker. Is a suspect who hacks and then threatens people a hacker (with a hacking profile), or a violent offender (and therefore a person with an 'offender profile' developed by other criminologists? This example shows how thin the ice is on which offender profiling is based.

Figure 7.6   The hackers circumplex of Rogers (2006)

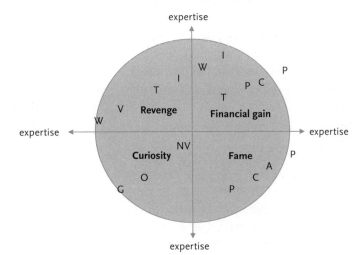

7.4   Modus operandi of hackers

The techniques used by hackers – and the things they have to do in order to achieve their goals – are constantly evolving. These developments are difficult to predict in advance because they depend not only on the hackers and ICT, but also on developments in the field of security (criminals adapt their *modus operandi* to the new investigative tools of law enforcement agencies).

Hackers often use social engineering. This method, where the aim is to persuade people into cooperating with an attack, is of all times (Mitnick et al. 2002). Social engineering plays a big role if the target is a specific organisation. It is an indispensable tool for obtaining information or access to systems. With undirected attacks in the form of malware such as viruses and worms, social engineering originally did not play a major role. These viruses and worms spread purely in a technical manner: the victim had no active role. Later, as technical dissemination mechanisms became less accessible due to improved security of computer systems, social engineering became a factor. The 'I love you' virus from 2000 was an early example of this. Today, the social engineering component is virtually indispensable in most targeted and undirected attacks: victims are tempted with exciting releases, movies of celebrities or alarmed by fake antivirus software (Govcert 2009, 2010). The victim plays an active role by opening a link or a document, movie or software. Chapter 12 deals extensively with social engineering.

Regarding the technique, hackers use weaknesses in software to penetrate systems. They do this by using design flaws or bugs. SQL injection is an example of a technique that abuses a design flaw: because the designers did not think through the interaction that an (untrusted) outsider could have with a database, it is possible to access data that ought to be protected. Design errors in standard products can be widely abused in an automated manner, but with the growth of custom-made web applications (including the growth of Web 2.0 applications that use user generated content) a lot of design flaws are website-specific.

Abuse of bugs (e.g. in the form of buffer overflows) is the basis of much of the malware that is currently in circulation, and enables hackers to gain access to systems.

Techniques used by hackers are not isolated and can be used in combination. Furthermore, it should be noted that when a hacker – by abusing a weakness in a system – has entered a system, he usually has not yet reached his end goal. After entering and (partially) controlling the system, the hacker is able to search for valuable information or abuse the system for the purpose of attacking others (e.g. sending spam or phishing mails of hosting malicious websites – see chapter 13).

7.5   Scope

In literature little is known about the extent of hacking. To determine the extent we refer to the scope of the cyber criminal techniques that are used by hackers. These techniques are discussed in chapter 12 and 13. However these figures must be interpreted with care. As shown in this chapter, different types of hacker use different techniques for different goals. Several sources, for example, indicate that a large proportion of computers worldwide are infected with malware, but the figures range from about 33% (Computer Security Institute 2007) to over 60% per cent (America Online et al. 2005). No information is available about techniques like Iframe injections, but several sources[35] have noted that attacks (which are in fact hacking attempts) are performed on hundreds of thousands of websites.

---

35 www.computerwold.com, ddanchev.blogspot.com and ww.symantec.com/enterprise/ security_response/weblog.

The above shows that there is ambiguity about how the extent of hacking is to be measured. Is it about attempts to enter a system, including all untargeted malware attempts to spread itself as much as possible? Is it successful hacks? In addition, a lot of the published figures come from organisations that play a role in information security. Realistically therefore it is not feasible to present reliable figures about the extent of hacking.

7.6   Trends

A shift has been reported in the motives of hackers since the beginning of this century, a shift from hacking for fame to hacking for fortune (KLPD 2007; Van der Hulst & Neve 2008). This move has not been backed up with empirical research, but is repeatedly referred to. Over the years, the purpose of malware has shifted from 'infect as many systems as possible' to 'infect systems as a way to make money'. In the early days, much of the malware could be placed in the 'fame' quadrant in Rogers' circumplex. The previously cited 'I Love You' virus is a good example. Much of the malware currently found includes components that aim to intercept financial information (bank, credit card information) (APWG 2010). The fact that the internet has become an important conduit for financial transactions has probably contributed to this development.

Another shift in hackers' motives is noted by Leukfeldt et al. (2010). They identify a move from hacking for fortune to hacking for revenge. Because the internet is increasingly becoming part of our everyday life, hacking seems to become more and more democratised. Hacking is not *only* for the whizz kids, but these days it also is a 'tool' for the common people and is used in everyday conflicts (which are often in the relational sphere with revenge as a motive).
Another trend is the emergence and growth of hacks that have power and influence as a goal. These include attacks on political targets like the office of the Dalai Lama (Information Warfare Monitor 2009) but also the DDoS attacks on commercial companies that stopped to support the Wikileaks site (Arbor Networks 2010).
Perhaps the largest problem in defining hackers and hacks, and in determining trends in this field, is that there are many schemes and hypotheses but not too much research providing us with valid empirical data on which to base our knowledge of this phenomenon.

Key concepts

Hacking
Hackers (old guard hackers or innovators)
Hackers (novice and newbies, script kiddies, copycatters and amateur fame seekers)
Hackers (internals)
Hackers (petty thiefs)
Hackers (professional criminals or organised cyber gangsters)
Hackers (information warriors and political activists)

8   E-Fraud

Rutger Leukfeldt & Johan van Wilsem

8.1   Introduction

Fraud is a generic term covering many forms of deviant behaviour. Fraud can therefore be defined in different ways (Doig 2006; Levi & Burrows 2008). The essence of fraud is however always the same, according to Leukfeldt et al. (2010): through deception people obtain money or property to which they are not entitled, whereby they infringe on the rights of others. Thus fraud can be defined as deception aimed at gaining financial profit. The essence of deception is that someone is deceived. This deception may be executed with the use of a false name, another person's identity or sly tricks (such as drawing up false documents or data carriers, or the use of a false key).[36] Based on this, we define the digital equivalent of fraud as deception with the aim of achieving financial gain, where ICT is essential for the execution.

With the advent of the internet and a new e-commerce economy, new ways of committing fraud have emerged. E-commerce is a rapidly growing sector that handles a lot of money. The easy access and global reach of the internet provides many opportunities to sell and purchase products and services. B2C (business to consumer) sales in the Netherlands alone amounted to six billion euros in 2009 (CBS 2009). Websites like eBay.com and other auction or selling sites have created a lively trade between individuals. eBay has 90 million active users globally and in 2009, the total worth of goods sold on eBay was $ 60 billion.[37] The economic sector has become increasingly dependent on online business traffic. Internet is now part of what is called the vital infrastructure for economic processes (Helmus et al. 2006; KLPD 2004). Loss of trust in the e-commerce sector can have major consequences for the economy and society as a whole (Sackers & Mevis 2000). The large sums of money that circulate in the digital economy also attract criminals, however. It is noted that cyber criminals are more and more financially motivated and that there

---

36 These elements are distilled from the articles in the Dutch Criminal Code which penalize fraud (see for an analyse Leukfeldt et al. 2010): artikel 326 Sr (scam), artikel 225 Sr (forgery), artikel 232 Sr (distort of a payment device (e.g. a credit card), artikel 310 Sr (theft), artikel 321 Sr (embezzlement) en artikel 416 Sr (healing).

37 http://www.ebayinc.com/who Lastly visited at December 9th 2010.

is a shift from 'hacking for fame' to 'hacking for fortune' (Boerman & Mooij 2006: 22)[38] – e-fraud is one of the possibilities.

8.2   Main categories of e-fraud

In literature we find five forms of e-fraud:

Online sale and auction fraud

The most common form of e-fraud is fraud through online sale and auction sites (Domenie et al. 2009). It is a fairly simple form of fraud. The victim buys goods or services via the internet, pays for the goods or services but never receives them (or, if s/he does receive them, they are of much lower quality than promised), or when during an online auction the price of an article is artificially increased by the owner (Europol 2003; Taylor et al. 2006).

Advance fee fraud

A common form of e-fraud is advance fee fraud. Spectacular stories surround these scams (scammers who dish up imaginative stories about a fortune in a distant land which can only be released if the victim is willing to help solve some financial obstacles first). Advance fee fraud is associated with large numbers of people being ripped off for large amounts of money (Van der Hulst & Neve 2008). There are hundreds of variants internationally (for an overview see Schoenmakers et al. 2009).

Corpelijn (2008) concludes that advanced fee fraud has four different stages that act as a funnel: gradually more and more potential victims fall off, and in the end a small group remains who are tricked out of big sums of money. (1) the first phase is the information phase: offenders contact the victims in a friendly and businesslike tone. Via email, but also by traditional mail, they gain the confidence of the victim. (2) The next is the interaction phase: only a small proportion of people who receive an email respond. Reminder mails are meant to ensure that the victim is persuaded to take part in the scam. Victims must provide personal information in order for the transaction to succeed. (3) Then the transaction phase begins. A request for an advance payment is sent, for example in order to cover administration costs. At this point the scam really starts. The victim is constantly asked to pay amounts for new contingencies. Sometimes even face-to-face meetings take place where the victim is

---

38 See chapter 7 for a more elaborate discussion about this.

shown a suitcase full of counterfeit money. (4) The final phase: the transaction phase continues until the victim realises he or she has been scammed.

Identity theft

Since e-fraudsters often do not use their own identity to commit their scams, identity theft is closely related to e-fraud. Identity theft is commonly defined as the unlawful use of another's identifying information for gain. With this infor-mation, offenders can access existing bank or credit card accounts or open new accounts in order to facilitate financial transactions under the victim's name (McNally & Newman 2005). In addition, personal information can be used for other criminal purposes, such as dodging a traffic charge, getting medical care or renting a house, though this type of fraud seems less prevalent (Lang-ton & Planty 2010; White & Fisher 2008). Identity theft is not a new crime, yet its prevalence has increased rapidly in recent years. According to Benson (2009), two developments are mainly responsible for this. First, he mentions the 'stunningly rapid advances surrounding networked computers, electronic databases, and most importantly, the internet' (p. 231), which has improved the connection between people and information. Second, the growth in con-sumer credit has increased the value associated with the personal information of many fraud targets.

Various types of personal documents or authentification sources can serve as the target of identity theft perpetrators, such as social security numbers, credit card accounts, energy and tax bills, employment records, birth records, email addresses, and social networking sites (Newman 2005). Ways to steal someone's identity includehacking someone's computer, phishing) or using personal information recorded on social networking sites (more about these subjects in chapters 7 and 13) (Newman 2005; Irani et al. 2009).

Other forms of e-fraud

Alongside the categories of e-fraud mentioned above, two other categories can be distinguished: the trade in counterfeit goods, and market manipula-tion. The first category includes trading fake products (for example, imitation LaCoste T-shirts which are offered as genuine) and internet piracy[39] (the trade of copyrighted material such as software, movies, books, etc.) (KLPD 2007). The second category – market manipulation – covers the insider trading and manipulation of shares by spreading (false) rumours and information (for example about possible takeovers or internal problems in organisations) in

---

39 More about internet piracy in chapter 10.

chat rooms, internet forums and via email (spamming) (Van Amersfoort et al. 2002). The manipulation of stock prices is also known as 'pump 'n dump' or 'trash and cash' (Morris 2004). These two categories are cited in literature, but little research into them has taken place. For that reason these two forms of e-fraud will not be discussed in this chapter.

8.3 Amount of e-fraud crimes

Asking how much e-fraud occurs does not lead to straightforward answers. In general, estimating the extent of the crime is difficult due to dark number problems – incidents that occur but are not reported to the police. With respect to e-fraud, the problem is exacerbated because victims have alternative agencies to report to, such as credit card companies and banks. As a central registration office of U.S. internet crime, the Internet Crime Complaint Centre (www.ic3.gov) has been issuing annual numbers of cyber crimes reported to them since 2000. These numbers suggest a rising trend between 2000 and 2008, with a count of approximately 275,000 complaints in 2008 (Internet Crime Complaint Center 2008). 'Not receiving products paid for on the internet' was the largest category of complaints. However, it is likely that these numbers reflect a disproportionate number of serious internet crimes, and that less serious incidents are not reported. Victim survey data offer an alternative and probably more reliable way to estimate internet crime volumes, as respondents can also report internet crime experiences not reported to official agencies.

Dutch figures on cyber crime offences registered by the Dutch police (both reports and official statements) show that around half of the files on cyber crime are about cases of e-fraud (in two police regions 51.4% and 48.6%) (Domenie et al. 2009). But relative to the total number of police registrations (about all types of crime), e-fraud represents only a fraction of the overall number of cases registered (the number of cyber crime cases registered in the Netherlands in 2009 was in fact less than 1%).

Online sale and auction fraud
The International Crime Victims Survey (ICVS) and European Survey of Crime and Safety (EU_ICS) offer comparative statistics on 'fraud with shopping on the internet', for more than 20 mainly Western countries (2003-2004). Relatively high rates were found for the U.S., Poland, Germany and Bulgaria, with annual prevalence estimates of 2.6% to 3.3%. In contrast, Italy,

Finland, Greece and Mexico had low annual occurrence rates of 0.0 to 0.2% (Van Dijk et al. 2007).

A recent victimisation study using representative survey data from the Netherlands found that during a one-year period approximately 2.5% of all respondents reported victimisation in the form of non-receipt of goods purchased on the internet (Van Wilsem 2010). A U.S. survey reported that 13.5% of all adults suffered from at least one instance of general consumer fraud (Anderson 2007). According to this study, 21.5% of all consumer fraud victimisation was perpetrated by internet or email.

Identity theft

Little is known too about the extent of identity theft. Studies show that between 3% and 5% of phishing attacks actually succeed in stealing personal information (Ollmann 2004; Stamm et al. 2006). How many phishing attacks are actually being carried out is however unknown. Citizens who have been the victim of phishing will firstly contact their bank or credit card company in order to get indemnification (Boerman et al. 2008). After that, there is no need to report to the police. If a victim has reported to the police, it is often difficult for researchers to identify a case as a phishing case, because victims do not always know whether or not they were a victim of phishing, and moreover the police do not register these types of offences well (Domenie et al. 2009).

Research into police files shows that most e-fraud cases are simple scams: paying, but not delivering goods through auction and sale sites (Leukfeldt et al. 2010). The Internet Crime Complain Centre (IC3) shows a similar picture: most reported cases are about scams through auction and sale sites and not about phishing. A possible explanation is that victims do not (instantly) know that they have been the target of a phishing attack and that the cyber criminal has stolen personal information. Indeed, phishing sites are designed to fool victims and pose as normal official websites. Only when the criminal is abusing the personal information is the victim alerted, for example because he receives an invoice for goods or services he has never ordered. But at that point, it is unclear whether the victims still know when and where their personal information has been stolen.

Scarcely any international comparative statistics are available on identity theft. Exceptions are the ICVS and EU-ICS reports of one-year victimisation prevalence rates for 'credit card fraud' covering 18 Western countries (Van Dijk et al 2007). The highest percentage was found for the U.S. (4.0%), while the U.K. scored second highest (separate surveys in specific parts of the U.K., each

121

revealing a victimisation rate of approximately 1.5%). In addition, U.S. surveys specifically tailored to measure the volume of identity theft are the Federal Trade Commission's survey (Synovate 2003, 2007) and the Identity Theft Supplement to the National Crime Victimisation Survey (NCVS-ITS). Langton and Planty (2010) report on two-year prevalence rates from the NCVS-ITS 2008 and show that 5% of persons aged 16 years or older were a victim of identity theft. Most common forms were frauds involving existing credit card of bank accounts (2% to 2.5% victimisation rate). Frauds involving new accounts or misuse of personal information such as getting government benefits or renting a house were quite rare (less than 1%). Estimates of the FTC (2007) put the victimisation rate for identity theft during the year 2005 at 3.7%.

8.4   Offender characteristics

Because of the different types of e-fraud, it is impossible to describe the general characteristics of the e-fraudster. In this paragraph, we will describe the characteristics of fraudsters who use online sale and auction sites, offenders of advance fee fraud and identity theft.

Online sale and auction fraud

Fraudsters who use online sale and auction sites to execute their scams usually work alone; there are no signs of organised criminal networks (Leukfeldt et al. 2010). Financial gain is the main motive and the offenders and their victims do not know each other. Furthermore offenders do not adopt complex criminal techniques, in most cases simply using social engineering to deceive victims (in buying and paying for a product).

Leukfeldt and Stol (2011) show that almost three-quarters of suspects are male (74.6%). The proportion of women in e-fraud cases is higher than in all other types of crimes (e.g. violence, drugs, traffic) (25.4 vs. 17.1, p<0.01) (see Prins 2008). Another study shows that the proportion of women is also higher in comparison to other cyber crimes (Leukfeldt et al. 2010). Table 8.1 shows a significant difference between the percentages of men and woman who commit fraud, hacking, child pornography, and hate crimes.

Table 8.1   Gender of suspects

Gender	Hacking (n=63)	E-fraud (n=218)	Child porn (n=167)	Hate crime (n=43)	# HKS (n=244.000)	## NL (n=16mlj)
	%	%	%	%	%	%
Man	79.4	o 73.4	* 98.2	86.0	82,9	* 49.5
Woman	20.6	26.6	1.8	14.0	17.1	50.5
Total	100.0	100.0	100.0	100.0	100.0	100.0

Source: Prins 2008; ## Source: Dutch Statistical Bureau: www.cbs.nl, reference year 2009.
* Significant difference with other percentages in the row; o Significant difference with Dutch Convictions Database (HKS) (steeds p<0,01).

Leukfeldt and Stol (2011) found furthermore that e-fraudsters are between 13 and 58 years old, with most between the ages of 18 and 24 (39.6%). This group is overrepresented (see Prins 2008). The group of suspects aged 12 to 18 years is underrepresented in the e-fraud cases. The authors suspect that, unlike offline property crimes without violence (e.g. car theft, shoplifting), e-fraud is not something for the youngest offenders, who may lack the social skills needed to scam other individuals. Persons aged between 18 and 34 are optimally equipped for e-fraud: they are old enough to have adequate skills for social engineering, and young enough to move with ease in cyberspace.

The criminal careers of e-fraudsters were also analysed by Leukfeldt and Stol (2011). Of the e-fraudsters, 44.1% are first offenders (in contact with the police for the first time in their lives).

Case 8.1   Online sale and auction fraud[40]

On the internet a mobile phone was offered on a selling site. The asking price was 120 euros. I was interested in the product and emailed the seller that I agreed on the price. I then transfer money. The seller emailed me that I would receive a track and trace code. I've never received the code. Subsequent correspondence yielded nothing more than excuses. The advertiser told me that he lived abroad, but I don't think he really does. The telephone is never delivered. I find that I'm scammed, especially since the telephone was offered on the same site again.

40 Source: Leukfeldt et al. (2010).

Advance fee fraud

According to Van der Hulst and Neve (2008), offenders of advance fraud are professional criminals who operate in groups, are part of a worldwide (criminal) network and are often derived and / or controlled from Nigeria. This type of fraud is also known as the 'Nigerian Scam' or '419 fraud' (based on Article 4.1.9 of the Nigerian Criminal Code). Such scams have been executed since the 1980s. In the early days scammers used letters, and with the technological developments in the decades thereafter, fax and email (Schoenmakers et al. 2009).

Perpetrators operate in flexible networks, consisting of separate cells[41] that are also guilty of many other forms of crime (Boerman et al. 2008). According to Boerman et al. (2008) and Schoenmakers et al. (2009) this loose structure is characteristic of West African criminal networks and allows the fraudsters to respond quickly to changing situations. Schoenmakers et al. (2009) conclude that advanced fee fraudsters are often young men. Also most offenders have a criminal record (forgery and fraud) and there is a high volume of recidivism: offenders simply restart after a conviction, if necessary in another country (Van der Hulst & Neve 2008). To hide their identity, the criminals frequently use forged or stolen (personal) documents.

Networks of fraudsters work in particular from the Netherlands, Spain and England, but also from other Western European countries. Victims are not made in the same country as where the scammers are resident. The networks that operated in the Netherlands, for example, made their victims in the United States and the United Kingdom. Dutch citizens were often the victims of fraudsters operating from other countries (Boerman et al. 2008; Schoenmakers et al. 2009).

---

41 According to experts of the Dutch National Police Agency (cited in Shoemaker et al. 2009) such networks consist of about eight to ten people. It is, however, also noted that in reality there are hundreds of 'cells' that are involved. It is, therefore, unclear what the true extent of these networks is.

Case 8.2   Advanced fee fraud (Schoenmakers et al. 2009)

----- Original Message -----
From: "United Nations Foundation" < notification@un.org>
To: <undisclosed-recipient>
Sent: Monday, July 21, 2008 10:56 PM
Subject: Grant Notification (Please Read)

This is to notify you that you have been chosen By the Board of trus-
tees of the above International (Charity & Human Developmental)
Organization, as one of the final recipients of a Cash Grant/Dona-
tion for your personal development of the sum of US$500,000.00
(Five Hundred Thousand United States Dollars) as developmental
aid from the UN Foundation. The I.T.I.L Foundation, UK has been
appointed to oversee this development affair. You are required to
expeditiously Contact the Executive Secretary of the I.T.I.L Foundation with the details below for documentation and processing of the
release of your cash aid, between the hours of 8.00 am – 7.00 pm on
Monday through Saturday. Please endeavour to quote your qualification numbers (UNF/FBF-816-1119 G-900-94) in all discussions.

Executive Secretary: ITIL Foundation – Dr Henry McCartney
Email: unofficer0003@gmail.com
Telephone: +44 701 113 862
United Nations Foundation.

Identity theft

Little is known about individuals engaged in identity theft. Copes and Vieraitis (2009) interviewed 59 offenders of identity theft detained in the United
States for their study into the mindset of these offenders. Copes and Vieraitis
conclude that the primary motivation of offenders is to make quick money in
a relatively easy way. They note that the offenders do not form a homogeneous group. Nevertheless, some characteristics can be distinguished: middle
class workers, criminal record (e.g. fraud, drugs), highly manipulative, technical skills and knowledge of financial systems (from banks and other financial
institutions). Some of the perpetrators obtained the specific knowledge during
work. These offenders worked, for example, in a mortgage institution or in
public or private companies that provide access to personal information like
credit card numbers (banks, department stores). Because there is little insight
into the offender characteristics of criminals engaged in identity theft, it is
difficult to establish whether they work in organised groups (Van der Hulst &
Neve 2008; National Police Agency 2007; Gordon & Ford 2006). A criminal

technique that can be used for identity theft is phishing. This technique is discussed in chapter 13.

> Case 8.3   Identity theft and abuse by means of a phishing attack[42]
>
> About 14 days ago I logged onto the site of my bank to make some transfers. I could not log on with my regular username and password. I had to create a new password and username at the site before I could log on again. After a week I heard nothing and I called an employee of the bank. He told me to request this on the site of my ... I did this and in the following days I received a new username and password by mail. After I logged on to the site of the bank I noticed that a transfer of € 25,000,- was made. I never instructed to do so. The transfer took place in the time when I could not log into the site from my bank.

8.5   Victims of e-fraud

Until now, studies on internet fraud victimisation and targeting are relatively rare. However more research has been conducted in the fields of online auction and sales frauds and identity fraud. We first discuss findings for auction and sales fraud, and then for identity theft. As we did not find empirical studies into victims of advance fee fraud, this category of e-fraud is not treated in this section.

Online sale and auction fraud

Victimisation through internet auction fraud appears to be no random event. Rather, the susceptibility to risk of fraud targets is determined by specific characteristics. As with offline fraud victimisation (Titus et al. 1995), there seem to be no clear socio-demographic differences between people being targeted for online fraud victimisation and those who are not (Pratt et al. 2010). Instead, routine activity theory argues that people's everyday online activities are important to understanding who is at higher risk of being contacted by internet perpetrators. Based on a victimisation survey among Florida residents, Pratt et al. (2010) concluded that people who spent many hours online and who made online purchases were more likely to be targeted (i.e. approached) by internet fraud offenders. After being targeted, some people are victimised because they respond to the fraudulent offer, while other targets check out before any harm is done. Using the same survey data, Holtfreter et al. (2008) found that low self-control is a major contributor to the subsequent stage of victimisation,

126

---

42 Source: Leukfeldt et al. (2010).

though this study pertained to the broader area of general consumer fraud, including offline variants. The authors argue that low self-control is relevant for the domain of fraud victimisation, because it involves seeking immediate gratification, little financial planning and risk taking with respect to commercial offers (Baumeister 2002). As such, they show that self-control theory is applicable outside the traditional criminological focus of street crime.

In a large-scale Dutch survey among the general population, Van Wilsem (2010) found patterns similar to the study by Holtfreter and colleagues. Focusing on the victimisation of not receiving products bought online, he found that internet shopping and low self-control were the two most important predictors of risk. More specifically, low self-control appeared to determine risk through mechanisms of selection as well as causation. As a mechanism of selection, low self-control affects who is active online, and thus, who is more likely to be targeted by online fraud perpetrators. Indeed, Van Wilsem (2010) found that people with poor impulse control do more online purchases and are more active in online forums. In turn, these activities increased online consumer fraud risk, thus suggesting a selection effect of low self-control by structuring the exposure to online fraudsters. However, when the effect of these activities was monitored, low self-control remained an independent contributor to victimisation, suggesting a causal influence as well. Impulsive people possibly react differently to suspect online commercial offers.

127

Identity theft

In the U.S., large-scale victimisation data on identity theft are available from the Identity Theft Supplement to the National Crime Victimisation Survey. Data on 2008 reveal that high-income households suffer from greater risk of attempted or successful identity theft, particularly with *existing* bank or credit card accounts (Langton & Planty 2010). These possibly result from differences in the use of these accounts. Higher rates among high-income households were also observed by Anderson (2006), using large-scale survey data from the Federal Trade Commission of 2003. In addition, he found higher rates for households with one adult, households with three or more children, females and old people.

In general however, socio-demographic differences in victimisation risk do not reveal which mechanisms are responsible for creating the degree of risk that people run. As one of the exceptions, Hutchings and Hayes (2009) conducted a small-scale Australian study of phishing victimisation by asking respondents if they had recently received fraudulent emails to obtain personal information   which is one of the ways identity theft can occur. It appeared that heavy users of computers and people frequently engaged in online banking suffered more risk of a phishing attack. A Dutch study among college and high school students by Van Wilsem et al. (2010) revealed that the risk of unauthorised cash withdrawals from one's existing bank account – the most common form of identity fraud – was higher among people who revealed their surname and phone number on their social networking site as well as among people who were perpetrators of digital crimes themselves. These results are in line with the general predictions of routine activity theory that crime targets become more suitable with increasing visibility and accessibility (Felson & Clarke 1998).

8.6   Trends

E-fraud covers a wide range of offences, therefore we cannot comment on general trends. In the case of online sale and auction fraud and advance fee fraud, too little information is available to identify trends. We can cautiously single out some trends in identity theft. The expectation is that identity theft will make large numbers of casualties and cause much financial damage in the coming years (Taylor et al. 2006). E-fraud through phishing is regarded as one of the fastest growing forms of non-violent crime (Rogers 2006). Several factors play a role. Firstly, with the growth of e-commerce and virtual money flows, it has become more and more attractive for criminals to engage in e-fraud (Taylor et al. 2006). The Western world is a very attractive field for phishers because of the high internet speeds and computers that are almost permanently online, (Van der Hulst & Neve 2008). In addition, attacking techniques are constantly being updated (Watson et al. 2005). Cybercriminals always invent new ways to make (phishing) attacks successful (Govcert 2010). This is reflected for example in the number of variants of phishing (vishing, smishing, spear phishing, see chapter 13). Finally, there is reason to believe that in the coming years the use of social engineering will increase (see chapter 12) and social events and personal interests will be exploited. Examples are the Olympics, World Cup and major disasters (Govcert 2010).

Key concepts

Fraud
Online sale and auction fraud
Identity theft
Advance fee fraud

9 Child Pornography

Rutger Leukfeldt & Anton van Wijk

9.1 Introduction

Creating and distributing child pornography is not new and existed before the advent of the internet (Finkelhor 1984). However, the phenomenon has become more visible since the mid-1990s and various disciplines have paid more attention to it (Van Wijk et al. 2009). In light of social indignation and police priorities, the spreading of child pornography can be regarded as one of the biggest cyber crime problems (Stol et al. 2008b).

The public concern is understandable, because we know from previous research that the internet contributes significantly to the spread of child pornography (Biegel 2001; Jenkins 2001; Bullens 2007). Paedophiles seem to be early adapters of new technology (Van Wijk et al. 2009). O'Donnell & Milner (2007) for example, claim that paedophiles used computer databases to download and distribute child pornographic material long before the general public did.

There is no general internationally accepted definition of child pornography. We define child pornography as follows: every image – or data carrier, which includes an image – of a sexual act in which someone who seemingly has not yet reached the age of 18 years is being involved, or appears to be involved (based on The Council of Europe Convention on Cyber crime – see Section 9.2). The phrase 'or appears to be involved' means that even if the impression is given that a minor is shown in these images, it is child pornographic material. This ensures that the so-called virtual child pornography also falls under this definition.

9.2 Penalisation

Child Pornography on the internet is by definition an international problem. The legislation on child pornography however varies from country to country. There are a number of international initiatives to harmonise child pornography legislation. The three main international legal instruments that address child pornography, according to the International Centre for Missing & Exploited Children (ICMEC) (2008), are: (1) the UN Convention on the Rights of the Child on the Sale of Children, Child Prostitution and Child Pornography,

(2) the Council of Europe Convention on Cyber crime,[43] and (3) the Council of Europe Convention on the Protection of Children against Sexual Exploitation and Sexual Abuse.

International Conventions aim to harmonise legislation regarding child pornography. In all three conventions, producing, distributing, accessing and possessing child pornography (through ICT) is made punishable. In addition, the treaties give a definition of child pornography. The European Cyber crime Treaty states that the following elements are mandatory in the definition: 'pornographic material that visually depict ... [], (a person appearing to be) a minor engaged in sexually explicit conduct [, or] ... realistic images representing a minor engaged in sexually explicit conduct'. The other two treaties define child pornography as 'any representation, by whatever means, of a child engaged in real or simulated explicit sexual activities or any representation of the sexual parts of a child for primarily sexual purposes.' Further important elements in the European Cyber crime Convention are the age of 18 years and the criminalisation of virtual child pornography.[44] By adding the phrase 'or apparently involved', virtual child pornography is brought under the operation of the law. Despite international conventions designed to further harmonise child pornography legislation, there are differences between national laws, including between those of European countries (Stol et al. 2008a) and the separate states in America (Wells et al. 2007). One reason is that not all countries signed or ratified the treaties. In 2008, for example, almost half of Interpol Member Countries had no legislation that addressed child pornography: only 94 out of 183 countries have legislation on child pornography in greater or lesser extent (ICMEC 2008). Of this latter group, 29 countries in total have legislation sufficient to combat child pornography offences. Of the remaining 65 countries that do have child pornography laws:

- 54 do not define child pornography in national legislation;
- 36 do not criminalise possession of child pornography, regardless of the intent to distribute;
- 24 do not provide for computer facilitated offences.

---

43 The Cyber crime Convention is open for signature by the Council of Europe Member States and the non Member States that have participated in its elaboration, and for accession by other non Member States. Currently, 23 countries (22 Member States and 1 non Member State) have ratified the Cyber crime Convention, and 22 other countries (19 Member States and 3 non Member States) have signed, but not ratified, the Cyber crime Convention.

44 Virtual child pornography is apparently real, but is not made with real children. It is created with the help of digital techniques, for example, by simple two-dimensional cutting and pasting or by advanced three-dimensional animation technology.

9.3 Forms of child pornography and images

The manifestations of child pornographic content vary. Besides individual photos, there are photo collections or photo series. Photo series are not just a collection of photos but they involve a series of photographs that tell a story or are arranged by theme, such as children in underwear (Taylor et al. 2001 Quayle & Taylor 2003). Images can be digitally altered (pseudo-photographs). Applying digital graphic changes in the images is termed morphing (Krone 2004; Van der Zee & Groeneveld 2007). With all new technical developments – namely the increased bandwidth and storage capacity – movies play an increasingly important role in the supply of child pornography on the internet. The films are also used to take still pictures (video prints of paused videos). Indeed, Taylor et al. (2001) note that images in an extensive database of child pornography images often seem to be similar to the films from the same databases. It is also possible to watch children being abused live via a webcam. People can log on to a website and use a chat room to make special requests (Taylor et al. 2001).

Not only the technical forms, but also the nature of child pornographic content can vary. A widely used classification is that of the Copine database, a European project launched in 1997 (Combating Paedophile Information Network in Europe). Here are 10 categories, ranging from not very serious to extreme forms of child pornography (figure 9.1).

Figure 9.1   The Copine Scale

1	Indicative	Non-erotic and non-sexualised pictures showing children in their underwear, swimming costumes from either commtercial sources or family albums. Pictures of children playing in normal settings, in which the context or organisation of pictures by the collector indicates inappropriateness.
2	Nudist	Pictures of naked or semi-naked children in appropriate nudist settings, and from legitimate sources.
3	Erotica	Surreptitiously taken photographs of children in play areas or other safe environments showing either underwear or varying degrees of nakedness.
4	Posing	Deliberately posed pictures of children fully clothed, partially clothed or naked (where the amount, context and organisation suggests sexual interest).

5	Erotic Posing	Deliberately posed pictures of fully, partially clothed or naked children in sexualised or provocative poses.
6	Explicit Erotic Posing	Pictures emphasising genital areas, where the child is either naked, partially clothed or fully clothed.
7	Explicit Sexual Activity	Pictures that depict touching, mutual and self-masturbation, oral sex and intercourse by a child, not involving an adult.
8	Assault	Pictures of children being subjected to a sexual assault, involving digital touching, involving an adult.
9	Gross Assault	Grossly obscene pictures of sexual assault, involving penetrative sex, masturbation or oral sex, involving an adult.
10	Sadistic/Bestiality	a. Pictures showing a child being tied, bound, beaten, whipped or otherwise subjected to something that implies pain. b. Pictures where an animal is involved in some form of sexual behaviour with a child.

According to Taylor & Quayle (2003), most photo series fall in the categories 'indicative' to 'explicit erotic posing' (1 to 6).

9.4 Scope and distribution methods

The international Wonderland case, which happened in 1998 (see figure 9.2), shows that large amounts of child pornography have been circulated on the internet for a long time (Klaver 1999). The Wonderland network on the internet was created for people who were interested in sex with children and child pornography. One of the members had 180,000 photographs in his possession. To become a member of this network it was obligatory to supply new child pornographic material (MKI 2008).

Interpol maintains a database of child pornographic material circulating on the internet. In 2008 the database contained approximately 500,000 images (MKI 2008). In the national database of the Dutch National Criminal Investigation department there are about 1.8 million images (Van Wijk et al. 2009). How much other material is still circulating on the internet is unknown. Also unknown is how often such images are transmitted and shared among paedophiles. In short, it is unknown how much child pornography the internet contains and how often material is downloaded. It is clear, however, that the number of images will not readily diminish. The increased technical capabilities (particularly cheap storage) will increase the supply. Until recently the fact that the police arrested a distributor of child pornographic material with millions of images in his possession was unthinkable (Van Wijk et al. 2009).

Figure 9.2   The Wønderland Club

In September 1998 the 'Wønderland Club' was nabbed by an international police operation called 'Operation Cathedral'. The 'Wønderland Club' existed only on the internet and was very well organised: there was a president, secretary and a thorough process for new members to be audited. The internet site had five different levels of security to keep unwanted viewers away from the illegal activities. One example is the use of complex passwords and using encryption technologies to protect files. Another method to make the site less accessible, was to use an alphanumeric character (Ø) in the name of the website. The existence of this online organisation was revealed only through another case of sexual abuse of children. The first case started with a man in California in 1996. This man abused a 10-year-old girlfriend of his daughter live on camera. During the abuse he received instructions from other members of the 'Orchid Club', which he was a member of, who were logged on and were watching. Some time later, another girl reported the man, and the police arrested him and searched his home and computer. On his computer contacts with other men were found. In the U.S. 12 others were arrested. Furthermore, the trail led to three men in Britain. On the computer of one of these three, information was found that led to the site of the 'Wønderland Club'. Source: Video The Wonderland Club.

133

Number of abused children

A question relating to child pornography and the internet, especially with the increasing amount of material that is circulating, is whether the number of abused children has risen. For a start, we do not know exactly how many children are victims of sexual abuse. The study by Wolak et al. (2008) shows that reality is more complicated than we sometimes tend to think. One can assume that the internet leads to an increase in child abuse. Larger paedophile networks may indeed be created and it has become easy to come into contact with new potential victims. Wolak et al., however, believe there are no studies that substantiate this speculation. There has even been a decline in the number of child abuse cases registered in the U.S. since the advent of the internet. Between 1990 and 2005, according to Wolak et al., the number of cases of child abuse reported by the child protective authorities in the U.S. dropped by more than half (51%). Wolak et al. (2008) suggest the possible explanation that child molesters have moved from the physical world to the virtual world. The factors that ensure that the internet facilitates child abuse may not be as powerful as assumed.

We cannot simply assume that the number of child abuse cases has increased because of the internet. However we can see that the internet is being used to disseminate child pornography and that it has become easier to disseminate material.

Method of distribution

For the dissemination of child pornography, all possible routes offered by the internet are used: websites, newsgroups, chat programs like MSN and ICQ, peer-to-peer networks and virtual hard disks (cloud computing) (Oosterink & Van Eijk 2006; Schell et al. 2007; Stol 2004; Stol et al. 1999, 2008a).

We do not know what proportion of child pornography on the internet is distributed via which routes. Clearly, the distribution routes are subject to change. This is due partly to continuous new technical opportunities (Deibert et al. 2008) and partly to the providers of child pornography responding to repressive measures (Stol 2004; Stol et al. 2008b). Efforts to combat child pornography have affected the working methods of the suppliers. In the mid-1990s the material was often found on easily approachable websites (free-networks). It then gradually shifted to the less public parts of the internet, which are hard for the police to control (from websites to newsgroups, peer-to-peer (P2P) environments) and closed domains (Stol et al. 2008a; Van Wijk et al. 2009).

9.5   Distributors

Two groups of distributors of child pornography can be distinguished: a commercial group and a group of 'enthusiasts' (Stol et al. 2008a). The commercial traders see child pornography as a new way to make money. Makers and distributors of child pornography are found in all layers of the population and often move in networks (Van der Werf 2003). There is a heterogeneous offender profile. It has however been established that offenders in this category quite often have a criminal record (mostly for sexual offences and / or child abuse). According to Van der Hulst & Neve (2008), the trade and production of child pornography is, increasingly a business of organised crime groups. Child pornography is a lucrative business and a lot of money can be made (NDB, 2004). According to several authors, such groups are mainly from Russia and Eastern Europe (KLPD, DNRI 2004; Lünnemann et al. 2006; McCusker 2006; Van der Werf 2003). However, little empirical research on such groups has been done and for that reason we do not know, for example, what the ratio between open and closed networks is, or how many networks exist.

The second group, the 'enthusiasts', are usually not money-driven. This group primarily wants to acquire new material. The sexual abuse of children (self or to exhort others) in order to produce new material is part of the core business of these offenders (Durkin, cited by Alexy et al. 2005; McLaughlin 2000). This second group forms a new subculture on the internet. They find each other on shielded parts of the internet (e.g. forums) to discuss and exchange material (Durkin & Bryant 1999; Jenkins 2001). Research into the online paedophile subculture shows that the online social world of paedophiles is shaped by four interrelated normative orders (Holt et al. 2010):

Marginalisation. One of the most significant normative orders in the paedophile subculture is the relationship between paedophiles and society at large. Paedophiles who use online forums recognise that their sexual orientations are different, which causes them to face extreme social stigma in the real world and means they constantly have to defend themselves against those who do not share their sexual orientations.

Sexuality. Paedophiles use forums to safely discuss their (sexual) attractions and desires within an online community of like-minded individuals. The forums contained conversations on fetishes, likes and dislikes, and experiences with children.

Law. Paedophiles also used forums to discuss the definitions and law on paedophilia and child pornography. Paedophiles appeared to be well versed in the laws that prohibit the behaviours they claim to have engaged in and warned each other about certain acts that may put them at risk of arrest or detection.

Security. Paedophiles discuss the best ways to structure individual behaviour on- and offline and how to protect their true identities and keep their computers secure. Restrictive guidelines are aimed at minimising negative attention for the forums and reducing the likelihood that members will use the site to exchange illegal materials. Furthermore, measures were taken to protect the forum users and moderators (e.g. the use of web proxies anonymisers to protect the location).

135

Journalist Van Kleef (2004) describes the virtual world of paedophiles in an article in the Dutch magazine 'Nieuwe Revu'. He infiltrated an active community where child pornography was distributed. The purport of this article is consistent with what experts in research of Stol et al. (2008a) have said in in-depth interviews about accessing online groups. The following description is based on Stol et al. (2008a), while the texts in boxes come from Van Kleef.

Step 1: finding the supplier
The first step in obtaining child pornography is to find the suppliers. This turns out to be more difficult than it initially appears.

> But someone who does not know where to look for child pornography cannot even find a picture of a naked toddler on the beach. Google produces 6.8 million hits on the term 'child porn', but all those results are linked to legal porn sites where the models are not under 18.

Hence, the average surfer does not just stumble on child pornography. But those who ask the right questions in the right place will end up in the corner right where the child pornography is distributed.

> In the chat room of Free Spirits, we find Nestor who has a tip: 'I have heard that the Alex BBS sometimes has these kinds of photos. That's all I know.' Alex is a digital bulletin board where links to free sex sites are exchanged. At first sight, there is no illegal porn. We decide to leave a message on the board. We write that we are looking for child pornography and leave a Hotmail address. An hour later, the mailbox is packed.

Step 2: taking security measures
Once directed to a website containing child pornography, a number of security measures has to be taken, in order to ensure that the suppliers and other users of the site cannot be traced by the police. Hence, if a new member of the network has been apprehended by the police, the other members are also at risk.

> Untraceable surfing is possible, but there it is necessary to take a couple of steps. We need a firewall, install software that can erase the memory of the computer and encrypt your IP number.

Step 3: entering a group

When the right precautions are taken, the supplier of the child pornography can be contacted.

> Twipsy mails a Web address, and writes that we need to log in with a certain code. We click on the link that links to a site called - 'or all your questions about this nice hobby!'. A login window appears. We enter the code that we have received from Twipsy. A few seconds later another web page opens. At the top is days: 'Welcome at K-Book, tops', 'Enjoy your stay!'.

Step 4: climbing in the hierarchy

Once you are inside a group of child pornography 'enthusiasts', firstly the trust of the other members has to be gained. The hierarchy within the group appears to be important. Members of the group who load up large amounts of new material on the network are, according to the article, honoured as heroes.

> 'Well, is this the child porn mecca?' we ask. 'Just wait', Sirax advises. 'The chat is very important here. Make sure you make some friends. Spread your nest odour. Then everything will be all right.' (...) Here Twipsy and the other select those who are allowed in the higher levels. There you will find better pictures and movies.

When asked why, despite all the safety measures, there have been numerous arrests of paedophiles, a member of the group replied: 'They were playing a whole different ballgame. They applied to commercial child pornography websites. They paid with their credit card. Indeed, they basically asked for the police' (Van Kleef 2004).

9.6 Child pornography offenders (the downloaders)

Downloading and distributing child pornography are not always strictly separated things. If, for example, a downloader joins a P2P network, s/he can be both downloader and supplier at the same time (every user can make folders on their computer that contain content which is accessible for all the people in the P2P network – usually, the 'download folder', in which new material is downloaded, is standard accessible for all users). Section 9.6 further shows that people who want to participate in a closed network should offer material themselves first and should continue doing that in order to gain a high status. So, also in this case, the downloader is also a distributor.

Several empirical studies show that downloaders are generally white men (e.g. Seto & Eke 2005). The age range varies, but the largest group seems to be between 25 and 45 years old (Burke et al. 2002; Kierkegaard 2008). Download-ers can live alone, but can also have a partner (Sullivan 2002). In the latter case, according to Van Wijk et al. (2009) who interviewed therapists of down-loaders, there are problems within the relationship or there is an unequal rela-tionship. The downloaders have had secondary to higher education (e.g. Webb et al. 2007). The professions are varied. When the downloader has a sexual preference for children, he often also has a job where he can come into contact with children, for example, education or health professions (e.g. Burgess et al. 2008) or he has a technical profession (Van der Hulst & Neve 2008; Schell et al. 2007). Downloaders will also tailor their leisure time to their sexual preferences, for example, by becoming a youth team coach or joining the Boy Scouts (Van Wijk et al. 2009). Downloaders may have all sorts of psychological problems. The addiction factor plays an important role in their deviant online behaviour. In these cases, it is referred to pathological internet use (Davis 2001). This behaviour is a substitute for 'normal' relations with other adults in the offline world. Downloaders are characterised by an inability to engage in intimate relationships, partly because of their low self-esteem and poor social skills. There may also be emotional deregulation (e.g. Quayle & Taylor 2003; Schell et al. 2007). Psychiatric disorders appear to be less frequent. Studies in which therapists of downloaders were interviewed show that sexual disorders and autism related disorders sometimes occur in the group of downloaders (Van Wijk et al. 2009). Sexual dysfunction usually implies paedophilia (Seto et al. 2006), but physical and sexual dysfunction (e.g. erectile dysfunction), with all possible additional psychological problems, also occurs. Downloaders do not seem to be addicted to alcohol or drugs (Webb et al. 2007).

A Dutch analysis of police files shows that there is usually only one suspect in cases of downloaders (Leukfeldt et al. 2010). These are mostly indigenous men, mainly in the 18-55 age group. Leukfeldt et al. (2010) conclude that curi-osity is the primary motive most frequently mentioned by suspects. Suspects who mentioned curiosity as their motive say they are not searching because of an established paedophile inclination, but want to explore their bounda-ries. Bullens (2007) and Seto et al. (2010) also conclude that most perpetra-tors claim that they had stumbled by chance on child pornography and that

they subsequently became curious and got excited (see, for example, case 9.1).
A qualification is needed here. Stol et al (2008a) show, for example, that
finding child pornography is not so easy and innocent internet users do not
find child pornography by accident. We also know that having child pornography is a good predictor of a paedophile preference, something which society finds so undesirable that perpetrators are not likely to admit to having
searched for this material.

Case 9.1   Curiosity as a motive (Leukfeldt et al. 2010)

'I know I am not obliged to answer. Since last year I sometimes have looked
at child pornography. I looked occasionally and sometimes I downloaded
and viewed pictures and movies. I have never touched children, let alone
exploited. I stumbled upon these child pornography web sites by clicking
and surfing on normal porn sites. Sometimes you got a list of passwords
you had to use to open pictures and movies. Sometimes you had to try
the password a couple of times. In some cases you could see what the
title of the photo or video meant and sometimes not. The files I received
were 'compressed' files like 'zip' and 'WinRAR'. After you unzipped these
files, you got to see the pictures and movies within. I have seen children
from about five years old on these sites. I have looked at them, but they
did nothing to me. I was not excited or anything. It was more curiosity for
me. I usually threw the files away later.'

Finally, the study of Leukfeldt et al. (2010) shows that a relatively new group
of offenders that produces and disseminates child pornography has emerged:
youngsters. Almost a quarter (23.8%) of the suspects in Dutch child pornography files are younger than 24 years (and, in total, 8.3% is younger than
18 years). This can be explained by the fact that minors, whether voluntarily
or not, take sexual photos and make videos of themselves and/or each other.
When this material is distributed via the internet (by the suspect him/herself,
a classmate or acquaintance, see case 9.2) it becomes – according to the Dutch
law – the distribution of child pornography. A new social problem arises: are
the accused simply ordinary young people who (as always) experiment with
their sexuality, and should the police and justice ignore these cases, or are they
committing criminal acts whereby perpetrators must be prosecuted because
otherwise a situation arises in which certain types of child pornography are

no longer punishable? The question of the extent to which self-produced child pornography by young people is actually harmful should be examined. More about this topic in chapter 15.

Case 9.2   Young child pornography producers and distributors
              (Leukfeldt et al. 2010)

A father and mother report a crime against their daughter at the desk of a local police bureau. Their underage daughter has taken part in some sexual acts with an underage boy. A movie of these acts was made and posted on the internet. The boy was 14 or 15 years old. The movie was made in [person x's] home; he was 16 or 17 years old. The victim did not know that the movies were being made. The persons all attend the same school. It was stated that all the children from the school had already seen the movie. The father wants to talk to a vice detective. The detective, however, was not clear whether the sexual acts were committed against the wishes of the victim.

140

9.7   Trends

A trend in the digital distribution of child pornography is that the material disappears into the less public parts of the internet. In these parts of the internet it is difficult for the police to observe, and therefore it is also difficult to collect evidence (see also section 9.3). The first shift was that of public websites to newsgroups (MKI 1997), the second movement was that of newsgroups to chat rooms (MKI 2002) and third movement to (closed) P2P systems (MKI 2004, 2005; Oosterink & Van Eijk 2006; Schell et al. 2007; Stol 2004; Stol et al. 2008a).

Technological developments will continue to shape this cyber crime. We have seen a shift from photos to movies. Webcams make the online production of child pornography possible and contribute, as do mobile phones with camera functions, to the production of child pornography by young people among themselves. Important in this respect is the sexual morality among the young. As mentioned in section 9.7, a new social problem is emerging and the question should be examined of the extent to which self-produced child pornography by young people is actually harmful.

Furthermore, digital imaging techniques continue to facilitate the production of virtual child pornography The quality of the content will undoubtedly increase further and for that reason the extent to which real images can be distinguished from virtual ones can be expected to decrease. We can also assume that providers of child pornography will develop new payment methods to ensure that recipients who pay for their material by credit card cannot be detected. Finally, it is expected that child pornography files will be encrypted more often in order to avoid filtering techniques (Leukfeldt et al. 2010).

Key concepts

Child pornography
Distributor of child pornography (commercial)
Distributor of child pornography (enthusiasts)
Distributor of child pornography (youngsters)

10 Unauthorised File Sharing[43]

Joost Poort & Paul Rutten

10.1 Introduction

This chapter deals with a fascinating, and for some disturbing, phenomenon in the domain of the media and entertainment industries: unauthorised file sharing, in some cases also referred to as piracy. The latter term, however, was originally used to refer to the organised production of a counterfeit product, i.e. illegal physical copies of games and DVDs (or Gucci bags and Rolex watches). On the internet, it is confined to those who practise file sharing with a straightforward criminal intent driven by commercial motives. This chapter deals exclusively with unauthorised file sharing by individual citizens. With the advent of broadband digital networks following up on the introduction of the internet, people have shown a great interest in acquiring digital content, in order to get to know it or to store their favourite works on their digital devices for immediate access. At first file sharing primarily related to music, later also to films, games and, since recently, books. Digital technology in the hands of citizens proved a powerful tool for sharing creative works online and get the better of rights holders, not asking for authorisation, giving consumers free access to a *mere à boire* of entertainment products. Although the unauthorised *distribution* of copyrighted works is a violation of copyright law, file sharing has proven to be an obstinate phenomenon. Media and entertainment companies have vigorously attempted to stop the unauthorised sharing of files on legal grounds, evoking copyright law in particular, with very limited success.

This chapter introduces the subject of file sharing, discussing its specific nature and its relevant legal and regulatory context as well as recent policy developments in Europe. Based on an extensive survey among Dutch citizens it provides insight into the specific behaviour and motivations of file sharers and assesses the consequences of these for the actual sales of entertainment products. Before concluding, it presents a short review of the opinions of authors and performers on rights protection and file sharing based on research conducted among creators of digital content.

---

45 This chapter is largely based on Huygen et al. (2009) and Van Eijk, Poort & Rutten (2010).

10.2 Legal and regulatory context

File sharing is the catchall term for uploading and downloading, and encompasses a range of technologies. The most popular forms are peer-to-peer (or P2P) file sharing networks such as Bittorrent, cyberlockers, and file hosting services. In *P2P file sharing*, users install software that connects to a peer-to-peer network to search for shared files on the computers of other users (i.e. peers) connected to the network. Files of interest can then be downloaded directly from other users on the network. Typically, large files are broken down into smaller chunks, which may be obtained from multiple peers and then reassembled by the downloader. By default, a peer who is downloading a file simultaneously uploads the chunks that he or she already has to other peers.[46] This ensures fast proliferation and wide availability of content. Hence, P2P networks contain no central database or servers on which copyright protected material is stored. *File hosting services* such as Usenet do have such servers from which material can be downloaded, even though these form a distributed network without a central server or dedicated administrator. *Cyberlockers* are websites that provide password protected online storage capacity. Cyberlockers can be used to store copyrighted content, which can subsequently be downloaded by anyone who has the required password.

The regulatory context of file sharing in most European countries is based on traditional copyright related concepts, but increasingly is an issue that is attracting national and international attention. File sharing logically breaks down into downloading and uploading, with the latter particularly relevant in terms of the law since any online offering of copyrighted content generally is not permitted without the prior consent of the rights holder. By contrast, *downloading* copyrighted material such as music, films and books is permitted in several countries, provided it is for the downloader's own use and meets certain requirements – sometimes regardless of whether the content comes from an 'illegal source'. Note that these rules do not apply to games. They are considered computer programs (software) and are therefore governed by different laws. In Europe, both up- and downloading of computer programs is considered a violation of copyright.

---

46 Downloaders may choose not to engage in uploading, but this will often lead to decreased download speeds as capacity is distributed on a quid-pro-quo basis.

Downloading and private copying

In the context of copyright law, downloading of copyrighted digital content constitutes a reproduction (copying). Every form of downloading (from P2P networks or a website, on a mobile phone, etc.) basically constitutes making a copy. In general, the permission of the rights holder is required for making a copy of protected content. However, in several countries downloading is permitted if the material is for private use. Whether or not content is paid for does not in itself indicate that the content is offered with or without the permission of the rights holder.

However, in certain cases consent to download content is not required. In some cases protection has expired,[47] as a consequence of which works are in the public domain and free to be used. Nor is consent required for downloading content that is not eligible for protection (facts, formulas and creations lacking their own original character). Likewise, 'torrent' files, which specify the name, size and location of a file, do not enjoy copyright protection.

Downloading of works that are not in the public domain can also be lawful without prior consent. That is the case if one of the copyright exceptions is applicable. The most relevant exception is private use. As a consequence citizens may *download* content from P2P networks, websites and social networks (Facebook, Hyves, MySpace, etc.) even without the consent of the rights holder, when they use the work in the private context. Both socio-cultural and economic arguments have been advanced for this private use exception. Socio-cultural arguments include privacy protection, promotion of participation in cultural and intellectual life, personal development and encouragement of creativity and freedom of expression. Economic arguments are the high costs and practical difficulties that would make it impracticable to enforce a prohibition on making copies for private use. Another consideration mentioned in the context of the private use exception is the need to strike a balance between, on the one hand, the aims of copyright (i.e. encouraging creativity, innovation and wider distribution) and the cost/benefit ratio (limiting the possibility for third parties to use existing creations) and, on the other, encouraging authors and producers. A specific condition for making digital copies for private use is that a fair levy is paid to the rights holders by way of compensation. In Europe,

145

47 See Goldstein & Hugenholtz (2010), par. 8.3.

the types of levy and the amount of compensation are typically based on the sale of blank tapes/CDs/DVDs/harddisks and/or recording devices.[48]

However, countries may also choose not to allow copying of certain types of works or limit the scope of it. For example, the private copying of games is not allowed or restricted to copies for the use and study of the work for professional purposes or for making a back up copy,[49] nor is breaking the protection schemes of DVDs. Private copying might also be limited to short parts of the work. More importantly, countries such as France and the United Kingdom have chosen not to allow private copying from a so-called 'illegal source'. A source is considered to be illegal if the content is *distributed* without the permission of the copyright holder or if the downloadable file has been produced without the consent of the copyright holder. Arguments against such a provision are that it is difficult for users to determine whether or not a source is 'legal' and that such a provision is difficult to enforce and can negatively affect the amount paid to the rights holders for private copying as part of the compensation for this practice.

Enforcement instruments and procedures

There is a relevant difference between *civil* and *criminal* instruments and procedures as far as the enforcement of copyright and action to prevent unlawful acts are concerned. The civil law rules are partly of a specific nature (e.g. the rules in copyright acts) and partly of a general nature (including tort law). Copyright can be enforced against anyone committing an infringement. Various instruments are available, including an injunction backed by a penalty for non-compliance (also in the case of imminent infringements), damages, surrender of profits, attachment, destruction of infringing content and means of production, claim for ownership of such content or means of production, recall of infringing products from the trade, and demands for personal information (name and address etc.) of infringers from the intermediaries (such as Internet Service Providers). Provisions on surrender of profits and attachment focus specifically on infringers who act in a commercial or professional capacity. When imposing enforcement measures, the courts must weigh the interests of the defendant (such as privacy and freedom of expression) against those of the rights holder.

---

48 1 See Goldstein & Hugenholtz (2010), par. 11.2.2.
49 The applicable regime has affects on file sharing.

As regards means of enforcement under criminal law, it should be noted that an individual user who infringes copyright (e.g. by uploading without authorisation) might be guilty of an indictable offence if he or she acted with intent. Not every instance of unauthorised uploading is committed with intent. Intent may be doubted, for example, when users make use of P2P or BitTorrent software and may upload unknowingly. Conditional intent may be held to exist in certain circumstances, namely where users "knowingly expose themselves to the far from negligible chance ..."[50] Users might possibly be presumed to realise that using P2P software can also result in the distribution of copyrighted content. The level of actual awareness is therefore a relevant element. Other aspects that have to be taken into account are questions such as proving that the publication was actually committed by the suspect or the question whether or not the offence is committed in a commercial or professional capacity. Finally, it should be noted that criminal law in general serves as an ultimate remedy, which is applied mainly where the public interest is affected by the infringement.

Policy developments

The introduction of a special law in France in 2009 – intended to criminalise *downloading* by individual users – generated a lot of discussion throughout Europe. The law, known as the 'Loi Hadopi', provides the possibility to cut off internet access because of copyright infringements (after two previous warnings). The original version of the law received substantial criticism and was turned down by the French constitutional court. It didn't provide enough legal guarantees, and more in particular it would have allowed cutting off internet users without a judicial procedure. The version that was finally accepted ruled that the intervention of a judge is obligatory. Nonetheless, it remains to be seen whether this legislation is enforceable in practice. It requires substantial resources (police, courts) and moreover criminalises large parts of the population. Also, there is a risk of file sharing going underground (by using encryption) or moving to alternatives (such as Usenet or cyberlockers). Some European countries are discussing whether they should introduce similar regulation. Others take a more cautious approach adopting a broader perspective by emphasising the need to implement new business models first.

The position of file sharing was heavily debated during the Review of the European communication framework. The European Parliament rejected proposals

---

50 Dutch Supreme Court, 9 November 1954, NJ 1955, 55.

for stricter rules on copyright infringements. Finally a compromise was concluded. Article 1, sub 3 of the Universal Service Directive now reads as follows:

> "This Directive neither mandates nor prohibits conditions, imposed by providers of publicly available electronic communications and services, limiting end-users' access to, and/or use of, services and applications, where allowed under national law and in conformity with Community law, but lays down an obligation to provide information regarding such conditions. National measures regarding end-users' access to, or use of, services and applications through electronic communications networks shall respect the fundamental rights and freedoms of natural persons, including in relation to privacy and due process, as defined in Article 6 of the European Convention for the Protection of Human Rights and Fundamental Freedoms."[51]

This text clearly aims at a more balanced approach although it doesn't entirely exclude the French solution. The issue remains a priority on the European agenda and is subject of further consultation.[52]

10.3 Profiles and motivations of file sharers

Downloading all sorts of works, from music to film and from games to books from unauthorised sources is a widespread and growing global phenomenon. The International Federation of Phonographic Industries states that in 2009, the proportion of file sharers was around 21% of the internet users in the top five European markets (IFPI 2010). In a French survey, 38% of the internet users admitted having downloaded music from torrent sites, whereas around 28% had downloaded in the last year (*Rapport au Ministre de la Culture et de la Communication* 2010). Statistics for the United States, where lawsuits against individual file sharers have drawn considerable media attention, are

---

51 Directive 2009/136/EC of the European Parliament and of the Council of 25 November 2009 amending Directive 2002/22/EC on universal service and users' rights relating to electronic communications networks and services, Directive 2002/58/EC concerning the processing of personal data and the protection of privacy in the electronic communications sector and Regulation (EC) No 2006/2004 on cooperation between national authorities responsible for the enforcement of consumer protection laws, Publ L337 d.d. 18/12/2009. (Article 1, sub 3, universal service directive).
52 See for example the recent Public consultation on "Content Online": http://ec.europa.eu/avpolicy/other_actions/content_online.

comparable. In December 2007, 37% of internet users admitted to having downloaded music; 27% downloaded video files (PEW 2009). File sharing figures tend to be higher in countries with higher broadband penetration and much higher among young people. A survey in the UK showed that 63% of young respondents download music (University of Hertfordshire 2008). In the United States, 58% of the age bracket from 18 to 29 years downloaded music (PEW 2009). File sharing of films and games is less common, but is rapidly catching up as residential bandwidth increases. Whereas estimates of the volume of download traffic vary strongly, it is clear that it accounts for many billions of files per year worldwide and makes up a substantial share of international internet traffic. File sharing of e-books is different again: the bandwidth required is almost negligible which makes e-books highly susceptible to unauthorised file sharing. However the popularity of e-books has until recently been limited. Given the current rapidly increasing penetration of e-readers and tablet computers, this is likely to change soon.

A file sharer profile

To gain a better understanding of consumers' file-sharing activity, their motivations, and its impact on the entertainment industries, a representative survey of a sample of the Dutch population was conducted in 2008 (Huygen et al. 2009). File sharing turned out to be a very common phenomenon across all socio-demographic groups of the Dutch population. Of the Dutch internet population over the age of 15 with internet access 44% admitted to file sharing on one or more occasions in the previous twelve months. Music is the most frequently downloaded entertainment category: 40% of those who have internet access do so. Note that this figure is remarkably in tune with figures in France and the United States. Films (13%) and games (9%) follow at some distance.

File sharers mainly stand out from the overall Dutch internet population by their age: they are younger. The proportion of downloaders among students in secondary schools and higher education is also higher. Males are overrepresented among file sharers (57-74%), particularly when downloading of films or games is concerned. Interestingly this cannot be explained by their consumption patterns of entertainment products: women and girls spend a comparable amount of time watching films or playing games. Regional differences are negligible. However file sharers typically own more state-of-the-art equipment than non-file sharers. In addition, file sharers rate their internet knowledge higher than do non-file sharers.

A notable finding is that almost 50% of file sharers are unable to say what method or technology they use for downloading, e.g. P2P, Usenet, newsgroups or FTP address. Most file sharers claim they only engage in *downloading* and do not *upload*. This would seem improbable as most P2P programs upload automatically. It seems likely that many file sharers are unaware that they are uploading. A mere one in twenty file sharers admit to adding new uploads.

File sharers are very often not aware of what is and what is not permitted. The majority of both file sharers and non-file sharers have no idea what the (Dutch) law allows in terms of downloading, uploading and/or adding. Nine per cent of file sharers, for instance, believe it is illegal to download for one's own use, 16% think automatic uploading is permitted and 12% are convinced that adding uploads is not against the law.

Motivations: downloading and buying

Contrary to the popular belief that file shares are 'lost to the industry', purchasing of music, film and games and file sharing go hand in hand. Music sharers are as likely to buy music as other people: 68% of file sharers also purchase music. File sharers buy as much music as non-file sharers. Moreover, file sharers spend more money on merchandise and go to concerts significantly more often. As for films, file sharers prove to buy significantly more DVDs than non-file sharers. On average, file sharers and non-file sharers go to the cinema equally often. Game sharers also buy games, and significantly more frequently too: 67% of file sharers are buyers as well. And if they buy, they buy significantly more games than non-file sharers. These results are summarised in table 10.1.

Table 10.1   Differences in purchasing behaviour between file sharers and non-file sharers

	Music	Films	Games
Buyers in the past 12 months: Yes/No	No difference	No difference	File sharers buy more often (61% vs. 57%)
If a buyer in previous 12 months: number	No difference	File sharers buy more (12.0 vs. 8.0 films)	File sharers buy more (4.2 vs. 2.7 games)
Related products	File sharers visit concerts more often and buy more merchandise	No difference in cinema visits	No difference in buying merchandise

Source: Huygen et al. (2009).

Interestingly 63% of music downloaders occasionally buy the music they first got for free online. The main reasons for buying are liking the music very much – a key motive for over 80% – or wishing to support the artiste (over 50%). Owning the CD sleeve and booklet are cited as motivation by one third of eventual buyers, as well as the perceived higher quality of the CD compared to the download. Forty-eight per cent of film sharers occasionally buy a previously downloaded film at a later date, citing such reasons as liking it a lot or wanting the extra features the DVD offers. Between 50% and 60% download to discover new genres and directors/actors. Some 63% of game sharers report sometimes buying a previously downloaded game at a later date. Their main reasons include thinking it a really good game. Wanting to own the original box and game were also frequently mentioned.

All in all, these figures show that there is no sharp divide between file sharers and others in their buying behaviour. On the contrary, when it comes to attending concerts and spending on DVDs and games, file sharers are the industry's largest customers. Note that no causal relationship is implied here. File sharers tend to be music, film or games aficionados who were more likely to consume content in the first place and might have consumed more if there had been no opportunities for file sharing. On the other hand, some might also have purchased *less* had there been no file sharing: several possible mechanisms concerning the effect of file sharing on sales are discussed below. Rather, the message here is that by declaring war on file sharers, the content industry would be declaring war on their largest customers, which could have serious adverse effects.

File sharers can have many different motivations for their activity: avoiding payment for the content they want to have (substitution) is just one of these. Other motivations are getting acquainted with the artiste and genres, known as 'sampling'. After sampling the content, consumers might decide to purchase it, to purchase other work from the same artiste, go to concerts or the cinema or to buy merchandise. Hence, the net effect of file sharing on sales is ambiguous: file sharing can have a negative, as well as a neutral or a positive effect on sales, depending on the effects that prevail. In general, this will vary between different media types and between famous and relatively unknown artistes. Well known artistes seem to profit less from sampling and suffer more from substitution, while the opposite holds for relatively unknown artistes (Blackburn 2004). Nine potential mechanisms discussed in the literature are summarised in table 10.2.

The survey also asked file sharers what they would consider a reasonable price for a CD, film or game they would really like to own. Please note that this is more than what they would be willing to pay on average for the products they are downloading. Three-quarters of music sharers are willing to pay at least eight euros for a CD. The average 'reasonable price' for music was higher than that for DVDs, which was five euros. Games are generally valued more highly.

Table 10.2　　Nine possible effects of file sharing on the sales of CDs, films, games and related products

Positive effect on sales	– File sharing introduces consumers to music, films and games (and to artistes and genres), thus creating demand. This is known as the sampling effect. – File sharing allows consumers to pool their demand, resulting in increased demand. (*) – File sharing enhances willingness to pay and demand for concerts and related products (complementary demand). – File sharing enhances the popularity of products, boosting demand driven by a lack of purchasing power (network effect). (**)
Neutral effect on sales	– File sharing meets the demand of consumers who are not, or not sufficiently, willing to pay and subsequently are not served by the manufacturer. – File sharing meets a demand for products that are not offered by manufacturers (e.g. film files for iPods).
Negative effect on sales	– File sharing substitutes the purchase of music, DVDs or games or cinema visits (substitution). – File sharing results in the deferred purchase of music, DVDs or games, at a lower price than the price at launch. – Sampling results in sales displacement as a result of fewer bad buys.

(*) This applies in particular to the exchange of content with friends rather than to the anonymous exchange through P2P networks.
(**) This applies in particular to the use of software for which network effects are clear. A (modest) network effect may also be found for lifestyle products such as music, films and games. Unauthorised use can also, under certain circumstances, have a positive effect on profits and investments without network effects as it can weaken competition between products.
Source: Huygen et al. (2009).

Table 10.3   Reasonable price according to file sharers

	Music	Films	Games
75 percentile	€ 8	€ 5	€ 7
Median	€ 9	€ 9	€ 19
Top qartile	€ 12	€ 11	€ 24

Source: Huygen et al. (2009).

Opinions and experiences of creators and performers

Despite the wide acceptance of file sharing within the general population and the ambiguous relationship between file sharing and revenues for the industry, a majority of *performers and creators* in the Netherlands think that action should be taken against both file sharers and file sharing websites (Weda et al. 2011). About 30% of all creators and performers claim financial damage from file sharing, primarily performers in the music industry.

Both performers' perceived financial damage from file sharing, and their opinions regarding (legal) action against file sharing were strongly age-related: older performers more often claim damages and endorse measures against file sharers and file sharing websites. Performers in the music industry are much less sympathetic towards such measures, despite the fact that file sharing has as yet been more disruptive to their industry than to any other creative industry.

153

Some 22% of performers and creators admit to downloading from illegal sources themselves.[53] Though a substantial percentage, this is significantly less than for the general population. This suggests that more involvement with copyright and the creative industries can influence downloading behaviour. It will not come as a surprise that performers who themselves download copyright protected content from illegal sources are much less sympathetic towards measures against consumers who engage in file sharing then those who do not download themselves.

---

[53] From those performers who download from illegal sources, 85% admit to downloading music, compared with some 40% for films, and less than 10% for games and books.

10.4 Conclusion

File sharing is a typical product of the confrontation between new ways of dealing with acquiring and gaining access to information and traditional and legal models from the pre-internet era. The advent of digital technology has effectively separated content and information carriers like CDs, Videocassettes and DVDs and more recently CD-ROMs and game consoles. The internet has introduced new forms of distribution of information, gaining access to content and sharing of entertainment products in broader communities on a scale and with a speed that was unimaginable in the pre-digital age. Digital technology, deeply penetrating in society, has provided opportunities to citizens to introduce new practices and to consequently undercut the business prospects of entertainment companies, whose operations were still based on traditional concepts. It seems that the recording industry was ill prepared for the new era. Instead of timely adapting their way of doing business to the new circumstances, the industry chose to head for a strategy in which criminalisation or even prosecution of supposed offenders of copyright law was a key element, together with lobbying for legal reform and a plea for higher compensation for private copying. The main argument of the industry was that file sharing should be prohibited because it was seriously harming the business prospects of the entertainment industry and the income of authors and performers.

The analysis of the legal and regulatory context of file sharing provided in this chapter shows that in many jurisdictions within the European Union, the law does not provide a clear-cut basis for prosecuting consumers who share files containing copyrighted material. Whereas uploading is a violation of copyright, downloading is often part of the private use exception, with the exception of games. As they are considered to be computer programs, games have a more extended protection then music and films. This situation is complicated further by the fact that in many cases consumers are unaware of the fact that they upload music in the technological context in which downloading takes place. Also, they are often confused about the legal status of their activities, and one might even claim this confusion is structurally nurtured by the entertainment industry. Moreover, it turns out that it is not always possible or easy for consumers to tell a legal source from an illegal one. The lack of any intent to download from an illegal source and to upload complicates prosecution.

At the same time legal regimes in different countries differ, in particular outside the European Union, which makes it hard to follow a clear-cut policy concerning the global network that is the internet. Lastly, the actual prosecution ol supposed offenders is extremely difficult to enforce and will in many cases prove disproportionate, as some cases in the United States have shown. This is also the background of scepticism about the effectiveness of the 'Loi Hadopi' in France. Moreover, a harsh policy towards file sharers has a detrimental effect on the reputation of the entertainment industries, leading to backlashes, harming sales. Note once more that in the Dutch survey, file sharers turned out to be the industries' best clients. The case of file sharing shows that in some circumstances technological developments and their social and cultural consequences can and should have consequences for laws and regulations and should be taken on as inducement for industries to reconsider their business models and to align them with the way people want to consume their products. Moreover the research reported here shows that the music industries' presupposition about the effects of file sharing being detrimental to sales and revenues needs serious revision. File sharing proves to be part of the culture and identity of music fans who do not stop spending money on their hobbies as a result of file sharing options. The industries' challenge is to tap into the new revenue streams.

Key concepts

File sharing
Unauthorised source
Copyright
Private copying exception

11 Cyberwar[52]

Lianne Boer & Arno Lodder

11.1 Introduction

Cyberwar is a fairly prominent concept. We can imagine what cyberattacks can lead to: outages, nuclear disasters, or the breakdown of the world's financial system. But although we have already come pretty close to catastrophe on a few occasions, these scenarios still belong for the most part to the domain of our imagination. However the very fact that cyberwar is considered to be within the realm of possibility has secured it a top spot on political and military agendas. Cyberspace has become something to be dominated, contested, and fought for, making it "reminiscent of the Pentagon's way of speaking of nuclear war in the 1960s" (Clarke 2009: 41). Some people have referred to it as "the fifth domain of warfare" (*The Economist* 2010).

If cyberwar is indeed the next type of warfare, how does it relate to public international law as we understand it today? Given the scope and purpose of this chapter, we have limited our discussion to two important areas that are challenged by the recurrence of cyberattacks. Firstly, we consider the harm that cyberattacks can potentially inflict, and the pressure that this puts on the logic of the laws of conflict management (Wingfield 2000). Cyberspace can be used, for example, to disable an opponent's military defences, its financial system, or its electricity grid. Although the consequences of cyberattacks could be equally severe as those caused by conventional military force, the laws of armed conflict are based exclusively on the use of the latter kind of force (Schmitt 1999). The way we interpret the central features of this body of law – the use of force, armed attacks, and the right to self-defence – is therefore challenged. Secondly, we discuss the difficulty of attributing cyberattacks to a state (Döge 2011). Even if attacks can be traced, this does not mean that the state in question can be held legally responsible for the attack. This defies the way we currently deal with wrongful acts between states.

---

54 The authors would like to thank Prof. dr. W.G. Werner for his valuable comments on this chapter. English-language editing: Alison Gibbs.

But first, the next section outlines cyberwar as a concept and provides a working definition. We pay particular attention to the differences between cyberwar, cyber crime and cyberespionage, as these are often confused. Next, in section 11.4, we examine the laws of conflict management and state responsibility in relation to cyberwar. We conclude with an overview of the key concepts.

This chapter contains three text boxes, each of which discusses a notorious cyberattack: the 2007 attack on Estonia, the 2008 attacks on Georgia, and the attack in 2010 on Iran's nuclear facility in Natanz. These are only a few examples out of many, and serve as an illustration of what cyberattacks involve and what they may lead to.

11.2 Defining cyberwar

Even though cyberspace has been declared by some to be the next domain of warfare, besides land, sea, air and space (see, for example, the 2006 United States National Military Strategy for Cyberspace Operations), there is no agreement yet on what we refer to when we talk about cyberwar. This ambiguity is partly due to the fact that the nature of cyberspace differs from that of the other domains. Our laws are based on geography, and as cyberspace is not connected to a particular geographical area it immediately defies the legal system as we know it (Johnson & Post 1996; Ziolkowski 2010). In 1993 two authors stated that "for now … [cyberwar] is too speculative for precise definition" (Arquilla & Ronfeldt 1993: 31). We have a sense of what it is, but almost 20 years later we do not seem to have made much progress when it comes to defining cyberwar (Carr 2009). An aspect that confuses matters even further is the fact that phrases such as 'cyberwar', 'information operations', and 'computer network attacks' are used interchangeably. One author, for example, defines cyberwar as "actions by a nation-state to penetrate another nation's computers or networks for the purpose of causing damage or disruption" (Clarke 2009: 6). This definition identifies an aggressor (a nation-state) a target (another nation-state) and a purpose (causing damage or disruption). However, it contains one major flaw in that it requires a cyberattack to be attributable to a state – which is seldom the case. Cyberattacks are difficult to trace, and even if governments or computer scientists succeed in doing so, it often proves hard to attribute the actions of those responsible for the attack to a specific state.

Considering a different viewpoint, a 2006 United States Joint Publication defined 'information operations' as "the integrated employment of electronic warfare (...) computer network operations (...) psychological operations (...) military deception (...) and operations security (...) in concert with specified supporting and related capabilities, to influence, disrupt, corrupt or usurp (...) human and automated decision making" (J.P. 3-13 Information Operations, 13 February 2006: 1). This definition brings us no further in limiting the scope of this chapter as, on closer examination, it covers the entire bandwidth of cyber operations. As such, it excludes the physical damage usually resulting from armed attacks in the military sense. And that is the specific context within which we want to look at cyberwar.

Thomas Wingfield meanwhile defines computer network attacks as "[o]perations that disrupt, deny, degrade, or destroy information resident in computers and computer networks or the computers and networks themselves" (Wingfield 2000: 374). This definition omits the inter-state element, as well as the hostile intent displayed by an adversary.

Given the above, we propose the following working definition of cyberwar for the purposes of this chapter:

> An attack, originating from abroad, employing virtual means, purporting to damage or disrupt a state's physical or digital infrastructure.

This definition contains the following elements: (1) hostile intent; (2) to damage or disrupt (Clarke 2009); (3) an opponent's infrastructure; (4) through non-physical means, and (5) involving at least one state.

Box 11.1   The Bronze Soldier of Tallinn (2007)

In September 1947, Russia erected a bronze statue of a soldier in the centre of Tallinn, the capital of Estonia. Russia wanted it to serve as a constant reminder to Estonians that the Soviet Union had liberated them from German rule in the Second World War (Stiennon 2010). However, as a result of the years of Communism that followed the Second World War, most Estonians came to regard the statue as a symbol of Soviet domination (Stiennon 2010). After Estonia regained its independence, its government decided in April 2007 to relocate authorities. In the weeks following the removal of the statue, Estonia suffered severe cyberattacks on its government sites, its banks and its newspapers (Carr 2009 - BBC News 2007).

> Given the severity of the attacks and the country's reliance on the internet, NATO and EU experts were asked to trace the attacks – while Russia continued to deny involvement (Traynor 2007). Eventually one person was arrested – involvement of the Russian government has, however, never been proven (Traynor 2007).

11.3 What is the difference between cyberwar, cyber crime and cyberespionage?

As cyberwar, cyber crime and cyberespionage are often confused, we need to clarify what cyber crime and cyberespionage are, and how they differ from cyberwar (Stiennon 2010), in particular with regard to the different legal regimes governing them. This section does not deal with cyberterrorism, as this is governed by the legal regimes applying to cyber crime and cyberwar, and therefore shares many of the characteristics already dealt with here.

Cyber crime

Cyber crime belongs to the domain of criminal law involving private perpetrators, and is punishable under national law. On the international level, the Convention on Cyber crime entered into force in July 2004, penalising both computer-related and content-related crimes, such as forgery (Article 7), fraud (Article 8), and the production, sale, transmission, procurement and possession of child pornography (Article 9) (Convention on Cyber crime 2001). Like cyberwar, cyber crime has a transnational dimension – the spread of child pornography being a salient example – but the purpose is not to damage or disrupt a state. As the hacking of e.g. credit card companies and corporate databases show, cybercriminals seek only personal gain (see, for example, Warman 2010; Osawa 2011).

One difficulty in differentiating between cyber crime and cyberwar is that developments in cyberwar are almost a direct result of developments in cyber crime (Farwell & Rohozinski 2011). Governments, as in the case of China, exercise (at the very least some measure of) control over private hackers for targeted cyberattacks (Ball 2011), thus transferring technical developments from the private sphere to the public domain. Farwell and Rohozinski aptly point out that the "'[b]otnets' harnessed by Russian criminal operators effected the denial of service that disrupted Estonia's national networks in May 2007" (Farwell & Rohozinski 2011: 26). The same phenomenon occurred during the Russian-Georgian border conflict in 2008 (Carr 2009). Although governed by different legal regimes, in reality cyber crime and cyberwar are not that far apart.

Cyberespionage

In a speech detailing his new cyber strategy, United States Deputy Secretary of Defense Lynn announced that "over the past decade, terabytes of data have been extracted by foreign intruders from corporate networks of defense companies", including some 24,000 documents taken in one go in March 2011. The extracted data related to "... our most sensitive systems, including aircraft avionics, surveillance technologies, satellite communications systems, and network security protocols". Lynn simultaneously announced that a joint pilot program had been launched with several of the targeted companies in order to strengthen the protection of their networks (Lynn 2011).

The 1907 Hague Convention considers someone a spy "when acting clandestinely or on false pretences, he obtains or endeavours to obtain information in the zone of operations of a belligerent, with the intention of communicating it to the hostile party" (Hague Convention 1907: Article 29). Wingfield employs a rather more recent definition, and cites from a Joint Publication by the United States Department of Defense: "[espionage is] the act of obtaining, transmitting, communicating, or receiving information about the national defense of a state with intent, or reason to believe, that the information may be used to the injury of that state or to the advantage of any foreign nation" (Wingfield 2000: 376).

161

Box 10.2   The battle for South Ossetia and Abkhazia (2008)

The Georgian provinces of South Ossetia and Abkhazia, both located on the border with Russia, were *de facto* independent of Georgian rule. In August 2008, tensions rose to the point that Russia countered a Georgian attempt to regain military control over the two provinces (BBC News 2008). Weeks of heavy fighting ensued, accompanied by carefully orchestrated cyberattacks by (supposedly) Russian authorities (Haddick 2011). Notably, Russian hackers launched websites encouraging attacks on Georgian websites and handing out quite practical advice on, for example, 'how to launch a DDoS' attack (Carr 2009). A few weeks before the physical attack, Russian authorities commenced 'cyber rehearsals' (Haddick 2011). The cyberattacks disturbed military communications but left important strategic targets intact – perhaps to leave the Georgians in doubt of what was yet to come (Haddick 2011).

Espionage during wartime is common, and governed by the laws of armed conflict, *inter alia* the 1907 Hague Conventions (Articles 30 and 31) and the 1977 First Additional Protocol to the Geneva Conventions (Article 46) (Chesterman 2006). Although espionage is prohibited under national law, *international* law has remarkably little to say on the subject during peacetime. It is sometimes simply seen as part of the *modus operandi* of international relations (Fleck 2007). As it is, there is no law prohibiting it (Wingfield 2000; Chesterman 2006). However, we can take some clues from, for example, the Friendly Relations Declaration (Fleck 2007). From this we can deduce that it is prohibited "to intervene, directly or indirectly, for any reason whatever, in the internal or external affairs of any other State" (Friendly Relations Declaration 1970, no numbering). There are many different kinds of espionage, varying in impact and degree of intrusion, but the purpose of cyberespionage differs from that of cyberattacks. There is no intent to cause damage or disruption; instead, the goal is to obtain information or to gain a competitive advantage. However, in technological terms the difference between the two may only be a few strokes on a hacker's keyboard.

11.4 Cyberwar as a legal concept

So far we have used the phrases 'cyberwar' and 'cyberattacks' interchangeably. But if we want to study cyberwar from the viewpoint of international law we immediately find that 'war' is not a legal concept (Neff 2005). Legally speaking, cyber*war* does not exist. International law prohibits the 'use of force' between states, except when a state falls victim to an 'armed attack' from abroad. In that case, the victim state can use force in self-defence. Therefore, we need to consider the question whether a single cyberattack can constitute an 'armed attack' under the laws of conflict management (Wingfield 2000).

Secondly, we need to consider the difficulty in tracing a cyberattack. A state needs to know who its attacker is. However, as we have pointed out earlier in this chapter, tracing a cyberattack is almost impossible. To highlight some of the legal difficulties involved, we will also discuss the relation between cyberattacks and state responsibility for those attacks.

Armed attack

The prohibition on the use of force by one state against another is laid down in Article 2(4) of the Charter of the United Nations: "[a]ll Members shall refrain in their international relations from the threat or use of force against the territorial integrity or political independence of any state, or in any other manner inconsistent with the Purposes of the United Nations" (Charter of the United

Nations 1945: Article 2(4)). As well as being treaty law, the International Court of Justice has declared it to be part of customary international law (Nicaragua Case, ICJ Rep. 1986 14 at 188). The only two exceptions to the prohibition on the use of force by states are found in Article 51 of the same Charter: "[n]othing in the present Charter shall impair the inherent right of individual or collective self-defence if an armed attack occurs against a Member of the United Nations, until the Security Council has taken measures necessary to maintain international peace and security" (Charter of the United Nations 1945: Article 51). This article states that the use of force is permissible only in the case of self-defence against an armed attack, or when permitted by the Security Council. For the sake of brevity, we will discuss only the first exception – the use of force in self-defence against an armed attack.

Traditionally, only the use of military (as opposed to diplomatic and economic) means "[engages] the normatively more flagrant act of using force" (Schmitt in Wingfield 2000: 118). This focus on instruments results from the "[extraordinary difficulty] to quantify or qualify consequences in a normatively practical manner", and therefore makes rather good sense (Schmitt 1999: 16, 17). Moreover, the consequences of the use of force are usually much greater than the consequences of applying diplomatic or economic measures. Consequences and means (conveniently) coincide (Schmitt 1999). However, a "[computer] network attack challenges the prevailing paradigm ... [the] dilemma lies in the fact that [it] spans the spectrum of consequentiality" (Schmitt 1999: 17). The International Court of Justice itself has placed particular emphasis on the 'scale and effects' of the use of force, not on the kind of force involved (Nicaragua Case, ICJ Rep. 1986 14 at 195). As the consequences of cyberattacks vary greatly, an approach based on effects or targets (Graham 2010) may be helpful in adjusting our interpretation of the use of force. This effects-based approach, however, "is as notable for what it leaves out of the "armed attacks" category as what it brings into it" (Hinkle 2011: 11). Considering merely the consequences of a particular act to determine whether an armed attack has taken place, broadens the scope of 'armed attacks', which leads to a loss in the discriminatory and thereby limiting impact this concept is supposed to have on the use of force.

Some authors point out the possible cumulative effect arising from multiple minor (cyber) attacks that in themselves then constitute something "short of armed attack" (Nicaragua Case, ICJ Rep. 1986 14 at 210). A 2003 ICJ ruling "implied that a series of acts may be weighed cumulatively and then categorized as an armed attack" (Dinstein 2011: 206). These 'series of acts', if considered to constitute an armed attack, in turn invoke the right to self-defence.

Concluding, it is important to note that we do not know yet whether a cyber-attack can constitute an armed attack. This also means that we do not know whether the use of force in response would be legitimate. Though there are some major proponents of the 'effects-based approach', this approach is not wholly undisputed and leaves us in doubt as to its actual applicability. It has hardly any limiting effect on the use of force by states, as the 'armed attack' concept loses its discriminatory character.

Box 11.3 Disabling Iran's nuclear facility (2010)

Stuxnet was a worm spread by USB-keys and identified weaknesses in a system in order to reprogram software and thus write new instructions for industrial mechanisms (Fildes 2010). It ended up in Iran's nuclear enrichment facility in Natanz. Once inside, it instructed the centrifuges to increase speed at short intervals, simultaneously feeding false data into the control mechanisms designed to set off the alarm once the centrifuges were out of control (Langner 2011). It was detected in June 2010 (Fildes 2010).

The code turned out to be so complex and deliberately targeted at the nuclear installation that suspicions were very strong that another state was behind this attack (Fildes 2010). It was simply too complicated to have been designed by individual hackers. Of all possible suspects, Israel is seen as being the most likely designer of Stuxnet (Farwell & Rohozinski 2011).

State responsibility

Any response to a cyberattack requires a target, but states that fall victim to a cyberattack seldom know who their opponent is. Developments in terrorism and cyberwar both seem to require a more lenient approach towards state attribution, perhaps even to the extent of not requiring attribution at all for the legitimate use of force in response (Ruys & Verhoeven 2005). The lines between private and public actors in cyberspace are often blurred, and the conduct of private actors cannot always be attributed to a state. A striking example is the Russian attack on Georgia described earlier in this chapter. At the outset of the conflict, a website called stopgeorgia.ru was launched. This included a forum containing practical advice on, *inter alia*, how to launch a DDoS attack on Georgian websites. One month later some 200 forum members were participating in such attacks (Carr 2009). Were these hackers acting under the instruction or control of the Russian government? And if not, would Georgia have been allowed to target the private hackers on Russian territory? These questions require an answer, and this is something that the current regulations on state responsibility do not seem to provide.

There is considerable debate on the extent to which an attack has to be attributable to a state in order for the right of self-defence to be legitimately invoked (Ruys & Verhoeven 2005). Traditionally, the language of the UN Charter has been interpreted in such a way that some measure of state attribution is required for this right to be exercised: "states invoking self-defence against private attacks have continuously placed the role of states at the core of their justification" (Ruys & Verhoeven 2005: 293). There are two situations – the exception rather than the rule – in which states can be held legally responsible for private attacks (Ruys & Verhoeven 2005). The first is when the private attacks are performed under the instruction or control of the state (Draft Articles on State Responsibility: Article 8). Instruction is a more obvious case than control. What, after all, is the threshold for determining the level of control required to create state responsibility? In the Nicaragua Case, the ICJ referred to "effective control" (Nicaragua Case, ICJ Rep. 1986 14 at 64). In 1999, the International Criminal Tribunal for the former Yugoslavia expanded the standard for attribution to 'overall control'; the ICJ, however, rejected this standard in its 2007 ruling on the crime of genocide and held to the 'effective control' threshold instead (Dinstein 2011). Although the question of whether the threshold is 'overall' or 'effective' control remains largely unresolved, it is a fact that certain private attacks can, under particular circumstances, be attributed to a state (Dinstein 2011).

The second exception to the rule is when a state "acknowledges and adopts the [private] conduct as its own" (Draft Articles on State Responsibility: Article 11). Both demands – acknowledgement and adoption – have to be met in order to meet the threshold for state attribution (Ruys & Verhoeven 2005). Even if attribution is impossible, a state still has an obligation "not to allow knowingly its territory to be used for acts contrary to the rights of other states" (Corfu Channel Case, cited in Dinstein 2011: 226).

With the rise of terrorism, this approach to state responsibility has become subject to scrutiny by authors who claim that the right of self-defence can indeed be exercised even if there is no state involvement whatsoever in a private attack (Ruys & Verhoeven 2005). Although this position is contested, so too is the argument that an armed attack has to be exclusively attributable to a state in order for the right to self-defence to be legitimately invoked. The first position is too lenient, whereas the second is too strict considering "state practice, security doctrines and legal literature" (Ruys & Verhoeven 2005: 319).

Recent years have seen "a loosening of the conditions" applying in respect of state attribution, but it "continues to be governed by a great amount of uncertainty" (Ruys & Verhoeven 2005: 319).

11.5 Concluding remarks

Our aim in this chapter was to provide an introduction to cyberwar from the perspective of public international law. We started by discussing the difficulties in defining cyberwar – a discussion we resolved by providing our own working definition for the purposes of this chapter. This first section showed the extent to which opinions differ on what cyberwar actually is. To differentiate between cyberwar and other 'events' in cyberspace, we elaborated on the distinction between cyberwar, cyberespionage and cyber crime.

As we discuss cyberwar within the context of international law, we proceeded to outline the laws of conflict management. This highlighted the challenges posed by incorporating "things cyber" (Hayden 2011: 3) into the laws of conflict management. If we consider cyberattacks to be a form of armed conflict between states, we simply do not know where to position them. Are they a particular kind of armed attack that invokes the right to self-defence? And how are states to respond to cyberattacks that cannot be classified as an armed attack, but that do cause damage or disruption to the target state? Are they then allowed to use force? The phenomenon of disrupting or damaging states through cyberspace gives rise to many questions. Questions we would like to see answered include what would happen if, for example, a Chinese hacker paralysed the financial system of the United States using Russian computers. Although the underlying questions – Why do we want to discuss cyberattacks within the framework of the laws of conflict management? What purpose does this characterisation serve? How did cyberattacks end up in this framework in the first place? – are beyond the scope of this chapter, they merit further investigation, given the current obscurity and the stakes involved in cyberwar.

Key concepts

Cyberwar
Armed attack
Use of force
International responsibility

166

12   Basic Cybercriminal Techniques & Techniques to Cause Damage

Rutger Leukfeldt, Marko van Eekelen, Erik de Jong & Harald Vranken

12.1 Introduction

Cybercriminals employ numerous criminal techniques. In this chapter two different types of technique are discussed. We start with some basic techniques that cyber criminals use to execute other attacks (section 12.2); then we will consider techniques that are specially designed to cause damage (section 12.3). Techniques are developing rapidly and it is impossible to cover all possible different forms of cybercriminal techniques. This chapter therefore does not give an exhaustive list of techniques, but describes the techniques that, according to experts, are most used by cyber criminals.

12.2 Basic techniques

Techniques used by cybercriminals to execute attacks are social engineering, shielding techniques and botnets. Social engineering is used in combination with other techniques (e.g. phishing) in order to better execute that technique. Criminals use shielding techniques to shield their criminal activity from crime fighters. Techniques are used by both individuals and organised groups and ensure that the user can operate reasonably anonymously. Botnets can be used as an infrastructure or tool to carry out other criminal techniques.

12.3 Social engineering

Social engineering is an attack on the weakest link in a system: the human being (KLPD 2007). It is simply persuading a user to do something he or she normally would not do, such as giving a password or other personal information.
Social engineering can be used in different ways. A cybercriminal may, for example, present himself as an employee of the IT help desk and steal the password of a user by telling him that the IT department is testing a new system. Once the criminal has obtained the password, he has access to the network. Social engineering may also be used to find out what type of hardware and software the company uses. Cybercriminals can use this information later

by exploiting well-known weaknesses in these systems. Social engineering is also used in combination with other criminal techniques. In a phishing email (see chapter 13), for example, the attacker uses social engineering to persuade the victim to click on a link or open an attachment. Choices made by a user to do something are determined by what he sees on his screen. By showing false information (click here, then ...) a user can be persuaded to do something he normally would not do: allow malware on his PC (Ianelli & Hackworth 2005). Furthermore, social engineering can be used to hack, to commit identity theft and e-fraud. There is also a connection with cyber extortion. One ways to extort from people is to threaten to reveal sensitive information. This information can be obtained through social engineering or social engineering can be used to break into a system with intent to steal sensitive information.

In the coming years, according to experts, social engineering will increasingly anticipate on social events (e.g. the World Cup), large (natural) disasters and personal interests (KLPD 2007; Websense 2007; Govcert 2010). Phishing attempts (see also chapter 13) will in the years ahead target specific user groups with the help of social engineering: written in their own language, sent to members of a particular social network with similar interests, or supposedly sent from the internal network (Symantec 2007; Govcert 2010).

12.4 Shielding techniques

In order to carry out their criminal acts, criminals need to stay out of the hands of the police. They do this by concealing their identity or adopting another digital identity and by erasing – or making inaccessible – their tracks. In this section we cover some of those techniques. First we deal with spoofing and anonymisers, and thereafter encryption. Just as in the real world, criminals in cyberspace leave traces as they operate. In any form of communication over the internet, for example, the IP address (Internet Protocol) of the sender and receiver are transmitted. This information on IP addresses can be used to detect criminals. Through ISPs (Internet Service Providers) information can be obtained that is linked with the IP addresses (e.g. information about someone's address or other contact information). Criminals are however aware of this and try to hide their IP addresses. This can be done by IP address spoofing, where the IP address of the sender is forged. That works for one-way traffic. The spoofed IP address can be chosen at random, or it can be deliberately chosen to pose as someone else's address. Apart from the IP address, other information may be falsified to conceal the identity of the sender. With two-way traffic, by which the sender and receiver exchange information, IP addresses can be masked by using anonymisers. An anonymiser is a proxy server that acts as an intermediary between two communicating parties. The sender makes contact through the proxy server, while the anonymiser shields the data (e.g. the IP address) from the sender. Only the proxy server knows who the sender is, the recipient sees the proxy server as the sender. Although anonymiser services claim that the identities of users are not revealed to police, it is possible for the police to retrieve the identity of users of anonymiser services. The Campina blackmailer, for example, used an anonymiser to send messages to Campina – a dairy concern – to poison their products in supermarkets. The FBI traced the blackmailer using data enhanced by an American anonymiser.[55] An example of an anonymiser is given in box 12.1

Box 12.1   The Onion Router

The Onion Router (TOR) (www.torproject.org). TOR is based on so-called onion servers, computers that serve as way stations between the sender and the destination. The principle is that messages travel to their destination through a random path and different onion-servers. Each server deciphers an encrypted layer of the routing information, similar to peeling an onion. This data is then forwarded to the next server until the fully decrypted data arrives at the receiver. For the receiver, it looks like the message came from the last onion-server. For the last server it is only possible to determine what the dates consist of, not where it came from.

169

Another way to shield information is the use of encryption. Before joining organised cybercriminal networks, such as a forum of criminals engaged in phishing or a network where child pornography is distributed, the use of such techniques is even required (Stol et al. 2008). There are ways to prevent that information being read by others. The basic idea is that information is encoded (*encrypted*) using a special code (the *key*) in such a way that it would take an unfeasibly long time (many years e.g.) to decode (*decrypt*) it when the key is not known. An example is given in box 12.2.

---

55 See, for example, *De Volkskrant*, August 23, 2003; http://www.out-law.com/page-3854 (last visited june 11th 2012).

Box 12.2   Encryption

> We want to encode the following text: "hello". As encoding mechanism, we take something simple: we shift each character 5 positions in the alphabet giving "mjqqt". This principle of shifting characters was first used by the Roman Emperor Caesar in the first century BC to send secret messages to his generals. This encryption method is not hard to crack. Just try with a computer every possible shift and a normal text pops up quickly. Every piece of information that is known about the text can help to decrypt it. If it is an English language text e.g. and the text is encoded character-by-character, then in a long text the most often occurring character is bound to be the encoding of the most often occurring character in the English language (the 'e'). Obviously, over the years and over the centuries many more encryption methods have been devised.

Modern encryption methods use mathematical transformations that are hard to reverse. They are directly applied on the bit-representation (sequences of ones and zeros) that underlies every piece of information on a computer. They are hard to crack. The encryption technique is usually publicly known, following Kerckhoffs' (1883) principle under the modern slogan "no security through obscurity" (see also chapter 21). These techniques take years to crack even when the technique is known. When the decoding techniques improve and the power of computers increases, the encryption can be broken by guessing the key. One of the standard solutions to strengthen the encryption technique further is to start using a longer key that makes it harder to guess the key.

Scientists are improving the state-of-the-art in cryptography all the time both in encrypting and in decrypting. With good, modern encryption methods, the code can normally only be broken when the key is known. This is not as impossible as it may seem. When the key is a pass phrase, it can often be guessed by quickly trying a vocabulary of frequently occurring words (or words derived from information about the person who invented the password) or simply trying all combinations of characters (this is called *brute force*).

Encryption tools are not only used by criminals and are available for everybody. Windows 7 and some versions of Vista have built-in drive encryption called *BitLocker Drive Encryption*. It can be used to encrypt the full hard disk or a partition of it. An example of a freely available and easy to use encryptions tool is given in box 12.3.[56]

Box 12.3   TrueCrypt

TrueCrypt (www.truecrypt.org). According to the TrueCrypt website, TrueCrypt is a software system for establishing and maintaining an on-the-fly-encrypted volume (data storage device). On-the-fly encryption means that data is automatically encrypted or decrypted right before it is loaded or saved, without any user intervention. A password defined by the user acts as the key for encryption and decryption. When the password is revealed, in principle the information becomes visible. However, some of the information might still be hidden. In some situations it may be very hard to figure out whether there is more encrypted information at all. No data stored on an encrypted volume can be read (decrypted) without using the correct password/keyfile(s) or correct encryption keys.

12.5 Botnet

A botnet is a remotely controlled network of infected computers that can be used for various criminal activities (KLPD 2007). The computers in a botnet can be infected in several different ways and can be computers of either individual users or organisations. Once infected the computer is called a bot or zombie. The computer can then receive commands from a criminal and perform these independently, without the user of the computer being aware of it. Creating a botnet is relatively simple and requires not too much technical knowledge (Ianelli & Hackworth 2005). The 'attacker community' shares information and knowledge with those who want to learn. There is also information available on how systems can be overtaken and what the simple commands are. IRC (Internet Relay Chat) channels even offer training sessions and provide advice for beginners (Van der Hulst & Neve 2008).

A cybercriminal can add computers to his botnet in different ways. In essence, the criminal uses flaws in the security of systems. This can be done auto-

---

56 We would like to emphasize here that the use of these programs is legal, and that the programs are not only used by criminals.

mated, for example, by a virus or trojan horse (NCSC 2012). Such malware is often 'offered' in an email or on a website where unsuspecting victims are tricked into clicking on links. A hacker can also attack a specific computer. Once a hacker has penetrated a system, the computer is infected in part of the botnet (NCSC 2012).

After a basis is made for the botnet, the criminal can start increasing the botnet. Infected computers in the botnet are controlled from a command and control centre, managed by the attacker or bot herder. A simplified version is shown in figure 12.1. It is common to give commands in a bot network through IRC channels, but cyber criminals are also using P2P networks and home-made protocols. The absence of a central place of command and unfamiliarity with the method of transmission makes it difficult to detect and disable botnets (KLPD 2007; Govcert 2008). Fast flux, a technique by which malicious servers hide behind rapidly changing network addresses, is another innovation that makes it difficult to detect botnets. The goal of the criminals is to extend the life of the botnets as long as possible (Govcert 2008). The longer a botnet remains operational, the more money it can earn. Once a botnet is created, cyber criminals have a powerful weapon to execute attacks and to gather information. Botnets can also be rented out to other cyber criminals.

Figure 12.1   Simplified representation of a botnet (Finjan 2007)

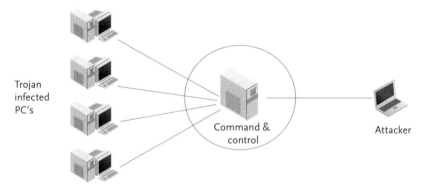

Trojan infected PC's

Command & control

Attacker

Botnet forms

A botnet can be used for different goals. Ianelli and Hackworth (2005) describe the following possibilities:

DDoS attack. A DDoS attack (Distributed Denial of Service attack, see section 12.3) is often executed out of revenge or for financial gain. The goal is to make a computer resource unavailable (e.g. a website or web shop).

Spyware. Infected computers are used to gain personal information (see also chapter 13).

Port scans. Botnets often have port scanners. These scanners are constantly searching for ports that are open in a system in order to exploit them. Known weaknesses in systems are also exploited by this malware.

Download and install function. This function is used to update the malware. It can also be used to download files that are of importance to the hacker.

Click fraud. Websites make money by renting banners and advertisement space. The owner of the website earns a certain amount for each click on a banner. Bots can be used to constantly click on banners. This generates an enormous amount of hits. Because the computers in a botnet are geographically spread, it is difficult to detect this form of fraud.

Server-class services. Botnets can be used to host http-[57] and ftp-traffic[58] or to send emails, if necessary on a large scale (e.g. for spam, phishing attacks or mails with links to other malware).

Gateway and proxy functions. A Proxy hides the identity of a cybercriminal. By using a gateway or proxy (proxy literally means middle man, a machine which is between two computers), the cybercriminal can remain anonymous on the internet.

Extent of botnets

173

There is little understanding of the exact extent of the botnet problem. It is very difficult to give an exact number of botnets and their size (Rajab et al. 2007; Van Eeten et al. 2010) and there is no agreement on what method should be used to measure them. In addition, commercial parties that monitor botnets do not reveal their measuring methods. Hence, estimates about the extent of the problem in the literature and media differ. The numbers that are known are difficult to evaluate and compare. An example of an attempt to measure the extent by Symantec is given in box 12.4.

---

57 HTTP (HyperText Transfer Protocol) is the protocol for the communication between a web client (usually a web browser) and a web server (Leukfeldt et al. 2010).
58 File Transfer Protocol (FTP) is a protocol for the exchange of files between (Leukfeldt et al. 2010).

Box 12.4   The extent of botnets according to Symantec

An indirect method of determining the number of bots and botnets is to measure the number of computers infected with the Trojan that gives the attacker control of the computer. The assumption here is that once a computer is infected with such malware it is almost certainly part of a botnet. Symantec defines an infected computer as a computer that executes an attack at least once a day. In 2009 Symantec recorded 46,541 active computers that were part of a botnet (Symantec 2010). Computers which were active at least once during the period of measurement are called 'distinct bot-infected' computers by Symantec. In 2009 there were 6,798,338 of these computers (Symantec 2010). Since the Symantec reports do not comply with the scientific standards of accountability, diligence, impartiality, integrity and confidentiality, we do not know what the value of these numbers is.

Botnet trends

For the past several years botnets are increasingly being used as a general tool: a botnet is set up as infrastructure and then rented to others who can use it for various purposes (see the section under the heading *forms*) (Govcert 2008). The rise of centrally controlled collections of infected COMputers (botnets) has now been going on for about 10 years. In the initial years, botnets were almost without exception based on and centrally controlled by IRC. In due course a greater variety of types of botnet have emerged, probably due to better protection measures and a firmer approach from detection companies and law enforcement. The original type of botnet is still around, but botnets increasingly use peer2peer technologies. These botnets are not centrally managed and can therefore no longer be centrally turned off. In addition, other methods of control have been identified, such as control through social network sites or Twitter. Finally, botnets are increasingly using encryption, to prevent eavesdropping and infiltration (KLPD 2007; Govcert 2008, 2010). A trend according to F-Secure is that botnets are becoming smaller (Simpson 2008). Large botnets are broken up and divided into smaller ones. There are still large bot networks, but new botnets are not being extended to the maximum. A number of small networks do not necessarily generate less money than a large one, yet they are harder to detect.

12.6 Techniques to cause damage

When talking about causing damage, we could be referring to shutting down systems so that, for example, a web shop can no longer be visited. But another form of attack is to change information on a (company) website in order to cause reputation damage. Techniques that can be used for this are Distributed Denial of Service attacks and defacing.

12.7 Distributed Denial of Service attacks

Denial of Service attacks are attacks on a system or service with the aim of overloading them and making them unavailable. Denial of Service can be initiated from a single system, but also from multiple systems simultaneously. Denial of service attacks from multiple devices is called Distributed Denial of Service. A denial of service attack is usually performed with infected computers that are part of a botnet (KLPD 2007). An advantage for the cybercriminal is that s/he is difficult to trace. A denial of service attack can also be performed with a group of friends or other internet users who together have the capacity to disrupt a service.

175

The disruption of services and systems that are connected with the internet is a daily occurrence. One example is the DDoS attacks from (presumably) Russians on websites in Estonia (following the removal of a war memorial by the Estonian authorities).[59] According to Estonia, the Russian government attacked websites of Estonian government institutions and banks. The mobile networks and rescue organisations were also under attack said Estonian Foreign Minister Urmas Paet according to news agency UPI. The IP addresses of the attacking computers came from the Russian government. A recent example is the 2011 attacks of Wikileaks supporters who attacked and temporarily shut down payment sites. These examples show the power of the DDoS attack and the vulnerability of systems on the internet.

Attacks on websites are pretty well known, but other computer systems are vulnerable as well. A classic example is sending a huge amount of email. If a person gets a lot of emails, the limit of his mailbox will be exceeded and s/he

---

59 *NRC Handelsblad* May 22th 2007 and *Trouw* May 12th 2007.

no longer receives new emails. File sharing services, authentication systems and DNS (Domain Name System) servers are also targets.

DDoS attack: forms and motives

In the earliest DoS attacks relatively simple tools were used that send packets from a source to a target. These tools have been further developed to single-source attacks (one attacker) with multiple targets, multiple source attacks (multiple attackers) with the same target, multiple source attacks (multiple attackers) to different targets (Houle & Weaver 2001). DoS services can also be provided to third parties (Damballa 2010). In addition, several variants of DoS and DDoS exist and motives vary, but in all these forms the goal is to make a service or system unavailable.

The most common motives for DDoS attacks are: (1) bragging, (2) revenge/hatred/terrorism and (3) cyber extortion. These motives will be discussed hereafter.

Bragging. This motive was particularly applicable to the early DDoS attacks (KLPD 2007). According to McAfee (2007) the enormous growth of the internet and the growing number of e-commerce transactions caused the attention of hackers to shift towards obtaining financial gain, particularly through fraud and extortion (McAfee 2007).

Revenge/hatred/terrorism. In 2007 a number of DDoS attacks were executed with this motive. One example is a DDoS attack by Turkish hackers on Swedish websites after the publication of a Mohammed cartoon. Swedish hackers answered by attacking Turkish sites (KLPD 2007). Another example is the attack on Estonia mentioned above. DDoS attacks are a problem for publicly accessible (governmental) websites (McAfee 2007). The attacks in late 2010 by Wikileaks adepts at PayPal also fall into this category (see figure 12.3).

Cyber extortion. A new form of old fashioned mafia protection: you pay money not to be targeted by DDoS. DDoS attacks can be a major threat to companies. A successful attack could cause the website or a network of a company to be inaccessible to both customers and staff. This can lead to heavy financial losses and reputational damage (Sophos 2007). Experts say that many businesses pay the requested ransom for that reason (Pappalardo & Messmer 2005). That might seem to be a cheap and quick solution, but one potential consequence is that the attacks keep returning.

An attack usually has different groups of victims (Rogers 2004). If a web shop is attacked and put out of action just before a busy period like Christmas, the first victim is the web shop itself. Hence, less profit is earned (*ibid.*). Furthermore, additional costs have to be incurred to restart the network and there is reputational damage. The second group of victims are the customers who cannot place their orders. A third group are the owners of the networks over which a DDoS attack is being executed. These networks have a maximum capacity. Because the DDoS attack takes up much of this capacity, the other users of the network are inconvenienced in the form of slower connections.

Figure 12.2   DDoS attack on PayPal[60]

> PayPal hit by DDoS attack after dropping Wikileaks
> Darren Pauli, ZDNet Australia | December 6, 2010 4:38 AM PST
>
> PayPal was hit by a denial-of-service attack on Sunday that took its blog offline for about eight hours, according to security researchers.
>
> The distributed denial-of-service (DDoS) attacks came in response to a move by the payment giant to stop providing services to whistle-blower website Wikileaks for donations. PayPal said Wikileaks had breached its user policies, which prevent its services from being used to support criminal activity. Wikileaks has been severely criticised for its decision to leak more than 250,000 US diplomatic cables.
>
> 'ThePayPalBlog.com is now back up after 75 service interruptions and 8 hours 15 minutes of total downtime. This report doesn't take into account the many hours that ThePayPalBlog.com resolved to a 403 error', PandaBlogs researcher Sean-Paul Correll said in a blog post.

DDoS attacks: extent

There are several figures about DDoS attacks. A Dutch study from 2005 (Den Hartog & Kouwenhoven 2005) shows that 12.7% of companies questioned in the past six months had been victim of a DDoS attack. The ECrime Watch Survey (CSO magazine et al. 2007) shows that 36% of the participating companies had been victims in 2006. In 2007, this number rose to 49%. A survey under U.S. companies (CSI Survey 2007) shows that 25% of respondents had been victims of such an attack in the past year. Furthermore, 13% of surveyed companies in an Australian survey suffered financial losses in 2006 through a DDoS attack (Auscert 2006). In 2005 the figure was 14% and in 2004, 20%.

177

---

60 http://www.zdnet.com/news/paypal-hit-by-ddos-attack-after-dropping-wikileaks/489237. Lastly visited on March 21st 2011.

The size of DoS attacks has grown the recent years, along with the growth of available bandwidth. The largest reported DDoS attack by Arbor (2010) was 10 times larger than the largest reported attack in 2005.

DDoS attack: trends

As more people use the internet, the impact of DDoS attacks increases (Rogers 2004). In the past, DDoS attacks were carried out as a form of vandalism. Such attacks are now increasingly carried out to protest against the viewpoints of companies and governments (Govcert 2005; 2010). Techniques for protection against DDoS attacks are becoming more sophisticated (Van der Hulst & Neve 2008). On the other hand, it is noted that DDoS attacks become more complex mainly because attacks are aimed at networks instead of specific applications (Arbor 2010). Good DDoS attacks are not easy to filter.

12.8 Defacing

Defacing is electronic graffiti, or the staining of the homepage of a site by hackers without permission from the owner (KLPD 2007). Growth in the number of defacings runs parallel with the growth of the internet (*ibid.*). Defacements of websites are a regular occurrence and may cause reputational damage. Databases that keep track of defacements are full of examples (Govcert 2008). Often these attacks have a political motive.

Defacing: forms

Defacing is the unauthorised changing of a website. There are two ways: mass-defacing, an automated attack where a large number of websites are being attacked, and 'normal' defacing, in which the cybercriminal focuses on one website. The goal may be to proclaim political messages, causing reputational damage to the company behind the website (Govcert 2008).

Defacing: extent

The direct financial damage caused by defacing is relatively minor, and more importantly, defacing yields little financial reward for cyber criminals. There is no real market potential (KLDP 2007). According to the Dutch National Police Agency, the trend of in recent years is that cybercriminals are paying less attention to defacing websites and more to trying to penetrate the website and use it as a springboard to infect visitors (*ibid.*). Research into cyber extortion of businesses with maximum 10,000 employees (Bednarski 2004) shows that of all companies that have been victims of cyber-extortion (17% of respondents), 19% were threatened with defacing. Figures in Australia (Auscert 2006) show that 7% of the responding companies were victims of defacement and the CSI Survey 2007 (Computer Security Institute 2007) shows that 10% of the respondents were victims of defacement.

Defacing: trends

According to literature defacing is currently mainly used for political motives and cyber extortions. There is a shift from defacing to Iframe injections,[61] because the latter technique can be used more efficiently for attacking a large number of websites simultaneously (KLPD 2007). It cannot however be ignored that defacing is also used for the extortion of businesses and that this problem will persist in the future.

Key concepts

Social engineering
Botnet
Distributed Denial of Service (DDoS) attack
Defacing
Iframe injection

---

61 An Iframe injection (an inline frame) is an invisible addition to a web page to ensure that the page loads a piece of (malicious) code from elsewhere.

13 Criminal Techniques to Steal Information

Rutger Leukfeldt & Erik de Jong

13.1 Introduction

Since the mid-1990s, with the growth of the internet, cybercriminals increasingly used automated attacks to steal user information (Watson et al. 2005). Cybercriminals may use many criminal techniques to steal information from individual computer users or companies. These techniques are often used by organised cybercriminals for financial gain. Computers of individual users can be infected and personal information, for example credit card information, can be stolen and used to commit fraud. Another way to make money is to steal trade secrets from commercial companies. These secrets can be sold to competitors, but the information can also be used to extort from the company from which the secret was stolen.

Because the criminal techniques are often available via the internet, 'ordinary people' can also use them. Leukfeldt et al. (2010) note that criminal techniques are not only used by technically savvy whizz kids. An example is an ex-partner who breaks into the computer of his (ex-)wife and steals information. In this case, the ex-partner wanted to obtain the correspondence between the lawyer and his (ex-)wife to gain advantage during the divorce hearing. It also appears that techniques to steal information are being used by youngsters who want to gain access to the accounts in virtual worlds of others in order to collect and sell digital belongings of the victim.

As indicated in chapter 12, it is important to emphasise that cyber criminals are able to use more criminal techniques than are described in this chapter (see, for example, Leukfeldt et al. 2010). We discuss the techniques which experts say are most used to steal information: phishing (section 13.2) and spyware (section 13.3). In each case the technique is defined, and different variations and its extent described.

13.2 Phishing

In literature, different definitions for phishing are given. But they have the gist of the matter in common, namely the retrieval of personal information from users. Phishing is often linked to email. Watson et al. (2005), for example, define phishing as sending fake emails composed in such a way that they appear to come from trusted organisations, and aimed at retrieving confidential information such as usernames, passwords and credit card numbers. This definition only considers sending emails as a means of conducting phishing attacks. However there are also variants where the means is not emails, but text messages or phone calls. A more complete definition is that phishing is the process that causes users to provide personal information to a criminal who acts as a trusted party (Ollmann 2004). It should be added that technical means have to be used; otherwise it is simply social engineering (see section 12.2).

The term phishing was coined in 1996. Computer criminals were targeting AOL (American Online) accounts. An account which had been stolen was referred to as a 'phish'. The accounts were traded among hackers. Accounts were exchanged, for example for hacking tools (Ollmann 2004). At the time the attacks on users of AOL were still quite simple. Users received a message stating that the user had to fill in personal information to ensure that their account would not be deleted. An example is shown in figure 13.1.

Figure 13.1   An example of the phishing attack on AOL users in 1996 (Watson et al. 2005)

Sector 4G9E of our database has lost all I/O functions. When your account logged onto our system, we were temporarily able to verify it as a registered user. Approximately 94 seconds ago, your verification was made void by loss of data in the Sector 4G9E. Now, due to AOL verification protocol, it is mandatory for us to re-verify you. Please click 'Respond' and re-state your password. Failure to comply will result in immediate account deletion (Watson et al. 2005).

Today, phishers prefer to send as many messages as possible, for example by email. The (email) message appears to originate from a known organisation that is trusted by the user (e.g. a bank), but in reality it is an attempt to gain personal information (Watson et al. 2005). These automated attacks still rely heavily on social engineering. Users must be persuaded to open attachments in emails or click on URLs. The execution of these attacks can be done in a variety of ways, from sending emails to hacking into a VoIP (Voice over IP) connection or to automatically guiding visitors of a website to a malicious web site, all with the intent to steal personal information.

Forms of phishing

Although the most common method is sending an email (KLPD, 2007) criminals use various forms of communication forms to carry out their phishing attacks. We describe the forms that are currently in use. As the following section will show, phishing attacks are continuously adjusted to new communication technologies.

Classical phishing. The first section of this chapter showed that phishing is an attack with technological resources with the aim of stealing confidential information from a user. In the classical form of phishing, criminals seek contact (mostly on a large scale) with potential victims. The most common means of communication is email (KLPD 2007). In this form an internet user receives a spoofed email that appears to come from a legitimate source (e.g. a financial institution) and in which the victim is asked to provide personal information (Van der Hulst & Neve 2008). The victim is enticed to click on a URL. The email states, for example, that the bank is performing a security check and that the user has to log on to a particular page. The URL leads to a malicious website that is a copy of the website of a legitimate organisation. On this website, the victim has to fill in personal information, for example, in order to log into his account. By doing so, the victim is sending personal information to the criminal. The user does not notice this and after the information has been sent to the computer of the criminal, the information is sent to the real login page of the bank and the user is simply logged on (KLPD 2007; Van Geest 2006; Ollmann 2004).

183

Figure 13.2   Dutch Police report of a probable phishing case (Leukfeldt et al. 2010)

'I want to report a scam, fraud or theft. About 14 days ago, [date], I logged onto the site of my bank in order to make a number of financial transfers over the internet. I noticed that I could not access the site with my regular username and password. I then requested a new password on the site because I could no longer log in. Then after about one week, when I still had not heard anything about my username and password, I phoned a bank employee. The employee told me to go to the site of bank. I did that the same day and I got my new username and password by mail yesterday. I then used the new username and password to log on to my bank. When I had done this, I noticed that on [date] a transfer had taken place with an amount of € 25,000,-. I never made this transfer. Indeed, the transfer took place at the time when I could not log on to the site of my bank via the internet.'

In some attacks, criminals use SMS to come into contact with potential victims (Ollmann 2007). In such cases, phone owners receive a text message which persuades them to visit a particular website. When the victim visits the site, his or her computer becomes infected with a trojan. This trojan subsequently sends information to the cybercriminal (KLPD 2007). It is also possible that the user is persuaded to enter personal information on the site. While phishing via SMS is not widespread, it is likely that with the rise of the smartphone the possibilities and use of this method will increase (KLPD 2007).

Finally, some phishing attacks are conducted by telephone. The victim is called by a seemingly legitimate organisation that uses a voice message system to ask for personal information. The number that appears on the display of the user can be spoofed, thus appearing to be from a trusted organisation (Ollmann 2007). This type of attack is carried out both through conventional telephone lines and VoIP systems. The high degree of trust that people have in the telephone (the dangers on the internet are becoming better known; the good old telephone therefore seems safer) and unfamiliarity with phishing ensures that people are more willing to give personal information by telephone (KLPD 2007; Ollmann 2007). In addition, the growth of VoIP ensures that telephone calls can be made at little cost all over the world. The retrieval of data from a VoIP caller is a lot more difficult than from a conventional telephone line (KLPD 2007). Because of the low costs and opportunities to act as a trusted party, this form will become increasingly attractive to cyber criminals (Ollmann 2007).

Various combinations of attacks are possible. Victims may also receive an email or text message stating that they have to call a certain number (Ollmann 2007). The message might be from his or her bank, for example, saying it was carrying out a security check because someone tried to attack the bank. Because of this check, the user cannot log on to the website and the user has to call the number of the bank and provide their old username and password so that the bank can automatically create a new password. The specified number is that of the cybercriminal.

Spear phishing. This form of phishing is different because the attacks are targeted at specific groups of users. By attacking a relatively small group of users, the messages can be personalised. This is intended to ensure that users believe the message and will provide confidential information (McGhee 2008; Ollmann 2007; Microsoft 2006a). The attacker may, for example, have spoofed the sender of an email, so that it appears to be an email from the IT department of a large organisation.

Pharming. Pharming is a combination of the words farming and phishing. Pharming uses a different technique to phishing, but has the same goal: gaining personal information. The difference is that classical Phishing uses social engineering to obtain certain information from users, while pharming only uses technology. A pharming attack is more difficult to perform, but is also harder to detect. The user does not have to make any mistakes (such as clicking on a URL in an email) and the user does not know that s/he is routed to another website (Violino 2005). Pharming ensures that the user is not directed to the website s/he actually wants to visit, but to a website that is under control of a criminal (KLPD 2007). This is possible without the user being aware of it, because the computer criminal has changed the IP address, which is linked to the URL or domain name. This can be done in two ways: by manipulating data in the Domain Name Server (DNS) or by modifying data in the host file on the computer of the user (National Police Agency 2007; Olmann 2007).

Trends

Identity fraud through phishing is considered one of the fastest growing forms of non-violent crime (Rogers 2006; Van der Hulst & Neve 2008). With the growth of e-commerce and virtual financial flows, internet fraud (and identity fraud) is expected to increase in the coming years, making large numbers of victims and causing the most financial damage (Taylor et al. 2006).

185

Cybercriminals are constantly innovating their attack techniques (Watson et al. 2005). They constantly invent new ways to execute phishing attacks more successfully: texts to trick users are becoming better and better and the actual locations of phishing sites are hidden as long as possible in order to stay online as long as possible (phishing by Proxy) (Govcert 2007). Another example is the use of stealth malware (or root kits), malware that is invisible and nests without a trace into a computer (AusCert 2006). AusCert saw an increase in such techniques in 2005 and 2006. The innovation of techniques is reflected in the number of variations of phishing (vishing, smishing, pharming, etc.). Another development in phishing is the *man in the middle phishing attack.* Authentication data that customers enter is passed directly on to the bank. This type of phishing makes it possible to access sites that are protected on the basis of two-factor authentication (Govcert 2007). The Anti-Phishing Work Group (APWG) saw an increase of these attacks in 2008 (APWG 2008).

Spear-phishing is used increasingly. An email is sent, for example, to certain social networks in their own language or as if sent by a colleague. In this email users are asked to confirm passwords and security codes (Symantec 2007; Van der Hulst & Neve 2008; Govcert 2010). Such targeted attacks are carried out on a smaller scale, making them less likely to be detected by anti-phishing software. Finally, in the years ahead criminals will continue to abuse social events and personal interests. Phishing messages are being sent for example after major disasters. Recent examples are the earthquake in Haiti and the tsunami in Japan (Govcert 2010).

Extent

Figures from the Internet Crime Complaint Centre (IC3, a partnership between the U.S. Federal Bureau of Investigation (FBI), the National White Collar Crime Centre (NW3C) and the Bureau of Justice Assistance (BJA)) show that 6% of reported e-fraud is related to identity theft (IC3 2008). Figure 13.3 shows statistics from the Anti-Phishing Work Group (APWG). It is a snapshot, but APWG reports from previous years show that the financial sector is often targeted by phishers (APWG 2008).

Figure 13.3   Statistics about phishing (APWG 2011)

- Unique phishing reports in Q2 2010 rose to an annual high of 33,617 in June, down 17% from the record high in August 2009 of 40,621 reports.
- The quarterly high of unique phishing websites detected was 33,253 in April, down 43% from the record high of 56,362 in August 2009.
- The number of phished brands reached a high of 276 in May, down 22% from the all-time record of 356 in October 2009.
- Payment Services accounted for nearly 38% of attacks in Q2, up from 37% in Q1.
- The United States continued its position as top country for hosting phishing websites during Q2.
- Spain's proportion of detected crimeware websites rose to 16% in Q2 from less than 4% in Q1.
- The percentage of computers infected with banking trojans and password stealers rose to 17% from 15% in Q1.

Not all phishing attacks succeed and make victims. Research of the Anti-Phishing Working Group (APWG) shows that about 5% of the attacks effectively succeed in stealing personal information (Ollmann 2004). Another study is comparable with these figures: 3% of attacks are successful (Stamm et al. 2006). In 2005 a study was conducted at the University of Indiana (Jagatic et al. 2005). A phishing attack was conducted by researchers targeting University students between 18 and 24 years old. There were two attacks, one using social engineering (in which the sender looked familiar) and one without social engineering (control group). An attack was considered successful if a student clicked on the link in the email and then entered his or her password and username on the website. In the case of nearly three-quarters of the students (72%) who were attacked with the help of social engineering, the attack was successful. When the attacks were carried out without social engineering, only 16% of the attacks were successful.

13.3 Spyware

Spyware is one of the many forms of malware (malicious software). Spyware is software that collects specific information from the user and sends this information to the cybercriminal. That may include keystrokes, screenshots, email addresses, surfing habits or personal information like credit card numbers (Microsoft 2006b; Hackworth 2005; Govcert 2010). The data may be used by cybercriminals but can also be sold to third parties. The use of spyware is not new. In the early 1980s keyloggers were first detected on computers at universities. Since then, the use of spyware has been growing (Hackworth 2005). Spyware does not need to be a separate piece of malware: much malware in circulation is modular and can include components to steal data.

There are various definitions of spyware. Van der Hulst & Neve (2008) see spyware as the generic term for programs that spy on a computer user's behaviour. However there is also software that sends information about the user for which the user has given his consent. When installing a program, the user can give permission to send information about his web browsing to a company that monitors online behaviour. The question is whether this is spyware. If a user knowingly consented to share such information with a company, one should not use the term spyware (Microsoft 2006b). Reading and understanding all the terms before installing a program is however quite difficult. They are often so lengthy and detailed that users do not even begin to read them

(Edelman 2005). We define spyware as a piece of software that, without the user's consent, sends information of that user to another party.

Spyware may monitor all data from a computer and is only limited by the (system) rights it has. If the spyware has user rights, then it can access all the data that the user can access. If the spyware runs with administrative rights, then it can access all data. This applies not only to files on the hard disk, but also screenshots, keystrokes and data packets in networks. The following is a list of information which spyware is usually looking for (Hackworth 2005):

- *Keystrokes.* The logging of keystrokes is one of the first methods used as spyware. The keystrokes of users are recorded by so-called keyloggers. There are both hardware and software keyloggers. The hardware version is usually located between the keyboard cable and the connector into the computer. Such applications can also be hidden in the keyboard. A problem with hardware keyloggers is that they have to be planted physically. Someone must have direct access to the computer. Just like other forms of malware, software keyloggers can be planted on the computer of a user in different ways (e.g. because the user opened an attachment from an email which secretly installed the keylogger). These loggers are often only active when certain keywords are used or certain programs are running (e.g. the website of a bank) (Ianelli & Hackworth 2005).

- *Screenshots.* In addition to keystrokes, spyware can capture screenshots. It makes a picture of what the user is currently seeing on his computer screen. Screenshots can also be activated when certain keywords are used or programs are run.
- *Internet activity.* Spyware keeps track of the websites a user visited, monitors online surfing and buying behaviour, and saves information that the user has entered on websites such as usernames and passwords, credit card numbers and identity.
- *Email and contact information.* Email addresses and other information from the user's electronic address book can be collected to be used for spam attacks.
- *Windows Protected Store data.* This Windows service stores some information such as usernames and passwords for programmes and encrypted websites. Because the spyware is on the computer while the user (with all its rights) is logged, it is able to access such data.
- *Clipboard content.* The contents of the clipboard may contain sensitive information. Users cut and paste their personal data that is used in the entry fields of websites. But even sensitive data from commercial firms can sometimes be found on the clipboard.

- *Network traffic.* By monitoring network traffic, information such as usernames, passwords, email messages or entire files can be intercepted.
- *Cookies.* Cookies contain bits of information about a user that are stored by a web server. If the user visits a web page the second time, the web server retrieves this information (and the web page is loaded faster). Cookies often contain sensitive information about user names and passwords.
- *Register and hard drive searching.* On the hard drive the spyware searches for information about passwords, usernames, email addresses, contacts, etc. (Ianelli & Hackworth 2005).

Hackworth (2005) describes a number of different groups that use spyware. Although not empirically supported, we describe the three groups here:
- *Online Attackers and organised crime.* Online attackers use spyware to collect personal information in order to commit identity fraud or e-fraud, or to sell the information to third parties that commit classic forms of crime. Such criminals can work alone, but may also have contacts with organised crime. Computers that are part of a botnet (chapter 12) are the most likely to be infected with spyware.
- *Marketing organisations.* These companies are interested in personal information such as email addresses, surfing and online purchasing behaviour, search queries and other information that can be used for marketing campaigns (usually in the form of spam, browser pop-ups, etc.).
- *Insiders.* Within a company, an employee can install spyware with the aim of obtaining confidential business information. This information can be sold to a competitor or the company can be targeted for extortion. Spyware can also be used to spy on family or friends. An example in Dutch police files is a woman who suspects her husband of cheating and uses spyware to find information about this on his computer (information about emails, chat sessions etc.) (Leukfeldt et al. 2010).

Trends

Spyware has been around since at least the early 1980s. In the meantime spyware has developed. For example spyware only comes into force when certain key words are given and spyware can be integrated into programs that seem legitimate to the user (Hackworth 2005). The use of keyloggers and spyware to gain access to classified information is expected to be discovered by criminals and become a lucrative crime in the future. (McAfee 2006, cited in Van der Hulst & Neve 2008).

189

Despite the fact that security measures against malware are steadily improving, security will always have weaknesses. Criminals are attempting to circumvent protections, and spyware and other malware are being adapted to every new vulnerability that emerges. One example is the database in which the existing patterns (digital signature) of known malware are registered. Antispyware and antivirus programs use such databases to detect malware. Cybercriminals develop ways to ensure that detection of digital signatures of the malware becomes more and more difficult (Computer Security Institute 2007). In addition, operating systems are becoming more complex and the number of variations in malware is growing. This makes it harder to halt new malware.

Distributers of malware have persisted with the trend of sending less malware in attachments of emails. Sophos reported in July 2007 that 1 in 337 emails contained unwanted software. In 2005 the ratio was 1 in 44 (Sophos 2008). Instead, more and more unwanted software is distributed through websites. Links to these malicious websites are distributed via spam messages.

Extent

Several sources show that a significant proportion of computers are infected with spyware. In an American study in 2005 (America Online et al. 2005), conducted among internet users, 46% of respondents indicated that their computer contained spyware. A scan for spyware by the researchers showed that 61% of respondents had spyware on their computers. Of this group, 91% had not given permission to install such software. Victim surveys conducted among companies in America have also demonstrated that a high percentage of computers are infected with spyware. CSO magazine et al. (2007) show a similar picture to the study of America Online et al. (2005). More than half of respondents (52%) who endured one or more attacks on their network in the last 12 months (66%) were said to have spyware on their systems. The CSI survey shows a different picture. This survey shows that 32% of respondents (U.S. companies) that were attacked in the recent months had spyware on their systems (Computer Security Institute 2007). The study from America Online et al. (2005) shows that users are not always aware that malware, or in this case spyware, is installed on their computer.

Key concepts

Phishing
Spear phishing
Pharming
Spyware

Part 3
Youth and
Cyber Safety

14 Adolescents Receiving Online Sexual Solicitations

Joyce Kerstens, Jurjen Jansen & Sander Veenstra

14.1 Introduction

Adolescents are the first and foremost users of online technologies, and this age group is also at the forefront in integrating the latest online technological developments into their daily lives (Bauwens, Pauwels, Lobet-Maris, Poullet, & Walrave 2009). Although the scientific demarcation of the period of adolescence in terms of age is not clear, adolescents are usually referred to as youth aged between 13 and 18 years, gender differences aside (e.g. Schrock & Boyd 2008). Traditionally, adolescents are associated with risk, an approach also prevailing in research on youth's usage of online technologies (Baumgartner, Valkenburg & Peter 2010). Kanuga and Rosenfeld (2004), for example, state that '[a]dolescence is a time that is characterized by numerous high-risk activities, and little attention to future consequences of current behaviors' (p. 122). The period of adolescence is furthermore considered to be the crucial phase for identity construction (Mitchell, Crawshaw, Bunton & Green 2001). Sexuality is an important part of every individual's identity. It is generally assumed that adolescents are particularly vulnerable and at risk, while discovering their sexuality and developing a sexual identity (Baumgartner et al. 2010; Potter & Potter 2001). Thus being at risk and developing a sexual identity seem to be characteristic of adolescents.

This brings us back to adolescents and the internet. Research has revealed that the internet serves as a means for adolescents' sexual development (Subrahmanyam & Greenfield 2008). However, in public discourse the internet is often perceived as hazardous, due for instance to its largely anonymous character (Bauwens et al. 2009; McKenna & Bargh 2000). Public anxiety about online sexual risks for adolescents focuses on sexual solicitations. These are perceived risks, because of the potentially severe consequences, such as sexual abuse (Livingstone, Haddon, Görzig & Ólafsson 2011). To summarise, the internet is perceived to be a potentially dangerous environment for adolescents since this age group is developmentally vulnerable and simultaneously inclined to take risks.

The subject of this chapter is online sexual solicitation, a term utilised in research. To complicate matters, the term 'sexual solicitation' is also used in legal provisions. Legally, the term 'sexual solicitation' is a synonym for 'grooming'. However the criminal definition of these terms vary slightly from jurisdiction to jurisdiction. To accurately interpret the findings from research, it is necessary to make a strict distinction between the uses of the term 'sexual solicitation' in research and in criminal law. For that reason the second section of this chapter deals with the delineation of the concept 'online sexual solicitation' in research, while the third section addresses 'online sexual solicitation' or 'grooming' in a legal context. The fourth section addresses the prevalence of online sexual solicitation, grooming and related topics such as internet-initiated offline contacts. Subjects dealt with in the fifth section are offender and victim characteristics. This chapter concludes with a few observations on the role of the internet with regard to sexual solicitation. The terms 'cybersex', 'stranger danger', 'paedophile' and 'online predator', which are often utilised in conjunction with online sexual solicitation, will be given consideration when relevant.

14.2 Delineation of online sexual solicitation in research

The verb 'to solicit' literally means 'try to obtain by urgent requests'. The term 'sexual solicitation' accordingly refers to a request to obtain something sexual. In research designs the definition of *online sexual solicitation* developed by Finkelhor, Mitchell and Wolak (2000: x) prevails – though with slight variation: 'requests to engage in sexual activities or sexual talk or give personal sexual information that were unwanted or, whether wanted or not, made by an adult' (e.g. Baumgartner et al. 2010; Wolak, Mitchell & Finkelhor 2006; Ybarra & Mitchell 2008). The constituents 'whether wanted or not' and 'made by an adult' were added to encompass possible adult-minor contacts, which are by definition considered to be inappropriate and potentially hazardous (Bauwens et al. 2009; Wolak et al. 2006). In research, therefore, the term 'online sexual solicitation' can refer to unwanted requests made by similar-aged youth or wanted and unwanted requests by adults. Perpetrators can be either minors or adults.

Online sexual solicitations range from relatively benign to serious, and they vary widely in appearance and underlying intentions. Finkelhor et al. (2000: 7) state that '[a] lot of it looks and sounds like the hallways of our high schools'. Online sexual solicitations largely mirror what is common in offline contexts. Some of the solicitations are merely invitations to engage in sexual conversations or can be interpreted as flirtatious remarks (Bauwens et al. 2009; Smith 2007). Others can be deduced as online sexual harassment (Finn 2004).

A sexual solicitation may also be a proposition for *cybersex*, 'a form of fantasy sex, which involves interactive (...) sessions where the participants describe sexual acts and sometimes disrobe and masturbate' (Finkelhor et al. 2000: 3). An invitation for cybersex does not exceed the boundaries of the online world. However personal boundaries can be violated (Döring 2000). Sexual solicitations may also involve requests for sexual photographs and performing sexual acts for the webcam (Wolak et al. 2006). Findings from research indicate that online sexual solicitations are predominantly benign incidents restricted to the online environment. Mitchell, Finkelhor and Wolak therefore also term these incidents 'online limited sexual solicitations' (2007: 532). In addition to the group online limited sexual solicitations, Finkelhor et al. (2000) distinguish the category 'aggressive sexual solicitations': 'sexual solicitations involving offline contact with the perpetrator through regular mail, by telephone, or in person, or attempts or requests for offline contact' (2000: x). These solicitations involve peers as well as adults. To conclude, research distinguishes between sexual solicitations limited to the online environment and sexual solicitations intended to establish offline contact, i.e., aggressive sexual solicitations.

14.3 Delineation of online sexual solicitation in criminal law

As mentioned earlier, the term 'sexual solicitation' is also utilised within legal contexts, where it refers principally to the offence of an adult enticing youth online into an offline sexual encounter. A synonym for the offence of online sexual solicitation is online *grooming*, grooming literally meaning 'to prepare'. Other terms used in law are 'to lure' and 'to entice'.

The first time online grooming or sexual solicitation was criminalised in an international treaty was in 2007. The Council of Europe was imbued with the necessity of guarantees to protect children from sexual exploitation and sexual abuse and specifically took into consideration society's increasing digitalisation and technological developments. The Council's efforts resulted in the *Treaty of the Council of Europe concerning the protection of children against sexual exploitation and sexual abuse*, also known as the *Treaty of Lanzarote* (CETS No. 201). Grooming is addressed in Article 23 of this Treaty:

'Each Party shall take the necessary legislative or other measures to criminalise the intentional proposal, through information and communication technologies, of an adult to meet a child who has not reached the age set in application of Article 18, paragraph 2, for the purpose of committing any of the offences established in accordance with Article 18, paragraph 1.a, or Article 20, paragraph 1.a, against him or her, where this proposal has been followed by material acts leading to such a meeting.'

Article 23 represents only minimum rules and parties may subsequently establish a stricter legislation (The Netherlands, for example, opted for stricter legal provisions: see box 14.1). The penalisation in Article 23 is expressly aiming at the misuse of computer mediated communications for the purpose of sexually seducing children. The constituent *'intentional proposal'* is a prerequisite for the liability of 'the offences established'; furthermore, the proposal has to be concretised by material acts, such as providing a child with directions leading to a prearranged meeting place. Flirting or sexual innuendos are not liable to punishment. Article 23 of the *Treaty of Lanzarote* also refers to Articles 18 and 20 in the Treaty. Article 18 addresses the penalising of intentional sexual activities with a child, and Article 20 makes the production, distribution and possession of child pornography a criminal act. Article 20 of the Treaty is of importance in this context, since asking minors for sexual pictures of themselves – these pictures by definition constitute child pornography – is another purpose of online grooming (Davidson & Martellozzo 2005).

Unfortunately, a comprehensive European policy of grooming is complicated. Article 23 of the *Treaty of Lanzarote* criminalises online grooming of a child. However, the *age of consent laws* (laws laying down the minimum age for sexual activity) differ from country to country. In Spain, for example, the age of consent is 13 years and the Cypriot law requires a minimum age of 17 years (Kierkegaard 2008). On the internet, obviously, communication crosses national boundaries. The disparities between European jurisdictions may impede a concerted law enforcement. To date, the Treaty has been signed by 27 countries and 15 countries have ratified it.

Legal provisions to address online grooming have also been laid down in countries outside Europe. The Federal Law of the United States, for instance, prohibits online sexual solicitation if an adult communicates intentionally in a sexually explicit manner with any individual who has not yet attained the age of 18 years (18 U.S.C. § 2422 b). As in Europe, the age of consent laws in the United States vary from jurisdiction to jurisdiction and, in some states the law calls for a minimum age difference between partners (Hines & Finkelhor 2007). In Canada, it is an offence to communicate with a child through a computer system for the purpose of luring a child (Criminal Code, section 172.1). In Australia, communicating through a carrier service with a person under the age of 16 or, exposing such a person to any indecent matter for the purposes of grooming, is prohibited (Criminal Code Act 1995, sections 474.26 and 474.27).

Box 14.1   Dutch criminal law and the treaty of Lanzarote

In consequence of Article 23 of the Treaty of Lanzarote, grooming became punishable in 2010 under Article 248e of the Dutch Penal Code. Grooming is defined as an active attempt to seduce somebody younger than 16 years through the internet with the ultimate aim of sexual abuse or producing child pornographic content. This provision enables the prosecution of a person who asks a minor to meet offline in order to realise the aforementioned goals, providing that the proposal has been followed by material acts. To fulfill the legal requirements, it is not necessary that contact on the internet leads to actual physical contact with a minor. Article 248e extends the purpose of Article 23 of the Treaty of Lanzarote: not only adults, but also minors are liable to punishment for this offence.

Certain forms of online grooming were already liable to punishment under Article 248a of the Dutch Penal Code. This article addresses active attempts made by a person to entice someone younger than 18 years to adopt sexual poses or to perform sexual acts – alone or with someone else – for the person concerned to look at on a webcam.

Article 240b of the Dutch Penal Code criminalises the production, distribution and possession of child pornography. In coherence with the provisions in Article 20 of the Treaty of Lanzarote, Article 240b was amended. Since January 2010 this article also prohibits looking at 'live' webcam images of sexual acts of somebody apparently younger than 18 years in a private environment – for example, at home – without saving these images on a data carrier, i.e., not possessing these images.

In The Netherlands a person is liable to punishment from the age of 12 onward (Article 77a of the Dutch Penal Code). With regard to online sexual risks for adolescents, it is important to note that, according to Dutch penal law, requests for offline sexual meetings, requests for webcam sex and, looking at 'live' webcam sex involving a minor may bring about legal actions for grooming or child pornography.

197

Research on offender online grooming behaviour is in its infancy. However, researchers have identified some characteristics of these online practices, mostly based on case studies. Kierkegaard (2008: 42) states that grooming is a time consuming strategy by which 'criminals contact children and gain their trust for the purpose of meeting them and engaging in sexual behaviour'. However, although time consuming, the internet facilitates grooming multiple children simultaneously. Based on a participant observation methodology involving a researcher – posing as a socially isolated child aged 8, 10 and 12 years old – entering communication channels used by youth, O'Connell (2005) distinguished six stages in the grooming process: victim selection (*sounds like you unhappy L... wanna chat?*), friendship forming *hiya...wanna be friends?*), relationship forming (*like chatting with you ...wanna go private?*), risk assessment (*who else uses this computer?*), exclusivity (*this is our secret...*) and the sexual stage (*have you ever been kissed?*). In the last stage the groomer brings up the suggestion of an offline meeting. The groomer executes the six-staged strategy in such a manner that the child assumes it is appropriate and acceptable to consent to the offline sexual encounter. O'Connell adds that not all perpetrators 'will progress through the stages in the conversations sequentially' (p. 6); they tailor their strategy as they learn more about the victim. It is important to bear in mind that the six-staged strategy developed by O'Connell is based on groomers' communications with a fictitious prepubescent child. To conclude, in criminal law the term 'online sexual solicitation' and its synonym 'online grooming' refer to a sexual offence characterised by a protracted set of behaviours by an adult directed at a minor.

14.4 The prevalence of online sexual solicitation

Large-scale research on the prevalence of online sexual solicitation is relatively sparse. The findings from current research – though varying, for example, in operationalisation – indicate that between 13% and 23% of adolescents received some form of online limited sexual solicitation (Baumgartner et al. 2010; Bauwens et al. 2009; Finkelhor et al. 2000; Livingstone 2006; Livingstone et al. 2011; Wolak et al. 2006; Ybarra & Mitchell 2008). The *EU Kids Online Survey* that collected findings from 25 European countries emerging from interviews conducted directly with children included a question on the frequency of online sexual solicitation. For most adolescents receiving a sexual solicitation was an infrequent experience (Livingstone et al.). The incidence of aggressive sexual solicitations was only questioned in the *Youth Internet Safety Surveys* (YISS-1 and YISS-2), telephone surveys of representative national samples of youth in the United States. The prevalence of these incidents is relatively small compared to online limited sexual solicitations; it did not exceed 5% (Finkelhor et al.; Wolak et al.). The likelihood of receiving an online sexual solicitation – limited or aggressive – increases when children grow older (Livingstone et al.; Wolak et al.).

Existing studies on online grooming primarily focus on the method and online technologies used by online groomers, using an experimental or sting-oriented approach (e.g., O'Connell 2005). In these studies the online groomer is defined as a paedophile, i.e. a person sexually attracted to prepubescent children (e.g., Frances, 2000; World Health Organisation 2007). No scientific research is available on the prevalence of grooming – a practically and ethically difficult research topic. Estimates of the prevalence of grooming therefore vary widely. The United States' *National Juvenile Online Victimization Study* – a national sample of law enforcement agencies about crimes by online predators in the years 2000 and 2006 (N-JOV Wave 1 and 2) – revealed that most arrested offenders of internet-initiated sex crimes conducted a protracted strategy to develop relationships with victims (12 through 17 years), a practice considered to be distinctive for online grooming. Wolak, Finkelhor, Mitchell and Ybarra (2008) compared the prevalence of these internet-initiated sex crimes against minors with the overall number of sex crimes against minors: the former account for a relatively low percentage (approximately 7 %).

An offline meeting with the solicitor is rarely the result of an online sexual solicitation, since many sexual solicitations aim at teasing or harassing the recipient. When a solicitation does result in an offline sexual encounter, this is mostly between two adolescents or an older adolescent and a young adult (Wolak et al. 2006; Wolak, Mitchell, Finkelhor & Ybarra 2008). A sizeable minority of youth, however, do meet people they initially met online: between 8% and 16%. These offline contacts were primarily non-sexual. The majority of the offline contacts are with persons belonging to the adolescents' social circle – a friend or relative of someone known face-to-face. Adolescents also met people offline with whom they shared similar interests online and who subsequently became friends. Most of the reported meetings were known to parents. (Finkelhor et al. 2000; Liau, Khoo & Ang 2005; Livingstone et al. 2011; Livingstone & Helsper 2007; Wolak et al. 2006).

A relatively new risk related to online sexual solicitation is *sexting*, a term most commonly used to denote the production and distribution of online sexual pictures or videos by minors. However no consistent definition exists. (Sacco,

199

Argudin, Maguire & Tallon 2010). Only a few studies addressed the prevalence of sexting and their outcomes vary widely. A national representative telephone survey released by the United States' *Pew Research Center* reveals that 15% of the adolescents received a sexual image and that 4% sent such an image (Lenhart 2009). Other more broadly framed surveys found higher percentages, ranging from 20% to 24 % (Sacco et al. 2010) Sexually explicit pictures posted online can generate social repercussions for involved youth, for instance, reputation damage. Furthermore, producing and distributing sexually explicit pictures of a minor – even if they make the images themselves – can result in legal charges of producing child pornography (Leukfeldt, Domenie & Stol 2010).

14.5 Perpetrators: views and facts

Online sexual solicitations and grooming are often bracketed together with the designations stranger danger, paedophile, and online predator, all of which refer to the person behind online sexual solicitations or grooming. The term *'stranger danger'* refers to the potential dangers threatening minors while communicating online with unknown persons. News coverage in the media primarily associates stranger danger with naive children receiving online invitations from adults for offline sexual contact (Schrock & Boyd 2008). In the media these offending adults are often referred to as *'paedophiles'* or *'online predators'*, a term first used in the mid-1990s and generated from the more widespread term 'sexual predator'. Due to the popularity of a television show in the United States entitled 'To Catch a Predator' the word became more and more prevalent (Marwick 2008). The sexual predator is stereotyped as an older male prowling online for children, searching for personal information to identify potential targets, and using deception to entice children into offline meetings (Wolak, Finkelhor, Mitchell & Ybarra 2008). However, research indicates that the portrayal of the sexual perpetrator by means of designations such as stranger danger, paedophile and online predator fails to reflect actual online practices (Palfrey et al. 2010; Wolak et al. 2009).

First of all, the term *'stranger danger'* fails to identify actual sex offenders, since the vast majority of sexual offences against adolescents (95%) are perpetrated by people they are related to or who belong to their social networks (Snyder & Sickmund 2006; Wolak et al. 2009). It is moreover difficult to demarcate the term 'stranger': from what point on is a person not a stranger anymore? The term 'stranger danger', therefore, reveals nothing about the perpetrators of online sexual solicitations.

Secondly, although there are a few examples of empirical evidence available regarding child molesters, 'there are indications that they occupy a narrow range on the spectrum of the sex offender population, one that largely excludes paedophiles' (Wolak et al.: 118). *Paedophiles* have by definition a sexual tendency towards prepubescent children, not adolescents (Frances 2000; World Health Organisation 2007). The *N-JOV studies* (Wave 1 and 2) revealed that none of the sexually offended youth were younger than eleven years (Wolak et al.). Findings from the *YISS surveys* reveal that all sexual solicitations were directed at youth above 10 years old (Finkelhor et al. 2000; Wolak et al. 2006). Sex offenders and adults who solicit minors are not a homogeneous group consisting of paedophiles.

Thirdly, except for the fact that arrested sex offenders are virtually always men (Wolak et al. 2009), the standard image of the *online predator* is seldom accurate. To begin with, according to respondents in the *YISS surveys* a not negligible part (19% in YISS-1 and 16% in YISS-2) of the solicitors was female (Finkelhor et al. 2000; Wolak et al. 2006). Furthermore, results from *N-JOV study* (WAVE 1) indicate that the ages of arrested offenders vary widely, from 18-25 (23 %) and 26-39 (41 %) to over 40 (35 %) years of age (Wolak et al. 2004). The perpetrators of online sexual solicitations in the *YISS surveys* were mostly peers and young adults (73%), although a significant portion of the respondents stated they were unable to identify the age of the person they were communicating with (Finkelhor et al.; Wolak et al.). Other research validates these findings in general (e.g. Bauwens et al. 2009). To recapitulate, many sexual solicitors on the internet are young, some are female and, the ages of sex offenders vary. Consequently, the portrayal of the sexual perpetrator as an older male must be modified.

The anxiety about sexual predators searching the internet for sensitive personal information – for example on social network sites – in order to subsequently approach potential targets offline is also overrated. Transmitting personal information online is widespread among youth, although adolescents' publication of contact information is seemingly rare and even declining (Bauwens et al. 2009; Patchin & Hinduja 2010; Schrock & Boyd 2008). No evidence has been found to support the idea that arrested offenders search for personal online information to establish contact with children (Wolak et al. 2009).

Finally, the so-called sexual predator seldom uses deception. Most arrested offenders in the *N-JOV studies* were frank about their sexual motives prior to the offline encounter. Only a minority of arrested sex offenders pretended to be minors, although the application of this strategy seems to be increasing

201

(Wolak et al. 2009). The most frequently applied deception entails 'promises of love and romance by offenders whose intentions are primarily sexual' (Wolak 2008, p. 113). Adults engaging in internet-initiated relationships with minors are more likely to pretend to be slightly younger or to alter certain aspects of their identity (Schrock & Boyd 2008). To conclude, the designations stranger danger, paedophile and sexual predator do not capture the actual practice of online sexual solicitation and internet-initiated offline sexual contact.

According to Potter and Potter (2001: 38) 'the profile of the solicitor [is] similar to those encountered in physical space by teens'. On the one hand, sexual solicitations predominantly occur between similarly aged youth, for whom experimenting with sexuality and sexual relationships is developmentally normal. On the other hand, there are adults who use the internet to establish sexual offline contacts with minors. However, the majority of adult sex offenders still predominantly operate in the offline world.

14.6 Victims: views and facts

What are the distinguishing features of youth victims of sexual solicitations and subsequent offline sexual encounters? First, research shows that gender differences are an important factor: girls receive the vast majority of online solicitations (Baumgartner et al. 2010; Finkelhor et al. 2000; Wolak et al. 2006). Most victims of arrested sex offenders were also girls (Wolak et al. 2009). Another factor is age. The YISS surveys revealed that older adolescents are more at risk for online sexual solicitation than early adolescents (Finkelhor et al. 2000; Wolak et al. 2006). Furthermore, the N-JOV studies (Wave 1 and 2) indicated that about three-quarters of the victims of internet-initiated sex crime arrests were aged 14 to 17 (Wolak et al. 2009). This also holds for youth reporting aggressive sexual solicitations (Finkelhor et al.; Wolak et al.). To summarise, being female and being between 14 and 17 years of age are salient factors for receiving online sexual solicitations. Other identified factors that increase the likelihood of receiving online sexual solicitations are being gay or being uncertain about sexual preferences, and being sexually or physically abused. Engaging in risky online behaviours, for instance searching for sexually explicit materials, also may increase adolescents' vulnerability. The more risky behaviours they show, the greater the likelihood of receiving online sexual solicitations (Wolak et al. 2008: 118).

The N-JOV studies further indicate that most victims of arrested offenders knew they were interacting online with an adult who was sexually interested in them. The offline sexual encounters were predominantly consensual and a substantial number of these compliant victims engaged in several offline sexual encounters with the adult (Wolak et al. 2009). The offenders were charged with breaking the age-of-consent laws; crimes referred to as *statutory rape*. The victims of these statutory rapes cannot be called naive or ignorant with regard to the sexual nature of their offline encounters with an adult. They might be called naive about the genuineness of the adult promising love and romance (Wolak et al. 2008).

14.7 Discussion

Much has been written in the media about the risks of online sexual solicitation, online grooming and the dangers associated with internet-initiated offline sexual contacts and as a result the internet is often portrayed as a dangerous environment for adolescents. However, it is justifiable to conclude tentatively that the internet does not facilitate an increase in sex crimes against minors (Wolak et al. 2008).

It is important to recognise that the percentage of adolescents who sexually solicit peers online is substantial. Most online sexual solicitations are relatively benign or intended to harass or bully others. Adolescents continue their offline conduct in the online world; the internet is just one of the existing social domains. For good reason, researchers state that youth have fully integrated online technologies in their daily lives (e.g. Mitchell et al. 2007). In general, youth at risk online appear to be the same as youth in danger offline, and negative life circumstances and experiences offline apparently can increase the vulnerability of youth online (Palfrey et al. 2010). A strict distinction between the offline and online world therefore appears to be artificial.

The internet, of course, has specific features not found in the offline world, such as the sense of being anonymous and reduced audio-visual cues. However, these features can play a role in harming as well as in protecting youth from online sexual solicitations. Bearing in mind that the factors influencing adolescents' vulnerability, increasing risk and causing harm are complex, multidimensional and inextricably connected, it is appropriate to quote McKenna and Bargh's dictum that '(...) the internet by itself is not a main effect cause of anything' (2000: 57).

203

Key concepts

Adolescents
Sexual solicitation (research context)
Sexual solicitation (legal context)
Stranger danger
Treaty of Lanzarote

15 Youth and Sexually Explicit Internet Material: Exposure and Effects

Joyce Kerstens, Sander Veenstra & Jurjen Jansen

15.1 Introduction

Every technological invention – from cave paintings to the internet – has been associated with sexually explicit material or pornography (Potter & Potter 2001). Sexually explicit material is often evaluated as evil, immoral, or developmentally inappropriate, or in other words, pornography is perceived to be harmful (Attwood 2007). Although young people have long since turned to pornography to satisfy their sexual curiosity (Brown & L'Engle 2009), adolescents' current exposure to sexually explicit internet material (SEIM) is an issue of parental, public and political concern. That concern is elicited by the juxtaposition of three factors. First, it is assumed that youth are 'vulnerable and underdeveloped, incapable of informed choice about mass media or sexual activity' (Critcher 2003: 156), while simultaneously sexual curiosity emerges in childhood to become distinctive for adolescents. If young people are exposed to SEIM, they may not be able to put the deviating sexual and social reality portrayed in these materials into perspective. Second, the anonymity (belief that one is unknown), affordability (low cost or cost-free) and accessibility (easy to get) of SEIM, together termed the *Triple A-Engine* (Cooper 1998), have fundamentally altered the ways in which pornography can be accessed. Today, internet access is near-universal, and sexually curious youths no longer have to openly purchase a magazine bearing sexual content only available at certain outlets (Brown & L'Engle 2009). Third, an effective management of youth's exposure to SEIM by educators is debatable, since the unsupervised use of the internet – in private rooms or through handheld devices – has increased and is expected to increase further. Moreover, the unguided use of the internet attributable to the disparity in digital literacy between adults and children remains substantial (e.g. Livingstone, Haddon, Görzig & Ólafsson 2011). The internet, along with other media technologies like digital cameras and cell phones, has not only altered youth's exposure to pornography, but adult authority over media access and usage as well.

Youth is leading the adoption and use of online technologies and, although a lifelong process, the formation of a solid and unique identity is distinctive for this age group. Subrahmanyam, Greenfield and Tynes characterise this developmental process as 'a quest for self-understanding' (2004: 654). Research has demonstrated that youth utilises media content, including SEIM, to explore two important aspects of their identity: sex and gender (Brown 2000; Steele & Brown 1995). However, content analyses indicate that SEIM is a predominantly stereotypical product representing sexual practices deviating from reality and employing scripts in which men are dominant and women sexually available (Brown & L'Engle 2009; Döring 2009; Peter & Valkenburg 2008). With regard to the risk and harm attributed to SEIM, this raises the question whether adolescents are capable of putting the portrayal of sexual behaviour and gender roles in SEIM into perspective.

This chapter addresses the behavioural and attitudinal effects of exposure to SEIM on the identity formation of adolescents with regard to sexuality and gender. First, exposure to SEIM will be situated in a broader context, emphasising the attention shift towards youth in the digital era alongside the sexualisation of mainstream media, followed by a discussion on the concept clarity of pornography and the operationalisation of SEIM in prevailing research. The next section outlines the prevalence of youth's exposure to SEIM with an emphasis on gender. This section will be followed by a brief outline of currently influential theoretical models describing the relation between media use and effects on users. The findings from research on the effects of SEIM will be described thereafter, and finally in the last section, research on SEIM and concern about SEIM are evaluated and placed in a broader context.

15.2   SEIM: context, concept and content

Although pornography use has been universal over time, particularly in the twentieth century when pornographic content became widely obtainable, for instance by means of the printed media, the supposed negative effects of this low cultural genre became a matter of public concern. This concern initially centred on the perverse – i.e. pornography consuming – adult being a threat to society's moral order; at presents the focus has shifted to the vulnerable child in danger of being corrupted by pornography (Attwood 2007).

The change of course in legislation is exemplary. From the 1960s onward, general or restricted bills to legalise adult pornography consumption have been passed in most, particularly Western, countries. The first country to take these laws into force was Denmark. A possible sociological explanation for this more liberal approach to pornography is the shift in democratic countries from control by means of authoritarian regulation – based on conservative experts' delineation of proper sexual behaviour – to reliance on individuals' choice for and experience with media use and sexual practice (Attwood 2007; see also Beck 2005).

Conversely, while the debate involving adult pornography consumption gradually quietened down, youth's exposure to pornography became a focus of political interest. The advent of the internet further reinforced this interest, attributable to the accessibility of unprecedented amounts of SEIM. The mainstream media in the United States even induced a *moral panic* – a sociological term for an exaggerated reaction to a perceived sharply increasing threat to accepted moral standards or vulnerable groups leading to injudicious efforts to secure safety – among the public (Jenkins 2009; Marwick 2008; Potter & Potter 2001). Since the 1990s several countries have attempted to regulate, ban or censor youth's exposure to SEIM. In the United States, for example, several congress and state legislatures have passed laws aimed at protecting youth, although most of these failed to pass the examination for compatibility with the Constitution (Marwick 2008). Public concern over the possible harm to youth's sexual and social development led to youth's exposure to SEIM being targeted.

However it is important to acknowledge that youth's exposure to sexual content is not limited to the internet. Analyses have shown that in the past 20 years, although varying by medium and genre, the quantity of sexualised material, sexual issues and references has increased in the mainstream media and; furthermore, the depiction of sex has become more explicit, especially in western culture (Flood 2007; Ward 2003). These analyses also reveal that the media overwhelmingly highlight heterosexual relationships in which women are portrayed as sexually available, passive and attractive and in which, subsequently, male virility, dominance and activeness are emphasised. Research moreover indicates that the portrayal of female sexuality is contradictory. Women are reduced to their bodily appearances and portrayed as sexual playthings – termed *objectification* – while simultaneously girls' and women's sexual responsibility and discretion are being emphasised. The media thus contribute to upholding a sexual double standard for women. The increased quantity and explicitness of gender stereotypical sexual content is termed the *sexualisation* of the media (e.g. APA 2007; Escobar-Chaves Tortolero, Markham, Low, Eitel & Thickstun 2005; Ward 2003).

Alongside the increase of sexualised content in the media, the iconography of pornography – codes and conventions – has proliferated in art, fashion and

207

popular culture. This iconography is also disseminated by the media (Træen, Nilsen & Stigum 2006). McNair termed this process 'the pornographication of the mainstream' (1996: 23). It has been suggested that the *pornographication* of culture distorts the distinction between perceived obscene and fashionable sexual representations (Attwood 2007). Since the media diet of youth is not limited to the internet and the traditional media are an important source of information about sex and gender roles (Ward 2003), it is questionable whether the possible effects of SEIM on youth's attitudes and behaviours can be seen in isolation from the influence of other sexualised content, or even a sexualised culture. It is open to debate whether the explicitness of sexual content in a single medium correlates more closely or strongly with stereotypical beliefs about gender and sex than implicit content in multiple media. Research has demonstrated that sexualised content in mainstream media can affect youth's attitudes and behaviours with regard to sex and gender roles and; and that the impact of this content differs for males and females (Brown & L'Engle 2009; Escobar-Chaves et al. 2005; Ward 2003). Peter and Valkenburg (2007: 382) have therefore proposed 'the concept of a sexualised media environment' to broaden the research on the effects of sexualised content. To conclude, it is important to keep in mind that SEIM is not an isolated phenomenon, but an explicit part of overall sexualised media.

Measuring the isolated effects of SEIM is one thing; the definition of pornography is another. In research the terms '(internet) pornography' and 'sexually explicit (internet) material' – the former repeatedly used pejoratively and the latter having a more neutral connotation – are used interchangeably (Brown & L'Engle 2009). Over the years the definitions of pornography or sexually explicit material have been adapted to contemporary social and cultural contexts, reflecting the prevailing opinions and beliefs of a specific period (Træen et al. 2006). A key feminist approach to defining pornography, for example, is that pornography is an expression of misogyny. A definition provided by Boies, Cooper and Osborne – 'images or written words that are sexually arousing or stimulating' (2004: 209) – extends the concept, making the term applicable to, for example, depictions on ancient Greek pottery or Shakespearean poetry. In other words, the definition of pornography has been directed by prevailing beliefs about human sexuality. A potentially enlightening observation stems from Stuart Potter, a former judge. He stated that although he could not give a definition of pornography, he would unquestionably recognise it when he saw it (*Jacobellis v. Ohio* 1964).

Although there is indisputably a case for this judge's practical approach to the problem, a definition proving insight in the digital representation of pornography is preferable. For this purpose the definition proposed by Peter and Valkenburg (2010b) is suitable. They define SEIM as:

> 'professionally produced or user-generated (audio)visual material on or from the internet that typically intends to arouse the viewer and depicts sexual activities and (aroused) genitals in unconcealed ways, usually with close-ups on oral, anal, and vaginal penetration' (p. 377).

This neutrally formulated definition describes what pornography is and what it intends to do, it includes user-generated and professionally produced content and, it covers online and downloaded material, thereby reflecting ongoing developments in online technology. It is important to state however that to date an internationally acknowledged definition of pornography or sexually explicit material is not available; and consequently, present studies do not meet the criterion of external validity, i.e. the comparability of data becomes an issue. To conclude, the concept 'internet pornography' or 'SEIM' is still under construction.

Besides definitional problems, it is also important to take into account that research on youth's exposure seldom operationalises the diverse manifestations of SEIM. According to Brown and L'Engle, pornography 'ranges considerably from depictions of rather traditional heterosexual behaviour to multiple sexual partners, coercion, and non-traditional sex including bestiality and sadomasochism' (2009: 130). In other words, the portrayed sexual activities as well as sexual preferences differ widely. The wording used to operationalise SEIM, however, is principally confined to seeing naked people, genitals and people having sex. After all, in research on children ethical reasons play a part, i.e. protecting unaware youth from phenomena thus far unheard of (e.g. Livingstone et al. 2011; Wolak, Mitchell & Finkelhor 2006; Peter & Valkenburg 2008). To conclude, research in general does not reveal what sexual content, from relatively innocent to deviant or even illegal, youth actually see and this calls for a cautious interpretation of the findings on the effects of SEIM.

15.3 Exposure to SEIM

The total amount of Internet pornography adds up to many millions of files. Youth can come into contact with SEIM through deliberate or inadvertent exposure. Reasons for deliberate exposure are curiosity and desire for sexual stimulation. The likelihood of inadvertent exposure is linked to the internet, since 'before development of the internet, there were few places youth frequented where they might encounter unsought pornography regularly' (Wolak, Mitchell & Finkelhor 2007: 248). Inadvertent exposure can occur through accidently stumbling upon the material, for instance, by mistyping a key word into a search engine or, through actions by others, for example, by means of pop-up advertisements or emails (Flood 2007). A relatively new phenomenon of actions by others is publishing sexual pictures of young people made by their peers on the internet. When executed via the text messaging function of cell phones, this is called *sexting*. This can have unintended consequences for the sender, such as prosecution under laws of child pornography, or it may be carried out with malice intent, for example, to sexually harass or to embarrass the recipient (Lenhart 2009).

The outcomes of research on the prevalence of exposure to SEIM differ considerably, reflecting methodological variance. Findings obtained from various countries indicate that a considerable proportion of youth is exposed to SEIM, although exposure prior to the age of 13 is relatively uncommon (Flood 2007; Livingstone et al. 2011; Lo & Wei 2005; Mesch 2009; Mitchell, Wolak & Finkelhor 2007; Peter & Valkenburg 2006a). Youth's exposure to SEIM can therefore be described as a quite common experience. Youth's reported inadvertent exposure to SEIM is higher than deliberate exposure, and there are indications that inadvertent exposure to SEIM is on the rise (Brown & L'Engle 2009; Sabina, Wolak & Finkelhor 2008).

However, youth are not a homogenous group, and up till now research provides insufficient insight into their individual variances; gender being an important exception to the rule. The evidence that males are significantly more exposed to SEIM than females is consistent, making gender the key variant to predict youth's exposure to SEIM. This finding is consistent with research on the use of traditional pornography (Escobar-Chaves et al. 2005; Livingstone et al. 2011; Mesch 2009; Wolak et al. 2006). There is insufficient evidence, however, to indicate that boys are exposed to different types of SEIM than girls. Do boys, for instance, see more violent pornography than girls?

A possible explanation for the gender variance is that SEIM mainly represents stereotypes of sexuality typically gratifying for men (Brown & L'Engle 2009). Another approach is that the female gender is socialised 'to perceive pornography in terms of morality rather than as a means to achieve sexual arousal'

(Treen et al.: 252) Also, traditionally the use of pornography is deemed more acceptable for males than for females. Research does not reveal to what extent the double standard on female sexuality might result in girls' underreporting exposure to SEIM.

15.4 The effects of SEIM from a theoretical perspective

The notion that media content potentially has an influence or effect on the attitudes and behaviours of its consumers is generally accepted in communication studies. As a result, several theories and models have been developed over the years to describe and explain this influence (e.g. Escobar-Chaves et al. 2005; Ward 2003). A frequently referenced theoretical model aiming at describing and explaining media's influence on *attitudes* is the *cultivation theory*. This theory derives from two underlying assumptions. Firstly, the media construct a homogeneous and stereotypical image of reality; and secondly, the users of these media create for themselves a subjective reality corresponding with the image of reality imposed by the media (Gerbner, Gross, Morgan & Signorielli 1994). As a consequence, frequently occurring stereotypical images in the media affect the attitudes of regular consumers; and concurrently, those consumers evaluate their own lives in view of standards shown in these stereotypical images. With regard to the consumption of SEIM, this implies that the more youth are exposed to SEIM, the more they – gradually and cumulatively – come to adopt attitudes about sexuality that coincide with the attitudes in online sexual content; and additionally, youth evaluate their own sexual experiences in the light of prevailing standards (Ward 2003).

A commonly used model to describe and explain media's impact on adopting specific *behaviours* is *social learning theory*. The basic assumption of this theory is that while observing the conduct of role models in the media, the consumers of these media learn and internalise which behaviours are rewarding and which will be punished. When the consequences of the observed behaviour are positive, users of media are inclined to copy this behaviour when a relevant situation elicits it. However, behaviour that is unappealing to the user and behaviour for which children are developmentally not yet ready will be overlooked or ignored (Bandura 1994). Content analyses have demonstrated that the negative consequences of irresponsible sex or degrading behaviour toward women are absent in SEIM and that deviant behaviour is portrayed in an appealing manner (Brosius, Weaver & Staab 1993). This implies that sexual

211

behaviour in SEIM is likely to be copied in related circumstances by developmentally ready youth.

The aforementioned theoretical models assume, however, that individuals are
predominantly passive consumers of the media, thus underestimating the
relevance of individuals' motivation to actively and deliberately choose content from competing media. However research has indicated that youth select
media content, for example relating to their pubertal status (Brown & Witherspoon 2002). The internet is exemplary for actively making choices: selecting
or searching content by typing key words in search engines and clicking on
links is the only way to navigate the internet. The *Uses and Gratifications theory*
hypothesises that the effects of media content vary depending on consumers'
motivations – reasons and goals – to use this content. It is likely that the effects
of SEIM will be different if the choice for SEIM is motivated by the need to
explore a gay or lesbian orientation, or if the motivation derives from a demand
for sexual arousal (Ruggiero 2000).

The Uses and Gratifications theory is embedded in the *Adolescents' Media
Practice Model* (AMPM) (Brown 2000). The AMPM assumes that youth are
not a *tabula rasa*; prior to media use they have already developed an identity
influenced by the conditions of their own life history, such as gender, family
life and social background. Together these conditions are termed '*lived experience*'. The *identity* of youth determines the motivation for the *selection* of media
content at a specific moment. The motivation then shapes the attention for
and the *interaction* with this chosen content, followed by the interpretation
and evaluation of the seen content proceeding from their present identity. The
evaluation produces two possible reactions: the incorporation of media content in youth's attitudinal and behavioural patterns, or not. The *application*
of incorporated media content will have an affect on youth's identity development and; therefore, on future media selection (Brown & Witherspoon 2002;
Steele 1999). The AMPM predicts 'that studies will find that effects are not
uniform' (Brown 2000: 38), since youth actively and consciously select media
content. Some adolescents will conform to the dominant depiction of sexuality in SEIM, while others will rebel against the stereotypic sexual portrayal
of women. According to Ward, the circular and reciprocal AMPM 'provides a
useful framework of *how* to study connections between sexuality and media
use' (2003: 362). This observation also applies to the relation between media
use and gender roles. The AMPM, however, does not take into account other
factors that might directly affect media's influence, such as school, friends,
and parents.

Figure 15.1   The Adolescents' Media Practice Model

Based on the model developed by Steele (1999).

15.5   Research on the effects of SEIM regarding sexuality and gender

According to Zillmann and Bryant, "[i]t would seem naïve, (...) to believe that pornography entertains without affecting perceptions of sexuality and behavioral dispositions toward sex and gender" (1982: 13). They have also stated that research on the effects of pornography is directed by prevailing notions about sexuality. These notions include gender-specific attitudes and behaviours. The United States and the Netherlands, for example, differ in their approach to youth's sexuality and gender roles. In the United States youth's sexuality is predominantly morally assessed with an emphasis on its possible negative consequences and, in the Netherlands youth's exploration of sexuality is primarily seen as developmentally normal and not restricted to marriage (Joshi, Peter & Valkenburg, in press). As a consequence, in some research premarital sex is listed among the negative effects of pornography (see Escobar-Chaves et al. 2005; Ward 2003), while in other studies it is emphasised that researchers by no means suggest that youth using SEIM are morally wrong (e.g. Peter & Valkenburg 2008). Although it is likely that SEIM can affect youth, prevailing notions in research make the external validity of studies questionable, i.e. findings are not simply generalisable.

It has already been noted that the likelihood of youth's exposure to SEIM – in most publications noted as the risk of being exposed – is substantial. The question is to what extent this 'risk' translates into negative effects or harm for youth. Since youth are not a homogenous group, and the frequency of exposure, dominating beliefs about sexuality and gender and the portrayed sexual preferences, for example, play a role in the complex correlates between exposure and effect, it is important to note that SEIM is not inevitably harmful. A contextualised interplay between various factors determines the possible effects of SEIM. Some youth may not be harmed at all, others may be upset or worried at the time of the incident or shortly after, or some may be negatively affected years later (Döring 2009). In summary, SEIM may have emotional, attitudinal and behavioural effects on youth depending on a number of variables.

With regard to emotional harm, sparse research indicates that approximately one in three of the children who have been exposed to SEIM stated that they felt bothered or upset immediately or shortly after a reported incident. Girls are significantly more likely to feel bothered or upset by these incidental exposures than boys. However, when they are upset, there is no difference between boys and girls as to how upset they feel. Feeling guilty or feeling ashamed after seeing SEIM was reported significantly more often by girls. Most youth who reported being upset said that they almost immediately got over it. There is no evidence that youth respond differently to the same or different type of content. If youth reported being embarrassed by exposure, this was often attributable to the expected reactions from adult should they learn about the exposure (Livingstone et al. 2011; Sabina et al. 2008; Wolak et al. 2006). Children in Australian focus groups conceived exposure to SEIM as a *rite de passage*, 'helping to mark transitions from childhood to early adulthood' (Potter & Potter 2001: 37). There is no research available on the translation of reported emotional responses into long-term harm. To conclude, most youth report no impact directly or shortly after exposure, and any emotional harm reported did not last for long. Girls are more likely to experience emotional harm than boys.

Based on the aforementioned theories, for instance, research postulates that exposure to SEIM can have long-lasting effects, i.e. attitudes and behaviours can be influenced by frequent exposure (Brown & L'Engle 2009: 132). Attitudes comprise the *beliefs* about sexuality and gender and the *values* placed on the diverse manifestations of sexuality and gender (Peter & Valkenburg 2008). The supposed relation between SEIM and behavioural effects derives from the question whether exposure to SEIM stimulates users to behave according to the social and sexual reality depicted in SEIM. Obviously, examining this relationship is difficult, since sexual behaviour is ultimately complex, and furthermore, using experimental studies to establish causality is impossible and, especially with young participants, unethical. Risk behaviour, such as having unprotected sex, is subject to research, however. SEIM's effect on behaviour is mostly expected to be indirect, working through the effects on youth's attitudes (Ward 2003: 369). The stereotypical, non-consequential depiction of sex and gender roles in the majority of SEIM may affect youth, for example in furthering sexual permissiveness, objectification of women, sexually harassing behaviour, instrumental sex, sexual activity at an early age, irresponsible sexual behaviour and, the belief in the so-called *rape myth*, i.e., that women would enjoy coercion while having sex (Brown & L'Engle 2009; Escobar-Chaves et al. 2005; Flood 2007; Mesch 2009).

The body of research on the effects of SEIM on youth's attitudes and behaviours is small. Findings on the effects of SEIM on attitudes are more consistent than those on the behavioural effect. Research has however established an association between exposure to SEIM and sexually harassing conduct or an earlier onset of sexual activities (Brown & L'Engle 2009). According to the social learning theory, this is explainable, since showing the negative consequences of sex or deviant behaviour is uncommon in SEIM. There is consistent evidence that exposure to SEIM can be associated with more permissive sexual attitudes and stronger beliefs that women are sex objects (Brown & L'Engle 2009; Lo & Wei 2005; Peter & Valkenburg 2006a; Peter & Valkenburg 2007; Peter & Valkenburg 2008a; Peter & Valkenburg 2008b). However the causal direction has not been established, and therefore the correlations found in research may reflect the fact that youth select content that validates their current attitudes and behaviours.

As the cultivation model predicts, the frequency of exposure is correlated to the effects of SEIM and, although conditional, evidence has recently been found to support a causal relation between frequency and effects of SEIM (Peter & Valkenburg 2010b). There is also initial evidence that the perceived realism of SEIM may play a mediating role in the effects of SEIM on youth's attitudes. When youth are more frequently exposed to SEIM, they perceive the portrayed activities in SEIM as more realistic. The increased perceived realism of SEIM subsequently leads to a greater acceptance of instrumental sex. The effects identified were however small (Peter & Valkenburg 2006b; 2010). Research tentatively indicates moreover a possible link between frequency of exposure, increased sexual uncertainty and the mediation role of involvement.

When youth are more exposed to SEIM, they become more involved in SEIM and, more involvement results in increased sexual uncertainty. There was no gender difference in the effects on sexual uncertainty. Here, the discovered effects were also small. (Peter & Valkenburg 2008; 2010a). To conclude, a relatively small body of research suggests that SEIM may have an effect on youth's attitudes and behaviours.

15.6 Discussion

Research on the effects of sexualised content has consistently found that, if asked about the effects of pornography, people perceive pornography to affect others more than themselves. This is termed the *'third-person effect'* (Escobar-Chaves et al. 2005). In the contemporary debate about SEIM it seems that adults are 'we', discussing the SEIM use of 'them', i.e., youth being the third person. In this context the wording in research is striking: while adults use pornography, youth are exposed to SEIM. Apparently, adult's use of SEIM – universal in the western world (Döring 2009) – is not a topic for debate, while SEIM is deemed to be only damaging to youth. Recent research, however, suggests that the frequency of SEIM use is largely the same among adolescents and adults. Other new research indicates that exposure to SEIM increases sexual risk behaviour for adults and not for adolescents (Peter & Valkenburg, in press a; Peter & Valkenburg, in press b). It is obvious that the debate about SEIM follows an adult discourse of sex and sexuality. Since adult concern on the effects of SEIM on youth is considerable and; conversely, the evidence on the (negative) effects of SEIM on youth's behaviour and attitudes is small, it is important to place the debate and the research on SEIM in a broader context. Some youth are not harmed at all, others may experience negative effects and, some might even benefit from obtaining information on sex and gender roles fitting to their sexual preferences.

Key concepts

> Adolescents' media practice model (AMPM)
> Cultivation theory
> Moral panic
> Sexual explicit Internet material (SEIM)
> Social learning theory
> Third person effect

16 Cyberbullying: Defining, Understanding and Intervening

Sander Veenstra, Heidi Vandebosch & Michel Walrave

16.1 Introduction

Information and communication technologies such as the internet and mobile phones play an important role in the daily lives of youngsters. These media provide them with opportunities to learn, to be entertained and – especially important amongst adolescents – to keep in touch with peers. There are, however, also some ICT-related risks. Youngsters might be the target of, for instance, aggressive e-commercial actions, or grooming practices. Another, relatively recent, phenomenon is cyberbullying, where youngsters are not only involved as victims but also as perpetrators or bystanders of online (peer) aggression. Cyberbullying has already received a lot of attention from both the mass media (which, for instance, report on serious incidences where young people commit suicide after being bullied online) and from scholars in the fields of (school) psychology, communication science and criminology. In this chapter we will sketch the state-of-the-art with regard to research on cyberbullying, and discuss the practical implications of the research findings.

16.2 Definitions

Bullying also occurred before the emergence of cyberspace. The Norwegian scientist Dan Olweus has conducted numerous studies on 'traditional' bullying. He developed a definition for bullying that still forms the basis for a multiplicity of definitions used in scientific literature (e.g. Smith & Brain 2000; Smith Cowie, Olafsson & Liefooghe 2002). According to Olweus (1993: 9):

> "A student is being bullied or victimised when he or she is exposed, repeatedly and over time, to negative actions on the part of one or more other students." He furthermore states that (1993: 10): "In order to use the term bullying, there should be an imbalance in strength (as asymmetric power relationship): The student who is exposed to the negative actions has difficulty defending him/herself and is somewhat helpless against the student or students who harass."

Olweus (1993) argues that bullying consists of three key elements: (1) the bullying has to be intended to hurt another person; (2) it has to occur repeatedly over time and (3) there has to be a power imbalance between the bully and the victim.

There is no unambiguous definition for cyberbullying. Nevertheless, the key elements in definitions of traditional bullying repeatedly form the basis for definitions of cyberbullying as well. However, one element is added to definitions of cyberbullying: the bullying behaviour has to be conducted via ICT. Smith et al. (2008: 376), for example, define cyberbullying as: 'an aggressive, intentional act carried out by a group or individual, using electronic forms of contact, repeatedly and over time, against a victim who cannot easily defend him or herself' (other examples: Slonje & Smith 2008; Vandebosch, Van Cleemput, Mortelmans & Walrave 2006; Williams & Guerra 2007). In some studies, definitions are used that contain merely one or two of these elements (e.g. Patchin & Hinduja 2006).

Critique on definitions

It is questionable whether elements that form the basis for definitions of traditional bullying are applicable for cyberbullying. Determining the elements of intention, repetition and power imbalance in bullying behaviour that exclusively takes place in cyberspace is no sinecure (e.g. Wolak, Mitchell & Finkelhor 2007; Slonje & Smith 2008).

Firstly, determining whether cyberbullying is intentional appears to be problematic. Due to the lack of relational cues in cyberspace, youth find it difficult to interpret online expressions and behaviour (e.g. Dehue, Bolman & Vollink 2008; Kowalski & Limber 2007; Smith 2008). As a result, online messages that are not meant to intentionally hurt the recipient might be perceived as bullying behaviour. On the other hand, the recipient could interpret intentional cyberbullying behaviour as funny.

Furthermore, according to the definition, cyberbullying has to occur repeatedly over time. However, determining 'repetition' in cyberspace is problematic. For example, if a victim rereads an aggressive posting on the internet about him or her or if such a message becomes widely disseminated in cyberspace, does it stop at one incident or does it become a repeated act (David-Ferdon & Feldman Hertz 2007)? Slonje and Smith (2008: 154) therefore argue that 'figures based on the victim's awareness of frequency may thus be less reliable than for traditional bullying; and the use of repetition as a criterion for more serious bullying may be less reliable for cyberbullying'. In addition, there is no unambiguous instrument for measuring the frequency of online bullying. The timeframe used to determine the repetitiveness of cyberbullying differs across the studies: while some studies ask about students' involvement with cyberbullying in the past (school)year (e.g. Ybarra & Mitchell 2007; Williams & Guerra 2007), other studies refer to experiences during the last couple of months (Kowalski & Limber 2007), ask whether respondents have ever been involved in cyberbullying (Hinduja & Patchin 2008), or do not mention a reference period at all (Li 2007). Moreover, most studies do not document how frequent aggressive incidents have to occur within the chosen timeframe to call it bullying. Some authors refer to the cut-off point for traditional bullying: in that case (online) incidents are only called bullying when they occur monthly or more often. Since it is difficult to determine repetition in cyberspace, it is questionable whether this cut-off point is applicable for cyberbullying.

Finally, there is no consensus about the elements that determine a power imbalance in cyberspace. In traditional bullying, factors such as physical strength and popularity elicit a power imbalance between the bully and the victim (e.g. Patchin & Hinduja 2006). It is possible that offline bullies also bully their 'weaker' victims online. In that case, as long as the victim knows the identity of the perpetrator, the power imbalance remains. However, when a victim is exclusively bullied (anonymously) in cyberspace, offline components do not play a role (Strom & Strom 2005). With regard to cyberbullying, some authors suggest that ICT related factors such as superior technological knowledge (Jordan 1999) or anonymity (Raskauskas & Stolz 2007; Ybarra, Diener-West & Leaf 2007) could cause a power imbalance. However, these suggestions do not seem to be widely accepted in cyberbullying literature.
Simply adopting elements that form the basis for definitions of traditional bullying in definitions of cyberbullying is thus problematic, because cyberspace has its own dynamics. Although this problem is signalled in the literature, so far there is still no integrative and applicable definition of cyberbullying that has been agreed upon.

16.3 Forms

The literature mentions a wide variety of cyberbullying forms. There have also been several attempts to categorise them. Smith, Mahdavi, Carvalho and Tippet (2006), for instance, introduced a categorisation that is based on the technological platform that is used to bully. However, considering the continuous progression in technological developments, it is expected that this categorisation will soon be outdated. Therefore, a categorisation that is based on the behaviour of individuals is preferable (Ortega, Mora-Merchán & Jäger 2007; Walrave, Demoulin, Heirman & Van der Perre 2009).

A commonly used categorisation differentiates between direct and indirect forms of cyberbullying (e.g. Raskauskas & Stolz 2007; Van Rooij & Van den Eijnden 2007; Walrave et al. 2009). This distinction is derived from literature on traditional bullying (e.g. Stassen Berger 2007). Direct cyberbullying is also called 'to my face bullying' (Stassen Berger 2007: 95). It contains forms of cyberbullying in which the victim is directly involved. As is the case with traditional bullying, a distinction can be made between property, verbal, non-verbal and social forms of direct cyberbullying (see table 16.1) (Vandebosch & Van Cleemput 2009).

Table 16.1   Types of (cyber)bullying

Traditional bullying	Cyberbullying
Direct bullying – Property (e.g. damaging someone's personal belongings) – Verbal (e.g. calling someone names) – Non-verbal (e.g. making obscene gestures) – Social (excluding someone from a group)	*Direct bullying* – Property: purposely damaging the ICT of the victim (e.g. by sending a virus infected file) – Verbal (e.g. using the internet or mobile phone to insult or threaten) – Non-verbal (e.g. sending threatening or obscene pictures or movie clips) – Social (e.g. excluding someone from an online group by, for example, banning someone from a online game)
Indirect bullying – Spreading rumours	*Indirect bullying* – Denigration: e.g. spreading rumours online – Outing: 'public posting, sending, or forwarding personal communications or images, especially communications or images that contain intimate personal information or are potentially embarrassing' (Willard 2007: 9). – Impersonation: 'occurs when the cyberbully gains the ability to impersonate the target and post material that reflects badly on the target or interferes with the target's friendships. This may occur in the target's personal web page, profile, blog, or through any form of communication.' (Willard 2007: 8) – Taking part in voting on a defamatory polling website

Source: Vandebosch & Van Cleemput 2009.

Also noteworthy are the numerous possibilities that the internet and mobile phone offer for 'indirect' bullying. Indirect forms of cyberbullying can take place without direct involvement of the victim. These forms of cyberbullying are identified as 'behind my back bullying' (table 16.1) (Stassen Berger 2007: 95).

Since a huge variety of forms of cyberbullying are differentiated in the literature and because a multiplicity of terms is used to describe these forms, it is beyond the reach of this chapter to summarise all forms of cyberbullying. Nevertheless, based on traditional bullying classifications, table 16.1 provides a framework to divide forms of cyberbullying and presents some of the main forms of cyberbullying identified in the literature.

To illustrate how cyberbullying takes place, box 16.1 briefly describes the case of 'Moshzilla': a true story about a girl who was bullied on the internet.

Box 16.1   cyberbullying in practice: the case of 'Moshzilla'

A picture of 'Sam', a girl who was moshing – dancing in an aggressive manner – at a punk rock concert in 2005, was posted on the web. Via Photoshop, an image-editing program, the picture was repeatedly altered in humiliating ways and redistributed in cyberspace numerous times. Many of the photoshopped images of 'Moshzilla' are still online. At the time of writing, Google, for example, finds 4270 pictures of Moshzilla within a second. Sam has been very upset by the pictures.

Source: Hinduja & Patchin 2009.

221

16.4 Prevalence of cyberbullying

A large number of studies have been conducted to determine the prevalence of cyberbullying. However, the results of these studies vary widely. For instance, with regard to cyberbullying victimisation, the percentages range between 5.3% (Slonje & Smith 2008) and 72% (Juvonen & Gross 2008). For cyberbullying perpetration, percentages vary between 4% (Kowalski & Limber 2007) and 29% (Ybarra & Mitchell 2007). These differences are caused by the fact that there is no unambiguous operational definition to measure the prevalence of cyberbullying. David-Ferdon and Feldman Hertz (2007: s2) signal this problem and conclude that 'the variety of terms used and the lack of a standardised operational definition make it extremely difficult to pool results and draw conclusions across the limited studies'.

Nevertheless, cyberbullying studies do reveal some common tendencies. It appears that the majority of aggressive incidents in cyberspace are incidental rather than repetitive in nature (e.g. Dehue et al. 2008; Juvonen & Gross 2008; Ybarra & Mitchell 2007). Since the use of repetition as a criterion for more serious bullying is questionable, all aggressive incidents – whether incidental or repetitive – are referred to as bullying in most studies. Dehue et al. (2008), for example, found that 17.2% of their Dutch respondents (N=1211) had been victims of cyberbullying once or twice in the previous school year whilst (only) 4.7% of their respondents had been victims of online bullying at least once or twice a month. In addition, studies that measure the monthly occurrence of either cyberbullying perpetration or cyberbullying victimisation commonly find that 10% or less of the respondents are either a bully or a victim (Cassidy 2009; Dehue et al. 2008; Hinduja & Patchin 2009; Van Rooij & Van den Eijnden 2007; Slonje & Smith 2008; Smith et al. 2006/2008; Wang et al. 2011; Ybarra et al. 2007).

Furthermore, it is commonly found that cyberbullying is less prevalent than traditional bullying (e.g. Juvonen & Gross 2008; Williams & Guerra 2007). Nevertheless, Mishna, Saini and Solomon (2009) conducted seven focus groups with 38 students aged 10 to 14 years old (between fifth and eight grades) and found that youth indicate cyberbullying as a serious problem. In addition, in a survey among 2,052 primary and secondary school children Vandebosch and Van Cleemput (2009) found that the majority of their respondents (63.8%) perceive cyberbullying as a 'big problem'.

16.5 Roles in cyberbullying

As in the case of traditional bullying, it is possible to distinguish between three types of role in cyberbullying. Apart from the cyberbullies and the victims, there are also the bystanders. Studies investigating the profiles of the individuals involved in these categories often concentrate on socio-demographic (gender, age) and psychosocial characteristics. Furthermore, researchers also focus on ICT-related variables (i.e. frequency of internet use, online risk behaviour, parental supervision of internet use) and involvement in traditional bullying.

Cyberbullies

The findings with regard to the gender of cyberbullies are inconsistent. While some studies found slightly more males among cyberbullies (e.g. Aricak 2008; Li 2006; Slonje & Smith 2008), others did not find significant gender differences (Patchin & Hinduja 2006; Smith 2008; Walrave & Heirman 2009), or reported that girls outnumbered boys (Kowalski & Limber 2007). Nevertheless this literature suggests that girls, who are less often bullies in real life (Ladd 2005), might catch up in cyberspace. They, more than boys, use the internet primarily for social reasons (e.g. Livingstone, Haddon, Görzig &

Olafsson 2010) and prefer indirect forms of bullying (Griffin & Gross 2004; Stassen Berger 2007) which, for example due to anonymity, are relatively easy to conduct in cyberspace.

There is also no consensus with regard to the typical age of cyberbullies. However, most studies seem to indicate that cyberbullying is more common amongst secondary school students than amongst primary school children, with a peak in early adolescence at the age of 14-15 years old (e.g. Vandebosch 2006; Williams & Guerra 2007; Slonje & Smith 2008).

As for internet use, cyberbullies are found to be youngsters who make more use of the internet in general (e.g. Smith et al. 2008; Aricak 2008; Twyman 2010; Walrave & Heirman 2009) or certain (social) applications in particular (e.g. Instant Messaging as in the study of Ybarra & Mitchell 2004). Regarding ICT related variables, some studies furthermore found that most cyberbullies anonymously bully their victims (e.g. Kowalski & Limber 2007; Williams & Guerra 2007). However, other studies found that most bullies do not hide their identities (Dehue 2008; Juvonen & Gross 2008). Cyberbullies also report significantly lower levels of parental monitoring (of their internet activities) than other youngsters (Ybarra & Mitchell 2004; Dehue 2008, Vandebosch & Van Cleemput 2009).

The psychosocial characteristics which have been positively associated with cyberbullies are moral approval of bullying, feeling disconnected from the school, lack of perceived peer support (Williams & Guerra 2007), lower scores at school and family measures of self-esteem (Patchin & Hinduja 2010) and a deficiency in affective and cognitive empathy (Ang & Goh 2010; Schultze-Krumbholz & Scheithauer 2009). The latter is partly attributed to the nature of ICT mediated communication: the absence of non-verbal communication cues may motivate people to share their most intimate emotions, fears and desires with each other (also called *benign* disinhibition (Suler 2004)), but also induce them to use rude language, hatred and threats (so-called *toxic* disinhibition (Suler 2004)). More particularly, the lack of immediate emotional feedback from the victim is argued to cause a *"cockpit effect"*. Just like fighter pilots who are not directly confronted with the suffering they cause and are therefore facilitated in their actions (e.g. De Laender 1996; Lorenz 1974), cyberbullies sitting at their computer feel disinhibited because direct emotional feedback from their 'target' is absent (Heirman & Walrave 2008).

Finally, there appears to be a strong overlap between being the perpetrator and being the victim of cyberbullying (Li 2007; Vandebosch & Van Cleemput 2009; Walrave & Heirman 2009), and between involvement in cyberbullying and traditional bullying as perpetrator (Li 2007; Raskauskas & Stoltz 2007; Smith 2008; Vandebosch & Van Cleemput 2009). Studies by Ybarra and Mitchell (2004) and Hinduja and Patchin (2008) furthermore show that 'online aggressors' are also more often involved in other types of problematic behaviour (such as purposefully damaging property, stealing and the consumption of cigarettes or alcohol).

Victims of cyberbullying

In accordance with the research results for cyberbullies, there are inconsistent findings with regard to the gender and age of cyberbullying victims. However, most studies and especially those that investigate the relationship between gender and cyberbullying, after controlling for a wide range of other variables, such as involvement in traditional bullying, find that the risks of becoming a victim of cyberbullying are equal for girls and boys (e.g. Hinduja & Patchin 2008; Vandebosch & Van Cleemput 2009). With regard to the age of the cyberbullying victims, most evidence (again) seems to point to 12-15 year olds as the age group with the highest risk of cyberbullying victimisation (e.g. Slonje & Smith 2008; Calvete et al. 2010).

Moreover, the total amount of internet use (Patchin & Hinduja 2006), the use of certain social applications such as Instant Messaging (IM) (Ybarra 2004) or IM and webcams (Juvonen & Gross 2008), the engagement in online risk behaviour – such as passing on passwords of email or IM accounts or publishing personal information on a blog (Walrave & Heirman 2009) – and internet dependency (Vandebosch & Van Cleemput 2009) are predictors of cyberbullying victimisation. However they seem to be less important predictors than the following (cyber)bullying related variables: involvement in cyberbullying as a perpetrator (or bystander), and being the victim of traditional bullying (e.g. Juvonen & Gross 2008; Li 2007, Vandebosch & Van Cleemput 2009).

Although most studies on the negative 'impact' of cyberbullying rely on cross-sectional data (which makes real causal inferences impossible), they seem to suggest that cyberbullying might have similar types of health and school related consequences as have traditional bullying. For instance, victims of cyberbullying often experience more stress and depressive-like symptoms (Ybarra 2004; Patchin & Hinduja 2006). Juvonen and Gross (2008) also found a positive relationship between the number of bullying experiences and the reported level of social anxiety. Mason (2008) mentioned that the related symptoms and issues included: low self-esteem, poor academic performance, depression, emotional distress, and, in some cases, violence or even suicide (see also: Finkelhor, Mitchell & Wolak 2000; Raskauskas & Stolz 2007, Hinduja & Patchin 2010).

The severity of the impact (compared to traditional bullying) seems however to be highly dependent on the form of cyberbullying that was used. In the study of Smith et al. (2008), for instance, picture/video clip bullying were perceived as having more impact than traditional bullying, while chat room bullying was perceived as having less impact (all other kinds of cyberbullying had similar impact factors to traditional bullying).

Bystanders of cyberbullying

In line with studies on traditional bullying, several cyberbullying studies have asked respondents whether they have witnessed cyberbullying behaviour (by and against others). These studies indicate that a large proportion of young-sters have indeed been 'bystanders' of cyberbullying. For instance, in a recent school survey in Taiwan (Huang & Chou 2010) 63.4% of 7th-9th grade students reported having witnessed or having been aware of cyberbullying. As in the case of traditional bullying, bystanders were not likely to take action. As a possible explanation, Huang and Chou (2010: 1588) mentioned that "A prevalent idea was that people considered the act of reporting neither their business nor their responsibility and that the cyberbullying itself was 'no big deal'". Another study found that peers are not always aware of strategies they can use to be helpful for the victim (Agatson et al. 2007).

225

16.6 Conclusion: which interventions to consider

In addition to the aforementioned research findings on the nature and extent of cyberbullying a discussion of possible interventions has emerged. It is argued that, given the overlap between traditional bullying and cyberbullying, existing anti-bullying programmes might be (partly) suited to tackle cyber-bullying (e.g. Mason 2008; Williams & Guerra 2007). This is for instance evident from the evaluation of the large-scale Finnish anti-bullying interven-tion "KiVa", which appears to be effective in reducing both traditional and cyberbullying (Salmivalli 2010). On the other hand, cyberbullying has some unique features, which seem to require an adjusted approach (within a global anti-bullying programme). The latter idea is also reflected in the current initia-tives specifically aimed at cyberbullying (from policy makers, educators, ISPs, internet safety organisations) and the emerging, more evidence-based, inter-ventions against cyberbullying (see for instance: Menisini & Nocentini 2010; Steffgen, König & Pfetsch 2009). These underline that cyberbullying inter-ventions may target actors that are not typically involved in traditional (school) bullying interventions. Besides children/adolescents, teachers, and parents, also Internet Service Providers, for instance, constitute an important actor. Since cyberbullying often takes place outside school (although both its causes and effects might still be found there), the role of parents and other actors are probably also more important than in cases of traditional bullying. Furthermore, these anti-cyberbullying actions, underline the need to promote "new media literacy" skills (necessary to act "correctly" in cyberspace, or to avoid or adequately handle online risks), apart from the (social or coping) skills that are typically enhanced in traditional anti-bullying programs.

When we look at the very limited number of evaluated intervention programs against cyberbullying, it is clear that most of them are small scale, and often not only focused on cyberbullying. Examples of these types of interventions are the I-SAFE cyber safety program (Chibnall, Walace, Leicht & Lunghofer 2006) and the Missing cyber safety program (Crombie & Trineer 2003). A major goal of these interventions was to create awareness amongst youngsters about different types of risks that are associated with the internet. While these programs did seem to be effective in increasing knowledge in students (e.g. regarding how to manage risks online, how to identify internet predators, how to protect personal information), they were unsuccessful in changing internet related safety attitudes or behaviour (such as disclosing personal information or participating in open chat rooms with strangers). In addition, the HAHA-SO program, an in-school program developed to tackle both traditional and cyberbullying, did not change the number of reported cyberbullying incidents experienced by the participants (Salvatore 2006). Another recent, unevaluated initiative is "CyberTraining", a research-based training specifically on cyberbullying. This manual primarily addresses trainers from across Europe working with schools, parents and young people affected by or dealing with cyberbullying on various levels (more information: http://www.cybertraining-project.org/).

The above initiatives seem to indicate an academic shift from problem-analytic to intervention oriented research about cyberbullying. At this juncture, however, it is still unclear how cyberbullying amongst youngsters could best be tackled.

Key concepts

Cyberbullying
Direct cyberbullying
Indirect cyberbullying
Disinhibition
Bystanders (cyberbullying)

17 The Perils and Pleasures of Playing Videogames

Jeroen Jansz & Tony van Rooij

17.1 Introduction

While videogames enjoy an increasing popularity among an ever-expanding audience, the public image of videogames is very much associated with controversy. In this chapter we aim to present a balanced perspective on the negative phenomena that are associated with gaming. A video, or computer game, is an interactive rule-based system for playing, enabled by computer processing power. We will focus on research covering three main 'perils' of gaming. We first address the relationship between violent game content and real life aggression. Secondly, we will deal with the risk of game addiction, and thirdly we will look at the negative consequences of cheating and other kinds of foul play. Our discussion of negative effects concentrates on entertainment games, which almost exclusively consist of so-called Commercial 'Off The Shelf' Games (COTS). We then look at the positive effects and pleasures of gaming in order to counterbalance the debate on negative aspects of gaming. We will present research on what motivates people to play, and what cognitive and social benefits can be attributed to gaming.

17.2 Who plays what?

The large majority of gamers are either children or adolescents (ISFE 2008; Pratchett 2005). Most enthusiasm was found in the youngest group of 6 to 12 year olds. They all played the short 'casual games' on the internet (for example, *Bejeweled* or *Minesweeper*). More than 40% of this age group played the more complicated *online multiplayer games*, such as *Runescape* (Mijn Kind Online 2009; Pratchett 2005). Some children lose interest in gaming as they grow older, but estimates are that about 80% of adolescents continue playing (Pratchett 2005; Van Rooij Schoenmakers, Meerkerk & Van de Mheen 2008). For most, gaming has become a common pastime. Adolescents report spending about one to one and a half hours per day on gaming. About 8% spend two and a half hours or more on games per day (ISFE 2008; Roberts & Foehr 2008; Van Rooij et al. 2008).

Contemporary video game culture is strongly gender biased. In general, boys play more often and longer than girls. During childhood the gender differences in time spent on gaming are not large, but from about 12 years on, female gamers become a minority (Krotoski 2004; Nikken 2003; Pratchett 2005). The gender bias is related to the fact that most video games are 'green-brown games' covering stereotypical male interests and targeted at a (young) male audience (Jansz & Vosmeer 2009). The green and brown colours of their packaging aptly reflect a content that is often about fighting wars in camouflage attire, or playing sports matches on green fields. Female characters are underrepresented, and generally appear in submissive positions with an emphasis on their virtual breasts and buttocks (Beasley & Collins Standley 2002; Jansz & Martis 2007). Girls' preferences are catered to with 'pink games' aiming to appeal to a (young) female audience with bright colours and game content relating to traditional female roles, like nursing and caring. Pink games are criticised for their traditional, if not stereotypical, portrayal of female gender roles (Jenkins & Cassell 2008; Vosmeer, 2010).

17.3   The perils of playing

Violence copied

A major issue of concern is the possible effect of playing games on behaviour in real life. Most research was dedicated to aggression, that is, acts in which someone intends to inflict pain or suffering on someone else. The earliest effect studies found that people, mostly male children and adolescents, who spent a lot of time on games scored higher on aggression scales than people who did not play video games. Heavy players were also found to receive lower grades in school (Anderson & Dill 2000; Funk et al. 2002). More recently, a wider range of effects was included in the studies. Researchers found, for example, an increase in aggressive feelings and thoughts towards peers, increasing levels of arousal as measured by heart rate and blood pressure, as well as a decrease in altruistic behaviour (Barlett, Anderson & Swing 2009; Lee & Peng 2006). Other researchers used the severity of punishment by students inflicted on fellow pupils as a measure for aggression. They found that players of violent games punished more severely that those playing non-violent games (Anderson, Gentile & Buckley 2007; Lemmens, Bushman & Konijn 2006).

The first meta-analyses underlined what was established in individual studies: playing violent video games has a small effect on aggression. Surprisingly, the effects of gaming were less than the effects of watching violent film or television content. Some attributed this to games being less realistic than film or TV, others argued that it was due to the difference between player and viewer.

As players pulled the trigger themselves, they may have felt the need to disso-ciate themselves from the killing (Jansz 2005). A recent meta-analysis expand-ed upon the primarily Western focus of previous research by also including studies from Asian countries. The meta-analysis confirmed the small effect established earlier and also reported that cultural differences in effects of vio-lent games were minimal (Anderson et al. 2010).

Game effects research has been seriously criticised by fellow researchers (Ferguson & Kilburn 2010; Goldstein 2005). The artificiality of playing in a research laboratory was a common point of criticism. In most studies research participants were briefly exposed to violent content with subsequent measure-ment of aggression. Obviously, research ethics prohibit inducing real aggres-sion in the laboratory, but some of the indirect measurements used were considered questionable. For example, rough physical play among boys after a gaming session may not be the best indicator of their aggression, as many boys tend to play roughly. Another critical issue is the duration of the effects. The level of aggression was typically measured immediately after play. As a result, there is hardly any evidence about long term effects. In one of the few longitudinal studies where verbal aggression among online gamers was meas-ured repeatedly, an increase in aggression could not be established (Williams & Skoric 2005).

229

The critical appreciation of effects research raises serious questions about whether playing violent video games increases real life aggression. This does not mean, however, that negative effects of gaming are non-existent. However, the effects may be indirect and as much dependent on playing violent games as they are on other factors, for example, on the ways in which families cope with aggressive behaviour (Nikken 2007).

Game addiction

Recently, public concern about the perils of playing video games shifted some-what from violence to addiction. Box 17.1 shows some examples of extreme behaviour involving gaming. Of course these incidents cannot be generalised to the gaming population since millions play without problems, but these dis-tressing news reports do raise concerns about the consequences of extended play. The Diagnostic and Statistical Manual of Mental Disorders (DSM-IV) issued by the American Psychiatric Association (2000) does not include exces-sive or compulsory forms of video gaming as an addiction in its current form. However, the current debate on the next incarnation of the DSM contains proposals for a more unified approach to addiction, which includes excessive behaviour such as internet and potentially game addiction (APA 2010).

Box 17.1   Some extreme cases

Shocking incidents are occasionally reported in the media such as the example of a 14 year old English boy who had to be treated for serious thrombosis after a full day of gaming, a 28 year old online gamer in South Korea died after playing for 50 hours with few breaks and a South Korean gaming couple that was arrested for neglect which allegedly caused their 3-month-old child to starve (Cho 2010). The most widely publicized was the death of 'Snowly' a young Chinese girl playing *World of Warcraft* (WoW) for days. Her death was virtually commemorated by an online funeral in WoW (Murano 2009).

At the behavioural level, 'game addiction' manifests itself as spending excessive amounts of time on gaming. However, this does not mean that all heavy gamers are addicted. In this regard, West provides a useful pragmatic definition of addiction: "Nowadays the term 'addiction' is applied to a syndrome at the centre of which is impaired control over a behaviour, and this loss of control is leading to significant harm. The fact that there is harm is important because otherwise addiction would be of limited interest." (West & Hardy 2006: 10). As such, researchers expect to see a variety of (self-reported) negative symptoms before even considering declaring cases of excessive gaming to be instances of 'addiction'.

Over time, researchers have developed various criteria to demarcate addiction from excessive play (Griffiths 2005; Lemmens, Valkenburg & Peter 2009; Van Rooij, Schoenmakers, Vermulst, Van den Eijnden & Van de Mheen 2011). The first is *mood modification*: games are used to create and regulate feelings. This includes inciting arousal (a 'high'), but also a tranquil sense of relaxation. The second is *withdrawal*. It is concerned with the unpleasant feelings gamers report when they cannot play. *Salience* is the third and it refers to mental preoccupation with gaming that extends to moments when gamers do not play. *Conflict* is the fourth and it points to interpersonal conflicts about gaming with, for example, parents, peers and teachers. It also points to conflicts occurring between gaming and other activities (e.g. school, work, other hobbies). The fifth criterion is *Relapse*: the gamer wants to minimise his game time, but repeatedly fails to succeed in doing so. *Tolerance* is the sixth criterion: an addicted gamer needs to invest an increasing amount of time in order to experience the desired mental effect.

The criteria were applied in survey research exploring the scope of game addiction. Researchers report slightly different estimates, but they agree on the relative proportion of addiction among adolescent gamers: a small group of about 1% to 3% can be labeled 'addicted' (Lemmens et al. 2009; Van Rooij et al. 2008, 2011). Boys were more likely to play excessively than girls and they also showed more signs of pathological involvement (Lemmens 2010). Other researchers pointed to the relation between game genre and the peril of addiction. Players of the open ended large scale online multi-player games (e.g., *World of Warcraft, Runescape*) are particularly prone to excessive time investment (Smyth 2007). Mental health institutions started offering professional treatment for addicted gamers (Rooij, Zinn, Schoenmakers & Mheen 2010; Van den Eijnden, Van Rooij & Meerkerk 2007). Thus far the clinics have not received a major influx of either gamers or concerned parents. While numbers are seemingly growing in anecdotic field reports, the professional treatment of video game addiction remains incidental for now (Meerkerk, Van Rooij, Amadmoestar & Schoenmakers 2009). While this could indicate that it may take some time before gamers in peril realise that professional help is available for their problem, it may also simply mean that this 'addiction' is a temporary phenomenon for most gamers.

Cheating

Cheating in play is about breaking the rules to gain an advantage. Most kinds of cheating are fairly innocent, for example when players use cheat-codes to take a shortcut in the game. Other kinds of cheating may have grim consequences for other players, for example in cases of theft and fraud. Researchers estimate that cheating is growing rapidly, but the empirical research backing this observation is very limited (Yan & Randell 2005). We will first characterise cheating in general terms and then discuss the insights we drew from the limited number of studies that were published. In the first systematic study of cheating in video games Mia Consalvo (2007) showed that cheaters engage in the activity for a wide range of reasons. Most were stuck in the game and used cheats to be able to play on or to save time. Others wanted to find out how far they could bend the rules or beat the game code. A small group used cheats to engage in "grief play", i.e. playing with the aim of disadvantaging others. Cheating in the virtual world employs practices that have much in common with crime in the real world (Yan & Randell 2005). Theft of virtual property is a major example. In 2007, a Dutch 17-year-old was arrested for stealing about

4,000 euros worth of virtual furniture in the online game Habbo (Murano 2009). Thieves generally exploit misplaced trust of fellow players to pursue identity theft. In the Habbo case, children were lured to a fake Habbo website where they had to log in with their username and password to receive attractive goods. Taiwan was among the countries where the popularity of massive multiplayer online role- playing games (MMORPG) such as *Lineage Online*, *Everquest*, *World of Warcraft* and *Runescape* peaked early. A systematic analysis of about 600 cases of online gaming crime in Taiwan provides more insight into what this type of crime amounts to (Chen et al. 2005). The majority of gaming crime was theft (74%) and fraud (20%). The offenders mostly used identity theft (43%) and "social engineering" (44%) that often amounted to persuading or tricking players into breaking normal safety procedures. About 64% of the offenders were between 15 and 20 years of age. The perpetrators committed their crimes almost exclusively in *Lineage Online* (94%), with internet cafés as the actual crime scene in more than half of the cases (55%). This context underlines the local situation, as Taiwan is one of the countries where MMORPGs are played in public spaces rather than at home.

It has been observed that the market for illegal property within MMORPGs is growing. It has led to 'gold farming' where people play just for the sake of acquiring in-game valuables (e.g. virtual gold) in order to sell it to players who would rather pay money than spend time on improving their avatar's qualities. A survey among almost 2,000 MMORPG players showed that 22% of the players said they had purchased virtual currency. It was also established that older players were slightly more active in this real money transfer (RMT) than younger players (Yee 2005). The epicenter of gold farming is China, where gold farmers often are exploited by bosses who force them to work long hours under dubious circumstances (Heeks 2008). In 2009 it was reported that the Chinese government issued regulations limiting the opportunities for gold farming (Claburn 2009). Game publishers have taken their own measures as well, for example by prohibiting gold farming and other kinds of RMT in the End User License Agreement (EULA) players must accept before they can start playing the game.

Game developers and publishers increasingly appear to take cheating seriously. Cheating hurts the publisher's reputation and it often has serious economic consequences, for example when access codes are hacked enabling gamers to play for free instead of paying their monthly dues (i.e. the case of the Playstation 3 root access keys becoming available on the internet in early 2011), or when players leave a game because they no longer feel safe. Most MMORPGs employ automated and human supervisors to police the virtual world and uphold the local rules. Some online games also use players themselves, by asking them to report on cheating, idling, botting, and other kinds of deviant behaviour. For example, Habbo hires bona fide players to help patrol the game for adults who impersonate children (Consalvo 2007; Slot 2009).

Dealing with the three perils

The perils of being a vicitim of cheating in an online game, developing a game addiction or imitating violent game content are unavoidably tied up with actually playing specific games. The possible perils could be dealt with in a crude fashion, for example by not going online, limiting the length of game sessions and only playing non-violent titles. One can safely assume that these coping strategies will not work in day to day practice as they seriously limit what makes gaming attractive in the first place. Thus parents and other caretakers may have to consider employing other ways to protect children and adolescents from possible negative consequences. Researchers of youth and media generally agree that parental involvement matters (Livingstone, Haddon, Görzig & Ólafsson 2011; Nikken & Jansz 2006; Rideout, Foehr & Roberts 2010). Knowing what children play, how long they play, with whom they play, and what their preferences are creates a common ground for discussing the consequences of gaming. If necessary, parents should not be afraid of complementing the discussion with home rules incorporating PEGI's ratings and rules about the length of play. Coping with the perils of cheating and other crimes requires more, however, than discussing games and restricting play. Basic security measures are necessary, for example never sharing personal account data online, running anti-virus software, and reporting suspicious online encounters. It is also advisable to raise child and adolescent awareness about their password quality. The game publisher could support this by online tests of username and password efficacy, providing alternative identity confirmation (i.e. the Warcraft mobile phone authenticator), as well as by requiring password changes at regular intervals (Chen et al. 2005).

17.4 The pleasures and benefits of play

While the previous three perils are very real and should be taken seriously, the majority of gamers will either never experience them, or only to a minor extent. We would therefore like to conclude this chapter by summarising recent research findings on the pleasures and benefits of play (see also box 17.2).

Video games are unique among entertainment media because they enable players to identify beyond identification: gamers can enact, or perform, a particular identity in the most literal sense of the word. The actual opportunities for assuming a virtual identity are of course dependent on the characteristics of specific genres and titles. For example, one could be a fighter pilot for as long as the game lasts, or embrace Niko Bellic's (*Grand Theft Auto 4*) violent performance of masculine identity, or temporarily assume Lionel Messi's professional identity as a striker in *FIFA12*. Controlling one's character opens up rich possibilities for experimenting with virtual identities. The video game itself turns into a laboratory providing a safe personal context where players interact individually with their personal computer or game console. Moreover, the game also provides a safe social context because experimenting is often done with like-minded individuals (Jansz, Avis & Vosmeer 2010).

The effects on the player's cognitive system have been well established. The earliest effect studies were mostly concerned with educational computer games showing positive effects on, for example, problem solving, memory and the processing of spatial information (Subrahmanyam, Greenfield, Kraut & Gross 2001). The positive cognitive effects were underlined in a meta-analysis showing also that benefits were highest in contexts where players were free to decide what to play and when (Vogel et al. 2006). Recent research also included Commercial Off The Shelf (COTS) entertainment games. For example, cognitive benefits were assessed in a series of studies among players of the complex 3-D war game *Medal of Honor* (Dye, Green & Bavelier 2009; Green & Bavelier 2003, 2007). The participants were trained for 1 hour per day for 10 consecutive days. A second group, the control group, played the puzzle game *Tetris* which is less cognitively demanding. After 10 days, only the *Medal of Honor* gamers showed a significant increase in their cognitive operations. Apparently, a relatively short period of playing was enough to provide positive results.

Video games are also linked to the improvement of various relationships. Playing a video game often teaches players tacitly how to interact with each other. The social effect is particularly evident at the end of primary school and is slightly stronger among boys than girls (Von Salisch, Oppl & Kristen 2006). Given the fact that boys (at least in US schools) tend to perform worse than girls, the benefits of gaming have led some authors to argue that a game oriented learning environment might well be extra beneficial for boys, given their preferred learning style (Carr-Chellman 2011). Moreover, online games provide ample opportunities for playing with – or against – each other.

234

Research among adolescent gamers showed that they were also drawn to their online games for social reasons. Some gamers, for example, appreciated the competition among friends, while others liked helping other players or collaborating on in-game missions (Axelsson & Regan 2006; Jansz & Tanis 2007; Yee, 2006). Online social worlds such as Whyville and Habbo were appreciated by their inhabitants because of the opportunity to meet old and new friends (Kafai, Fields & Cook 2010; Slot 2009). These positive social effects challenge the stereotype of the adolescent *nerd* who is totally involved in gaming with no discernible social life. Game researcher Durkin (2006) affirmed the social benefits by arguing that he, personally, would be worried if a young adolescent did not play (online) games.

Box 17.2   Motives for playing

When players like to be challenged, they can pick fast paced games on football, or shooting and killing, but also simulation games like Sim City or ZooTycoon. Some titles promise to gratify specific needs. The Sims, for example, was appreciated because the game offers ample opportunities for tinkering and building (Jansz et al. 2010). On the other hand, players of the online First Person Shooter Counterstrike were motivated by competition. However, satisfying this need went hand in hand with satisfying social needs as gamers really liked to team up with their mates in a *clan* to fight other, enemy *clans* online (Jansz & Martens 2005; Jansz & Tanis 2007). American researchers included different game genres in their study of the motivations of young players. They found that challenge was the most important motive, followed by competition, diversion, arousal, fantasy and social interaction. Furthermore, the boys scored higher on all motives than the girls, but the order of ranking of motives was the same for both genders (Sherry, Lucas, Greenberg & Lachlan 2006). In a Dutch study carried out among 300 children, it was apparent that being challenged was clearly an important element of the games. The young players were asked what was important in a good game. The challenge of being able to 'win' a game was ranked as the number one reason to play, followed closely by the possibility of being able to determine the course of the game themselves (Nikken 2000).

235

17.5 Conclusions

The research results we discussed in this chapter show that playing video games is not without risks and involves several perils. Young or otherwise vulnerable players may run the risk of being incited to aggressive thoughts or feelings when they play violent titles meant for an older audience. In their enthusiasm, they may also develop a compulsive gaming habit that, in some cases, could be labeled as an addiction. In the case of social, online gaming there is the potential peril of being victimised by cheaters. By contrast, the research has also shown that gaming can result in cognitive and social benefits. In developing a balanced view on the perils and pleasures of gaming we must take the scale of these phenomena into account. Millions of young people habitually play video games without any problem.

Moreover, given the shocking incidents that are occasionally linked by the media to video game play it can be quite a challenge to maintain a balanced perspective, and not be led astray by these extreme examples. We believe that game researchers have an obligation to contribute their understanding of these phenomena to the public, providing a 'big picture' in which to contextualise the incidents. Our hope is that this chapter will be appreciated as a contribution to this aim.

Key concepts

Addiction (to gaming)
Aggression
Cheating (in gaming)
Videogame
Violent video game

Part 4
Internet & Regulation

18 Fighting Cyber Crime: an Integral Approach

Rutger Leukfeldt & Evelien de Pauw

18.1 Introduction

To function well, a society needs to maintain a certain degree of order and continuity. Safety is an important precondition in that context. In years past, safety was purely a question of protection against dangers from the tangible world. A world alongside that old world emerged in the form of 'cyberspace' in the 1990s (Stol 2008). Since then the classical offline world and the new online world have become increasingly intertwined (Leukfeldt et al. 2010). A safe internet is an internet where (and with which) no crime can be committed, where the safety of persons is not otherwise in jeopardy, and which provides a predictable continuity. That last is important not only for the safety or well-being of individual internet users, but also for the untrammelled functioning of the economic system – and thus for a well-functioning society as a whole.

Boutellier (2005) uses football as metaphor to distinguish three main groups of players involved in ensuring safety. For a start, citizens in the forward line play a significant role in fighting cyber hazards. They can themselves demonstrate safe behaviour, by taking precautionary measures for instance, exercising social control and signalling problems. Then there is a midfield consisting of institutions that do not have safety as their primary objective, but play a role in the safety paradigm. Examples of these are housing corporations and schools. Lastly there is a line of defence in the form of institutions that have safety as their prime concern. These players are the police, the judiciary and private security companies.

Safety is an area in which diverse organisations and disciplines work side by side. That is equally true with regard to safety in cyberspace. Jewkes and Yar (2008) note that many of the monitoring, regulatory, protection and enforcement activities relating to cyber crime are not the sole responsibility of state-controlled police forces. 'The scope, scale and structure of the internet outstrip the capacity of any single enforcement or regulatory body' (Jewkes & Yar 2008: 582). These two researchers, but also others like Stol (2008) argue that tackling cyber crime requires a joined up approach between individuals, private sector agencies and the police.

If we take Boutellier's football metaphor as our starting point, we see that various kinds of player indeed have a role in tackling cyber crime. In the front line, private individuals safeguard the security of their own computers by installing virus scanners, firewalls and the like. At midfield, Internet Service Providers (ISPs) ensure that spam emails don't reach their customers, and managers of weblogs and discussion forums remove undesired reactions to postings. At defence we find commercial companies whose job is to protect computer networks or supply protective aids such as virus scanners. Police and the courts also play their part in this backline.

In this chapter we focus on that integral approach to the fight against cyber crime. We identify the parties occupying the forward line, midfield and defence (paragraphs 18.2, 18.3 and 18.4 respectively). We then discuss a form of collaboration that plays a significant part in combating cyber crime: the public-private partnership (PPP). We describe a PPP of this kind in paragraph 17.5. Lastly we describe what implications cyber crime has by its very nature for the parties participating in the battle to curb it.

18.2 The forward line

Individual internet users (termed 'end users') in the forward line play an important role. In this paragraph we first indicate what we mean by 'informal social control' and then describe what end users themselves can do to make the internet safe or safer.

Informal social control

Wherever people get together, instrumentation is needed to maintain social order. Informal social control is a form of order maintenance that is undertaken by citizens. This kind of control is given shape by the reactions of individuals and groups to norms and laws, and includes peer and community pressure to act in certain ways. In our society today, informal social control is eroding under the impact of individualism. In an online environment, informal social control can be well organised. People in the virtual world are often participants in online communities like Facebook, MSN Messenger or online discussion groups. One of the most common regulatory procedures in such communities is shaming or online reputation management. The virtual offender is given a bad reputation or a bad comment. In these social spaces where the constraining effects of the family are lacking (unless family members are also present online), the bonds with other 'netizens' and the online community are just as significant as offline ties. In commercial online spaces like eBay and Amazon, for example, forming good relationships with buyers is key to gaining a reliable reputation as a seller. Similarly, in purely social spaces like Cyberworlds and Secondlife, strong relationships are important to sustaining a favourable reputation and status. Online acts of shaming invariably draw on such ties, seeking either to humiliate the wrongdoer or to draw on their classical conditioning in an attempt to induce feelings of guilt (Wall 2007). This procedure can restrain perpetrators from certain acts. It creates a kind of moral censure, although in more extreme cases the offending behaviour is reported to relevant authorities (Wall 2005). Depending on the types of behaviour that are betrayed, internet users will react through their own mechanisms or ask for help from other actors. More about this in chapter 1.

The role of individual internet users

End users can themselves take an important step in protecting themselves against cyber criminals. First, they should maintain the security of their own computers, for example by installing virus scanners and firewalls and keeping these up to date. End users also need to give conscious thought to their online activities (e.g. concerning the type of personal information they share online through social media, and the type of websites they download from). That way end users not only protect their own computer, but can also guard against their computer becoming part of a botnet that is used by criminals to commit other forms of cyber crime, to name one example (see chapter 12).

241

Box 18.1   influencing individual internet users

Although end users must above all be alert to their own behaviour, national governments and private sector parties also have a role in this. For example they can put safer computer equipment on the market, draw up new legislation, or launch awareness campaigns concerning internet safety. Many European governments are currently taking action on awareness campaigns. These may be effective in making end users more cautious about the dangers of the internet and ways of protecting themselves. One example at European level is the Safer Internet Programme, whose aims are to support legislative initiatives, establish a registration desk for network users, raise the awareness of target groups and develop a knowledge centre (Leeuw 2009).

18.3 Midfield

Midfield is where different players have a role in exercising secondary informal social control. Among these players are ISPs, hardware and software manufacturers, internet reporting sites, pressure groups, schools and libraries. In this paragraph we explain what we understand by this form of informal social control. We then look briefly at the part played by ISPs and some international initiatives by interest groups.

Secondary informal social control

Alongside informal social control exercised by individual citizens on grounds of rules in society, informal social control may also be exercised by organisations where internet safety is not their primary concern. Because exercising control is only one aspect of their activity, we define their function as 'secondary informal social control'.[62]

Most virtual communities employ moderators or online security managers (often from within the virtual community itself) to monitor the behaviour of their online community in terms of compliance with the specific norms of that community. Moderators ensure that community members adhere to acceptable codes of behaviour, and prevent discussions from becoming disruptive or libellous, or from being hijacked (Wall 2007).

Some communities or programs lay down a code of conduct. Before users register in a community, they must read a code of conduct and promise to respect these rules. If someone breaks these rules (for example, with smutty language or by damaging virtual property) a moderator will maintain order online. In discussion forums participants are not allowed to be rude or offensive to others. Moderators ensure that community members adhere to acceptable behaviour and prevent discussions from becoming disruptive.

A useful example of online moderation is found in the virtual world Habbo Hotel, which describes itself as a virtual hotel where teenagers can hang out and chat. It is constantly monitored by trained moderators. The sanctions that moderators can invoke when community norms or rules are broken include time-outs, the temporary removal of access rights if the offence is minor, and permanent exclusion and reporting to the police if it is serious (Wall 2007). A

---

62 To be clear, the word 'secondary' here relates to 'control' and not to 'informal'.

common example is the Dutch teenager who stole thousands of euros worth of furniture in Habbo Hotel and was excluded from the virtual community. The moderator then contacted the police to take further action (figure 18.1).

Figure 18.1   Theft of virtual goods from Habbo Hotel

Goods belonging to the victim were stolen from a virtual world on internet. This virtual world is known as Habbo Hotel. The victim had acquired these goods by transferring money through text messages. (...) 'I have been playing on Habbo Hotel since 16 February 2005. This is a virtual hotel on the internet. I took out an account with Habbo Hotel through my Hotmail. I left behind all my personal data there."
'I began at Habbo Hotel with an avatar (online character) and after that I started dressing this avatar. Then I always telephoned or sent a text message and after doing this I could buy new things on Habbo Hotel. I had built up 25,000 credits which would have a value of 4,000 euros if I had called by telephone or about 4,583 euros if I had sent a text message.'

'When I logged in on [date] I saw that my rooms on Habbo Hotel were empty. I saw that my furniture had disappeared. The furniture I had had, including a purple ice cream machine, were worth a lot. I know that in the illegal circuit there are bids of about 900 euros for this machine. I also had two golden dragons and about 200 euros each is being bid for these. And I had a big lot of grass and there are bids of about 400 euros for that.'

243

These forms of informal social control in online communities work fairly efficiently because nobody wants to have a bad reputation within his community. Besides appointing a moderator, some communities use a complaints service. Users can report illegal content or, for example, hate speech. Sanctions imposed in such cases are determined later by the provider or administrator (De Pauw 2010).

Secondary informal social control in practice
An important midfield role is reserved for Internet Service Providers (ISPs) (e.g. Stol et al. 2008; Alberdingk Thijm 2008). ISPs can influence online behaviour through contractual governance (Wall 2007; Crawford 2003), which is effected through the terms and conditions of their contracts with individual clients, namely internet users. Because of their strategic position in communication networks, ISPs can moreover employ a range of software

solutions to curb offensive online behaviour. These are typically robust security systems alongside sophisticated professional spam filters.

Van Eijk et al. (2010) conclude that internet safety, and in particular the relationship between ISP and end user, are still in their infancy. This is not to say that nothing happens in practice, but there is still not much of a formal framework or self-regulation. The researchers note that developments are still in full flight. In this paragraph we discuss the role of ISPs in brief. More on this subject in chapter 20.

Under European rules, internet providers are not responsible for data traffic that they did not initiate or influence with respect to content. They are not required to verify whether or not they host punishable information or information that is illegal, but they are expected to act in the event they are aware of the punishable or illegal nature of the information (Stol et al. 2008). ISPs are furthermore are subject to Article 4 of the Directive on Privacy and Electronic Communication.[63] This directive obliges providers of public telecommunications services (thus also ISPs) to take appropriate technological and organisational measures to safeguard the security of that service. A measure is taken to be 'appropriate' if it safeguards a level of security that is proportionate to the risks against which it would safeguard (Eijk et al. 2010). The article also stipulates that providers must inform their subscribers of special risks relating to breaches of network security.

International initiatives

As well as ISPs there are numerous interest groups directed towards making the internet safe or safer. Here we discuss several international interest organisations.

– *European Network and Information Security Agency (ENISA) (www.enisa.europa.eu)*

ENISA is the 'pace-setter' for Information Security in Europe. ENISA is a body of expertise set up by the EU to carry out specific technical scientific tasks in the field of Information Security. The Agency's Mission is to achieve a high and effective level of Network and Information Security within the

---

63 Directive 2002/58/EC of the European Parliament and Council of Europe of 12 July 2002 concerning the processing of personal data and the protection of privacy in the electronic communications sector (Directive on Privacy and Electronic Communication) PB L 201/37 (31/07/2002).

European Union. The objective is to make ENISA's website the European hub for the exchange of information, best practices and knowledge in the field of Information Security.

ENISA's goal is to help the European Commission, the EU Member States and business community to address, respond to and especially to prevent Network and Information Security problems. The Agency also assists the European Commission in the preparatory technical work for updating and developing Community legislation in the field of Network and Information Security.

– *Internet Crime Complaint Center (IC3) (www.ic3.gov)*

The US Internet Crime Complaint Center (IC3) was established as a partnership between the Federal Bureau of Investigation (FBI) and the National White Collar Crime Center (NW3C). Is serves as a channel for receiving internet related criminal complaints and then researching, developing, and referring these complaints to federal, state, local, or international law enforcement and/or regulatory agencies

The IC3, formerly known as the Internet Fraud Complaint Center, was renamed in 2003 to better reflect the broad character of such complaints. It has became increasingly evident that, regardless of the label placed on a cyber crime matter, the potential for it to overlap with another referred matter is substantial. IC3 now receives complaints crossing the spectrum of cyber crime matters, including online fraud in its many forms, matters of Intellectual Property Rights (IPR), Computer Intrusions (hacking), Economic Espionage (Theft of Trade Secrets), Online Extortion, International Money Laundering, Identity Theft, and a growing list of internet facilitated crimes.

– *International Association of Internet Hotlines (INHOPE) (www. inhope.org)*

INHOPE was founded in 1999 under the EC Safer Internet Action Plan. Today, there are 42 hotlines in 37 countries worldwide, including members from Europe, Asia, North America and Australia. By meeting regularly to share knowledge and best practice, INHOPE and its members are working to tackle the global problem of illegal content online (primarily child pornography).

The mission of the INHOPE Association is to support and enhance the performance of internet hotlines around the world, ensuring swift action is taken in response to reports of illegal content to make the internet a safer place. To achieve this mission, INHOPE has multiple objectives: to (1) exchange expertise, (2) support new hotlines, (3) interface with relevant initiatives outside the EU and (4) educate and inform policy makers, particularly at the international level.

245

- *International Network Against Cyberhate (INACH) (www.inach. net)*

INACH seeks to counter and address all forms of online discrimination and bring the online world into line with Human Rights. INACH wants to do this by uniting and empowering organisations to promote respect, responsibility and citizenship on the internet through countering cyber hate and raising awareness concerning online discrimination. INACH tries to reach its goals by:

- uniting organisations fighting against cyber hate;
- exchanging information to enhance effectiveness of such organisations;
- lobbying for international legislation to combat discrimination on the internet;
- supporting groups and institutions that want to set up a complaints bureau;
- creating awareness and promoting attitude change about discrimination on the internet by giving information, education.

18.4 Line of defence

In the defence line are commercial companies focusing on protecting computer networks or providing technological aids like virus scanners, but also police forces and the law, whose job is to trace and prosecute criminals. Awareness of the fact that security is also an issue in the online world has meanwhile penetrated to national governments. But academics observe time and again that police and the courts are unable to stay abreast of developments on the internet and are behind the times, notably in cases of more or less everyday cyber crime that do not fall within the remit of specialised national police units (Jewkes & Yar 2008; Van der Hulst & Neve 2008; Leukfeldt et al. 2010; Stol et al. 2012; Struiksma et al. 2012). The policing of cyber crime is discussed in greater depth in chapter 19. In this paragraph we deal only briefly with international cooperation in the area of policing. First let us see what we mean by formal social control.

Formal social control

We refer to social control as formal when that control is exercised by people who are specifically responsible for that task on grounds of regulations in society. Such control is authorised by mandate, as it were, and the people who control, the mandate holders, act primarily on behalf of third parties. Policing is the preeminent example of formal social control. (e.g. Cachet 1990; Stol 1996). Chapter 19 addresses the role of police. In this paragraph we only look in greater depth at international police cooperation, a prerequisite in tackling cyber crime, which obviously in many cases has an international component. (see for example Leukfeldt et al. 2010).

International police cooperation
In 1995 the G8 (Group of Eight) – a group of the world's major industrial nations: Canada, Germany, France, the United Kingdom, Italy, Japan, Russia, and the USA – set up an expert group on transnational crime. Within this group, a subgroup on High Tech Crime was established in 1996 (Verdelho 2008). For the first time, multiple nations established general principles for tackling cyber crime and drew up an action plan. An important principle was that there must be no 'safe havens' for cyber criminals. When certain activities are criminal under one country's law code and not in that of another, the discrepancy creates a safe haven: electronic sanctuaries where someone, under the protection of the local law, can commit facts that have an effect in other states (Kasperen 2004). In Europe, national law codes are being harmonised through the Council of Europe's Convention on Cyber Crime (see chapter 4).

Alongside the network of G8 countries, Interpol (see figure 18.2) built the Interpol National Central Reference Points (INCRP) (Verdelho 2008). EU Member States that are not part of the G8 network have joined Interpol's 'National Central Reference Point System' (NCRP). The two networks will work side by side in a spirit of cooperation. In addition, Member States that are not represented in the G8 network should be able to link a 24-hour function to their specialist units that form part of the Interpol network. In 2012, Interpol announced the creation of a cyber crime centre at the IGCI (Interpol Global Complex for Innovation). The Interpol Digital Crime Centre (IDCC), previously called Innovation, Research and Digital Security Directorate (IRDSD), will complement the current activities of Interpol in this area by strengthening member countries' cyber security programmes and tools.[64]

In response to the European Commission's communication 'Tackling Crime in our Digital Age: Establishing a European Cyber crime Centre', the Council of the EU has endorsed the establishment of a new European Cyber crime Centre (EC3) at Europol in The Hague (the Netherlands). According to Europol, the Centre will become the focal point in the EU's fight against cyber crime,

247

64 Interpol Global Complex for Innovation Newsletter /03 April 2012. https://www.europol.europa.eu/ec3, last visited June 2nd 2012.

contributing to faster reactions in the event of cyber attacks. It will support Member States and the European Union's institutions in building operational and analytical capacity for investigations and cooperation with international partners.

Figure 18.2   Interpol

Interpol is the world's largest international police organisation, with 188 member countries (www.interpol.int). Interpol was founded in 1923 to facilitate cross-border police cooperation, and now supports and assists all organisations, authorities and services whose mission is to prevent or combat international crime. Interpol has been actively involved in combating cyber crime for a number of years. The Interpol General Secretariat has harnessed the expertise of its members in the field of Information Technology Crime (ITC) through the vehicle of a 'working party' or a group of experts. In this instance, the working party consists of the heads or experienced members of national computer crime units. These working parties are designed to reflect regional expertise, and have been set up in Europe, Asia, America and Africa.

18.5 Case study: CPNI.NL

This chapter shows that the fight against cyber crime is not the responsibility of only one organisation. Different public and private organisations should work in harness to make the internet safe or safer. Public-private partnerships can be expected to have an important role in the future. In this section we discuss the Dutch public-private partnership CPNI.NL.

In the Netherlands, the Centre for Protection of the National Infrastructure (CPNI.NL) (formally known as the National Infrastructure against Cyber crime (NICC)[65]) is a public-private partnership which aims to integrate separate activities and establish and facilitate collaboration between all parties involved in the fight against cyber crime (CPNI.NL, 2011). Although CPNI.NL is not involved in the actual fight against cyber crime – that is the responsibility of all the public and private stakeholders involved – the programme

---

65 The Dutch NICC changed its name to CPNI, emulating CPNI.UK.

supports, facilitates and finances initiatives by other public and private organisations that contribute to safer computer-supported work processes.

The Cyber crime Information Exchange is the beating heart of the CPNI.NL, in which public and private organisations share sensitive information in socalled Information Sharing and Analysis Centers (ISACs). The informationsharing model adopted by the Dutch Cyber crime Information Exchange is based on that used by the UK's Centre for the Protection of National Infrastructure (CPNI). Information Exchange is pictured as a 'flower model' (see figure 18.3). The heart of the flower is made up of governmental bodies. They meet with participants from the critical industry sectors. Meeting face-to-face, a trusted community is built.

Figure 18.3   The Flower model of the Cyber crime Information Exchange
(CPNI.NL 2011)

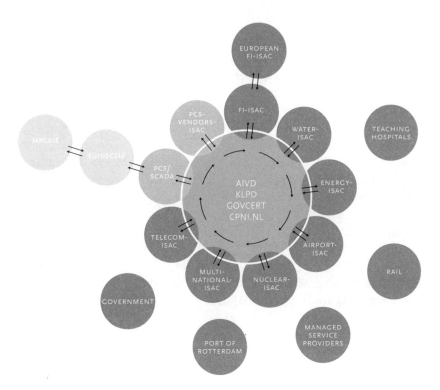

According to CPNI.NL (2011), 80% of the vital infrastructure in the Netherlands is in the hands of the private sector. It bears its own responsibility for taking measures to combat cyber crime. Considerable knowledge about cyber crime is held within public organisations such as the National Police Services Agency *(Korps Landelijke Politiediensten, KLPD)*, the General Intelligence and Security Service *(Algemene Inlichtingen- en Veiligheidsdienst, AIVD)* and the NCSC (National Cyber Security Centre). This group of governmental services consults with representatives of critical industry sectors on the risks of cyber crime and the measures to be implemented. The sectors themselves select representatives to participate in these meetings. Trust and Value are fundamental success factors for the Cyber crime Information Exchange. Valuable information can only be shared in a trusted environment. For this purpose a 'traffic-light protocol' is used, where 'red' information must not be disseminated outside the exchange, 'amber' information may be shared within the organisation on a need-to-know basis, and 'green' information may be circulated more widely within a particular community. This sharing of information is beneficial for both industry and government. By learning from each other, all participants can improve their level of security.

The fight against cyber crime can be undertaken not only at national level. Participants in various Information Sharing and Analysis Centers (ISACs, consultation centres where representatives of companies can exchange confidential information per business sector) are initiating contact with each other because the international component of cyber crime poses specific problems for them. The CPNI.NL programme fosters international knowledge exchange by establishing and strengthening contacts with comparable organisations in other countries, such as the CPNI.UK, SEMA (Sweden), Melani (Switzerland) and the Bundesamt für Sicherheit in der Informationstechnik (Germany). The CPNI.NL programme also collaborates with other initiatives in the area of ICT security, such as the European Network and Information Security Agency (ENISA), the SANS Institute and the Meridian.

18.6 The nature of cyber crimes: some implications for the fight against cyber crime

There is a diversity of problems involved in combating cyber crime. In the following chapters we discuss various players that play a role in combating cyber crime (police, ISPs, information security) and thus address the problems these players encounter. In this paragraph we deal only with the implications that cyber crime has by its very nature for the various players.
Cyber crime brings a new dimension to the relationship between organisations that fight crime, technology and the public. Many of these organisations

focus on combating organised cyber crime. It has been observed however that cyber crimes are not committed only by organisations, but are often crimes committed by the 'common people' (Leukfeldt et al. 2010). The fact that cyber crime is also perpetrated by 'people' has implications for different players (see also Leukfeldt, De Pauw, Domenie & Stol 2011).

First of all the public must become aware of the fact that danger in the form of virusses or hackers aiming for financial gain is not the only threat, but that cyber criminals may be motivated in the area of relations. An example is an ex-partner trying to blacken the name of the other, or seeking to obtain personal information that could be useful in divorce proceedings. The suspect and his or her victim are often acquainted with each other: former lovers, jealous husbands, school friends, or (former) business relations. These dangers should thus be taken (even more clearly) into consideration in information campaigns targeting the public or specific groups such as young people.

In the case of the midfield players, the findings of Leukfeldt et al. (2010) have implications predominantly for popular trading sites like Markplaats and eBay. For example e-fraud is apparently the most frequently occurring form of cyber crime in police records. Most of concern relatively simple cases of swindling (see chapter 7). That indicates not only that people should be very wary, but that online trading sites should be even more active in warning their customers about fraudsters on these websites, how they operate and how to recognise an attempted fraud.

In the backline of defence the implications specifically relate to police policy. Cyber crime is committed not only by organised groups from beyond our borders. Fighting cyber crime must therefore *not only* be the domain of specialist teams (as is currently almost always the case). Knowledge and expertise in the area of cyber crime must be available right across the force: every police officer must have at least some basic knowledge of cyber crime. Police personnel have to deal not only with individual cyber crimes, traditional offences will also have a cyber crime element with increasing frequency. Take for example hacking into the email account of someone who is already a victim of stalking. This certainly applies in the case of younger generations who are growing up at a time when a world without computers and the internet is inconceivable. They will increasingly more often be confronted with cyber crime (whether as victim or perpetrator) and with traditional offences like threat, defamation and libel involving a digital element. That means police forces will have to deal more often with cyber crime across the full breadth of their activities: for example in social problems for neighbourhood police officers, in reports for intake, in questioning by tactical detective officers and in the formulation of policy at senior command level.

Key concepts

Informal social control
Secondary informal social control
Formal social control
Online moderation

19 Policing Cyber Crime

Yvonne Jewkes & Rutger Leukfeldt

19.1 Introduction

Since the mid-1990s, the internet has been incorporated into nearly every aspect of everyday life (in advanced industrial nations, at least) and has brought with it previously unimaginable challenges for the police. It took the World Wide Web just three years to reach its first 50 million users and this potential audience, which is now over one billion users, provides limitless opportunities for those who are criminally inclined. Cyberspace is also largely anonymous and reconfigures time and space, so that offences can be initiated, and their consequences felt, in entirely different parts of the world. Not only do these inherent characteristics – immediacy, anonymity and global yet 'borderless' reach – make investigating cyber crime immensely difficult, but its sheer pervasiveness and mundaneness have made numerous offences – e.g. buying and selling counterfeit goods on online auction sites – a common practice and almost impossible to police. In addition, lack of cooperation and divergent practices between law enforcement agencies across geographical boundaries and legal jurisdictions are a significant obstacle to policing cyber crime. This chapter will explore some of these problems and discuss both pan-European initiatives to tackle cyber crime and the responses of three individual countries: the UK, the Netherlands and Belgium.

19.2 'Policing' bodies

First of all, it must be underlined that while cyber crimes of the breadth and nature described in Part 2 of this Volume undoubtedly pose significant challenges for police services across Europe and internationally, much of the monitoring, regulation, protection and enforcement related to cyber crime is not the responsibility of state-controlled public police forces at all (see chapters 18 and 20). Individual users protect their own computers, for example, by installing virus scanners and firewalls. Internet Service Providers (ISPs) make sure that spam emails do not reach their customers and administrators of blogs and discussion forums delete inappropriate comments. In addition there are a growing number of interest groups – such as Internet Hotline Providers in Europe or INHOPE (https://www.inhope.org/) and Cyberangels (http://www.

cyberangels.org/) – who support a particular cause or aspect of regulation. Finally, there are commercial companies who focus on the protection of computer networks or offer technical solutions, such as virus scanners. And in recent years there has been a proliferation of private security firms set up to protect corporate data for commercial businesses who place a premium on discretion and privacy when it comes to their computerised records and data systems.

These developments may be symptomatic of a situation in which the scope, scale and structure of the internet outstrips the capacity of any single enforcement or regulatory body (Wall 2007; Yar 2008) and the police themselves have become part of a more diverse and diffused assortment of bodies within and between nation states. Just as the policing of terrestrial space has demanded a 'joined-up approach' between individual citizens, private sector agencies and the police, so too has the policing of cyberspace become a pluralistic endeavour. This pluralism has two facets. First, new laws introduced in individual countries are increasingly supported by international harmonisation and police coordination treaties such as the Council of Europe's Convention on Cyber crime (2001). Second, in some countries 'policing' functions have been awarded to other state-funded organisations that work alongside the police. For example, in New Zealand, the Censorship Compliance Unit (CCU) within the Government's Department of Internal Affairs has responsibility for regulating and detecting some cyber offences. Because the CCU investigates a relatively narrow range of offences, including the policing of internet child pornography, it has developed a pro-active strategy based on specialist intelligence and technical expertise and claims higher success rates than comparable police units (Jewkes & Andrews 2007).

So, when commentators talk of 'policing' cyber crime, they may be referring to a wide range of different bodies or strategies encompassing those whose primary aim is to *protect* and those whose primary aim is to *enforce*.

When it comes to state-funded policing, the names and precise operational remits of specialist units dealing with cyber crime vary from country to country (and in countries with separate regional forces, such as the UK, The Netherlands and Belgium, from force to force). In the main, however, they fall into four categories:

First are scientific support units or forensic investigation units which carry out forensic examinations of seized computer equipment and data recovery, as well as investigating cases involving DNA, fingerprints and so on.

Secondly, there are departments that gather intelligence on major crimes, usually in support of a force Criminal Investigations Department (CID) or fraud squad. Personnel in these units tend to work on major, cross-boundary investigations such as terrorism and fraud, and they gather intelligence on persistent, known, 'career' offenders.

The third group of specialist units are those with a broader remit to investigate offences committed against computer systems as well as to investigate traditional crimes that have a 'high-tech' element. These include force hi-tech crime units, computer crime units or telecoms and computer crime units.

Finally, there are units that deal with obscene images of children and/or investigate paedophile networks. These include child protection and investigation units, paedophile units, abusive images units, obscene publications units and vice squads. The names of these departments indicate some of their differing functions but, while all may have a duty to investigate sexual images of children on the Net, not all of them will include within their remits the safeguarding of children in chat rooms or the more general welfare of children in the community.

The section that follows will discuss the differing approaches to policing cyber crime in three countries: the UK, the Netherlands and Belgium.

19.3 Policing cyber crime across Europe: different approaches

The United Kingdom

In the UK, several policing initiatives have been tried, although many appear to have been implemented rather half-heartedly. In January 2000, the Home Office allocated what we now know to be a woefully inadequate £ 337,000 (approximately 400,000 euro) to the National Criminal Intelligence Service (NCIS) to target fraud, money laundering, pornography, cyber-stalking, email viruses, paedophilia and hacking. The following year the National Hi-Tech Crime Unit (NHTCU) was established. This team was made up of representatives from the National Crime Squad, the National Criminal Intelligence Service, HM Customs and Excise, the Ministry of Defence and seconded police officers. In 2006, the NHTCU was absorbed into the new Serious and Organised Crime Agency (SOCA) which has a very broad remit, but includes the investigation of 'cyber' offences such as online frauds and scams. In the same year the Child Exploitation and Online Protection (CEOP) Centre was launched which, in addition to investigating cases in the ways outlined earlier, has a remit to educate young people and their parents about the dangers of online activities (http://www.ceop.gov.uk). The most recent policing cyber crime initiative in the UK came into operation in 2009. Based within the Metropolitan Police Service, the Police Central e-crime Unit (PCeU) provides specialist officer training and coordinates cross-force initiatives in support of the new National Fraud Reporting Centre (NFRC) and the National Fraud Intelligence Bureau (NFIB). PCeU was created in response to calls by the Association of Chief Police Officers (ACPO) for increasing capacity and capability within the police service to get to grips with internet crime and is jointly funded by Government (to the tune of £3.5 million) and the Met (£3.9 million), though it also seeks support from industry partners (http://press.homeoffice.gov.uk/press-releases/new-specialist-ecrime-unit).

While financial constraints are clearly going to have an impact on all policing activities in times of global recession, there are in addition more 'micro' reasons why the policing of cyber crime has not been regarded as a priority in the UK. The specialist organisations mentioned above employ individuals with the highest level of technical expertise, but the UK police in general are renowned for their resistance to change and progress. The vast majority of UK police forces do not have their own distinct and easily identifiable 'cyber crime unit' dedicated to investigating only computer-mediated crimes. Some forces employ one or two specialist personnel with 'high-tech' expertise within the much broader context of, for example, a Serious Crime Unit, Scientific Support Unit or Forensic Investigation Unit. Other forces have departments that gather intelligence on major crimes, usually in support of a force CID or Fraud Squad. However, even within units that amass expertise within the broad field of cyber crime, the officers working within them may not have sufficient specialist skills and training.

The Netherlands

These days the Dutch government gives high priority to detecting and combating cyber crime, employing various legal and organisational measures. Examples include the Law on Computer Crime-II (2006), a result of the European Convention on Cyber crime (2001), the penalization of grooming (2010), the Treaty of Lanzarote (2007), the establishment of the Police Hotline Cyber crime and the Team High Tech Crime (THTC) at the National Police Services Agency and the National Program Against Cyber crime (PAC) of the Council of Chief Commissioners, which was recently extended by three years. The latter program initiated several local pilots, which might be implemented nationally if proven successful (e.g. the Internet Fraud Centre, which aims to analyse all reports of internet fraud from different regional police departments in order to more effectively detect fraudsters with multiple victims, or the child pornography pilot, which aims to detect online paedophiles). In spring 2011, the Dutch government presented a National Cyber Security Strategy (NCSS), including a strategy against cyber crime. Many parties were involved in drafting the strategy, including governmental bodies, banks, universities, the Dutch Govcert, the police, ICT security companies and software developers.

The Dutch police first developed a 'three echelon model' for organising the fight against cyber crime in the mid-1990s (Stol et al. 1999). This included:

- semi-experts at the lower layers of the organisation for simple digital detective work;
- scientific support units (so-called 'bureaus of digital expertise' – BDEs) at a regional or interregional level (the first three of these started in 1990);
- cyber crime experts at a national level.

Although the police have abandoned the term 'three echelon model', today one can still recognise the three levels. At local level there are basic units which are responsible for general policing duties such as surveillance, registering statements of victims and small criminal investigations. These basic units form the vast majority of the police organisation: 36,057 of the total of 53,348 full-time police officers. Although they are responsible for regular criminal investigations, these officers are not trained in the field of cyber crime. A recent study shows that police employees responsible for registration – which forms the basis of the criminal investigation process – have a lack of knowledge about cyber crime and are unable to register these offences properly, suggesting that the police would benefit from officers in the role of semi-experts in the field of cyber crime (Toutenhoofd et al. 2009),

At the middle level we find a digital detective unit in every force, with the number of officers ranging from three to 25 (the Netherlands has 25 regional police forces). Furthermore, at this middle level we still find the above-mentioned inter-regional bureaux of digital expertise (Stol 2008). Their objective is to support criminal investigation teams; for example, by securing suspects' computers and searching for illegal digital material. At a national level are Team High Tech Crime units (THTC) whose goal is to fight cyber crimes that threaten the vital infrastructure of the Netherlands, and the National Forensic Institute which provides technological support and develops new tools for investigating cyber crime. In 2008, around 65 detectives specialising in cyber crime worked at a national level.

There is an important difference in the organisation of the Dutch police with regard to the combating of cyber crime and other forms of (non-IT) crime. The organisation of the police has always been like a pyramid: most officers work at a local level; fewer officers at a regional level; and the least number of officers are available at a national level. The organisation of the combating of cyber crime, however, has a somewhat different shape. A relatively large proportion of all police officers fighting cyber crime – and, consequently, a large proportion of cyber crime knowledge – are at the national level. Regionally and locally, relatively few police officers are available. This means that policing cyber crime in the Netherlands focuses on high-tech organised crime and not on the more common low-tech crimes such as internet auction fraud, cyber stalking or simple hacking cases.

Belgium[66]

In recent years, Belgium's government has given priority to combating cyber crime. The Belgian law on cyber crime was established in 2000 and a series of cyber crimes were made punishable. The law covers both criminal attacks against computers and networks, such as computer hacking, and the spreading of computer viruses, as all sorts of 'old' crimes are now being executed with the help of computers (e.g. internet fraud). Furthermore, based on the European Convention on Cyber crime, the law on child pornography and hate crimes (including discrimination, racism and xenophobia) were amended to take account of the new technologies.

Since 1992 Belgium has had a Computer Crime Unit (CCU), which was part of the Judicial Police. Three years later, in 1995, the former Gendarmerie also set up a specialised unit: the BOGO Team (Team for Assistance and Investigation in Automated Environments, in Dutch: *Team voor Bijstand en Opsporingen in Geautomatiseerde Omgevingen*). Because of the reorganisation of the police in Belgium at federal level, the CCU and BOGO Team merged into the Federal Computer Crime Unit (FCCU) (Beirens 1998). Furthermore, 22 Regional Computer Crime Units (RCCU) were founded. The aim of the federal and the regional teams is to assist police forces. Their main task is forensic research into ICT, giving (technical) assistance in investigations involving the internet (the identification and localisation of targets) and cases involving hacking, cyber espionage and sabotage (Beirens 2010). Finally, victims of cyber crime can make a report through the FCCU's website: www.e-cops.be. The FCCU

---

66 This section is based on Leukfeldt, De Pauw, Domenie & Stol (2011).

examines reports and either passes them on to a regional RCCU or self-initiates an investigation (De Pauw 2010; Belren 2010).

Pan-European and Global Initiatives

In addition to these national policing efforts, several new pan-European and global initiatives have been introduced in an attempt to effectively police cyber crime. In 2001 the Council of Europe introduced the Cyber Crime Convention, an international legal mechanism for cooperation in law enforcement and harmonisation of laws. Aside from enhancing mutual legal assistance, the Convention – activated in 2004 – provides comprehensive powers: to expedite the preservation of stored computer data and partial disclosure of traffic data; to seize stored data and enable real-time collection of traffic data; and to intercept the content of 'questionable' data (Broadhurst 2006). Today 44 countries have signed the Convention (including non-member states such as the US and Canada) and, as of February 2009, 23 had ratified it. At the level of the European Union and its member states, ENISA(the European Network and Information Security Agency) has been established (www.enisa.europa.eu/). Operational since May 2005, it aims to 'enhance the capability of the European Union, the EU Member States and the business community to prevent, address and respond to network and information security problems' (ENISA 2008). In addition, the international police coordination body Interpol, and its European equivalent Europol, also support cross-border investigation and act as conduits for the pooling of intelligence and expert knowledge. European police also cooperate in the fight against cyber crime on a more operational level, such as in the so-called Circamp project against child pornography on the internet in which police officers from about 20 European countries cooperate.

Unfortunately there are numerous obstacles facing all these initiatives. Although aimed at harmonising cyber crime laws around the world, ratification of the Cyber Crime Convention is not a priority in many states. In attempting to pave the way for cross-border cyber crime investigation, it obliges signatories to cooperate with one another, which means making private national data available to governments around the world, with little oversight or control over how it is used. It also means that countries with considerable political and legislative clout can place limits on other countries' investigations on their data. For instance, the US can deny assistance in a variety of circumstances, e.g. if it would violate the First Amendment (www.i-policy.org/2010/06/council-of-europe-convention-on-cybercrime.html). Being somewhat smaller in scope, the hopes for ENISA might be a little better, though with an initial annual budget of € 6.9 million, its impact on computer crime across the 27 member states has been somewhat derided (Jewkes & Yar 2008). An increase in the budget is planned to € 19 million a year by 2016, but the sheer size and scope of the internet, the volume of electronic traffic it facilitates, the varying legal responses to cyber crime in different countries and other inter-jurisdictional difficulties combine to ensure that the police feel they remain in a perpetual game of 'catch-up' with cybercriminals. For example, the fact that ENISA's 'mission' places it at a considerable remove from the day-to-day operational business of policing should come as little surprise, as it is perhaps a recognition of the overwhelming nature of the demands faced by any purported 'internet police'.

In reality, then, a globally effective policing operation is still some way off. It is often claimed that efforts to police cyberspace are futile because the internet's global reach and inherent pliancy allow individuals and organisations to evade authorities. As Broadhurst (2006) observes, although "globalisation" continues to accelerate, a fully global response to the problems of policing, regulation and security in the digital age has yet to emerge. Cooperation between member states is undoubtedly desirable, but in reality it is hard to achieve and investigations can be held up for months while law enforcement officers from different countries struggle to find compatible *modus operandi*. It is not just language and operational differences that create obstacles; the problem is also one of organisational culture and parochialism: as Lenk (1997: 129) observes: "letting foreign police tread a square metre of their soil in hard pursuit of criminals is still anathema to ... national governments". The difficulties facing internet regulators are compounded by different moral codes and divergent legal responses in different countries: for example, material that is considered mildly pornographic in the UK and Ireland may not be censured at all in Sweden or the Netherlands but may be subject to much stricter regulation in China or the Middle East. This diversity in definition is brought even more sharply into focus in relation to communications between countries with a tradition of freedom of speech and those that are more repressive, or when an internet connection may provide a link to 'freedom' for political dissidents.

19.4 Policing cyber crime: challenges for the future

There are clearly no easy solutions to the problems of policing and prosecuting cyber crimes. But, as an initial step forward, progress could arguably be made in four areas.

The first is legislation, so that not only is there international agreement on what constitutes criminal activity in cyberspace but also an adequate legal framework to allow the police to investigate it and bring a strong case to prosecution. An example is legislation on internet child pornography (see chapter 9) which is a global problem by definition. Despite several international conventions, legislation on child pornography varies by country, including between those within Europe (Stol et al. 2008a) and between US states (Wells et al. 2007). This disparity exists partly because not all countries have signed or ratified the international treaties, and it can take a long time to change existing laws in a country.

Another problem with legislation is that the boundaries between legal and illegal seem to be blurred. For example, one of the most obvious outcomes of the ICT revolution is its creation and distribution of unimaginably more information-based products that, in turn, pose new legal challenges to defining the definition and protection of copyright. Put simply, the electronic transmission and reproduction of information has become so commonplace that many of those who routinely transfer, copy, and store material on their own machines may not even be alert to the fact that they are stealing. Another consequence of the vast scope and pervasiveness of digital technologies is that new areas of social vulnerability have emerged, such as hate crime. While internet-facilitated 'hate propaganda' (e.g. targeting specific racial or religious groups) has been relatively common for some time and its publication and distribution have been criminalised by law in several countries, the internet remains largely unregulated in this area. Furthermore, the lines between hate crime, abuse, bullying and mischief-making are frequently indistinct and – when directed at individuals rather than large groups – they can have even more devastating effects, as witnessed by the recent much-publicised case of a young man in the US who committed suicide after a video featuring him in a sexual encounter with another man was filmed on a webcam and broadcast via the internet from his college dorm. His roommates at Rutgers University were charged with invading the victim's privacy although charges of hate crime may not be brought unless evidence of the victim's state of mind and motivation for taking his own life can be proved (http://www.nydailynews.com/ny_local/2010/10/05/2010-10-05_hate_crime_may_not_be_option_in_rutgers_case.html).

Secondly, in order to give high priority to tracking and fighting cyber crime, better police intelligence and knowledge is required about the nature of offences, offender characteristics and *modus operandi*. Unfortunately, at the present time, the police cannot easily offer attractive salaries to recruit technically

261

skilled staff in what is a very competitive market, and the costs of ongoing training in a fast-moving, constantly evolving technological environment may be prohibitive[67] (Jewkes & Andrews 2005). Consequently, specialist units have been forced to concentrate on what have been termed 'low-hanging fruit', which need fewer resources and may require less complicated investigations in order to yield results (Goodman 1997). For example, in the case of online abuse of children, police have had some success in investigating individuals who download and pass on abusive images of children, or who use internet chat rooms to prey on young victims, but the more difficult task of policing the producers and distributors of child pornography has yielded little success. In general, then, scientific research into cyber crime should be the first step in fighting it.

sFourthly, as well as reviewing and updating their legal statutes which will help the police build a case for prosecution when cyber crimes are committed, and providing sufficient resources for the police to be able to attract highly-skilled technicians, governments must also do more to prevent such offences occurring in the first place. Their collective failure to do so is part of a wider neglect of the potential scope and costs of cyber crime and the harm that it can cause. Thus far, governments have been considerably more adept at introducing *reactive* measures (those that provide for the prosecution of offences after they occur) than pioneering *preventive* initiatives. Once again, investigators' tendency to concentrate on low-hanging fruit has attracted criticism but equally concerning is the power and authority that governments award themselves, which many regard as a 'licence to snoop'. For example, when the UK government introduced its 'Foresight' project on Cyber Trust and Crime Prevention in 2003, the Minister for Crime Reduction and Policing claimed that the initiative would "help ensure that technology is used to benefit society and ... police officers have the latest tools and technology to protect and police our communities and to minimise criminal misuse" (www.foresight.gov.uk). But many critics are wary of a government initiative designed, as its press release states, to ensure that "long term financial information is held in a consistent and compatible format that allows its retrieval in 20 years or more". And while few would question the need for the police to "protect and detect in the virtual world as in the real" (www.foresight.gov.uk), especially in their efforts to counter terrorist and cyber-terrorist threats, more may be troubled by the use of technology to hold sensitive or confidential information about individual citizens. As Aas (2007) observes, the internet has vastly extended the

---

67 One possible solution is a public-private partnership; see chapter 18.

scope and efficiency of regulatory practices and the increasingly sophisticated technological capacity for monitoring, tracking down and identifying individuals raises important questions not only regarding the 'policing' of cyberspace but also the implications of the internet's capacity to allow wide-scale regulation and surveillance of *everyone* who uses it. This begs the question, who defines and identifies 'miscreants' and with what consequences to notions of citizenship and civil liberties?

All in all, it is clear that the police face considerable challenges in policing cyber crime. By way of illustration, Figure 19.1 describes the recent 'Wikileaks' saga, which crystallises the issues discussed in this chapter and demonstrates how ineffective the police and other regulatory authorities can be when faced with illegal activities facilitated by the internet. This case study highlights the ways in which technology can alter the balance of power in society and present new obstacles to the police.

Figure 19.1   Wikileaks, the attacks of Anonymous & the powerlessness of the police

'Wikileaks' is a non-profit media organisation dedicated to bringing 'secret' information to the public, which first found fame when it published damaging US files relating to the Afghan war in July 2010, and which has continued to achieve further notoriety ever since. Providing an "innovative, secure and anonymous way for independent sources around the world to leak information to our journalists", according to its website (http://wikileaks.org.uk), Wikileaks has become a huge political embarrassment for many governments, notably that of the United States who claim that the site may be breaking US espionage laws and have vowed to pursue Wikileaks and its founder, Julian Assange, with all the vigour and commitment they have devoted to trying to bring down al-Qaida (*Guardian*, 11 December 2010). While Assange has been designated Public Enemy Number One by the US government, his site has galvanised a global network of 'information libertarians' who are committed to free speech and have the technological wherewithal to disrupt the online activities of anyone they perceive to be against them.

'Anonymous' – an amorphous army of online hackers – has now turned its attention to the US government and multi-national corporations including Mastercard, Amazon and Facebook (*ibid*.). The original target of Anonymous's 'Operation Payback' was America's recording industry, chosen for its prosecutions of music file downloaders, but now they have explicitly allied themselves to Wikileaks, even though Assange, himself a former hacker, has attempted to distance himself from their activities to avoid further reprisals from the American authorities. But even if the US government is successful in prosecuting Assange, questions concerning the public's right to information are not going to go away. Regardless of the fate of its founder, WikiLeaks will continue releasing more of the 250,000 declassified cables it has at its disposal and the police have little effective means at their disposal of tracking down the hacktivists that align themselves to Payback. While the British press report that police have been conducting an ongoing investigation into the activities of Anonymous for several months, no arrests have yet been made (*Daily Mail*, 10 December 2010). The outcome of this case is difficult to predict but it is being dubbed the 'first world information war' (*Guardian*, 11 December 2010). Whatever its long-term trajectory, the Wikileaks saga has graphically illustrated the potential of the internet to bring together a global community of people prepared to break the law and the inadequacy of authorities, including the police, to do anything about it.

Key concepts

Policing
Three echelon model
Cyber Crime Convention
Hate crime
Reactive measures
Internet characteristics

20 Duties of Care on the Internet[66]

Nico van Eijk

20.1 Introduction

Internet Service Providers currently find themselves in the spotlight, in both a national and international context, with regard to their relationship both with governments and other private parties, on for example questions of (civil) liability. This chapter focuses on duties of care in respect of the relationship between government and Internet Service Providers (ISP). It provides an overview of specific forms of duties of care in the Netherlands, France, Germany and the United Kingdom. These countries were selected based on the fact that they represent different policy/regulatory systems or because they are known for interesting developments. The European context is also taken into account. The analysis of duties of care takes place from the perspective of three themes. The first theme relates to breaches of internet security.[69] What kinds of duty of care are provided for in order to deal with privacy breaches or malware placement? The second theme relates to child pornography. Child pornography on the internet is among the subjects that required attention at an early stage in the development of the online environment; ISPs have been closely involved in this aspect.[70] Copyright is the third theme. The focus is not on copyright as such but on the possible involvement of the Internet Service Provider when it comes to observing and protecting applicable copyrights.

---

68 This chapter is based on the study *Moving Towards Balance: A study into duties of care on the Internet*, N.A.N.M. van Eijk, T.M. van Engers, C. Wiersma, C.A. Jasserand and W. Abel, WODC/University of Amsterdam, 2010, 125 p. Online: http://www.ivir.nl/publications/vaneijk/Moving_Towards_Balance.pdf.
69 On security, see for instance Coupez (2010).
70 About child pornography: Stol et al. (2008).

Box 20.1   ISPs, mere conduit, caching and hosting

ISPs' is understood to mean market parties engaged in providing access to the internet to end-users. In terms of telecommunications regulation, the activity in question consists of a 'public telecom service'. The E-commerce Directive ('Directive on electronic commerce') of 2000 comprises a system in which three activities are distinguished: 'mere conduit', 'caching' and 'hosting'. Mere conduit (Article 12) consists of the unmodified transfer of, or providing access to, information. Mere conduit thus includes the core activity of Internet Service Providers, i.e. providing access to the internet. If they do not make any further selections or changes to the information, the Directive excludes liability for such activity. Nevertheless, a court or an administrative authority may demand that a service provider terminates or prevents an infringement. Caching (Article 13) refers to the temporary but unmodified storage of information. Hosting (Article 14) refers to activities associated with the storage of information provided by a recipient of the service. This includes hosting a website or personal pages. With regard to caching and hosting, it is stipulated in the Directive that liability is avoided when providers remove information after they have obtained actual knowledge (with respect to information that is – evidently – unlawful/illegal, or where appropriate, by an order to that effect). This is also called 'notice and take down'.

In the provisions of the Directive on mere conduit, caching and hosting, nothing is stated about duties of care. Parties acting in conformity with the Directive, however, can claim a limitation of their liability. Yet, if member states opt for prescribing the 'notice and take down' principle as binding, the Directive would not oppose this. Market parties can make notice and take down part of self-regulation. In either situation, there is a duty of care.

20.2 Internet security

By virtue of Article 4 of the Directive on privacy and electronic communications adopted in 2002, providers of publicly available electronic communication services (which include Internet Service Providers) are required to take appropriate technical and organisational measures to safeguard the security of the services provided.[71] If necessary, this should happen in conjunction with the provider of the public communication network on which the service is provided. The measures to be taken should ensure a security level that is proportionate to the state of the technology and the costs of its execution. In the second paragraph of the article, it is stipulated that providers are to inform their subscribers of the special risks of network security breaches. If the risk lies outside the scope of the measures to be taken by the service provider, the latter must inform the users of any possible remedies, including an indication of the expected costs.

Article 4 was extended in the context of the revision of the European framework for the communication sector.[72] A new paragraph 1a has been added to the article, imposing obligations on the providers regarding access to personal data, protecting stored or transmitted personal data and introducing a security policy with respect to the processing of personal data. The national authorities need to be able to audit the measures taken and to issue recommendations. In a new third and fourth paragraph, a notification obligation is introduced as to breaches related to personal data. Breaches are to be reported to the competent national authority. When the personal data breach is likely to have adverse effects on the personal data or the privacy of a subscriber or individual, the provider shall also notify the subscriber or individual of the breach. Further rules can be laid down at a national level. In addition, the European Commission can adopt technical implementing measures.

269

In all four countries, the content of Article 4 of the Directive on privacy and electronic communications can be found in the national telecommunication Acts. In each instance, reference is made to the importance of the protection of privacy and personal data in electronic communications. However, hardly anything substantial can be found on duties of care. It is clear, however, that Internet Service Providers are understood to have mainly two duties of care. The first pertains to taking suitable technical and organisational measures to safeguard internet security. The second pertains to informing end-users about

---

71 Directive 2002/58/EC of the European Parliament and of the Council of 12 July 2002 concerning the processing of personal data and the protection of privacy in the electronic communications sector (Directive on privacy and electronic communications or e-privacy directive) OJ L 201/37 (31 July 2002).
72 Amendments to the Framework Directive and the Universal Service Directive: Directive 2009/136/EC of 25 November 2009, OJ L 337/11 (18 December 2009) ('Citizens' Rights Directive') and Directive 2009/140/EC of 25 November 2009, OJ L 337/37 (18 December 2009) ('Better Regulation Directive').

specific risks and measures that can be taken to minimise these risks, in so far as the Internet Service Provider does not have the obligation itself to take measures. In most countries, the minimum requirements or best practices have not been defined any further in regulations or jurisprudence.

In the Netherlands, on the initiative of the Independent Post and Telecommunication Authority (*Onafhankelijke Post en Telecommunicatie Autoriteit*, OPTA), a process has been started to put the duties of care as laid down in Article 11.3 of the Telecommunications Act into practice. This has resulted in the analysis of relevant issues for the establishment of policy rules. Currently, only rules on the obligation of informing end-users about certain risks have been formulated. The new European rules, as described at the beginning of this paragraph have been implemented in the Dutch Telecommunications Act. OPTA, together with the Radiocommunications Agency ('Agentschap Telecom')[73] are responsible for supervision the rules.

OPTA is working with the Dutch National Police Services Agency (*Korps Landelijke Politiediensten*, KLPD) on the basis of a protocol containing agreements on information exchange. The KLPD can act against security breaches to the extent that the national penal law allows for sanctions related to this. In addition, OPTA has its own powers to impose administrative sanctions. Studies have shown that the Netherlands is a pioneer in Europe concerning various internet security aspects.[74]

Many Dutch internet service providers have entered into a covenant in which intentions have been laid down for the joint combat against botnets. The exchange of information on the basis of the covenant plays a major role in this. End-users should be helped to clear their computers, before they obtain access to the internet again.

In the United Kingdom, the Internet Services Providers' Association (ISPA UK) has formulated 'best current practices', specifically for the secure handling of email. This document is not compulsory for the members.
In Germany, a provision in the national telecommunications act deals with the organisational measures required of Internet Service Providers; the provision focuses on the prevention of interruptions, the effects of external attacks and

---

73 www.agentschaptelecom.nl.
74 Dumortier & Somers (2008).

catastrophes. Here, too, further implementation is left to the stakeholders. In addition, an anti-botnet website has been developed on the initiative of ECO (*Verband der deutschen Internetwirtschaft* – Association of the German Internet Industry) and the federal government, through which Internet Service Providers play an active role in dealing with reported and detected botnets, by means of a call centre that actively helps to clear the computers of the reporting clients. The costs are partly carried by the government.

The French Government has drafted a proposal for a statutory regulation that will oblige Internet Service Providers to report certain security breaches with respect to personal data to the French supervisory authority in this field (CNIL – *Commission nationale de l'informatique et des libertés*). This proposal can be regarded as a response to the recently extended Article 4 of the Directive on privacy and electronic communications. In both the Netherlands and France, the government has expressed its intention to make this notification mandatory for other services of the information society, and not only for Internet Service Providers (e.g. web transactions, financial services).

Respondents in our study (Van Eijk et al. 2011) emphasise that further concrete steps towards putting in place the duties of care arising from the (new) European directive framework are necessary. The interviewed parties generally indicated that internet traffic inspections[75] might be in conflict with privacy legislation and principles regarding the confidentiality of (tele)communication. From a technical perspective, however, there are various possibilities. Additionally, on the basis of agreements with customers, Internet Service Providers filter information because of viruses and spam. Several parties have expressed their concern about the lack of clarity of the legal framework concerning the admissibility of such methods. There is little transparency as to who is affected by these methods and to what extent.

Botnets are clearly a concern for Internet Service Providers. Internet Service Providers may face blacklisting due to botnets, causing certain services, such as email, to be disrupted. Although many public sources with location data on botnets are currently available, it is difficult to catch all of them, and extensive work is required to deal with botnets in this way. Establishing the reliability

---

75 By using Deep Packet Inspection (DPI), for instance. For research on the deployment of DPI, see: http://dpi.ischool.syr.edu/Home.html.

of the public sources mentioned is also difficult.[76] Quarantine measures for such computers seem to be necessary, but limiting internet access also has an adverse impact. Furthermore, differences in available resources imply that not all Internet Service Providers would (like to) act against botnets for their customers.

Risks associated with the use of wireless routers have received special attention. The interviewees were asked if the current duties of care in the field of internet security also cover this issue. It is clear that besides internet service providers there are several other market parties supplying wireless routers. These parties are not within the scope of the current telecommunication-related legal framework.

Another question in the interviews was to what extent the effectiveness of the measures taken to implement the obligation to provide information as set out in Article 4 of the Directive on privacy and electronic communications is being supervised. The question arose whether the national government could play an active role in instructing end-users about the safety and security of the internet or whether it could at least be more closely involved in ensuring that the information actually reaches the end-users.

20.3 Child pornography

Child pornography has been on the European agenda for some time. In the Framework Decision of 22 December 2003, it is stipulated that member states are to take measures against the proliferation of child pornography.[77] A special Directive has been adopted.[78] Article 25, section 2 of the directive provides that member states should take measures to block access to child pornography.[79] This blocking should come with the necessary guarantees. Furthermore, member states are to take measures to remove child pornography from the

76 In this context, see Van Eeten et al. (2010).
77 Council Framework Decision 2004/68/JHA of 22 December 2003 on combating the sexual exploitation of children and child pornography, JO L 13/44, 20.1.2004.
78 Directive 2011/92/EU of 13 December 2011 on combating the sexual abuse and sexual exploitation of children and child pornography, and replacing Council Framework Decision 2004/68/JHA, JO L335/1 (17 December 2011).
79 On blocking, i.e.: Callanan et al. (2009).

internet. As stated in the preamble, blocking is important when the information originates from countries outside the European jurisdiction.

In the field of child abuse, the police authorities in Europe are already collaborating intensively in the CIRCAMP[80] programme, and various forms of cooperation between Europe and the United Stated (where apparently most child pornography is hosted) have been put into plac. Which form is used for blocking, is left to the member states. Self-regulation by Internet Service Providers on the basis of codes of conduct is mentioned as an option (besides blocking by order of the judiciary or the police on the basis of possibilities to that effect within the civil and/or penal law). The choices for alternatives are partly based on what is permitted by national regulation.

20.4 Copyright

The regime of the E-commerce Directive was partly implemented to establish the position of parties such as Internet Service Providers with regard to copyright. Supplementary to this, we can refer to the discussion in the context of the New Regulatory Framework (NRF)[81] for the communication sector about the 'three strikes' – or graduated response – issues.[82] Proposals to assign a specific role to Internet Service Providers in enforcing copyright (with respect to downloading music, video, e-books and games in particular)[83] have not led in the end to European regulations. It should also be noted that Article 3a of the Framework Directive[84] stipulates that fundamental rights and freedoms are to be observed by member states when taking measures on access to, or the use of, services and applications by end-users.

---

80 Cospol Internet Related Child Abusive Material Project (www.circamp.eu).
81 The New Regulatory Framework concerns the existing directives for the communication sector and can be found in two directives: Directive 2009/136/EC of 25 November 2009, OJ L 337/11 (18.12.2009) and Directive 2009/140/EC of 25 November 2009, OJ L 337/37 (18.12.2009).
82 See also TNO/SEO/IVIR (2009) and Van Eijk (2011).
83 In some countries, e.g. the Netherlands, downloading is not punishable; in other countries it is. See the literature in the previous note.
84 Directive 2002/21/EC of the European Parliament and of the Council of 7 March 2002 on a common regulatory framework for electronic communications networks and services (Framework Directive), OJ L 108/33 (24.04.2002), amended by Directive 2009/140/EC of 25 November 2009, OJ L 227/37 (18.12.2009).

The regulations laid down in the E-commerce Directive are the decisive legal framework for the copyright theme in all four countries. On the basis of this, the duty of care of Internet Service Providers only pertains to measures for the removal of offending content, in the form of 'notice and take down' procedures in the context of caching and hosting activities.

In the Netherlands, a number of court decisions establishing the liability of certain Internet (Service) Providers for copyright infringement have given rise to a further discussion on the limits of the duty of care of Internet Service Providers. These cases were primarily heard in courts of lower instance and were mostly about websites that were not entitled to the status of hosting services and the corresponding liability restrictions contained in the E-commerce Directive. In each case, the involvement in copyright breaches was such that the limited definition of hosting activities in this directive did not apply. In one case, the court ordered an Internet Service Provider in a provisional relief procedure to intervene by denying access to a website holder who had unlawfully facilitated a copyright breach. In the literature, there is much criticism of this decision.

In the Netherlands, the private use exception in the current Copyright Act, on the basis of which copying, including downloading, of copyright-protected material for private purposes is a permitted act, has recently been under discussion at parliamentary level. Such an exception (where copying for private use also covers downloading) cannot be found in the copyright legislation in the other countries under study. A parliamentary commission in the Netherlands has proposed to delete the current exception with respect to downloading. This discussion also dealt with the question of whether and how Internet Service Providers can play a part in enforcing the proposed new prohibition. New regulations might include the abolition of the private use exception and the introduction of enhanced enforcement mechanisms (primarily aimed at commercial and large-scale infringements).

In the United Kingdom, the duty of care of Internet Service Providers has hitherto been based on the liability restrictions of the E-commerce Directive, as implemented in national legislation. By virtue of the Digital Economy Act, however, Internet Service Providers are to forward notifications of rightful claimants to alleged infringers actively. On the basis of the new provisions, the providers also need to keep lists of end-users who have been the subject of such notifications. They also need to make these lists with identifiable data available to rightful claimants to help detect repeated breaches by end-users.

The internet user's identity is not to be disclosed by means of these lists. If forwarding the notifications does not result in bringing an end to the infringements, Internet Service Providers can be obliged to impose technical restrictions on the use of internet connections.

In Germany, the implementation of the E-commerce Directive is decisive for the duty of care of Internet Service Providers with regard to the protection of copyright on the internet. The German regulations implement the provisions of the Directive literally.

In France, the new legislation, known as the HADOPI laws (*Haute Autorité pour la Diffusion des Oeuvres et la Protection des Droits sur Internet*), has introduced obligations for internet access providers. These obligations are new in comparison with the existing duties of care arising from the E-commerce Directive regarding mere conduit, caching and hosting activities by Internet Service Providers.

Due to the end-users' obligation to secure their internet connection to prevent copyright infringements – an obligation laid down in the French Code of Intellectual Property – Internet Service Providers must propose efficient technical measures that are suitable for that purpose. Such measures are included in a list prepared by the HADOPI authority, which was set up pursuant to the new legislation. Additionally, Internet Service Providers must inform end-users in their user agreements about the possible sanctions in the event of non-compliance with the aforementioned obligation. If the HADOPI authority, together with the judicial authorities, decides to intervene, internet service providers can be required to send warning emails to end-users (stating that the unauthorised use has been detected) or, in the event of ongoing negligence, to cut off internet connections. If Internet Service Providers fail to cooperate, they may be subject to a penalty.

In French jurisprudence the interpretation of the duties of care of Internet Service Providers has focused primarily on the limitation of liability for hosting activities, as defined in the implementing legislation of the E-commerce Directive. As in the Netherlands, the interpretation is usually made by courts of lower instance – and not confirmed by higher courts.

Many cases concern the actual knowledge of hosting providers about the presence of unlawful material, which is required to establish intervention as an obligation for hosting providers, pursuant to the formulation of the liability restriction. In a few cases, hosting providers received an injunction, on the basis of their duty of care, to prevent any attempt to put the same content on the internet again after it had been removed from a website for the first time. Concerning the HADOPI legislation, interviewed stakeholders in the study by Van Eijk and Van Engers (2010) expressed many doubts. They warned that such stringent legislation might lead to the development and use of encryption technology for the distribution of copyright-protected material. The same technology could then be used to share illegal content. Some emphasised that Internet Service Providers should not be put in the position of having to monitor internet traffic or contribute to punitive measures against end-users. There is also much doubt about the capacity of Internet Service Providers and of the judicial authorities to support the active approach of copyright protection prescribed by the HADOPI legislation. Investigating authorities also questioned the proportionality of the measures and pointed to the relationship with other investigating authorities with respect to cyber crime. Many parties also pleaded for restraint when it comes to adopting HADOPI-like legislation.

Similar questions were raised in the context of the Digital Economy Act in the UK. Another issue with respect to the regulations in France and the UK is how they relate to the new Article 1, paragraph 3a of the Framework Directive, which stipulates that measures taken by member states regarding end-users' access to, or use of, services and applications through electronic communications networks shall respect the fundamental rights and freedoms of natural persons, as guaranteed by the European Convention for the Protection of Human Rights and Fundamental Freedoms and general principles of Community law. This includes the right to privacy and rules on due process.

20.5 Internet Service Providers: general observations and conclusions

The environment of the subject under study – duties of care on the internet – is dynamic. Nevertheless, some general observations are provided here, and conclusions formulated.

Value chain

Internet Service Providers are among the players who are active in the (economic) value chain between end-users and the providers of services. This is confirmed when we hold the three themes up against the light. In several parts, specific duties of care for Internet Service Providers can be discerned, arising from the sector-specific regulation or in consequence of the rules on

E-commerce. At first sight, placing the responsibility on the Internet Service Providers seems to be a simple option. After all, it is Internet Service Providers who control the end-users' access to the internet. Internet Service Providers are gatekeepers, and they fulfil a bottleneck job.

At the same time, it becomes clear that this approach is becoming increasingly less compatible with the dynamics of the internet (such as the involvement of many – interacting – parties), with the associated business models, with considerations of efficiency and with aspects of general interest. It is true that internet service providers are pivotal, but they constitute just one of the parties in a complex value chain. Imposing the duties of care only on the Internet Service Providers causes an imbalance, which on the one hand does not do justice to the providers' position, and on the other hand brings with it some adverse effects for the provision of services and innovation, for instance. After all, Internet Service Providers will assess their risks on the basis of their own business model. If this allows only a limited risk margin, it is likely that the risks will be ruled out or mitigated, with the result that services that increase the risk will no longer be accessible for end-users or that new services will not be developed. Efficiency considerations are also important: after further testing, seemingly obvious solutions may appear to be inefficient or may appear to lead to high costs (this is the case with filtering or deep packet inspection, for instance). The general interest plays a role when it comes to securing access to the internet for everybody at affordable rates.

The importance of a value-chain oriented approach is gaining attention in the literature.[85] Internet Service Providers in particular are critical of the extent to which they are considered to have duties of care. They blame this partly on their high profile and their direct relationship with end-users. At any rate, other parties in the value chain agree that in many cases Internet Service Providers are not the party on whom the duties of care should rest, and take a stand themselves as well. This is apparent, for instance, in their involvement in the fight against child pornography and in enforcing copyright.

Internet access/service providers

Internet Service Providers provide access to the internet to end-users and additionally perform various other tasks, such as hosting personal pages on websites or supplying added-value services, such as email. It is clear that sufficient

---

85 OECD (2010); Dommering & Van Eijk (2010); Rand Europe (2008); Ofcom (2008).

importance should be attached to this distinction. In their capacity as access providers, the Internet Service Providers are subject to the light E-commerce regime of 'mere conduit' anyway, but they also claim that the message/content is of no concern to them and that they, as distributors, cannot be held responsible for the content of what they transport.

As distributors the Internet Service Providers are required to respect the confidentiality of communications, it is stated, and therefore they cannot actually bear any responsibility for what internet users (or service providers) do on the internet. Some access providers suggestthat, in principle, they are obliged to allow spam to pass through, for instance – after all, the traffic between providers and users is not to be hampered with – but they use spam filters on the basis of a "separate" contractual relationship with the end-users. In this context, it is important to ascertain where the protection that goes with the 'mere conduit' regime of the E-commerce Directive begins and ends. Can the Internet Service Providers as an access provider be strictly separated from the Internet Service Providers as a provider of additional services, such as spam filtering? Are such services to be regarded as a separate category or is this a matter of activities that are subject to (or are to be included in) the rules for hosting/caching?

These arguments partly coincide with the viewpoints that are generally expressed in the discussion about net neutrality. Supplementary to this, it is argued that internet access can be regarded more and more as a universal service. Even though providers are each other's competitors, they believe that end-users are entitled to internet access and that in principle they cannot discriminate against users at admission.

Local context

From the stocktaking and analysis of national regulations, it becomes clear that national circumstances are to some extent decisive for the way in which the regulations are set up. In the United Kingdom, self-regulation has traditionally been highly developed. This is also reflected in the system adopted for combating child pornography, which goes beyond merely a notification system. In France, the emphasis is rather on regulation through statutory legislation, and self-regulation is clearly less developed than in the United Kingdom. Germany's position is closer to that of the United Kingdom than to the French position. In broad outline, the Dutch practice seems to be close to the German position. There is self-regulation, and it works, more particularin the case of child pornography. The code of conduct for 'notice and take down' provides some added value but also has its weak aspects, such as a wide potential for interpretation and the absence of an enforcement mechanism.

Conclusions

A varied picture emerges, which indicates that developments, including improving the balance within the value chain, are still in progress. Internet security, more particularly with regard to the relationship between the Internet Service Provider and the end-user, is still in its infancy. This does not mean that nothing is happening in practice, but formally a framework has scarcely yet been defined, and there is little self-regulation at this stage. On the other hand, there is a virtually identical system for child pornography in the countries under study, where parties are prepared to provide far-reaching assistance in combating this phenomenon. The (INHOPE) notification system is found in all four countries, either on the basis of self-regulation or in consequence of a legally defined duty of care. The use of filtering is a recurring issue in the prevention of the proliferation of child pornography. Much attention is devoted to copyright, and in two countries the regulations on copyright have been tightened, so that it has become possible to restrict internet access or to cut end-users off from the internet. There is strong criticism of the new rules, and Van Eijk et al. (2011) show that the actual enforcement possibilities are also subject to much criticism.

279

Key concepts

Mere conduit
Caching
Hosting
Internet security
Child pornography
Copyright

21 Information Security

Pieter Hartel & Nanna Suryana Herman

21.1 Introduction and definitions

Information security is all about the protection of digital assets, such as digital content, personal health records, state secrets etc. These assets can be handled by a party who is authorised to access and control the asset or a party who is *not* authorised to do so. *Authorisation* determines who is trusted to actually handle an asset. Two concepts complement authorisation. *Authentication* determines who makes a request to handle an asset. To decide who is authorised, a system needs to authenticate the user. There are three different ways in which users can be authenticated. You can use something you know (e.g. password, pin code), something you have (e.g. smart card, RFID tag) or something that is a personal physical property (e.g. fingerprint, your gait). These methods can be combined to provide stronger authentication than when they are applied individually. *Auditing* makes it possible to determine who handled an asset and how, so that ultimately an attacker can be prosecuted. The three concepts are known collectively as the 'gold standard', since 'Au' is the chemical symbol for gold (Lampson 2004).

There are three important security properties of digital assets. *Confidentiality* is the ability of a system to stop unauthorised users from handling protected assets. *Integrity* is the assurance that every asset or system component is exactly as the last authorised party to modify it has left it. *Availability* is the assurance that authorised users may find the system to work as they expect it to, when they expect it to. These properties (collectively known as the CIA) are true security properties and the focus of this chapter.

21.2 Design and attacks

One should design security into a system right from the start, rather than backstitching it later on. Still, a good design is difficult to achieve because one weak link is enough to spoil everything. The engineer can apply a multilayer approach or 'defence in depth'. If one line of defence fails, there will be another in place. Still, one hundred per cent security does not exist. Therefore the engineer should estimate the residual risk and decide what to do about it (e.g. take out insurance).

Regardless of the security precautions taken, systems will be attacked. The most common attacks exploit the weakest link, which is the human. People are notoriously careless, which makes life easy for the attacker. The second most common problem is the software, which is full of bugs that attackers can exploit. For example the Windows system consists of hundreds of millions of lines of code. The likelihood that there are errors in this complex code is high (Tanenbaum et al. 2006), and indeed, once a month Microsoft issues a long list of patches, that computers must install to be protected against the latest vulnerabilities. The most common problems that arise in software are again human errors. Computer owners who do not install the patches in good time run a serious risk of having their computers broken into. Many PCs all over the world are actually hijacked by attackers who have exploited software bugs. The hijacked PCs are now part of so-called botnets, which can be controlled by the attackers for a variety of purposes (such as identity theft or sending spam). Finally there are many interesting technical problems, such as badly designed encryption algorithms (for example both the encryption of the GSM phone system and the encryption of the DVD content protection are broken). However, exploiting such more technical vulnerabilities requires more effort than those mentioned above; hence they are less often exploited.

21.3 Some building blocks of information security

Cryptography and Artificial Intelligence offer the basic building blocks for information security. These building blocks are functions that are easy to compute if some secret key is available, but hard to computer without the key. The Kerckhoffs Principle of information security states that the functions and protocols should be publicly known, and that the strength of the security should depend only on the properties of the key (Kerckhoffs 1883). The idea is that it is easier to replace a compromised key than it is to redesign and implement a system once the design has been compromised.

Artificial intelligence

The most important computation from Artificial Intelligence is a CAPTCHA: a Completely Automated Public Turing tests to tell Computers and Humans Apart (Von Ahn 2004). Many websites use this to avoid automated scripts performing actions that only humans should do. A CAPTCHA usually looks like a word spelled in distorted letters, which you are asked to read and then type. If you type the letters correctly, the web site assumes that it is not some program that has recognised the distorted letters but a human. The underlying assumption is that humans are much better at recognising images than computers, which so far has not been disproved. If someone comes up with an efficient method for recognising a CAPTCHA the security of this method will instantly broken.

Cryptography

One of the most important computations from Cryptography is the discrete logarithm. This is the opposite of modular exponentiation in the same sense as division is the opposite of multiplication.

To be more precise, by modular exponentiation we mean, given suitable large numbers g, x and n calculate g to the power x modulo n and call the result c, (or as a formula $c=g^x$ *mod n*). By the discrete logarithm we mean to calculate x again from c, g and n. It is unknown whether calculating the discrete logarithm is really hard, but this is assumed to be the case because nobody has ever discovered an efficient way of doing it. As soon as someone discovers an efficient solution, then all systems based on the hardness assumption of the discrete logarithm (i.e. basically everything we do on the internet) will be instantly broken. This is unlikely to happen but cannot be excluded.

283

Cryptography: ciphers

Cryptography can be defined as secret writing, for which symmetric and asymmetric ciphers as well as hash functions are used.

Symmetric ciphers allow a message to be encrypted and subsequently decrypted, both with the same secret key. In general a symmetric cipher must satisfy the following requirement: for all messages m, and all keys k, it must be the case that first encrypting m to a e, and then decrypting e should produce m again, or in a formula: if e = *encrypt(m, k)* then *decrypt(e, k)* = m. Practical algorithms, which are widely used, are DES and AES. DES requires a key of 56 bits, and AES supports keys of 128, 196 and 256 bits. See for more detail Menezes et al. (2001).

To break a cipher, an attacker could use the brute force method. This means trying each possible key until the decryption succeeds. To make attacks infeasible the key should be long. When DES was first introduced, computers were so slow that a key of 56 bits was sufficiently long to make the brute force attack infeasible. At the time of writing this is no longer the case, hence DES is being replaced by AES with longer keys.

Asymmetric ciphers *allow a message to be encrypted with one key of a key pair, whereas the decryption requires the other half of the key pair. Normally one the keys of the pair, let's call it p, is made public, whereas the other, let's call it s, is kept secret. This makes it possible to communicate securely in a number of clever ways that cannot be achieved with symmetric ciphers (Menezes et al. 2001). For all messages m, and all key pairs (s, p), it must be the case that encryption followed by decryption gives back m, or in a formula: if* e = encrypt(m, s) *then* decrypt(e, p) = m.

An asymmetric cipher can be used to sign a message. Let us suppose that Alice has a secret key s and a public key p. If she now encrypts the message m with her secret key, i.e. by computing the $e = encrypt(m, s)$, then everyone else will be able to decrypt the e with Alice's public key p, i.e. by computing $d = decrypt(e, p)$. If the decryption succeeds, we know that Alice must have encrypted it, as only she holds the secret key s. Encrypting a message with a secret key is thus similar to signing a document: only the signatory could have done it, and everybody else can check it.

For this mechanism to work properly, the party verifying the signature must be absolutely certain that he is using the public key p of Alice. This is the purpose of a public key certificate, which contains a public key, as well as information identifying the person to whom this public key belongs. And guess how we can check that the certificate is not forged? We can do so by having the certificates signed by a trusted third party, such as VeriSign. And how do we then check the signature of the trusted third party? Well in the most common application of signatures this has been solved in a simple way: your web browser contains the public keys of a large number of trusted third parties, including VeriSign.

Asymmetric ciphers are usually significantly slower than symmetric ciphers, so in practical systems we need both.

Cryptography: Hash functions

Hash functions calculate a kind of 'fingerprint' of a digital asset. A hash function maps an arbitrary length message to a bit string of fixed length with the following properties:

- it is easy to calculate the hash of a given message;
- it is practically impossible to invert;
- it is extremely unlikely that two different input messages give the same hash.

A typical application of a hash function is signing long messages. As we indicated above, an asymmetric cipher is usually quite slow, so instead of signing the message itself, it is faster to sign the hash of the message. The properties of hash functions as listed above ensure that signing the hash is as secure against forgery as signing the original message. The most commonly used hash function is SHA-1, which hashes any input to a string of 160 bits. However, its design has shown some weaknesses and currently the US National Institute of Standards and Technology (NIST) are in the process of selecting a new standard hash function.

Cryptographic Protocols

Protocols allow a sequence of messages to be exchanged in a secure fashion. For example de Diffie-Hellman key exchange protocol (Diffie & Hellman 1986) can be used by two people (Alice and Bob) to agree a secret key in such a way that:

- the eavesdropper Eve does not learn the key;
- Alice and Bob do not need to know each other beforehand;
- Alice and Bob do not need the assistance of someone else.

Such a protocol cannot be built using symmetric ciphers alone. The protocol assumes that Alice and Bob agree on two numbers, n and g. There is no need to keep n and g secret; one could imagine that a government publishes them in a newspaper to ensure that all citizens who wish to communicate securely with each other using the Diffie-Hellman key exchange protocol have access to n and g.

Step	Alice (knows n and g)	Bob (knows n and g)
1	pick a random number $x < n$	
2	compute $a=g^x$ and send it to Bob	
3		receive a from Alice
4		pick a random number $y < n$
5		compute $b=g^y$ and send it to Alice
6	receive b from Bob	
7	$k = b^x$	$k = a^y$

At step 3, Bob receives the value that Alice has computed by raising g to the power of x and Bob remembers this value as a. When the protocol completes, at step 7, both Alice and Bob have the same key k, and nobody else has this key. Why? Let us first check that $b^x = a^y$ as required by computing $b^x = (g^y)^x = (g^x)^y = a^y$. Eve will only see g^x and g^y from which she cannot easily compute either x or y, unless Eve has solved the discrete log problem.

The protocol as described above is not secure against a man-in-the-middle attack (Menezes et al. 2001). A variant that is secure against this attack is used when a web browser connects to a web site using links that begin with 'https://'.

21.4 Biometrics

Biometrics can be defined as 'using measurable biological characteristics to identify people'. Biometrics can be based on physiological traits (face, finger-print) or behavioural traits (gait). We will focus on physiological biometrics, as these are used most. Biometric technologies can be used for verification of a claimed identity and for recognition of a specific person from a collection of people. The latter is harder than the former; we cannot explain the technical reasons here (Jain et al. 2000). For a biometric to be useful it must be:

– universal, i.e. the majority of people should be able to use it;
– unique, i.e. the probability that two people have exactly the same biometric should be small;
– permanent, i.e. it should be difficult to remove a biometric. Sandpaper applied to a finger is a relatively painless method to destroy a finger print, albeit temporarily;
– collectable, i.e. people should not normally object to their biometric being used. DNA is an example of a biometric that most people would object to. Fingerprints have a crime connotation and are often objectionable too.
– live, i.e. it must be hard to create a fake biometric. See Van der Putte & Keuning (2000) for a detailed account of how to create a fake fingerprint.

A biometric system is never perfect. A biometric system can make two essen-tially different types of error. The first is False Accept, i.e. an imposter is accepted as a genuine user. The second error is False Reject, i.e. a genuine user is rejected. To compensate for the errors, a biometric system can be optimised for the application. For example a high security application, such as the launch control of a nuclear missile should never falsely accept, but it might regularly falsely reject. This means that when the president really wants to launch the missile, he may have to try a few times. On the other hand, a home banking application should not annoy the user with too many false rejects, and may on occasion let an imposter use your bank account.

A biometric system operates in two modes. The first is enrolment mode: the biometric is captured and stored in the database, along with the identification of the person. This must be done under controlled circumstances, so that only genuine users are enrolled into the system. The second is authentication mode: the biometric is captured and compared to the biometric found in the database for the person wishing to be authenticated. Since a biometric is a permanent feature of a person, we must make sure that it cannot fall into the hands of the attackers. For this a range of template protection technologies are available (Jain et al. 2008). Biometrics cannot be lost or forgotten, which in principle makes it possible to create a user friendly and secure authentication system.

21.5 Physical security

Software is full of bugs and so flexible that it can be changed easily. This makes software an ideal target of attack. The attacker does not even have to be near the software to change it. A physical system (such as a PC, server or smartcard) can be complex too, but it is quite inflexible, hence hard to change, and certainly not easy to change remotely. This gives physical security an advantage over software (Anderson & Kuhn 1996). Physical security does not only apply to computers but also to the real world around us. We will discuss this aspect of physical security too.

Smart cards and RFID tags

A smart card is an inexpensive, tiny computer with some non-volatile memory, which can perform cryptographic, and other operations, and which can store keys and passwords. Smart cards are better at protecting secrets than PCs because they have been designed specifically for that purpose. A smart card has specific security features, such as a tamper resistant design, and a true random number generator that uses physical measurements as a source of randomness. A smart card communicates with the card reader via a number of (gold) contacts. Smart cards are heavily used in Banking and pay TV applications. Smart cards exist with batteries, biometric sensors, displays, keypads etc. but these are non-standard as the cost of such cards is relatively high (Praca & Barral 2001).

An RFID tag (Radio Frequency Identification) is a smart card that has an antenna instead of a contact pad. When an RFID tag is held near the reader, the energy of the electro magnetic field emitted by the reader is used to power the tag. At the same time the antenna is used to send and receive information from the tag to the reader and vice versa. RFID tags have many uses; we give a few examples. They are embedded in our modern e-Passport. The US retailer Wall Mart uses RFID tags for every box or crate that enters or leaves their warehouses for inventory control. Many institutions and businesses require staff and students to carry an RFID tag to enter and leave buildings.

An RFID tag does not have an on/off switch because it switches itself on when the tag is near the reader. This means that it is also possible to read any tags that people carry around with them without the victim being able to notice this. This is not good for privacy (Garcia et al. 2008). The e-Passport at least offers some protection against privacy leaks, as the immigration officer must first put the machine-readable zone of your passport in a machine before the RFID tag in the passport will disclose sensitive information. There have been rumours that the European Central Bank wanted to embed RFID tags in banknotes to make forgery harder. This would clearly have been bad for privacy (Juels & Pappu 2003).

Physical attacks

Poorly designed or badly implemented technology is a good target for attackers too. There are too many attacks to mention them all here, but we will mention one ingenious class of attack, called a side channel attack. The idea is that the transistors in an electronic device draw varying amounts of current when they switch. A computer contains millions of transistors that switch all the time. By analysing the amount of current drawn from the power supply, it is in principle possible to work out what the computer is doing. This includes finding out what the secret keys are. Side channel attacks are surprisingly difficult to defend against, and in any case a good defence only makes the attack only harder to commit, and never impossible (Witteman 2002).

Physical attacks include attacks on people. An attacker may blackmail a system administrator, or bribe the cleaning staff to get hold of secret information. Social engineering works well too. A thief can steal a laptop by convincing his victims that they should give the laptop to him (Dimkov et al. 2010), for example by pretending to belong to the IT department.

21.6 Storage security

To reduce the cost of ownership, businesses hire storage and computing capacity at specialised companies, a practice known as cloud computing. How should we then store confidential data, such as electronic health records, or intellectual property? Would it not be naïve to expect that the cloud computing service provider that looks after our data is not curious to see what is being stored? And why would cloud service providers want to know what data they are storing? This could be a serious liability too (Schneier 2005b).

The problem then arises of storing data in such a manner that the data base server can search the data for the client, but in such a way that even a curious server does not learn very much from the data. We call this an honest-but-curious data base server: it is honest in the sense that it can be trusted to answer the queries of the client truthfully, but it is curious in the sense that it cannot be trusted not to look at our data. There are many problems that have been published recently, which would not have occurred if people had assumed that the data base server might be curious. For example in 2007 the Heartland Payment processor lost 130 million credit card numbers that were stored in plaintext on their systems. As a result the company went bankrupt.

289

21.7 Internet banking

So far the most reliable way for someone to be authenticated on the internet is by the technology used by banks: with two factor authentication a customer uses his username and password to log into an internet backing server, and for every transaction the bank will send a transaction authorisation code (TAC) by SMS to the mobile phone of the customer. A hacker would have to intercept the username and password and he would have to intercept the TAC. The hacker might find it relatively easy to do one or the other, but to do both for the same user would certainly be harder. Two factor authentication is a good example of the principle of defence in depth that we mentioned in section 21.2. It works well because the username and password and the TAC travel over different networks (i.e. the internet and the mobile phone network). Two factor authentication is better than one factor authentication, but it too can be attacked (Schneier 2005a). The increasing popularity of smart phones which integrate the networks can be expected to undermine the security of this form of two factor authentication.

While we are on the subject of internet banking it is useful to reiterate that the security of any process is as strong as the weakest link, which as usual is the user, or more specifically in this case the PC of the user. Banks require their customers to adhere to the five golden rules:

– check the padlock of the https request on your browser;
– keep virus scanner and firewall up to date;
– don't open suspect attachments;
– don't install suspect software;
– check your statements.

21.8 Critical infrastructure security

Recently, the sector that manages the nation's critical infrastructure (e.g. water, gas, oil, electricity, railways) has started to switch over to internet and PC based technology because of the relatively low cost (Igure et al. 2006). To ensure reliable operation, process control systems are usually built with redundant components, so that if one component breaks down, another can take over. A second (back up) control network can be built alongside the system. However, the cost of building a back up control network is high so the temptation is to use the internet.

For the attackers this is good news. Where before they had to drive to one of the installations, cut the fence and break in to get access to the control network, now they can attack a nuclear power plant from the comfort of their own house. This is exactly what happened recently with the Stuxnet virus, which was specifically designed to attack Iranian nuclear power plants (Grier 2010). We believe that the risks of using the internet for critical infrastructures are underestimated.

21.9 Conclusions

We have painted a somewhat gloomy picture of the security of the internet, and the PCs that we all use to connect to the network, and we have not yet even mentioned (the lack of) privacy. Privacy is a concept that is closely related to security. It is the right of an individual to determine what information about oneself to share with others (Warren & Brandeis 1890). Sometimes security can improve privacy, for example when Alice encrypts her email, her privacy is more likely to be maintained than when she sends it unencrypted. Sometimes security hinders privacy, for example when Alice installs new software on her PC, which 'calls home' to check that the licence is valid. In this case the vendor learns that Alice has just installed their software, without Alice being able to control it.

We believe, like the designers of the current internet, that the time is ripe to build a new internet with security properties built into it. The most important property would be that when armed with a court order it should be possible to trace the origin of any attack to the person who did it. The attacker should not be able to hide from the law. Without such a court order no such tracing should be possible to offer privacy. It is a formidable challenge to design such a network, but it is better to start working on it rather than to wait until hackers discover how to take an entire continent or even the global internet out of the air.

Key concepts

Asymmetric cipher
Auditing
Authentication
Authorisation
Availability
Biometrics
Confidentiality
Cryptography
Integrity
Symmetric cipher

Key concepts

Addiction (to gaming)	A loss of control over the behaviour which results in significant harm, thought to be identifiable through the components loss of control, conflict, preoccupation/salience, coping/mood modification, and withdrawal symptoms.
(Additional) Protocol	An agreement with which states supplement an earlier treaty or convention.
Adolescents	Although the scientific age demarcation of the period of adolescence is not clear, adolescents are usually referred to as youth in between the ages of 13 and 18 years, gender differences aside.
Adolescents' media practice model (AMPM)	The AMPM assumes that youth already have developed an identity influenced by the conditions of their own lives' history. The identity of youth determines the motivation for the selection of media content at a specific moment. The motivation then shapes the attention for and the interaction with this chosen content, followed by the interpretation and evaluation of the seen content proceeding from their present identity. The evaluation produces two possible reactions: the incorporation of media content in youth's attitudinal and behavioural patterns or not.
Advance fee fraud	Scams in which people are ripped off for large amounts of money that has to be paid in advance. Typically, victims are convinced that they will receive large sums of money (e.g. an inheritance or lottery) but in order to get the money they have to pay a certain amount of money (for example to cover legal costs).
Aggression	Individual or group behaviour that purposively aims to inflict pain or suffering on other people.
Anonymity	The ability to engage in social action and communication without having one's identity available to others.
Armed attack	"A use of force that rises to a certain scope, duration, and intensity threshold within the meaning of Article 51 of the Charter of the United Nations that invokes a state's inherent right of self-defence" (Wingfield 2000: 373).
Asymmetric cipher	Method that allows a message to be encrypted with one key from a pair, whereas the decryption requires the other key from the same pair.
Auditing	Strategies to determine who handled an asset and how, so that ultimately an attacker can be prosecuted.
Authentication	Strategies to determine who makes a request to handle an asset.

293

Authorisation	Strategies to determine who is trusted to actually handle an asset.
Availability	The assurance that authorised users may find the system to work as they expect it to, when they expect it to.
Biometrics	Using measurable biological characteristics to identify people
Botnet	A remotely controlled network of infected computers that can be used for various criminal activities.
Bystanders (cyberbullying)	Witnesses of cyberbullying (see also 'cyberbullying').
Caching (ISP)	The temporary but unmodified storage of information.
Cheating (in gaming)	Cheating involves breaking the regular rules of the game environment in order to gain an unfair advantage.
Child pornography	Each image – or data carrier, which includes an image – of a sexual act in which someone who seemingly has not yet reached the age of 18 years is being involved, or appears to be involved.
Confidentiality	The ability of a system to stop unauthorised users from handling protected assets.
Convention	An agreement between a large number of states, reflecting positions that are shared among many. Other states can join later on.
Copyright	The exclusive right to the publication, production, or sale of the rights to a literary, dramatic, musical, or artistic work to an author, composer, artist, distributor or publisher, indicated by the symbol ©.
Crime	Any act that contravenes law and is subject to prosecution and punishment by the state.
Cryptography	Secret writing.
Cultivation theory	Cultivation theory takes its departure from two underlying assumptions. Firstly, the media construct a homogeneous and stereotypical image of reality; and secondly, the users of these media create for themselves a subjective reality corresponding with the image of reality imposed by the media. As a consequence, frequently occurring stereotypical images in the media affect the attitudes of regular consumers; and concurrently, those consumers evaluate their own lives in view of standards shown in these stereotypical images.
Cyberbullying	Bullying via ICT.

294

Cyber crime	(1) Used as; the umbrella concept for all forms of crime in which ICT plays a crucial role. There are two distinct subcategories. The first subcategory is 'cyber crime in the narrow sense' This subcategory includes all forms of crime in which ICT is used both as a means and a target, such as hacking and the spread of viruses. The second subcategory is 'cyber crime in the broad sense', a category including all crimes where ICT is essential for the execution, but where ICT is not a target. (2) Sometimes used as: crime in which ICT is used both as a means and a target, such as hacking and the spread of viruses. (3) Maybe in the future: it is not a key concept; the term is not needed to study crime and the way technology is used to commit it, nor is the term needed to fight crime in the internet era.
Cyber-crime Convention	An international legal mechanism for cooperation in law enforcement and harmonisation of laws (see also 'convention').
Cyber safety	Safety within the social structure of the internet.
Cyber space	The social structure within the internet.
Cyberwar	An attack, originating from abroad, employing virtual means, purporting to damage or disrupt a state's physical or digital infrastructure.
Data Protection	The right to control the release of personal information about oneself, even when that data is already collected and stored by a third party.
Defacing	Electronic graffiti, or the staining of the homepage of a site by hackers without the permission of the owner.
Deviance	Behaviour that may not necessarily be criminal, but which may transgress collective norms about appropriate or acceptable behaviour. While crimes are subject to formal, legal sanctions, those actions deemed deviant may be subject to informal sanctions such as social stigmatisation and denunciation.
Direct cyberbullying	Forms of cyberbullying in which the victim is directly involved (see also 'cyberbullying').
Disinhibition	The absence of non-verbal communication cues in cyberspace may motivate people to share their most intimate emotions, fears and desires with each other (also called *benign* disinhibition), but also induce them to use rude language, hatred and threats (so-called *toxic* disinhibition).
Distributed Denial of Service (DDoS) attack	Attacks on a system or service with the aim of overloading them and making them unavailable.
Distributor of child pornography (commercial)	Organised networks that trade in child pornography and see this as a new way to make money (see also 'child pornography').

295

Distributor of child pornography (enthusiasts)	This group wants to acquire new child pornographic material and is not primarily aimed at earning money. The sexual abuse of children (self or to exhort others) in order to produce new material is part of the core business of these offenders (see also 'child pornography').
Distributor of child pornography (youngsters)	A new group of producers and distributors of child pornography. Youngsters – with or without the consent of each other – make sexually explicit pictures and movies of each other. Once this content has landed on the internet, it becomes, according to the law, child pornography (see also 'child pornography').
EU Directive	A regulatory text from the competent EU institutions that is binding for the member states to implement minimum rules or a minimum situation for a common purpose.
EU Framework Decision	A regulatory text from the competent EU institutions, that is binding for the member states to implement minimum rules or a minimum situation for a common purpose (under the law before the Lisbon Treaty, used for justice and home affairs).
File sharing	Catchall term for uploading and downloading of (entertainment) content, encompassing a range of technologies, from peer-to-peer file sharing networks such as Bittorrent and file hosting services such as Usenet.
Formal social control	Control exercised by people who have this specific control function based on the rules of society. The control is as it were mandated and the controllers acts on behalf of third parties. The police is a form of formal social control.
Fraud	Deception aimed at gaining financial profit. The essence of fraud is: through deception people obtain money or property to which they are not entitled, whereby they infringe on the rights of others.
Function creep	The notion that, over time, the functionality of a system may change and grow, encompassing functions that are different from the original purposes of the system.
Globalisation	The social, economic, political and cultural processes in which local and national spatial limits on interaction are overcome, and come to span the globe.
Hacking	The intentional and unlawful intrusion into an automated work.
Hackers (information warriors and political activists)	Politically motivated hackers (see also 'hacking').
Hackers (internals)	(Ex-)employees with feelings of revenge (see also 'hacking').

Hackers (novice and newbies, script kiddies, copycatters and amateur fame seekers)	These hackers are characterised by a lack of technical knowledge. They thrive on copying the scripts of others. In this group we find the unskilful hackers who are exploring their possibilities and try to expand their knowledge. They are not worried or ignorant about potential damage their actions might cause (see also 'hacking').
Hackers (old guard hackers or innovators)	The group is driven by intellectual challenge and curiosity. The hackers in this group are probably those who have most to do with old hacking values such as freedom of information (see also 'hacking').
Hackers (petty thieves)	These are hackers who act like petty criminals (or petty criminals who have mastered digital technology) (see also 'hacking').
Hackers (professional criminals or organised cyber gangsters)	Groups of organised criminals. The 'virus writers or coders' can be hired by the organised cyber criminals (see also 'hacking').
Harmonisation	The development to change national law and/or policy towards similarity to an agreed standard; example: introduction of uniform descriptions of criminal behavior.
Hate crime	Internet-facilitated 'hate propaganda' (e.g. targeting specific racial or religious groups).
Hosting (ISP)	Activities associated with the storage of information provided by a recipient of the service. This includes hosting of a website or personal pages by an ISP.
Identity theft	The unlawful use of another's identifying information for gain.
Iframe injection	An inline frame-injection is an invisible addition to a web page to ensure that the page loads a piece of (malicious) code from elsewhere.
Indirect cyberbullying	Forms of cyberbullying that can take place without direct involvement of the victim (see also 'cyberbullying').
Informal social control	A form of order maintenance that is undertaken by citizens.
Information Society	A stage of socio-economic development in which the importance previously allocated to the production of material goods and resources is superseded by the centrality of knowledge and information in economic activity.
Integrity	The assurance that every asset or system component is exactly as the last authorised party to modify it has left it.
International responsibility	"[The] new legal relations which arise under international law by reason of the internationally wrongful act of a State" (Draft Articles on State Responsibility, p. 32).

Internet	Global infrastructure of interconnected computer networks that can be used for all kinds of online services and applications.
Internet characteristics	Immediacy, anonymity and global yet 'borderless' reach.
Internet security (ISP)	The security of the services provided by providers of publicly available electronic communication services.
IP address	Internet Protocol address. Numerical label assigned to each network interface of a host (e.g., computer or device) that is connected to the internet. An IP address is used as identifier and address of the host.
Legal pluralism	The divergences and differences in criminal law between different sovereign nations.
Mere conduit (ISP)	Consists of the unmodified transfer of, or providing access to, information includes the core activity of Internet Service Providers, i.e. providing access to the internet.
Moral panic	A sociological term for an exaggerated reaction to a perceived, suddenly increasing threat to accepted moral standards or vulnerable groups leading to injudicious efforts to secure safety among the public.
Mutual assistance	The activity of state authorities to help their colleagues from other countries in the investigation, prosecution and adjudication of crime and the execution of sentences; example: collection and surrender of information, obtained from a computer search
Online moderation	A form of secundary informal social control (see also secundary informal social control).
Online sale and auction fraud	The victim buys goods or services via the internet, and pays for the goods or services, but never receives them (or, if s/he does receive them, they are of much lower quality than promised), or when during an online auction the price of an article is artificially increased by the owner.
Orwellian society	A government that uses information technology to discipline its citizens.
Packet switching	Communication method for digital networks in which data is transmitted in sized blocks, called packets, which are routed independently through the network from sender to receiver. Packet switching contrasts with circuit switching, a communication method in which a dedicated connection is established between sender and receiver for exclusive use during the communication session.
Personal Identifiable Information (PII)	Information that can be linked, with reasonable effort, to a natural person.
Pharming	An attack with technological resources in order to steal confidential information from a user. Unlike phishing, social engineering is not deployed.

Phishing	An attack that combines social engineering and technological resources in order to steal confidential information from a user.
Policing	A wide range of activities that serve to monitor and control social behaviour. Policing may be undertaken by official state-sanctioned bodies (such as the police), by private organisations, by communities or individuals.
Policing	To regulate, control, or keep in order with, or as if with, a law enforcement agency.
Privacy by design	The concept that privacy should already be adopted as one of the *design parameters* of a system in the early stages of systems design.
Privacy Enhancing Technologies (PET)	Technical measures to protect privacy.
Privacy (in the context of information systems)	The right to control the release of personal information about oneself, even when that data is already collected and stored by a third party.
Private copying exception	Clause in many copyright laws in Europe stating that the copying of protected works for private use is allowed without prior consent of rights holders. This clause implicates, as stated in many court cases, that the downloading of protected works of art and literature from unauthorised sources is not illegal.
Protocol layer	Complex communication protocols, such as the internet protocols, are organised into a layered stack of protocols. Each layer performs a certain communication function. A layer provides services to its upper layer while receiving services from the layer below.
Reactive measures	Measures that provide for the prosecution of offences after they occur.
Revocable privacy	The method for designing systems in such a way that no personal information is available, unless a user violates the pre-established terms of service.
Router	Network device in a packet switching network that forwards data packets between computer networks. A router reads the address information (IP address) and forwards the packet to the next hub in the network, which is either another router or the destination node.
Safety	The effective protection against personal suffering: protection against the infringement of physical or mental integrity.
Secondary informal social control	Activities that are being undertaken by organisations or people in order to control behaviour of people by – without it being their primary task.

299

Sexual explicit Internet material (SEIM)	Professionally produced or user-generated (audio)visual material on or from the internet that is typically intended to arouse the viewer and depicts sexual activities and (aroused) genitals in unconcealed ways, usually with close-ups on oral, anal, and vaginal penetration.
Sexual solicitation (legal context)	Sexual solicitation – in a legal context – refers to the offence of an adult enticing youth online into an offline sexual encounter. Synonym of the offence 'online sexual solicitation' is 'online grooming'.
Sexual solicitation (research context)	Sexual solicitations – in a research context – are defined as requests to engage in sexual activities or sexual talk or give personal sexual information that were unwanted or, whether wanted or not, were made by an adult. The term can refer to unwanted requests made by similarly aged youth, or wanted and unwanted requests by adults.
Social engineering	Persuading a user to do something s/he normally would not do, such as providing a password or other personal information.
Social learning theory	The basic assumption of social learning theory is that while observing the conduct of role models in the media, the consumers of these media learn and internalise which behaviours are rewarding and which will be punished. When the consequences of the observed behaviour are positive, users of media are inclined to copy this behaviour when a relevant situation elicits it. However, behaviour unappealing to the user and behaviour children are developmentally not ready for will be overlooked or ignored.
Social structure	The sum of all more or less fixed patterns of human interrelationships
Spear phishing	A phishing attack targeting a specific group of users.
Spyware	A piece of software (malware) that collects certain information from users and sends the information to the cyber criminal.
Stranger danger	The term 'stranger danger' refers to the potential dangers threatening minors while communicating online with unknown persons. Research however indicates that the portrayal of the sexual perpetrator by means of designations such as stranger danger, paedophile and online predator fails to reflect actual online practices.
Symmetric cipher	Method that allows a message to be encrypted and subsequently decrypted, both with the same secret key.
TCP/IP	The Transmission Control Protocol (TCP) and the Internet Protocol (IP) are the most important communication protocols for the internet. TCP/IP refers to these two main protocols, but it is also used for referring to the entire internet protocol stack consisting of five layers.
Theory of technological enforcement	A theory that states that technology primarily regulates the behaviour of those who actually use it

Third person effect	Research on the effects of sexualised content has consistently found that people perceive pornography to affect others more than themselves. This is termed the 'third-person effect'. In the contemporary debate about SEIM it seems that adults are 'we', discussing the SEIM use of 'them', i.e. youth being the third person.
Three echelon model	A model for organising the fight against cyber crime including semi-experts at the lower layers of the organisation for simple digital detective work, scientific support units at a regional or interregional level and cyber crime experts at a national level.
Trans-national crime and policing	Criminal activities that span the borders of national territories, and crime prevention and control initiatives designed to tackle or reduce such offences.
Treaty	An agreement between a limited number of states, usually with a limited content and purpose.
Treaty of Lanzarote	This is the 'Treaty of the Council of Europe concerning the protection of children against sexual exploitation and sexual abuse'. The Council of Europe was imbued with the necessity of guarantees to protect children from sexual exploitation and sexual abuse. The Council especially took into consideration society's increasing digitalisation and technological developments.
Unauthorised source	Stock or repository of information or content made available online without the necessary consent of the rights holders, used by downloaders to get access to for instance music, film, games or e-books.
Use of force	"A state activity that threatens the territorial integrity or political independence of another state within the meaning of Article 2(4) of the Charter of the United Nations" (Wingfield 2000: 382).
Video game	A video, or computer game, is an interactive rule-based system for playing, enabled by computer processing power.
Violent video game	The content of violent video games is concerned with aggression. Game play amounts to intentionally harming other game characters (human, human-like or animal) and/or the destruction of objects.
World wide web	System of interlinked hypertext documents accessed through web browsers via the internet.

301

References

Aas, K. F. (2007). *Globalization and Crime*, London: Sage.

Alberdingk Thijm, C. (2008). Wat is de zorgplicht van Hyves, XS4ALL and Marktplaats? [Duties of care for Hyves, XS4ALL and Marktplaats] *Ars Aequi*, 57, 7/8, 573-580.

Alexy, E.M., Burgess, A.W. and Baker, T. (2005). Internet offenders: Traders, travelers, and combination trader-travelers. *Journal of Interpersonal Violence*, 20/7, 804-812.

America Online and National Cyber Security Alliance (2005). *AOL/NCSA Online Safety Study*. www.staysafeonline.info/pdf/safety_study_2005.pdf. Last visited 19 May 2008.

American Psychiatric Association. (2000). *Diagnostic and statistical manual of mental disorders (DSM-IV TR)* (4th ed.). Washington DC: American Psychiatric Association.

American Psychological Association, Task Force on the Sexualisation of Girls (2007). *Report of the APA Task Force on the Sexualisation of Girls*. Washington, DC: American Psychological Association.

Anderson, C. A. and Dill, K. E. (2000). Video games and aggressive thoughts, feelings, and behavior in the laboratory and in life. *Journal of Personality and social psychology*, 78(4), 772-790.

Anderson, C. A., Gentile, D. A., and Buckley, K. E. (2007). *Violent video game effects on children and adolescents: Theory, research, and public policy*. Oxford University Press, USA.

Anderson, C. A., Shibuya, A., Ihori, N., Swing, E. L., Bushman, B. J., Sakamoto, A., Rothstein, H. R., et al. (2010). Violent video game effects on aggression, empathy, and prosocial behavior in Eastern and Western countries: A meta-analytic review. *Psychological Bulletin*, 136(2), 151-173. doi:10.1037/a0018251.

Anderson, K.B. (2006). Who are the victims of identity theft? The effect of demographics. *Journal of Public Policy & Marketing*, 25, 160-171.

Anderson, K.B. (2007). *Consumer Fraud in the United States: The Second FTC Survey*. Washington: Federal Trade Commission.

Anderson, R.J. and Kuhn, M. G. (1996). Tamper resistance - A cautionary note. In *2nd Int. Usenix Workshop on Electronic Commerce*, Oakland, CA: USENIX Association; pp. 1-11.

Ang, R.P., and Goh, D.H. (2010). Cyberbullying among adolescents: the role of affective and cognitive empathy and gender. *Child Psychiatry & Human Development*, 41/4, 387-397.

APA. (2010, February). Substance-related Disorders. Retrieved 10 February 2010 from http://www.dsm5.org/ProposedRevisions/Pages/Substance-RelatedDisorders.aspx. Accessed: 2010-02-10. (Archived by WebCite? at http://www.webcitation.org/5nR8AitLs).

APWG (2008). *Phishing Activity Trends – Report for the month of January, 2008.* www.antiphishing.org. Last visited 11 May 2009.

APWG (2010). *Phishing Activity. Trends Report.* 2nd *Quarter 2010.* www.anti-phishing.org/reports/apwg_report_q2_2010.pdf. Last visited 17 February 2011.

APWG (2011). *Phishing Activity Trends Report. 2nd Quarter 2010.* http://www.antiphishing.org/reports/apwg_report_q2_2010.pdf Last visited 1 March 2011.

Arbor Networks (2010). *Worldwide Infrastructure Security Report, 2010 Report. http://www.arbornetworks.com/report. Last visited 16 February 2011.*

Aricak, T., Siyahhan, S., Uzunhasanogly, A., Saribeyogly, S., Ciplak, S., Yilmaz, N., and Memmedov, C. (2008). Cyberbullying among Turkish Adolescents. *CyberPsychology & Behavior*, 11/3, 253-361.

Arquilla, J., and Ronfeldt, D. (1993). Cyberwar is Coming! *Comparative Strategy*, 12/2, 141-165.

Article 29 WP 'Opinion 2/2010 on online behavioural advertising', June 22, 2010. http://ec.europa.eu/justice/policies/privacy/docs/wpdocs/2010/wp171_en.pdf.

Attwood, F. (2004). Pornography and Objectification: Re-reading 'the picture that divided Britain. *Feminist Media Studies*, 4/1, 7-19.

Attwood, F. (2007). 'Other' or 'one of us'?: The porn user in public & academic discourse. Participations. *Journal of Audience and Reception Studies*, 4/1. Available from http://www.participations.org/Volume%204/Issue%201/4_01_attwood.htm. Accessed 20 January 2011.

AusCert (2006). *2006 Australian Computer Crime and Security Survey.* www.auscert.org.au. Last visited 19 April 2008.

Axelsson, A. S., and Regan, T. (2006). Playing online. In P. Vorderer and J. Bryant (eds.), 291-306. London: Lawrence Erlbaum Associates.

Ball, D. (2011). China's Cyber Warfare Capabilities. *Security Challenges*, 7/2, 81-103.

Bandura, A. (1994). Social cognitive theory of mass communication. In J. Bryant and D. Zillman (Eds.), *Media effects: Advances in theory and research* (pp. 61-90). Hillsdale, NJ: Erlbaum.

Barlett, C. P., Anderson, C. A., and Swing, E. L. (2009). Video Game Effects-Confirmed, Suspected, and Speculative. *Simulation and Gaming*, 10/3, 377-403.

Baudrillard, J. (1983) *Simulations*. Boston, Mass: MIT Press.

Baumeister, R.F. (2002). Yielding to temptation: Self-control failure, impulsive purchasing, and consumer behavior. *Journal of Consumer Research*, 28, 670-676.

Baumgartner, S. E., Valkenburg, P. M., and Peter, J. (2010). Unwanted online sexual solicitation and risky sexual online behavior across the lifespan. *Journal of Applied Developmental Psychology*, 31, 439-447.

Bauwens, J., Pauwels, C., Lobet-Maris, C., Poullet, Y., and Walrave, M. (2009). *Cyberteens, cyberrisks, cybertools: Tieners en ICT, risico's en opportuniteiten*. Gent: Academia Press.

BBC News, Europe (2007). Estonia hit by 'Moscow cyber war'. Available at http://news.bbc.co.uk/2/hi/europe/6665145.stm (November 2011).

BBC News, Europe (2008). West condemns Russia over Georgia. Available at http://news.bbc.co.uk/2/hi/europe/7583164.stm (November 2011).

Beasley, B., and Collins Standley, T. (2002). 'Shirts vs. Skins: Clothing as an Indicator of Gender Role Stereotyping in Video Games'. *Mass Communication & Society*, 5/3, 279–93.

Beck, U. (1992). *Risk Society: Towards a New Modernity*. London: Sage.

Beck, U. (2005). *Risk Society: Towards a New Modernity*. London: Sage.

Bednarski, G.M. (2004). *Enumerating and reducing the threat of transnational cyber extortion against small and medium size organizations*. Research thesis. Pittsburgh: Carnegie Mellon University.

Beirens, L. (1998). 'Op zoek naar criminele bits, digitaal rechercheren' [Looking for criminal bits, digital investigation], *Politeia*, 8, 9-12.

Bell, D. (1999, orig. 1973). *The Coming of Post-Industrial Society*. 3rd Edition. New York: Basic Books.

Benson, M.L. (2009). Editorial introduction: Offenders or opportunities: Approaches to controlling identity theft. *Criminology & Public Policy*, 8, 231-236.

Biegel, S. (2001). *Beyond our control? Confronting the limits of our legal system in the age of cyberspace*. Cambridge, MA: MIT Press.

Blackburn, D. (2004). *Does File Sharing Affect Record Sales*. Working Paper. Cambridge, MA, Harvard University, Department of Economics.

Boerman, F. and Mooij, A. (2006). *Vervolgstudie nationaal dreigingsbeeld: Nadere beschouwing van potentiële dreigingen en witte vlekken uit het nationaal dreigingsbeeld 2004*. Zoetermeer: KLPD, DNRI.

Boerman, F., Grapendaal, M. and Mooij, A. (2008). *Nationaal Dreigingsbeeld 2008. Georganiseerde Criminaliteit.* Rotterdam: Thieme MediaCenter.

Boies, S. C., Cooper, A., and Osborne, C. S. (2004). Variations in Internet-Related Problems and Psychosocial Functioning in Online Sexual Activities: Implications for Social and Sexual Development of Young Adults. *CyberPsychology & Behavior, 7/2,* 207-230.

Boutellier, H. (2005). *Meer dan veilig. Over bestuur, bescherming en burgerschap.* [More than safe. About governance, protection and citizenship] The Hague: Boom Juridische uitgevers.

Brissy, J.F. (1990). Computers in organizations, the (white) magic in the black box. In B.A. Turner (ed.), *Organizational symbolism,* Berlin: Walter de Gruyter.

Broadhurst, R. (2006). 'Developments in the global law enforcement of cyber-crime', *Policing: An International Journal of Police Strategies and Management* 29/2: 408-433.

Brosius, H-B., Weaver, J. B., and Staab, J. F. (1993). Exploring the social and sexual reality of contemporary pornography. *Journal of Sex Research, 30,* 161-170.

Brown, J.D. (2000). Adolescents´ Sexual Media Diets. *Journal of Adolescent Health, 27S,* 35-40.

Brown, J.D., and L'Engle, K.L. (2009). X-rated: Sexual Attitudes and Behaviors Associated With U.S. Early Adolescents' Exposure to Sexually Explicit Media. *Communication Research, 36,* 129-151.

Brown, J.D., and Witherspoon, E.M. (2002). The Mass Media and American Adolescents' Health. *Journal of Adolescent Health, 31,* 153-170.

Bullens, R. (2007). Kijken naar kinderporno op internet: 'onschuldige' drang? [Looking at child pornography on the Internet: innocent or urge?] In Wijk, A. P. van, Bullens, R.A.R., and Eshof, P. van den (eds.), *Facetten van zeden-criminaliteit.* The Hague: Reed Business Information.

Callanan, C., Gercke, M., Marco, E. de, and Dries-Ziekenheiner H. (2009). *Internet Blocking, balancing cybercrime responses in democratic societies,* research commissioned by the Open Society Institute, 2009.

Calvete, E., Orue, I., Estévez, A., Villardón, L., and Padilla, P. (2010). Cyberbullying in adolescents: Modalities and aggressors' profile. *Computers in Human Behavior, 26/5,* 1128-1135.

Capeller, W. (2001). 'Nor such a neat net: Some comments on virtual crimina-lity', *Social & Legal Studies, 10,* 229-42.

Carr, J. (2009). *Inside Cyber Warfare.* Sebastopol: O'Reilly Media.

Carr-Chellman, A. (2011, January). Gaming to re-engage boys in learning.

Casey, E. (2002). Cyberpatterns: Criminal behaviour on the internet. In B.E. Turvey, *Criminal profiling: An introduction to behavioral evidence analysis*. San Diego: Academic Press.

Cassidy, W., Jackson, M. and Brown, K.N. (2009). Sticks and stones can break my bones but how can pixels hurt me. *School Psychology International,* 30/4, 383-402.

Castells, M. (1996). *The Rise of the Network Society: The Information Age: Economy, Society and Culture Vol. I.* Oxford: Blackwell.

Castells, M. (1997). *The Power of Identity, The Information Age: Economy, Society and Culture Vol. II.* Oxford: Blackwell.

Castells, M. (1998). *End of Millennium, The Information Age: Economy, Society and Culture Vol. III.* Oxford: Blackwell.

Castronova, E. (2007). *Exodus to the Virtual World: How Online Fun is Changing Reality.* New York/Houndmills: Macmillan.

Cavoukian A. (2010). Privacy by design – the 7 foundational principles. Available at http://www.ipc.on.ca/images/Resources/7foundationalprinciples.

Cavoukian A. (2011). *Whole body imaging in airport scanners – building in privacy by design.* http://www.ipc.on.ca/images/Resources/wholebodyimaging.pdf.

CBS (2009). *De digitale economie 2008.* Voorburg/Heerlen: Centraal Bureau voor de Statistiek.

Centraal Bureau voor de Statistiek (2010). *ICT gebruik van huishoudens naar huishoudkenmerken.* www.cbs.nl.

Chen, Y.-C., Chen, P. S., Hwang, J.-J., Korba, L., Song, R., and Yee, G. (2005). An analysis of online gaming crime characteristics. *Internet Research, 15/3,* 246-261. doi:10.1108/10662240510602672.

Chesterman, S. (2006). The Spy Who Came in From the Cold War: Intelligence and International Law. *Michigan Journal of International Law, 27/4,* 1071-1130.

Chibnall, S., Wallace, M., Leicht, C., and Lunghofer L. (2006). *I-safe evaluation.* Final Report. Caliber Association, Fairfax. (http://www.ncjrs.gov/pdffiles1/nij/grants/213715.pdf).

Cho, J. (2010, March). Game addicts arrested for starving baby to death. *ABC News,* p. 1. SEOUL.

Claburn, T. (2009, June). China limits use of virtual currency. *InformationWeek.*

Clarke, R.A., and Knake, R.K. (2010). *Cyber war: the next threat to national security and what to do about it.* New York: Harper Collins.

COM (2010). Communication from the Commission to the European Parliament and the Council. 'Overview of information management in the area of freedom, security and justice'. COM(2010)385 final.

Computer Security Institute (2007). *CSI Survey 2007: The 12th Annual Computer Crime and Security Survey*. www.gocsi.com. Last visited 10 April 2008.

Consalvo, M. (2007). *Cheating: gaining advantage in videogames* (p. 241). MIT Press.

Convention on Cybercrime (entry into force: 2004). Council of Europe. Budapest. 2296 UNTS 167.

Cooper, A. (1998). Sexuality and the Internet: Surfing into the new millennium. *CyberPsychology & Behavior*, 1/2, 181-187.

Copes, H. and Vieraitis, L. (2009). Bounded rationality of identity thieves: Using offender-based research to inform policy. *Criminology & Public Policy*, 8, 237-262.

Corpelijn, C. (2008). *Rijk worden? Eerst betalen! Een profielschets van het 419-slachtoffer. Thesis*. Utrecht: Universiteit van Utrecht.

Coupez, F. (2010) '*Obligation de notification des failles de sécurité: quand l'Union européenne voit double...*', François Coupez, www.juriscom.net, 30 January 2010.

Critcher, C. (2003). *Moral Panics and the Media*. Buckingham: Open University Press.

Crawford, A. (2003). Contractual governance of deviant behaviour. *Journal of law and society*, 30, 479-505.

Crombie, G., and Trinneer, A. (2003). *Children and Internet Safety: An Evaluation of the Missing Program. A Report to the Research and Evaluation Section of theNational Crime Prevention Centre of Justice Canada*. Ottawa: University of Ottawa.

CPNI.NL (2011). Jaarbericht 2011. [Annual Report 2011] CPNI.NL.

CSO magazine, U.S. Secret Service, CERT Program, Microsoft Corp. (2007). *2007 ECrime Watch Survey*. www.cert.org. Last visited 19 April 2008.

Dahl and Sætnan (2009). 'It all happened so slowly – On controlling function creep in forensic DNA databases. *International Journal of Law, Crime and Justice* 37/3, 83-103.

Daily Mail (2010). 'Police probe UK links to cyber attacks on WikiLeaks enemies as teen "hacktivist" is arrested in Holland', 10 December.

Damballa Threat Research (2010). *The IMDDOS Botnet: Discovery and Analysis. http://www.damballa.com/knowledge/downloads.php*. Last visited 16 February 2011.

Danziger, J.N. (1985). Social science and the social impact of computer technology, *Social Science Quarterly*, 66/1, 3-21.

Dasseluur, A. (2005). *Digitale Criminaliteit: Over daders, daden en opsporing.* [Digital Crime: about offenders, acts and investigation] Culemborg: Van Duuren Media.

David-Ferdon, C., and Feldman Hertz, M. (2007). 'Electronic Media, Violence and Adolescents: An Emerging Public Health Problem' *Journal of Adolescent Health* 41 /6, s1-s5.

Davidson, J. and Martellozzo, E. (2005). *The Internet And Protecting Children From Sex Offenders Online: When Strangers Become 'Virtual Friends'.* Available at http://www.oii.ox.ac.uk/research/cybersafety/extensions/pdfs/ papers . Accessed at 10 February 2011.

De Hert, P., Gonzales Fuster, G., and Koops, B.J. (2006). Fighting cybercrime in the two Europes. The added value of the EU Framework decision and the council of Europe Convention. *Revue Internationale de Droit Pénal*, 503-524.

De Pauw, E. (2010a). De aanpak van overlast en criminaliteit in cyberspace. Uitdagingen met betrekking tot internationale samenwerking. [Tackling nuisance and crime in cyberspace. Challenges related to international cooperation] In: *Cahier Integrale Veiligheid, Europa en integrale Veiligheid.* Politeia, 139-149.

De Pauw, E. (2010b). Sociale controle in online gemeenschappen. Een taak van de overheid of volstaat zelfregulering? [Social control in online communities. A duty of the government or self regulation?] *Orde van de Dag*, Kluwer, 49, 5-15.

De Sola Pool, I. (1983). *Technologies of freedom.* Cambridge: The Belknap Press of Harvard University Press.

De Sola Pool, I. (1984). *Communications flows.* Tokyo: University of Tokyo Press.

De Vries, U.R.M.Th., Tigchelaar, H., Linden, M. van der, and Hol, A.M. (2007) *Identiteitsfraude; een afbakening, een internationale begripsvergelijking en analyse van nationale strafbepalingen.* WODC/Universiteit Utrecht, 2007. [Identity Fraud; a demarcation, an international comparison of terminology and an analysis of national criminal offences]. English Summary: http://www.wodc.nl/onderzoeksdatabase/identiteitsfraude. aspx?cp=44&cs=6796).

Declaration on Principles of International Law, Friendly Relations and Co-operation among States in Accordance with the Charter of the United Nations (1970), GA Res. 2625 (XXV). 24 October 1970. UNYB 787.

Dehue, F. Bolman, C. and T. Vollink (2008). 'Cyberpesten: wat doen kinderen en wat weten ouders?' *Pedagogische studiën: tijdschrift voor onderwijskunde en opvoedkunde* 85/5, 359-370.

Deibert, R.J., Palfrey, J.G., Rohozinski, R. and Zittrain, J. (2008). *Access Denied; The Practice and Policy of Global Internet Filtering.* Cambridge, MA: The Mitt Press.

Den Hartog, H., and Kouwenhoven, V.P. (2005). *Cybercrime, Digitaal vandalisme en sabotage. Naar een cyberveilige onderneming.* [Cyber crime. Digital vandalism and sabotage] The Hague: Hogeschool INHOLLAND Rotterdam.

Denning, D. (2009). 'Terror's Web: How the Internet is Transforming Terrorism', in Y. Jewkes and M. Yar (eds.), *Handbook of Internet Crime.* Cullompton: Willan.

Diffie, W., and Hellman, M. E. (1986). New directions in cryptography. *IEEE Transactions on Information Theory,* 22/6, 644-654.

Dimkov, T., Pieters, W., and Hartel, P.H. (2010). Laptop theft: a case study on effectiveness of security mechanisms in open organizations. In *17th ACM Conference on Computer and Communications Security (CCS),* 4-8 October 2010, Chicago, Illinois; 666-668.

Dimkov, T., Pieters, W., and Hartel, P.H. (2010). Portunes: representing attack scenarios spanning through the physical, digital and social domain. In *Joint Workshop on Automated Reasoning for Security Protocol Analysis and Issues in the Theory of Security (ARSPA-WITS).* LNCS, vol. 6186, 112-129.

Dinstein, Y. (2011). *War, Aggression and Self-defence.* Cambridge: Cambridge University Press.

Directive 2002/58/EC of the European Parliament and of the Council of 12 July 2002 concerning the processing of personal data and the protection of privacy in the electronic communications sector (Directive on privacy and electronic communications).

Directive 2009/136/EC of the European Parliament and of the Council of 25 November 2009 amending Directive 2002/22/EC on universal service and users' rights relating to electronic communications networks and services, Directive 2002/58/EC concerning the processing of personal data and the protection of privacy in the electronic communications sector and Regulation (EC) No 2006/2004 on cooperation between national authorities responsible for the enforcement of consumer protection laws.

Directive 95/46/EC of the European Parliament and of the Council of 24 October 1995. On the protection of individuals with regard to the processing of personal data and on the free movement of such data.

Döge, J. (2010). Cyber Warfare: Challenges for the Applicability of the Traditional Laws of War Regime. *Archiv des Völkerrechts,* 48/4, 486-501.

Doig, A. (2007). *Fraud.* Devon: Willan Publishing.

Domenie, M.M.L., Leukfeldt, E.R. and Stol W.P. (forthcoming). *Slachtofferschap onder burgers in een gedigitaliseerde samenleving. [Victimisation in a digital society.]*. Leeuwarden: NHL Hogeschool.

Domenie, M.M.L., Leukfeldt, E.R., and Stol, W.P. (2009). *Werkaanbod cybercrime bij de politie. Een verkennend onderzoek naar de omvang van het geregistreerde werkaanbod cybercrime.* Leeuwarden: Noordelijke Hogeschool Leeuwarden.

Dommering E.J. and Eijk, N.A.N.M. van (2010). *Convergentie in regulering: Reflecties op elektronische communicatie,* Ministry of Economic Affairs, The Hague, March 2010. (Convergence in regulation: Reflections on electronic communications).

Döring, N.A. (2000). Feminist views of cybersex: victimisation, liberation, and empowerment. *CyberPsychology & Behavior, 3,* 863-884.

Draft Articles on Responsibility of States for Internationally Wrongful Acts, with commentaries 2001. Available at http://untreaty.un.org/ilc/texts/instruments/english/commentaries/ 9_6_2001.pdf (November 2011).

Dumortier J. and Somers, G. (2008). *Study on activities undertaken to address threats that undermine confidence in the Information Society, such as spam, spyware and malicious soft*ware, Time.lex CVBA, Brussels, 2008.

Dunn, M., and Wigert, I. (2004). *International CIIP Handbook: An Inventory and Analysis of Protection Strategies in Fourteen Countries.* Zurich: Swiss Federal Institute of Technology.

Durkin, K. (2006). Game playing and adolescents' development. In P. Vorderer and J. Bryant (eds.), 415-428. London: Lawrence Erlbaum Associates.

Durkin, K. F., and Bryant, C. D. (1999). Propagandizing pederasty: A thematic analysis of the on-line exculpatory accounts of unrepentant pedophiles. *Deviant Behavior, 20,* 103-127.

Dye, M. W., Green, C. S., and Bavelier, D. (2009). Increasing Speed of Processing With Action Video Games. *Current Directions in Psychological Science, 18/6,* 321-326.

Eeten, M. van, Bauer, J.M., Asghari, H., Tabatabaie, S. and Rand, D. (2010). *The Role of Internet Service Providers in Botnet Mitigation An Empirical Analysis Based on Spam Data. www.oecd.org.* Last visited 16 February 2011.

Eijk, N.A.N.M. van, Engers, T.M. van, Wiersma, C., Jasserand, C.A. and Abel, W. (2010). *Op weg naar evenwicht. Een onderzoek naar zorgplichten op het internet.* [On the way to equilibrium. A study of duties of care on the Internet] The Hague: WODC.

Elkin-Koren, N. (2006). 'Making Technology Visible: Liability of Internet Service Providers for Peer-to-Peer Traffic', 9 *N.U. J. Legis. & Pub. Pol'y* 15 (2006).

Ellul, J. (1964, orig. 1954). *The technological society.* New York: Vintage Books.

ENISA (2008). 'ENISA Mission', http://www.enisa.europa.eu/pages/01_01. htm.

ENISA Ad Hoc Working Group on Privacy & Technology (2008). Technology-induced challenges in privacy & data protection in Europe.

Escobar-Chaves, S.L., Tortolero, S.R., Markham, C. M., Low, B.J., Eitel, P, and Thickstun, P. (2005). Impact of the Media on Adolescent Sexual Attitudes and Behaviors. *Pediatrics, 116,* 303-326.

Espiner, T. (2007). 'EU To Launch Scam Crackdown', 26 February, http://news.zdnet.co.uk/security/0,1000000189,39286068,00.htm.

European Commission (2003). *First Report on the application of Directive 2000/31/EC of the European Parliament and of the Council of 8 June 2000 on certain legal aspects of information society services, in particular electronic commerce, in the Internal Market (Directive on electronic commerce),* COM(2003)702 def.

Europol (2003). *Computer-related crimes within the EU: Old crimes new tools, new crimes new tools.* Luxembourg: Office for Official Publications of the European Communities.

Farwell, J.P., and Rohozinski, R. (2011). Stuxnet and the Future of Cyber War. *Survival, 53/1,* 23-40.

FBI (2008b). *Gone Phishing.* Global Ring Gets Rather Slick. www.fbi.gov/page2/may08/phishing_052008.html. Last visited 26 May 2008.

Felson, M. and Clarke, R.V. (1998). *Opportunity Makes the Thief: Practical Theory for Crime Prevention.* London: Home Office.

Ferguson, C. J., and Kilburn, J. (2010). Much ado about nothing: The misestimation and overinterpretation of violent video game effects in Eastern and Western nations: Comment on Anderson et al. (2010). *Psychological Bulletin, 136/2,* 174-178. doi:10.1037/a0018566.

Fildes, J. (2010). Stuxnet worm 'targeted high-value Iranian assets'. *BBC News.* Available at http://www.bbc.co.uk/news/technology-11388018 (November 2011).

Finjan (2007). *Web Security Trends Report Q4 2007.* www.finjan.com. Last visited 21 March 2011.

Finkelhor, D. (1984). *Child sexual abuse: New treatment and research.* New York: Free Press.

Finkelhor, D., Mitchell, K.J., and Wolak, J. (2000). *Online victimization: A report on the nation's youth.* Alexandria, VA: National Center for Missing and Exploited Children.

Finn, J. (2004). A Survey of Online Harassment at a University Campus. *Journal of Interpersonal Violence, 19/4,* 468-483.

Fleck, D. (2007). Individual and State Responsibility for Intelligence Gathering. *Michigan Journal of International Law, 28/3, 687-709.*

Flood, M. (2007). Exposure to pornography among youth in Australia. *Journal of Sociology, 43/1,* 45-60.

Foresight (2000). *Turning the Corner. Report of the Crime Prevention Panel.* London: Department of Trade and Industry.

Foucault, M. (1979, orig. 1975). *Discipline and punish.* New York: Vintage Books.

Frances, A. (2000). *Diagnostic and Statistical Manual of Mental Disorders.* Washington DC: American Psychiatric Association.

Freid, C. (1968). Privacy. *Yale Law Journal* 77/3, 475-493.

Frissen, V., and Lieshout, M. van (2003). Tussen dwang en drang. OOV, ICT en ontgrenzing van het gedrag [Between coercion and persuasion. OOV, IT and liberating behaviour]. Delft: TNO.

Fukuyama, F. (2002). *De nieuwe mens: onze wereld na de biotechnologische revolutie [The new human being: our world after the biotechnological revolution].* Amsterdam/Antwerpen: Contact.

Funk, J. B., Hagan, J., Schimming, J., Bullock, W. A., Buchman, D. D., and Myers, M. (2002). Aggression and psychopathology in adolescents with a preference for violent electronic games. *Aggressive Behavior, 28/2.*

Furnell, S.M. (2002). *The problem of categorising cybercrime and cybercriminals (paperpresentatie) 2nd Australian Information Warfare (IW) and Security Conference (SC) Perth, Australia, 29-30 November 2001.* www.ieee-security. org/Cipher/ConfReports/2002/CR2002-Ianelli & Hackworth, 2005.

Gagnon, B. (2008). Cyberwars and Cybercrimes. In: Leman-Langlois, S., *Technocrime. Technology, crime and social order.* Willan Publishing.

Garcia, F., Gans, H. G. de Koning, Muijrers, R., Rossum, P. van, Verdult, R., Schreur, R. Wichers, and Jacobs, B. (2008). Dismantling MIFARE classic. In *13th European Symp. on Research in Computer Security (ESORICS),* LNCS, vol. 5283, 97-114.

Geest, E. van (2006). *Van herkenning tot aangifte. Handleiding cybercrime.* [From recognition to reporting. Handbook of cyber crime]. The Hague: Govcert.nl.

General Assembly, A/RES/41/38, 20 November 1986. 78th Plenary Meeting. Available at http://www.un.org/documents/ga/res/41/a41r038.htm (November 2011).

Gerbner, G., Gross, L., Morgan., and Signorielli, N. (1994). Growing up with television: The cultivation perspective. In Bryant, J. and Zillman D. (eds.), *Media effects: Advances in theory and research* (pp. 17-41). Hillsdale, NJ: Erlbaum.

Giddens, A. (1984). *The constitution of society.* Cambridge: Polity Press.

313

Giddens, A. (1990). *The consequences of modernity.* Cambirdge: Polity Press.

Goldstein, J. (2005). Violent video games. In J. Raessens and J. Goldstein (eds.), 341-358. Cambridge, MA: MIT Press.

Goldstein, P., and Hugenholtz, P.B. (2010). *International Copyright. Principles, Law, and Practice,* Second Edition, New York: Oxford University Press 2010, ISBN 9780199737109, 592 pp.

Goodman, M. (1997). 'Why the police don't care about cybercrime', *Harvard Journal of Law and Technology,* 10: 465-94.

Gordon, S., and Ford, R. (2006). On the definition and classification of cyber-crime. *Journal in Computer Virology,* 1/2, 13-20.

Govcert (2005). *Aanbevelingen ter bescherming tegen denial of service aanvallen.* www.govcert.nl. [Recommendations for protecting against denial of ser-vice attacks] Last visited 14 April 2008.

Govcert (2007). *Trendrapport 2007. Cybercrime in trends en cijfers.* [Trend report 2007. Cyber crime in trends and figures] The Hague: Govcert.nl.

Govcert (2008). *Trendrapport 2008. Inzicht in cybercrime: trends & cijfers.* [Trend Report 2008: trends and figures]. The Hague: Govcert.nl.

Govcert (2009). *Trendrapport 2009. Inzicht in cybercrime: trends & cijfers.* [Trend Report 2009: trends and figures]. The Hague: Govcert.nl.

Govcert (2010). *2010 National Cyber Crime and Digital Safety Trend Report.* The Hague: Govcert.nl.

Grabosky, P. (2001). 'Virtual criminality: Old wine in new bottles?', *Social & Legal Studies,* 10, 243-9.

Grabosky, P. (2004). The global dimension of cybercrime. *Global Crime,* 6/1 (2004), 146-157.

Graham, D.E. (2010). Cyber Threats and the Law of War. *Journal of National Security Law and Policy,* 4/87, 87-102.

Green, C. S., and Bavelier, D. (2003). Action video game modifies visual selec-tive attention. *Nature,* 423(6939), 534-537.

Green, C. S., and Bavelier, D. (2007). Action-video-game experience alters the spatial resolution of vision. *Psychological Science,* 18/1, 88-94.

Grier, D.A. (2010). Sabotage! *Computer,* 43/11, 6-8.

Griffin, R.S., and Gross, A.M. (2004). Childhood bullying: Current empirical findings and future directions for research. *Aggression and Violent Behavior* 9/4, 379-400.

Griffith, R.E. (2005). How Criminal Justice Agencies Use The Internet. In A. Pattavina (Ed.), *Information Technology and the Criminal Justice System* (59-77). Thousand Oaks: Sage.

Griffiths, M.D. (2005). A 'components' model of addiction within a bio-psychosocial framework. *Journal of Substance Use*, 10/4, 191-197. doi:10.1080146598905001114359.

Guardian (2010) 'WikiLeaks backlash: The first global cyber war has begun, claim hackers', 11 December.

Ha.ckers.org (2006). *How Phishing actually works*. http://ha.ckers.org/blog/20060609/how-phishing-actually-works/. Last visited 15 May 2008.

Hackworth, A. (2005). *Spyware*. www.cert.org. Carnegie Mellon University.

Haddick, R. (2011) This Week at War: Lessons from Cyberwar I. *Foreign Policy*. Available at http://www.foreignpolicy.com/Articles/2011/01/28/this_week_at_war_lessons_from_cyberwar_i?page=0,0 (November 2011).

Haraway, D. (1994, orig. 1991). *Een cyborg manifest [A cyborg manifest]*. Amsterdam: De Balie.

Hayden, M.V. Gen. (2011). The Future of Things 'Cyber'. *Strategic Studies Quarterly*, 5/1, 3-7.

Heckmann, D. (2011). 'Kapitel 8: Strafrecht', in: D. Heckmann (Ed.), *Juris PraxisKommentar Internetrecht*, Saarbrücken: Juris 2011, nos. 170-172; BT-Drs. 16/3656, p. 9-10.

Heeks, R. (2008). Current Analysis and Future Research Agenda on 'Gold Farming': Real-World Production in Developing Countries for the Virtual Economies of Online Games. *Development Informatics Group, Institute for Development Policy and Management* (Working Paper Series).

Heirman, W. and Walrave, M. (2008). Assessing Concerns and Issues about the Mediation of Technology in Cyberbullying. *Cyberpsychology: Journal of Psychosocial Research on Cyberspace*, 2/2, 1-1.

Helmus, S., Smulders, A. and Zee, F. van der (2006). *ICT Veiligheidsbeleid in Nederland – Analyse en overwegingen bij Herijking*. TNO (unclassified), no. 035.31231.

Hildebrandt, M. (2008). *A Vision of Ambient Law Regulating Technologies*. Ed. Roger Brownsword and Karin Yeung. Oxford: Hart, 175-191. Available at: http://works.bepress.com/mireille_hildebrandt/4.

Hinduja, S., and Patchin, J.W. (2008). 'Cyberbullying: an exploratory analysis of factors related to offending and victimization' *Deviant Behavior* 29/2, 129-156.

Hinduja, S. and Patchin, J.W. (2009). *Bullying Beyond the Schoolyard: Preventing and responding to cyberbullying*. Thousand Oaks: Corwin Press.

Hinduja, S. and Patchin, J.W. (2010). 'Bullying, Cyberbullying, and Suicide' *Archives of Suicide Research* 14/3, 206-221.

315

Hines, D.A., and Finkelhor, D. (2007). Statutory sex crime between juveniles and adults: A review of social scientific research. *Aggression and Violent Behavior, 12,* 300-314.

Hinkle, K.C. (2011) Countermeasures in the Cyber Context: One More Thing to Worry About. *Yale Journal of International Law Online, 37,* 11-21.

Holt, T.J., Blevins, K.R., and Burkert, N., (2010). Considering the Pedophile Subculture Online. *Sex Abuse* 22/1, 3-24.

Holtfreter, K., Reisig, M.D. and Pratt, T.C. (2008). Low self-control, routine activities, and fraud victimization. *Criminology, 46,* 189-220.

Home Office (2006). Updated Estimate of the Cost of Identity Fraud to the UK Economy', at http://www.identity-theft.org.uk/ID%20fraud%20table.pdf.

Houle, K.J. and Weaver, G.M. (2001). *Trends in Denial of Service Attack Technology.* www.cert.org/archive/pdf/DoS_trends.pdf. Last visited 28 February 2008.

Huang, Y.Y., and Chou, C. (2010). An analysis of multiple factors of cyberbullying among junior high school students in Taiwan. *Computers in Human Behaviour* 26/6, 1581-1590.

Hulst, R.C. van der (2008). Sociale netwerkanalyse en de bestrijding van criminaliteit en terrorisme. [Social network analysis and the fight against terror] *Justitiële verkenningen* 34/5 3-20.

Hulst, R.C. van der, and Neve, R.J.M. (2008). *High-tech crime: Inventarisatie van literatuur over soorten criminaliteit en hun daders.* [High Tech Crime: literature review about crimes and their offenders] The Hague: WODC.

Hutchings, A. and Hayes, H. (2009). Routine activity theory and phishing victimisation: Who gets caught in the 'Net'? *Current Issues in Criminal Justice, 20,* 433-451.

Huxley, A. (1986, orig. 1932). *Heerlijke nieuwe wereld [Brave new world].* Amsterdam: Bert Bakker.

Huygen, A., Rutten, P., Huveneers, S., Limonard, S., Poort, J., Leenheer, J., Janssen, K., Van Eijk, N., and Helberger, N. (2009). *Ups and downs. Economic and cultural effects of file sharing on music, film and games,* TNO/SEO/IViR, Delft/Amsterdam.

Ianelli, N., and Hackworth, A. (2005). *Botnets as a Vehicle for Online Crime.* www.cert.org/archive/pdf/Botnets.pdf. Last visisted 26 February.

IC3 (2008). *2007 Internet Crime Report.* www.ic3.gov. Last visited 19 May 2008.

ICMEC (International Centre for Missing & Exploited Children) (2008). Child Pornography: Model Legislation & Global Review. Fifth Edition. www.icmec.org. Last visited 7 December 2010.

IFPI (2010). *Digital Music Report 2010, Music how, when, where you want it.*

Igure, V.M., Laughter, S.A., and Williams, R. D. (2006) Security issues in SCADA networks. *Computers & Security*, 25/7, 498 506.

Information Warfare Monitor (2009). *Tracking Ghostnet: investigating a cyber espionage network*.

International Conferences (The Hague), Hague Convention (IV) Respecting the Laws and Customs of War on Land and Its Annex: Regulations Concerning the Laws and Customs of War on Land, 18 October 1907. Available at: http://www.unhcr.org/refworld/docid/4374cae64.html (November 2011).

Irani, D., Webb, S. Li, K. and Pu, C. (2009). Large online social footprints – An emerging threat. *Conference proceedings of the 2009 International Conference on Computational Science and Engineering*, 271-276.

ISFE. (2008). *Video gamers in Europe – 2008*.

Jacobs, B. (2005). Select before you collect. *Ars Aequi* 54, 1006-1009.

Jagatic, T., Johnson, N., Jakobsson, M., and Menczer, F. (2005). *Social Phishing*. Bloomington: School of Informatics Indiana University.

Jain, A.K., Hong, L. and Pankanti, S. (2000). Biometric identification. *Commun. ACM*, 43/2, 90-98.

Jain, A.K., Nandakumar, K., and Nagar, A. (2008). Biometric template security. *EURASIP J. on Advances in Signal Processing*, 2008:579416.

Jansz, J. (2005). The Emotional Appeal of Violent Video Games for Adolescent Males. *Communication Theory*, 15/3, 219-241.

Jansz, J., and Martens, L. (2005). Gaming at a LAN event: the social context of playing video games. *New Media & Society*, 7/3, 333-355. doi:10.1177/1461444805052280.

Jansz, J., and Martis, R. G. (2007). The Lara phenomenon: Powerful female characters in video games. *Sex Roles*, 56/3, 141-148.

Jansz, J., and Tanis, M. (2007). Appeal of playing online First Person Shooter Games. *Cyberpsychology & Behavior*, 10/1, 133-6. doi:10.1089/cpb.2006.9981.

Jansz, J., and Vosmeer, M. (2009). The unlikely serious gamer. In U. Ritterfeld, M. Cody and P. Vorderer (eds.), *Serious games: Mechanisms and effects*, 36-247. London: Routledge/Taylor & Francis Group.

Jansz, J., Avis, C., and Vosmeer, M. (2010). Playing The Sims 2: An Exploration of Gender Differences in Players' Motivations and Patterns of Play. *New Media & Society*. doi:10.1177/1461444809342267.

Jenkins, H., and Cassell, J. (2008). From Quake Grrls to Desperate Housewives: A Decade of Gender and Computer Games. In Kafai, Y., Heeter C., Heeter J., and Sun J. (eds.). Cambridge, MA: MIT Press.

Jenkins, P. (2001). *Beyond tolerance: Child pornography on the Internet*. New York: New York University Press.

Jenkins, P. (2009). Failure to Launch: Why Do Some Social Issues Fail to Detonate Moral Panics? *British Journal of Criminology, 49*, 35-47.

Jewkes, Y. (2009). 'Public Policing and Internet Crime', in Y. Jewkes and M. Yar (eds.), *Handbook of Internet Crime*. Cullompton: Willan.

Jewkes, Y. and Andrews, C. (2005). 'Policing the filth: the problems of investigating online child pornography in England and Wales', *Policing & Society* 15/1, 42-62.

Jewkes, Y. and Andrews, C. (2007). 'Internet child pornography: international responses' in Y. Jewkes (ed.), *Crime Online*, Cullompton: Willan.

Johnson, D.R. and Post, D. (1996). Law and Borders – The Rise of Law in Cyberspace. *Stanford Law Review, 48/5*, 1367-1402.

Joint Publication 3-13, Information Operations, 13 February 2006. Available at http://www.dtic.mil/doctrine/new_pubs/jp3_13.pdf (November 2011).

Jordan, T. (1999) *Cyberpower. The Culture and Politics of Cyberspace and the Internet*. London: Routledge.

Jordan, T. and Taylor P. (1998). A sociology of hackers. *The Sociological Review*, 46/4, 757-780.

Juels, A. and Pappu, R. (2003). *Squealing euros: Privacy protection in RFID-Enabled banknotes*. In 7th Int. Conf. on Financial Cryptography (FC), LNCS, vol. 2742, 103-121.

Juvonen, J. and Gross, E.F. (2008). 'Extending the School Grounds? Bullying Experiences in Cyberspace' *Journal of School Health* 78/9, 496-505.

Kafai, Y. B., Fields, D. A., and Cook, M. S. (2010). Your Second Selves. *Games and Culture*, 5/1, 23-42. doi:10.1177/1555412009351260.

Kanuga, M., and Rosenfeld, W.D. (2004). Adolescent Sexuality and the Internet: The Good, the Bad and the URL. *Journal of Pediatric and Adolescent Gynecology*, 17, 117-124.

Kaspersen, H.W.K. (1990). *Strafbaarstelling van computermisbruik*. Antwerpen/Deventer: Kluwer.

Kasperen, R. (2004). Bestrijding van cybercrime en de noodzaak van internationale regelingen [Combating cybercrime and the need for international regulations]. *Justitiële Verkenningen*, 30/8, 58-75.

Kerckhoffs, A. (1883). 'La cryptographie militaire.' *Journal des sciences militaires*, vol. IX, pp. 5-83, Jan. 1883, pp. 161-191, Feb. 1883. http://www.petitcolas.net/fabien/kerckhoffs/.

Kestermans, J., and De Maere, T. (2010). Tien jaar wet informaticacriminaliteit. [Ten years of computer crime law] *Rechtskundig weekblad*, 562-568.

Kerstens, J., and Stol W.P., (eds.) (forthcoming). *Youth and cybersafety*. The Hague: Boom Lemma.

Kerstens, J., Toutenhoofd, M. and Stol, W.P. (2008). *Wie niet weg is, is gezien. Gevalstudie over een proef met cameratoezicht in de Leeuwarder binnenstad [Hide and seek. Case study of an experiment with camera surveillance]*. The Hague: Boom Juridische uitgevers.

Kierkegaard, S. (2008). Cybering, online grooming and ageplay. *Computer Law & Security Report, 24*, 41-55.

Klaver, M.J. (1999). *UNESCO wil Internet zuiveren van kinderporno*. [UNESCO wants to clear the internet of child pornography] www.nrc.nl. Published on 23 January 1999, 00:00. Amended on 14 December 2005, 20:29.

Kleef, J. van (2004). Kinderporno kinderspel. [Child pornography: childs play] *Nieuwe Revu*, no. 52.

KLPD (2004). *Nationaal dreigingsbeeld zware of georganiseerde criminaliteit: een eerste Proeve*. [National Threat Analysis of Organised Crime] Zoetermeer: Dienst Nationale Recherche Informatie.

KLPD (2007). *Cybercrime – Focus op High Tech Crime: Deelrapport Criminaliteitsbeeld 2007*. [Cybercrime – Focus on High Tech Crime] Rotterdam: Thieme MediaCenter.

Koops, B.J. (2010). 'Het failliet van het grondrecht op dataprotectie', in: J.E.J. Prins et al. (eds.), *16 Miljoen BN'ers? Bescherming van Persoonsgegevens in het Digitale Tijdperk*, Leiden: Stichting NJCM-Boekerij, 99-110.

Kowalski, R., and Limber, S. (2007). 'Electronic Bullying Among Middle School Students' *Journal of Adolescent Health* 41/6, s22-s30.

Krotoski, A. (2004). *Chicks and Joysticks. An Exploration of Women and Gaming*. London.

Kuner, C., Burton, C., Hladjk J., and Proust, O. (2009). *Study on Online Copyright Enforcement and Data Protection in Selected Member States*, Study commissioned by the European Commission, Hunton & Williams, 2009.

Kurose, J.F. and Ross, K.W. (2009). *Computer networking: a top-down approach featuring the internet (5th edition)*. Addison Wesley.

Ladd, G. W. (2005). *Children's peer relations and social competence*. New Haven: Yale University Press.

Laender, J. de (1996). *Het hart van de duisternis: psychologie van de menselijke wreedheid*. Leuven: Davidsfonds.

Lampson, B.W. (2004). Computer security in the real world. *IEEE Computer*, 37/6, 37-46.

Langner, R. (2011). Cracking Stuxnet, a 21st-century cyber weapon. Talk delivered at TED 2011. Available at http://www.ted.com/talks/lang/eng/ralph_langner_cracking_stuxnet_a_21st_century_cyberweapon.html (November 2011).

Langton, L. and Planty, M. (2010). *Victims of Identity Theft, 2008*. Bureau of Justice Statistics.

Lee, K. M., and Peng, W. (2006). What do we know about social and psychological effects of computer games? A comprehensive review of the current literature. In P. Vorderer and J. Bryant (eds.), 325-346. Mahwah, NJ: Lawrence Erlbaum.

Leeuw, H.B.M. (2009). *High-tech crime en voorlichting. Een inventarisatie van voorlichtingsinitiatieven in Nederland en een analyse van kansen en mogelijkheden.* [High-tech crime and awareness. An inventory of information initiatives in the Netherlands and an analysis of opportunities and possibilities.] The Hague: WODC.

Lemmens, J. S. (2010). *Causes and Consequences of Pathological Gaming [PhD thesis].* Amsterdam.

Lemmens, J. S., Bushman, B. J., and Konijn, E. A. (2006). The appeal of violent video games to lower educated aggressive adolescent boys from two countries. *CyberPsychology & Behavior, 9/5*, 638–641. doi:10.1089/cpb.2006.9.638.

Lemmens, J. S., Valkenburg, P. M., and Peter, J. (2009). Development and validation of a game addiction scale for adolescents. *Media Psychology, 12/1*, 77-95. doi:10.1080/15213260802669458.

Lenhart, A. (2009). *Teens and Sexting: How and why minor teens are sending sexually suggestive nude or nearly nude images via text messaging.* Washington, D.C.: Pew Internet & American Life Project.

Lenk, K. (1997). 'The challenge of cyberspatial forms of human interaction to territorial governance and policing' in B. Loader (ed.), *The Governance of Cyberspace: Politics, Technology and Global Restructuring*, London: Routledge.

Lentz, Susan A., and Chaires, Robert H. (2007). 'The invention of Peel's principles: A study of policing 'textbook' history'. *Journal of Criminal Justice* 35: 69-79.

Lessig, L. (1999). *Code and other laws of cyberspace.* Basic Books.

Leukfeldt, E.R., De Pauw, E., Domenie, M.M.L. and Stol, W.Ph.(2011). Oude wijn in nieuwe zakken? De aard van cybercrime en de implicaties voor de opsporingspraktijk. [Old wine in new bottles? The nature of cybercrime and the implications for police practice] *Panopticon* 32/2 xx-xx.

Leukfeldt, E.R. and Stol, W.P. (2011). *De internetfraudeur: een criminologisch perspectief.* De Bilt: Programma Aanpak Cybercrime.

Leukfeldt, E.R., Domenie, M.M.L. and Stol, W.Ph. (2010). *Verkenning Cybercrime in Nederland 2009.* [Cyber crime in The Netherlands 2009] The Hague: Boom Juridische uitgevers.

Levi, M., and Burrows, J. (2008). Measuring the impact of fraud in the UK: a conceptual and empirical journey. *British Journal of Criminology* 48/3, 293-318.

Li, Q. (2006). 'Cyberbullying in Schools: A research of Gender Differences' *School Psychology International* 27/2, 157-170.

Li, Q. (2007). 'New bottle but old wine: A research of cyberbullying in schools' *Computers in Human Behavior* 23/4, 1777-1791.

Liau, A.K., Khoo, A., and Ang, P.H. (2005). Factors influencing adolescents' engagement in risky internet behaviour. *CyberPsychology & Behaviour, 8/2*, 513-520.

Lieshout, M. van, Kool, L., Jonge, M. de, and Schoonhoven, B. van, (2011). 'Privacy by Design: an alternative to existing practice in safeguarding privacy'. *INFO, The Journal of policy, regulation and strategy for telecommunications, information and media. 13/6*, 55-68.

Livingstone, S. (2006). Drawing conclusions from new media research: Reflections and puzzles regarding children's experience of the Internet. *Information Society, 22*, 219-230.

Livingstone, S., and Helsper, E.J. (2007). Taking risks when communicating online: The role of offline social-psychological factors in young people's vulnerability to online risks. *Information, Communication & Society, 10/5*, 619-644.

Livingstone, S., Haddon, L., Görzig, A., and Ólafsson, K. (2010). *Risks and safety on the internet: The perspective of European children. Initial Findings.* LSE, London: EU Kids Online.

Lo, V.-H., and Wei, R. (2005). Exposure to Internet pornography and Taiwanese adolescents' sexual attitudes and behaviour. *Journal of Broadcasting and Electronic Media, 49*, 221-237.

Lorenz, K. (1974). *Das sogenannte Böse. Zur Naturgeschichte der Aggression.* Amsterdam: Ploegsma.

LPDO (Landelijk Project Digitaal Rechercheren) (2003). *Visie op digitaal opsporen* [A vision of digital investigating]. Zoetermeer: LPDO.

Lünnemann, K., Nieborg, S., Goderie, M., Kool, R. and Beijers, G. (2006). *Kinderen beschermd tegen seksueel misbruik. Evaluatie van de partiële wijziging in de zedelijkheidswetgeving.* [Children protected against sexual abuse. Evaluation of changes in the vice law] The Hague/Utrecht: WODC/Verwey Jonker Instituut.

Lynn III, W.J., Remarks on the Department of Defense Cyber Strategy. As Delivered by Deputy Secretary of Defense William J. Lynn III. National Defense University. Washington, D.C., 14 July 2011. Available at http://www.defense.gov/speeches/speech.aspx?speechid=1593 (November 2011).

Lyon, D. (1994). *The electronic eye, the rise of surveillance society.* Cambridge: Polity Press.

Lyotard, J-F (1984). *The Postmodern Condition: A Report on Knowledge.* Manchester: Manchester University Press.

Marcuse, H. (1980, orig. 1964). *De eendimensionale mens [the one dimensional person]* Bussum: Paul Brand.

Marwick, A. (2008). Catch a predator? The Myspace Moral Panic. *First Monday,* 13(6), article 3.

Mason, K. L. (2008). 'Cyberbullying: A preliminary assessment for school personnel'. *Psychology in the Schools* 45/4, 323-348.

McAfee (2006). *Virtual Criminology Report. Organised Crime and the Internet.* www.mcafee.com. Last visisted 19 April 2008.

McAfee (2007). *Virtual Criminology Report: Cybercrime The Next Wave.* www.mcafee.com. Last visited 19 April 2008.

McCusker, R. (2006). Transnational organised cyber crime: distinguishing threat from reality. *Crime Law and Social Change, 46/4-5,* 257-273.

McGhee, K. (2008). *Beware of Spear Phishing by 'U.S. Tax Court'* www.avertlabs.com/research/blog/index.php/2008/05/22/us-tax-court-spear-phishing. Last visited 29 May 2008.

McKenna, K.Y.A., and Bargh, J.A. (2000). Plan 9 from Cyberspace: The implications of the Internet for personality and social psychology. *Personality and Social Psychology Review, 4,* 57-75.

McLaughlin, J.F. (2000). *Cyber child sex offender typology.* www.ci.keene.nh.us/police/Typology.html. Last visited 19 April 2008.

McNair, B. (1996). Mediated Sex: Pornography and Postmodern Culture. London & New York: Arnold.

McNally, M. and Newman, G.R. (2005). Editorial introduction. In M.M. McNally and G.R. Newman (eds.), *Perspectives on Identity Theft. Crime prevention Studies Vol. 23.* Monsey, NY: Criminal Justice Press, 1-8.

Meerkerk, G.-J., Van Rooij, A. J., Amadmoestar, S. S., and Schoenmakers, T. M. (2009). *Nieuwe Verslavingen in Zicht. Een Inventariserend Onderzoek naar Aard en Omvang van 'Nieuwe Verslavingen' in Nederland [New Addictions in Sight. A Survey into the Nature and Prevalence of 'New Addictions' in the Netherlands].* Rotterdam: IVO Reeks 63.

Menesini, E., and Nocentini A. (2010). Reti di supporto tra gli studenti nel mondo reale e virtuale: Valutazione di un progetto di prevenzione del cyberbullismo realizzato a Lucca. Paper presented at the *'Always-on-generation: risks and benefits of new technologies'* conference. Florence, 21 October.

Menezes, A.J., Oorschot, P. C. van, and Vanstone, S.A. (2001). *Handbook of applied cryptography.* CRC Press.

Merton, R.K. (1968). Social Theory and Social Structure. New York: The Free Press.

Microsoft (2006a). *Spear phishing: Highly targeted scams*. www.microsoft.com/protect/yourself/phishing/spear.mspx. Last visited 15 May 2008.

Microsoft (2006b). *What is spyware?* www.microsoft.com/protect/computer/basics/spyware.mspx. Last visited 16 May 2008.

Mijn Kind Online. (2009). *Next Level – Dossier over online spelletjes voor kinderen*. The Hague.

Military and Paramilitary Activities in and against Nicaragua (*Nicaragua* v. *United States of America*). Merits, Judgment. I.C.J. Reports 1986, p. 14.

Mills, C.W. (1983, orig. 1959). *The sociological imagination*. Harmondsworth: Penguin Books.

Mishna, F., Saini, M., and Solomon, S. (2009). 'Ongoing and online : Children and youth's perceptions of cyberbullying' *Children and Youth Services Review* 31/12, 1222-1228.

Mitchell, K.J., Finkelhor, D., and Wolak, J. (2007). Online Requests for Sexual Pictures from Youth: Risk Factors and Incident Characteristics. *Journal of Adolescent Health*, 41, 196-203.

Mitchell, K.J., Wolak, J., and Finkelhor, D. (2007). Trends in Youth Reports of Sexual Solicitations, Harassment and Unwanted Exposure to Pornography on the Internet. *Journal of Adolescent Health*, 40, 116-126.

Mitchell, W.A., Crawshaw, P., Bunton, R., and Green, E.E. (2001). Situating young people's experiences of risk and identity. *Health, Risk, & Society*, 3/2, 217-233.

Mitchell, W.J. (1995). *City of bits: Space, place and the Infobahn*. Cambridge, MA: MIT Press.

Mitnick, K., Simon, W.L., and Wozniak, S. (2002). *The Art of Deception: Controlling the Human Element of Security* Indiana: Wily Publishing.

MKI [Meldpunt Kinderporno op Internet] (2008). *Jaarverslag 2007*. Amsterdam: Stichting ter bestrijding van kinderporno op internet. [Foundation for the combating of child pornography on the internet].

More, T. (1987, orig. 1516). *Utopia*. Harmondsworth: Penguin Books.

Morris, S. (2004). *The future of nectarism now: Part 1 – threats and challanges*. UK Home Office online report no. 62/04, 2004. www.homeoffice.gov.uk/rds/pdfs04/rdsolr6204.pdf. Last visited 13 March 2008.

Mumford, L. (1963, orig. 1934). *Technics and civilization*. New York: Harcourt Brace Jovanovich.

Murano, G. (2009, January). 10 Most Bizarre Gaming Incidents. Retrieved 7 February 2011 from http://www.oddee.com/item_96657.aspx.

323

Accessed: 2011-02-07. (Archived by WebCite? at http://www.webcitation. org/5wK56ONao).

NCSC (2012). Cybercrime. *Van herkenning tot aangifte*. [Cybercrime. From recognition to reporting.] The Hague: NCSC.nl.

Neff, S. (2005). *War and the Law of Nations*. Cambridge: Cambridge University Press.

Newburn, T. (2008). Policing. Key Readings. Cullompton: Willian Publishing.

Newman, G.R. (2005). Identity theft and opportunity. In M.M. McNally and G.R. Newman (eds.), *Perspectives on Identity Theft. Crime prevention Studies Vol. 23*. Monsey, NY: Criminal Justice Press, 9-32.

Newman, G.R. and McNally, M.M. (2005). *Identity Theft Literature Review*. Paper prepared for the U.S. Department of Justice, United States. Newark: University of Albany, Rutgers University.

Nikken, P. (2000). Boys, girls and violent video games: The views of Dutch children. In C. Von Feilitzen and U. Carlsson (eds.), 93-102. Göteborg, Sweden: UNESCO International Clearinghouse on Children and Violence on the Screen.

Nikken, P. (2003). *Computerspellen in het gezin*. Hilversum.

Nikken, P. (2007). *Mediageweld en kinderen*. Amsterdam: SWP Books.

Nikken, P., and Jansz, J. (2006). Parental mediation of children's videogame playing: a comparison of the reports by parents and children. *Learning, Media and Technology, 31/2*, 181. doi:10.1080/17439880600756803.

Nykodym, N., Taylor, R. and Vilela, J. (2005). Profiling of cyber crime: criminal profiling and insider cybercrime. *Computer law & security report, 21/5*, 408-414.

O'Connell, R. (2003). *A typology of child cybersexploitation and on-line grooming practices*. Preston: University of Central Lancashire.

O'Donnell, I., and Milner, C. (2007). *Child pornography: crime, computers and society*. Willan: Cullompton.

OECD (2010). *The Economic and Social Role of Internet Intermediaries*, Paris, April 2010.

OECD Guidelines on the protection of privacy and the transborder flows of personal data (2011). http://www.oecd.org/document/18/0,3343, en_2649_34255_1815186_1_1_1_1,00.html (last visited 29 January 2011).

Ofcom (2008). Ofcom's Response to the Byron Review, (http://www.ofcom. org.uk/research/telecoms/reports/byron/).

Oil Platforms (*Islamic Republic of Iran* v. *United States of America*), Judgment, I.C.J. Reports 2003, p. 161. Dissenting Opinion of Judge Simma, Oil Platforms Case, 324-361.

Ollmann, G. (2004). *The Phishing Guide (Part 1) Understanding and Preventing Phishing Attacks.* NGSSoftware Insight Security Research: www.ngscon sulting.com.

Ollmann, G. (2007). *The Vishing Guide. A close look at voice Phishing.* NGSSoftware Insight Security Research: www.ngsconsulting.com.

Olweus, D. (1993). *Bullying at School: What We Know and What We Can Do.* Oxford: Blackwell Publishers.

Oosterink, M. and Eijk, E.J. van (2006). *Opsporing Kinderpornografie op inter-net. Een statusoverzicht.* [Detecting child pornography online] The Hague: Ministry of Justitie.

Ortega, R., Mora-Merchán, J.A., and Jäger, T. (2007). *Acting against school bullying and violence. The role of media, local authorities and the Internet* [E-book]. Landau: Verlag Empirische Pädagogik.

Osawa, J. (2011). PlayStation Takes New Hit. *The Wall Street Journal.* Available at http://online.wsj.com/Article/SB1000142405297020363310457662597197 6475508.html (November 2011).

Oudejans, M. and Vis, C. (2008). *Slachtoffers van (Poging tot) Oplichting.* The Hague: WODC.

Palfrey, J., Gasser, U., and Boyd, D. (2010). *Response to FCC Notice of Inquiry 09-94: Empowering Parents in Protecting Children in Evolving Media Landscape.* Berkman Center for Internet & Society. Available at http://cyber. law.harvard.edu/sites/cyber.law.harvard.edu/files/Palfrey_Gasser_boyd_ response_to_FCC_NOI_009_94_Feb2010.pdf. Accessed at 1 December 2010.

Pappalardo, D., and Messmer, E. (2005). *Extortion via DDoS on the rise: Criminals are using the attacks to extort money from victimized companies.* www.com-puterworld.com/networkingtopics/networking/story/0,10801,101761,00. html. Last visited 29 February 2008.

Patchin, J. W. and Hinduja, S. (2006). 'Bullies Move beyond the Schoolyard: A Preliminary Look at Cyberbullying' *Youth Violence and Juvenile Justice* 4/2, 148-169.

Patchin, J. W. and Hinduja, S. (2010). Cyberbullying and Self-Esteem. *Journal of School Health* 80/12, 614-621.

Patchin, J.W., and Hinduja, S. (2010). Changes in adolescent online networking behaviors from 2006 to 2009. *Computers in Human Behavior, 26,* 1818-1821.

Pauw, E. de, Pleysier S., Van Looy J. and Soetaert R. (2008). *Game on! We krijgen er niet genoeg van* [Game on! We can't get enough of it]. Brussel: ViWTA.

Peter, J., and Valkenburg, P.M. (2006a). Adolescents' exposure to sexually explicit material on the Internet. *Communication Research, 33/2*, 178-204.

Peter, J., and Valkenburg, P.M. (2006b). Adolescents' exposure to sexually explicit online material and recreational attitudes toward sex. *Journal of Communication, 56,* 639-660.

Peter, J., and Valkenburg, P.M. (2007). Adolescents' Exposure to a Sexualized Media Environment and Their Notions of Women as Sex Objects. *Sex Roles, 56,* 381-395.

Peter, J., and Valkenburg, P.M. (2008). Adolescents' Exposure to Sexually Explicit Internet Material, Sexual Uncertainty, and Attitudes Toward Uncommitted Sexual Exploration: Is There a Link? *Communication Research, 35/5,* 579-601.

Peter, J., and Valkenburg, P. M. (2009). Adolescents' Exposure to Sexually Explicit Internet Material and Sexual Satisfaction: A Longitudinal Study. *Human Communication Research, 35,* 171-194.

Peter, J., and Valkenburg, P.M. (2010a). Adolescents' Use of Sexually Explicit Internet Material and Sexual Uncertainty: The Role of Involvement and Gender. *Communication Monographs, 77/3,* 357-375.

Peter, J., and Valkenburg, P. M. (2010b). Processes Underlying the Effects of Adolescents' Use of Sexually Explicit Internet Material: The Role of Perceived Realism. *Communication Research, 37/3,* 375-399.

Peter, J., and Valkenburg, P. M. (in press a). The Influence of Sexually Explicit Internet Material on Sexual Risk Behavior: A Comparison of Adolescents and Adults. *Archives of Sexual Behavior.*

Peter, J., and Valkenburg, P.M. (in press b). The Use of Sexually Explicit Internet Material and Its Antecedents: A Longitudinal Comparison of Adolescents and Adults. *Archives of Sexual Behaviour.*

Peter, J., Valkenburg, P.M., and Schouten, A.P. (2007). Precursors of adolescents' use of visual and audio devices during online communication. Computers in Human Behavior, 23, 2473-2487.

PEW (2009). PEW Internet Project 'Usage over time'.

Pfitzmann, A., and Hansen, M. (2010). Anonymity, unlinkability, undetectability, unobservability, pseudonymity, and identity management – a consolidated proposal for terminology. http://dud.inf.tu-dresden.de/Anon_Terminology.shtml.

Poster, M. (1990). *The Mode of Information.* Cambridge: Polity Press.

Potter, R.H., and Potter, L.A. (2001). The Internet, Cyberporn, and Sexual Exploitation of Children: Media Moral Panics and Urban Myths for Middle-Class Parents? *Sexuality & Culture, 5/3,* 31-48.

Praca, D. and C. Barral (2001). From smart cards to smart objects: the road to new smart technologies. *Computer Networks*, 36/4, 381-389.

Pratchett, R. (2005). *Gamers in the UK. Digital play, digital lifestyles.*

Pratt, T., Holtfreter, K., and Reisig, M.D. (2010). Routine online activity and Internet fraud targeting: Extending the generality of routine activity theory. *Journal of Research in Crime and Delinquency*, 47, 267-296.

Prins, L. (2008). *Landelijke Criminaliteitskaart. Populatieprofielen 2007.* Zoetermeer/Driebergen: KLPD.

PWC (Profit for the Worlds Children) (2001). *Kinderpornografie en internet in Nederland. Een overzicht van de huidige situatie, knelpunten in de bestrijding, suggesties voor verbeteringen* [Child pornography and the internet in the Netherlands. An overview of the current state of affairs, bottlenecks in combating it, suggestions for improvement]. Haarlem: PWC.

Rajab, M.A., Zarfoss, J., Monrose F. and Terzis, A. (2007). *My Botnet is Bigger than Yours (Maybe, Better than Yours) : why size estimates remain challenging.* www.usenix.org. Last visited 16 February 2011.

Rand Europe (2008). *Responding to Convergence: Different approaches for Telecommunication regulators,* 2008.

Rapport au Ministre de la Culture et de la Communication (2010): *Creation et Internet,* http://www.culture.gouv.fr/mcc/Espace-Presse/Dossiers-de-presse/Rapport-Creation-et-Internet.

Raskauskas, J., and Stolz, A.D. (2009). 'Involvement in Traditional and Electronic Bullying Among Adolescents' *Developmental Psychology* 43/3, 564-575.

Reiner, R. (2000). *The politics of the police (3rd ed.).* Oxford: Oxford University Press.

Rideout, V. J., Foehr, U. G., and Roberts, D. F. (2010). *Generation M2. Media in the Lives of 8- to 18-Year-Olds.* Menlo Park, California.

Roberts, D. F., and Foehr, U. G. (2008). Trends in media use. *The Future of Children,* 18/1, 11-37.

Rogers, M. (2000). *A New Hacker Taxonomy* (revised version). Manitoba: University of Manitoba, Dept. of Psychology.

Rogers, M. (2001). *A social learning theory and moral disengagement analysis of criminal computer behaviour: an explorative study.* Winnipeg: University of Manibota.

Rogers, M. (2004). *What is a Distributed Denial of Service (DDoS) Attack and What Can I Do About It?* www.cert.org/homeusers/ddos.html. Last visited 29 February 2008.

Rogers, M. (2006). A two-dimensional circumplex approach to the development of a hacker taxonomy. *Digital Investigation, 3* (2006), 97-102.

Rooij, A. J., Zinn, M. F., Schoenmakers, T. M., and Mheen, D. (2010). Treating Internet Addiction With Cognitive-Behavioral Therapy: A Thematic Analysis of the Experiences of Therapists. *International Journal of Mental Health and Addiction.* doi:10.1007/s11469-010-9295-0.

Rooij, T. van, and Eijnden, R. van den (2007). *Monitor internet en jongeren 2006 en 2007: ontwikkelingen in internetgebruik en de rol van opvoeding.* Rotterdam: IVO.

Ruggiero, T.E. (2000). Uses and gratifications theory in the 21st century. *Mass Communication and Society, 3,* 3-37.

Ruys, S., and Verhoeven, S. (2005) Attacks by Private Actors and the Right of Self-defence. *Journal of Conflict and Security Law, 10/3,* 289-320.

Sabina, C., Wolak, J., and Finkelhor, D. (2008). The nature and dynamics of Internet pornography exposure for youth. *CyberPsychology & Behavior, 11,* 691-693.

Sacco, D. T., Argudin, R., Maguire, J., and Tallon, K. (2010). *Sexting: Youth Practices and Legal Implications.* Cambridge, MA: Berkman.

Sackers, H.J.B. and Mevis, P.A.M. (eds.) (2000). *Fraudedelicten.* Deventer: W.E.J. Tjeenk Willink.

Salmivalli, C. (2010). *KiVa anti-bullying program.* [Powerpoint slides]. Unpublished manuscript, University of Turku, Finland.

Salvatore A.J. (2006). *An Anti-bullying strategy: action research in a 5/6 intermediate school* (Doctoral dissertation, University of Hartford, 2006).

Schellekens, M.H.M., Koops, B.J., and Teepe, W.G. (2007). *Wat niet weg is, is gezien. Een analyse van art. 54a Sr in het licht van een Notice-and-Take-Down-regime,* Tilburg, November 2007.

Schmitt, M.N. (1999). Computer Network Attack and the Use of Force in International Law: Thoughts on a Normative Framework. *Research Publication 1 Information Series.* Available at http://www.usafa.edu/df/iita/Publications/Computer%20Network%20Attack%20and%20the%20Use%20of%20Force%20in%20International%20Law.pdf (November 2011).

Schneier, B. (2005a). Two-factor authentication: too little, too late. *Commun. ACM, 48/4,* 136-136.

Schneier, B. (2005b). Risks of third-party data. Commun. *ACM, 48/5,* 36.

Schneier, B. (2008). What our top spy doesn't get: Security and privacy aren't opposites. *Wired.*

Schoenmakers, Y.M.M., Vries Robbé, E. de, and Wijk, A.P. van (2009). *Mountains of gold. An exploratory research on 419 fraud.* Amsterdam: SWP Publishers.

Schrock, A., and Boyd, D. (2008). Online Threats to Youth: Solicitation, Harassment, and Problematic Content. In Internet Safety Technical Task

Force, *Enhancing Child Safety and Online Technologies: Final Report of the Internet Safety Task Force to the Multi-State Working Group on Social Networking of State Attorneys* (pp. 73-145). Durham, NC: Carolina Academic Press.

Schultze-Krumbholz, A., and Scheithauer H. (2009). Social-Behavioral Correlates of Cyberbullying in a German Student Sample. *Journal of Psychology*, 217/4, 224-226.

Seto, M.C., Reevers, L., and Jung, S. (2010). Explanations given by child pornography offenders for their crimes. *Journal of Sexual Aggression* 16/2, 169-180.

Sherry, J. L., Lucas, K., Greenberg, B. S., and Lachlan, K. (2006). Video game uses and gratifications as predictors of use and game preferences. In P. Vorderer and J. Bryant (eds.), 213-224. London: Lawrence Erlbaum Associates.

Simpson, G. (2008). *F-Secure sees smaller botnets on the rise.* www.news.com/F-Secure-sees-smaller-botnets-on-the-rise/2100-7349-6210900.html?part=dtx. Last visited 29 February 2008.

Slonje, R. and Smith, P.K. (2008). 'Cyberbullying: Another main type of bullying' *Scandinavian Journal of Psychology* 49/2, 147-154.

Slot, M. (2009). Exploring user-producer interaction in an online community: the case of Habbo Hotel. *International Journal of Web Based Communities*, 5/1, 33-48.

Smith, A. (2007). Teens and Online Stranger Contact. Pew Internet & American Life Project. Available at http://www.pewinternet.org/PPF/r/223/report_display.asp Accessed 1 December 2010.

Smith, P., Mahdavi, J., Carvalho, M., and Tippett, N. (2006). *An investigation into cyberbullying, its forms, awareness and impact, and the relationship between age and gender in cyberbullying.* London: University of London.

Smith, P.K., and Brain, P. (2000). 'Bullying in schools: Lessons from two decades of research', *Aggressive Behavior,* 26/1, 1-9.

Smith, P.K., Cowie, H., Olafsson, R.F., and Liefooghe, A.P.D. (2002). 'Definitions of Bullying: A comparison of Terms Used, and Age and Gender Differences, in a Fourteen-Country International Comparison', *Child Development* 73/4, 1119-1133.

Smith, P.K., Mahdavi, J., Carvalho, M., Fisher, S., Russel, S., and Tippett, N. (2008). 'Cyberbullying: its nature and impact in secondary school pupils' *Journal of Child Psychology and Psychiatry* 49/4, 376-385.

Smyth, J. M. (2007). Beyond Self-Selection in Video Game Play: An Experimental Examination of the Consequences of Massively Multiplayer

Online Role-Playing Game Play. *CyberPsychology & Behavior*, 10/5, 717-721. doi:10.1089/cpb.2007.9963.

Snyder, F. (2001). 'Sites of criminality and sites of governance', *Social & Legal Studies*, 10, 251-6.

Snyder, H.N., and Sickmund, M. (2006). *Juvenile Offenders and Victims: 2006 National Report*. U.S. Department of Justice, March. Available at http://ojjdp.ncjrs.gov?ojstabb/nr2006/index.html. Accessed 6 December 2010.

Sola Pool, I. de (1983). *Technologies of freedom*. Cambridge: The Belknap Press of Harvard University Press.

Solove, D. J. (2007). 'I've got nothing to hide' and other misunderstandings of privacy. *San Diego Law Review*, 44, 745-772.

Solove, D. J. (2010). Understanding privacy. Harvard University Press.

Sophos (2007). *Security threat report. Update 07/2007*. www.sophos.com. Last visited 14 April 2008.

Stamm, S., Ramzan, Z., and Jakobsson, M. (2006). *Drive-By Pharming*. www.symantec.com/avcenter/reference/Driveby_Pharming.pdf. Last visited 19 May 2008.

Stassen Berger, K. S. (2007). Update on bullying at school: Science forgotten? *Developmental Review* 27/1, 90–126.

Steele, J.R. (1999). Teenage Sexuality and Media Practice: Factoring in the Influences of Family, Friends, and School. *The Journal of Sex Research*, 36/4, 331-341.

Steele, J.R., and Brown, J.D. (1995). Adolescent room culture: Studying media in the context of everyday life. *Journal of Youth and Adolescence*, 24, 551-576.

Steffgen, G., König, K., and Pfetsch, J. (2009). Does Banning Cell Phones in Schools Reduce Cyberbullying? *Poster presented during the COST Action IS0801 Workshop 1: Cyberbullying: Definition and Measurement*, 22-23 August 2009, Vilnius.

Stiennon, R. (2010). *Surviving Cyberwar*. Lanham: Government Institutes.

Stol, W. (2010). Cyberspace Cybersafety overwogen. Een introductie in twee lezingen. [Cyber Safety Considered] The Hague: Boom Juridische uitgevers.

Stol, W.P. (1988). *Automatisering bij de politie: meldkamerwerk en kwaliteit van de arbeid*. [Computerizing the police] Amsterdam: Gemeentepolitie Amsterdam.

Stol, W.P. (1996). *Politie-optreden en informatietechnologie. Over sociale controle van politiemensen*. [Police actions and information technology] Lelystad: Koninklijke Vermande.

Stol, W.P. (2003). Sociale controle en technologie. De casus politie en kinderporno op het Internet [Social control and technology. Case study of police and child pornography on the Internet]. *Amsterdams Sociologisch Tijdschrift*, 30/(1/2), 162-182.

Stol, W.P. (2004a). *Handhaven: eerst kiezen, dan doen. Technische mogelijkheden en beperkingen.* [Maintaining law and order: decide before you act. Technological possibilities and limitations] The Hague: Ministry of Justice.

Stol, W.P. (2004b). Trends in cybercrime. [Trends in Cyber Crime] In *Justitiële Verkenningen 8* (2004), 22-33.

Stol, W.P. (2008). 'Cybercrime'. In: W.P. Stol and A. van Wijk (eds.) *Inleiding criminaliteit en opsporing* [Introduction to crime and detection of crime]. The Hague: Boom Juridische uitgevers.

Stol, W.P. (2008). 'Veiligheid en cyberspace'. [Safety and cyberspace] In: Stol, W.P., Rijpma, J., Veenhuysen, H., and Abbas, T. (eds.), *Basisboek Integrale Veiligheid.* Bussum: Uitgeverij Coutinho.

Stol, W.P. (2012). *Cyber Safety Considered. An introduction in two readings.* The Hague: Eleven International Publishing.

Stol, W.P., and Velt, C.J.E. In 't (1991). Politie en informatietechnologie. Veranderingen in politieoptreden? [The police and information technology: changes in police work?] *Tijdschrift voor criminologie, 33/3,* 256-278.

Stol, W.P., Kaspersen, H.W.K., Kerstens, J., Leukfeldt, E.R., and Lodder, A.R. (2008b). Internetcriminaliteit: kinderpornografie in meervoudig perspectief. [Internet Crime: Child Pornography from Multiple Perspectives]. *Ars Aequi 57* (07/08), 531-540.

Stol, W.P., Treeck, R.J. van, and Ven, A.E.B.M. van der (1999). *Criminaliteit in cyberspace – een praktijkonderzoek naar aard, ernst en aanpak in Nederland.* [Crime in Cyber Space: a study into the nature and approach in the Netherlands] The Hague: Elsevier.

Struiksma, N., Mestdagh, C.N.J. de Vey, and Winter, H.B. (2012). *De organisatie van de opsporing van cybercrime door de Nederlandse politie.* [The organization of the investigation of cybercrime by the Dutch police.] Amsterdam: Reed Business.

Strom, P. S., and Strom, R. D. (2005). 'Cyberbullying by Adolescents: A Preliminary Assessment' *The Educational Forum 70,* 21-36.

Subrahmanyam, K., and Greenfield, P. (2008). Online Communication and Relationships. *The Future of Children, 18/1,* 119-146.

Subrahmanyam, K., Greenfield, P., Kraut, R., and Gross, E. (2001). The impact of computer use on children's and adolescents' development. *Journal of Applied Developmental Psychology, 22/1,* 7-30. doi:10.1016/S0193-3973(00)00063-0.

331

Subrahmanyam, K., Greenfield, P.M., and Tynes, B. (2004). Constructing sexuality and identity in an online teen chat room. *Applied Developmental Psychology, 25,* 651-666.

Suler, J. (2004). The online disinhibition effect. *CyberPsychology and Behavior,* 7/3, 321-326.

Sullivan, C. (2005). *Internet traders of child pornograhpy: Profiling research New Zealand.* Department of internal affairs: www.lgc.govt.nz/pubforms.nsf/ URL/Profilingupdate2.pdf/$file/Profilingupdate2.pdf.

Surveillance and Securitization of Everyday Life. London: Routledge.

Svensson, J., and Wijk A.P. van (2004). Gratis zullen we alles delen [We'll share everything that's for free]. In J. Svensson and S. Zouridis, *Waarden en normen in de virtuele wereld* (15-81). Enschede: Universiteit Twente.

Symantec (2007). *Symantec Global Internet Security Threat Report. Trends for 2009.* www.symantec.com. Last visited 21 March 2010.

Symantec (2007). *Symantec Internet Security Threat Report. Trends for July – December 06.* www.symantec.com. Last visited 14 April 2008.

Symantec (2010). *Symantec Global Internet Security Threat Report. Trends for 2009.* www.symantec.com. Last visited 21 March 2011.

Synovate (2003). *Federal Trade Commission – Identity Theft Survey Report.* McLean, Virginia: Synovate.

Synovate (2007). *Federal Trade Commission – 2006 Identity Theft Survey Report.* McLean, Virginia: Synovate.

Tanenbaum, A.S., Herder, J. N., and Bos, H. (2006). Can we make operating systems reliable and secure? *IEEE Computer,* 39/5, 44-51.

Tanenbaum, A.S. and Wetherall, D.J. (2010). *Computer Networks (5th Edition).* Prentice Hall.

Taylor, R.W., Caeti T.J., Loper, D.K., Fritsch E.J., and Liederbach, J. (2006). *Digital crime and digital terrorism: The criminology of computer crime.* New Jersey: Pearson Prentice Hall.

The Economist (2010). *War in the fifth domain: Are the mouse and keyboard the new weapons of conflict?* Available at http://www.economist.com/ node/16478792 (November 2011).

Titus, R., Heinzelmann, F. and Boyle, J.M. (1995). *The anatomy of fraud: Report of a nationwide survey.*

TNO/SEO/IVIR (2009). *Ups and downs. Economische en culturele gevolgen van file sharing voor muziek, film en games,* a study by TNO Information and Communication Technology, SEO Economic Research and the Institute for Information Law, commissioned by the Dutch Ministries of Education, Culture and Science, Economic Affairs and Justice, February 2009.

332

Toutenhoofd-Visser, M.H., Veenstra, S., Domenie, M.M.L., Leukfeldt, F.R. and Stol, W.P. (2009). *Politie en Cybercrime. Intake en Eerste Opvolging. Een onderzoek naar de intake van het werkaanbod cybercrime door de politie.* [Police and Cybercrime. The registration of cybercrime offences] Leeuwarden: NHL.

Træen, B., Nilsen, T.S., and Stigum, H. (2006). Use of Pornography in Traditional Media and on the Internet in Norway. *The Journal of Sex Research, 43/3*, 245-254.

Traynor, I. (2007). Russia accused of unleashing cyberwar to disable Estonia. *The Guardian.* Available at http://www.guardian.co.uk/world/2007/may/17/topstories3.russia (November 2011).

Turgeman-Goldschmidt, O. (2005). Hacker's accounts: Hacking as a social entertainment. *Social Science Computer Review, 23/1*, 8-23.

Twyman, K., Saylor, C., Taylor, L.A., and Comeaux, C. (2010). Comparing Children and Adolescents Engaged in Cyberbullying with Matched Peers. *Cyberpsychology, Behavior and Social Network, 13/2*, 195-199.

United Nations (24 October 1945) Charter of the United Nations. 1 UNTS XVI.

United States Department of Defense (December 2006) The National Military Strategy for Cyberspace Operations. Washington, D.C. 20318. Available at http://www.bits.de/NRANEU/others/strategy/07-F-2105doc1.pdf (February 2012).

University of Hertfordshire (2008): *Music Experience and Behaviour in Young People,* Spring 2008.

Van den Eijnden, R. J. J. M., Van Rooij, A. J., and Meerkerk, G.-J. (2007). *Excessief en Compulsief Internetgebruik. Een Kwalitatieve Analyse [Excessive and Compulsive Internet Use. A Qualitative Analysis].* Rotterdam: IVO.

Van der Meulen, N. (2006). *The Challenge of Countering Identity Theft: Recent Developments in the United States, the United Kingdom, and the European Union.* Tilburg: International Victimology Institute Tilburg, 2006.

Van der Putte, T., and Keuning, J. (2000). Biometrical fingerprint recognition: Don't get your fingers burned. In *4th Int. IFIP wg 8.8 Conf. Smart card research and advanced application (CARDIS),* Boston (MA): Kluwer Academic Publishers, 289-303.

Van Dijk, J., Van Kesteren, J., and Smit, P. (2007). *Key Findings from the 2004-2005 ICVS and EU ICS.* Meppel: Boom Juridische uitgevers.

Van Eijk, N., Poort, J., and Rutten, P. (2010). Legal, Economic and Cultural Aspects of File Sharing. *Communications & Strategies, 77,* (1st Q. 2010), 35-54.

333

Van Eeten, M, Bauer, J.M., and Tabatabaie, S. (2009). *Damages from Internet Security, A framework and toolkit for assessing the economic costs of security breaches*, research commissioned by OPTA, TU Delft, February 2009.

Van Eeten, M., Bauer, J.M., Hadi Asghari, Shirin Tabatabaiea, and Dave Rand (2010). *The Role of Internet Service Providers in Botnet Mitigation: An Empirical Analysis Based on Spam Data*, http://weis2010.econinfosec.org/papers/session4/weis2010_vaneeten.pdf.

Van Eijk, N.A.N.M. (2011). File Sharing, note written at the request of the European Parliament's Committee on Legal Affairs, 2011 (http://www.ivir.nl/publications/vaneijk/pe432775_en-rev-fin.pdf).

Van Eijk, N.A.N.M. T.M. van Engers, C. Wiersma, C.A. Jasserand and W. Abel, *Moving Towards Balance: A study into duties of care on the Internet*, The Hague/ Amsterdam: WODC/ University of Amsterdam.

Van Hoboken, J.V.J. (2009). 'Legal Space for Innovative Ordering. On the Need to Update Selection Intermediary Liability in the EU', *International Journal of Communications Law & Policy*, 2009/13, 1-21.

Van Rooij, A. J., Schoenmakers, T. M., Meerkerk, G.-J., and Van de Mheen, D. (2008). *Factsheet Monitor Internet en Jongeren. Videogames en Nederlandse jongeren [Monitor Internet and Youth. Video games and Dutch Youth]*. Rotterdam: IVO.

Van Rooij, A. J., Schoenmakers, T. M., Vermulst, A. A., Van den Eijnden, R. J. J. M., and Mheen, D. van de (2011). Online video game addiction: Identification of addicted adolescent gamers. *Addiction, 106/1*, 205-212. doi:10.1111/j.1360-0443.2010.03104.x.

Van Wilsem, J. (2010). Gekocht maar niet gekregen. Slachtofferschap van online oplichting nader onderzocht. *Tijdschrift voor Veiligheid, 9*, 16-29.

Van Wilsem, J., Arnold, E., Van Buren, C., Cerdijn, L., Missler, R., Van der Plicht, D., and Valentini, A. (2010). Is online zichtbaarheid riskant? Onterechte bankafschrijvingen en persoonlijke informatie op sociale netwerksites. *Proces, 89*, 344-354.

Vandebosch, H., and Van Cleemput, K. (2009). 'Cyberbullying among youngsters: profiles of bullies and victims' *New Media & Society 11/8*, 1349-1371.

Vandebosch, H., Cleemput, K. van, Mortelmans, D. and Walrave, M. (2006). *Cyberpesten bij jongeren in Vlaanderen*. Brussel: ViWTA.

Verbiest, T. and Spindler, G. (2007). *Study on the Liability of Internet Intermediaries*, study commissioned by the European Commission (contract ETD/20-06/IM/E2/69), November 2007.

Verdelho, P. (2008). *The effectiveness of international co-operation against cybercrime: examples of good practice (discussion paper)*. Council of Europe (Project on Cybercrime): www.coe.int/cybercrime.

Violino, B. (2005). *After Phishing? Pharming! Security experts are concerned about pharming, a technically sophisticated DNS-based attack.* www.csoon-line.com, 1 October 2005.

Vogel, J. J., Vogel, D. S., Cannon-Bowers, J., Bowers, C. A., Muse, K., and Wright, M. (2006). Computer gaming and interactive simulations for learning: A meta-analysis. *Journal of Educational Computing Research, 34/3,* 229-243.

Von Ahn, L., Blum, M., and Langford, J. (2004). Telling humans and computers apart automatically. *Commun. ACM, 4/2,* 56-60.

Von Salisch, M., Oppl, C., and Kristen, A. (2006). What attracts children. In P. Vorderer and J. Bryant (eds.), 147-164). London: Lawrence Erlbaum Associates.

Vosmeer, M. (2010). *Videogames en Gender. Over Spelende Meiden, Sexy Avatars en Huiselijkheid op het Scherm.* Amsterdam.

Wall, D. (2005). The internet as a conduit for criminal activity. In: Pattavina, A. *The Criminal Justice System and the internet.* Thousand Oaks, Sage, 77-98.

Wall, D.S. (2001). 'Introduction', in D.S. Wall (ed.), *Crime and the Internet: Cybercrimes and Cyberfears.* London: Routledge.

Wall, D.S. (2007). *Cybercrime: The Transformation of Crime in the Information Age.* Cambridge/Malden MA: Polity.

Wall, D. (2007b). Policing cybercrimes. Situating the public police in networks of security within Cyberspace. *Police Practice & Research, an international journal,* 183-205.

Walrave, M., and Heirman, W. (2009). 'Cyberbullying: predicting victimization and perpetration' *Children and society* 25/1, 59-72.

Walrave, M., Demoulin, M., Heirman, W. and Van de Perre, A. (2009). Cyberpesten: pesten in bits en bytes. Brussels: Federal Public Service Economy. Internet Rights Observatory, 261 p.

Wang, J., Nansel, T.R., and Iannotti, R.J. (2011). Cyber and Traditional Bullying: Differential Association With Depression. *Journal of Adolescent Health* 48/4, 415-417.

Ward, L. M. (2003). Understanding the role of entertainment media in the sexual socialization of American youth: A review of empirical research. *Developmental Review, 23,* 347-388.

Warman, M. (2010). Wikileaks supporters hack mastercard.com. *The Telegraph.* Available at http://www.telegraph.co.uk/news/worldnews/wikileaks/8188797/WikiLeaks-supporters-hack-Mastercard.com.html (November 2011).

Warren, M. and Leitch, S., (2009). Hacker Taggers: A new type of hackers. *Information System Frontiers* (11) 12:425-431.

335

Warren, S. and Brandeis, L. (1890). The right to privacy. *Harvard Law Review.*

Warren, S.D., and Brandeis, L. D. (1890). The right to privacy. *Harvard Law Review,* 4/5, 193-220.

Watson, D., Holz, T. and Mueller, S. (2005). *Know your Enemy Phishing Behind the Scenes of Phishing Attacks. The Honeynet Project & Research Alliance.* www.honeynet.org. Last visited 20 May 2008.

Weber, M. (1990, orig. 1922). *Wirtschaft und Gesellschaft.* [Economy and Society] Tübingen: J.C.B. Mohr (Paul Siebeck).

Websense (2007). *Websense Predicts 2008's Top Ten Security Threats: Olympics, Online Advertisements and Web 2.0 Threats Top Hacker's To-Do Lists.* www. websense.com. Last visited 21 April 2008.

Webster, F. (2002). *Theories of the Information Society.* 2nd edition. London: Routledge.

Weda, J., Akker, I., Poort, J., Rutten, P., and Beunen, A. (2011). *Wat er speelt. De positie van makers en uitvoerend kunstenaars in de digitale omgeving.* [What's at play. The position of makers and performing artistes in the digital environment]. Amsterdam: SEO Economisch Onderzoek.

Wells, M., Finkelhor, D., Wolak, J. and Mitchell, K.J. (2007). Defining Child Pornography: Law Enforcement Dilemmas in Investigations of Internet Child Pornography Possession. *Police Practice and Research,* 8/3 269-282.

Werf, J. van der (2003). *Cybercrime. Deel 2 Een verkennende analyse.* [Cyber Crime. Part 2. An explorative analysis] Zoetermeer: KLPD.

West, R., and Hardy, A. (2006). *Theory of addiction* (p. 225). Wiley-Blackwell.

Westin, A. (1967). *Privacy and Freedom.* Atheneum, New York.

Whine, M. (2000). 'Far Right Extremists on the Internet', in D. Thomas and B. Loader (eds.), *Cybercrime: Law Enforcement, Security and Surveillance in the Information Age.* London: Routledge.

White, M.D. and Fisher, C. (2008). Assessing our knowledge of identity theft. The challenges to effective prevention and control efforts. *Criminal Justice Policy Review, 19,* 3-24.

Wijk, A.P. van, Nieuwenhuis, A., and Smeltink, A. (2009). Achter de schermen. Een verkennend onderzoek naar downloaders van kinderporno. [Behind the scenes. An explorative study into downloaders of child pornography]. Arnhem: Bureau Beke.

Willard, N. E. (2007). *Cyberbullying and Cyberthreats: responding to the challenge of online social aggression, threats and distress.* Champaign, Illinois: Research Press.

William, K. (2009). 'Transnational Developments in Internet Law', in Y. Jewkes and M. Yar (eds.), *Handbook of Internet Crime.* Cullompton: Willan.

Williams, D., and Skoric, M. (2005). Internet Fantasy Violence: A Test of Aggression in an Online Game. *Communication Monographs*, 72/2, 217-233. doi:10.1080/03637750500111781.

Williams, K.R., and Guerra, N.G. (2007). 'Prevalence and Predictors of Internet Bullying' *Journal of Adolescent Health* 41/6, s14-s21.

Wingfield, T.C. (2000). *The Law of Information Conflict: National Security Law in Cyberspace*. Falls Church: Aegis Research Corporation.

Witteman, M. (2002). Advances in smartcard security. *Information Security Bulletin*, July 2002, 11-22.

Wolak, J., Finkelhor, D., and Mitchell, K.J. (2004). Internet-initiated sex crimes against minors: Implications for prevention based on findings from a national study. *Journal of Adolescent Health*, 35/5, 424.e11-424.e20.

Wolak, J., Finkelhor, D., and Mitchell, K. J. (2008). Is talking online to unknown people always risky? Distinguishing online interaction styles in a national sample of youth Internet users. *Cyberpsychology & Behavior*, 11, 340–343.

Wolak, J., Finkelhor, D., and Mitchell, K. (2009). *Trends in arrests of 'online predators'*. Crimes against Children Research Center. Available at http://www.edu.ccrc/pdf/cv194.pdf. Accessed at 5 December 2010.

Wolak, J., Finkelhor, D., Mitchell, K.J. and Ybarra, M.L. (2008). Online 'Predators' and Their Victims. Myths, Realities, and Implications for Prevention and Treatment. *American Psychologist* 63/2, 111-128.

Wolak, J., Mitchell, K.J., and Finkelhor, D. (2006). *Online victimization of youth: Five years later*. Alexandria, VA: National Center for Missing and Exploited Children.

Wolak, J., Mitchell, K.J., and Finkelhor, D. (2007). Unwanted and Wanted Exposure to Online Pornography in a National Sample of Youth Internet Users. *Pediatrics*, 119/2, 247-257.

Wolak, J., Mitchell, K., and Finkelhor, D. (2007a). 'Does Online Harassment Constitute Bullying? An exploration of Online Harassment by Known Peers and Online-Only Contactsbullying'. *Journal of Adolescent Health* 41/6, 51-58.

World Health Organization (2007b). International Statistical Classification of Diseases and Related Health Problems, 10th Revision. Available at http://www.who.int/classifications/apps/icd/icd10online/. Accessed 10 February 2011.

Yan, J., and Randell, B. (2005). A systematic classification of cheating in online games (pp. 1-9).

Yar, M. (2005a). Computer hacking: Just another case of juvenile delinquency? *The Howard Journal*, 44/4, 2005b, 387-399.

Yar, M. (2005b). 'The Novelty of 'Cybercrime' An Assessment in Light of Routine Activity Theory', *European Journal of Criminology*, 2/4, 407-428.

Yar, M. (2006). *Cybercrime and Society*. London: Sage.

Yar, M. (2008). 'The Computer Crime Control Industry: The Emerging Market in Information Security', in K. Franko-Aas, et al. (eds.), *Technologies of Insecurity: Surveillance and Securitization of Everyday Life*. London: Routledge.

Yar, M. (2009). 'The Private Policing of Internet Crime', in Y. Jewkes and M. Yar (eds.), *Handbook of Internet Crime*. Cullompton: Willan.

Ybarra, M.L. (2004). 'Linkages between Depressive Symptomatology and Internet Harassment among Young Regular Internet Users', *Cyberpsychology and Behavior* 7/2, 247-57.

Ybarra, M. L., and Mitchell, K. (2004). 'Online aggressor/targets, aggressors and targets: a comparison of associated youth characteristics'. *Journal of Child Psychology and Psychiatry* 45/7, 1308-1316.

Ybarra, M.L., and Mitchell, K. (2007). 'Prevalence and Frequency of internet harassment Instigation: Implications for Adolescent Health'. *Journal of Adolescent Health* 41/2, 189-195.

Ybarra, M.L., and Mitchell, K.J. (2008). How Risky Are Social Networking Sites? A Comparison of Places Online Where Youth Sexual Solicitation and Harassment Occurs. *Pediatrics, 121*, e350-e357.

Ybarra, M.L., Diener-West, M., and Leaf, P.J. (2007). 'Examining the Overlap in Internet Harassment and School Bullying: Implications for School intervention'. *Journal of Adolescent Health* 41/6, s42-s50.

Yee, N. (2005, October). The Daedalus Project: Buying Gold. Retrieved 7 February 2011, from http://www.nickyee.com/daedalus/archives/001469.php. Accessed: 2011-02-07. (Archived by WebCite? at http://www.webcitation.org/5wK5LAyG5).

Yee, N. (2006). Motivations for Play in Online Games. *CyberPsychology & Behavior, 9/6*, 772-775. doi:10.1089/cpb.2006.9.772.

Ziolkowski, K.J. (2010). Computer Network Operations and the Law of Armed Conflict. *The Military Law and the Law of War Review, 49/1-2*, 47-90.

Zouridis, S. and Frissen P.H.A. (2004). Over virtuele vrijplaatsen en civilisatie in cyberspace [On virtual refuge and civilisation in cyberspace]. In J. Svensson & S. Zouridis, Waarden en normen in de virtuele wereld (85-140). Enschede: Universiteit Twente.

Zureik, E. and Harling Stalker, L., (2010). The cross-cultural study of privacy. In *Zureik, E. et al. (eds.), Surveillance, privacy and the globalization of personal information*. McGill-Queen University Press, Montreal/London/Ithaca, 10.

Index

344

About the authors

L.J.M. (Lianne) Boer is PhD candidate (cyber warfare) at the Faculty of Law, VU University, Amsterdam (Netherlands).

M.C.J.D. (Marko) van Eekelen is Professor of Software Technology at Radboud University Nijmegen (Netherlands) and the Open University of the Netherlands.

N.A.N.M. (Nico) van Eijk is Professor of Media and Telecommunications Law and Director of the Institute for Information Law at the University of Amsterdam (Netherlands).

P.H. (Pieter) Hartel is Professor of Computer Science at the University of Twente (Netherlands).

N. (Nanna) Suryana Herman is Director of the International Office at Technical University of Malaysia, Malacca.

J.H. (Jaap-Henk) Hoepman is Senior Scientist at TNO and Radboud University Nijmegen (Netherlands).

J. (Jurjen) Jansen is researcher at the cyber safety research group of NHL University of Applied Sciences and the Dutch Police Academy (Netherlands).

J. (Jeroen) Jansz is Professor of Communication and Media at Erasmus University Rotterdam (Netherlands).

Y. (Yvonne) Jewkes is Professor of Criminology at the University of Leicester (UK).

E. (Erik) de Jong is senior security expert at Fox-IT (Netherlands).

A.G.H. (Arno) Kentgens is PhD candidate (liability for ICT offences) at the Open University of the Netherlands.

J.W.M. (Joyce) Kerstens is researcher at the cyber safety research group of NHL University of Applied Sciences and the Dutch Police Academy (Netherlands).

E.R. (Rutger) Leukfeldt is PhD candidate in organised cybercrime at the Open University of the Netherlands and researcher at the cyber safety research group of NHL University of Applied Sciences and the Dutch Police Academy (Netherlands).

M.J. (Marc) van Lieshout is Senior Researcher with TNO (an independent research organisation) (Netherlands).

A.R. (Arno) Lodder is Professor of Internet Governance and Regulation at VU University, Amsterdam (Netherlands).

E. (Evelien) de Pauw, MSc, is coordinator and lecturer at the research centre in public safety and security at the Catholic University of Applied Science, southwest Flanders (Katho) (Belgium).

J. (Joost) P. Poort is senior economical researcher at the Institute for Information Law at the University of Amsterdam (Netherlands).

A.J. (Tony) van Rooij is researcher at IVO (a scientific bureau for research, expertise, and consultancy in the field of lifestyle, addiction, and related social developments).

P.W.M. (Paul) Rutten is Visiting Professor of Creative Industries and Innovation at Antwerp University and independent researcher (Belgium).

E.F. (Evert) Stamhuis is Dean of the Faculty of Law at the Open University of the Netherlands.

W.Ph. (Wouter) Stol is Professor of Police Studies at the Open University of the Netherlands, and chairholder for cyber safety at NHL University of Applied Sciences and the Dutch Police Academy (Netherlands).

H. (Heidi) Vandebosch is Associate Professor at the Department of Communication Studies, the University of Antwerp (Belgium), specialising in media sociology and health communication.

S. (Sander) Veenstra is researcher at the cyber safety research group of NHL University of Applied Sciences and the Dutch Police Academy (Netherlands).

H.P.E. (Harald) Vranken is Associate Professor Computer Science at the Open University of the Netherlands.

M. (Michel) Walrave is Associate Professor and head of the Department of Communication Studies at the University of Antwerp (Belgium) and is responsible for the research group MIOS which conducts research on ICT use among young people.

A.P. (Anton) van Wijk is a criminologist and director of Bureau Beke (Netherlands).

J. (Johan) van Wilsem is Associate Professor of Criminology at Leiden University (Netherlands).

M. (Majid) Yar is Professor of Sociology and Associate Director of the Centre for Criminology & Criminal Justice (CCCJ) at the University of Hull (UK).